PIMLI

410

THE BURNING BLUE

Paul Addison teaches history at the University of Edinburgh where he is Director of the Centre for Second World War Studies. He is the author of *The Road to 1945*, *Churchill on the Home Front* and editor (with Angus Calder) of *Time to Kill: The Soldier's Experience of War in the West 1939–45*.

Jeremy A. Crang is Lecturer in History and Assistant Director of the Centre for Second World War Studies at the University of Edinburgh. He is the author of a forthcoming book on *The British Army and the People's War 1939–45*.

THE BURNING BLUE

A New History of the Battle of Britain

Edited by

PAUL ADDISON and
JEREMY A. CRANG

PIMLICO

Published by Pimlico 2000

2 4 6 8 10 9 7 5 3 1

First published in Great Britain by
Pimlico 2000

Pimlico
Random House, 20 Vauxhall Bridge Road,
London SW1V 2SA

Random House Australia (Pty) Limited
20 Alfred Street, Milsons Point, Sydney,
New South Wales 2061, Australia

Random House New Zealand Limited
18 Poland Road, Glenfield,
Auckland 10, New Zealand

Random House (Pty) Limited
Endulini, 5A Jubilee Road, Parktown 2193, South Africa

The Random House Group Limited Reg. No. 954009
www.randomhouse.co.uk

A CIP catalogue record for this book
is available from the British Library

ISBN 0–7126–6475–0

Typeset by Palimpsest Book Production Limited,
Polmont, Stirlingshire
Printed and bound in Great Britain by
Mackays of Chatham PLC, Chatham, Kent

Contents

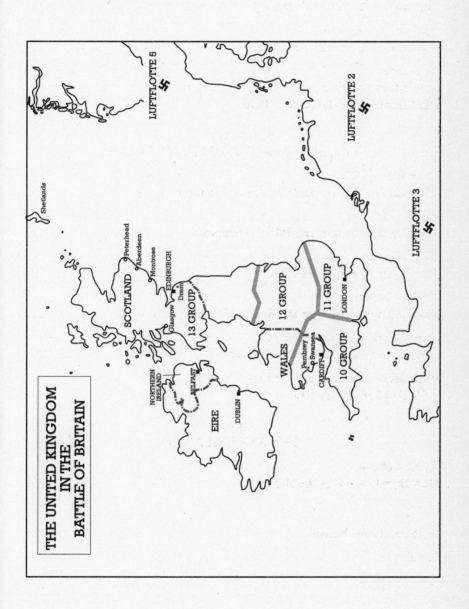

THE UNITED KINGDOM
IN THE
BATTLE OF BRITAIN

LUFTFLOTTE 5

LUFTFLOTTE 2

LUFTFLOTTE 3

Shetlands

SCOTLAND

Peterhead
Aberdeen
Montrose
EDINBURGH
Drem
Glasgow

13 GROUP

NORTHERN
IRELAND

BELFAST

EIRE

DUBLIN

WALES

12 GROUP

11 GROUP

LONDON

Pembrey
Swansea
CARDIFF

10 GROUP

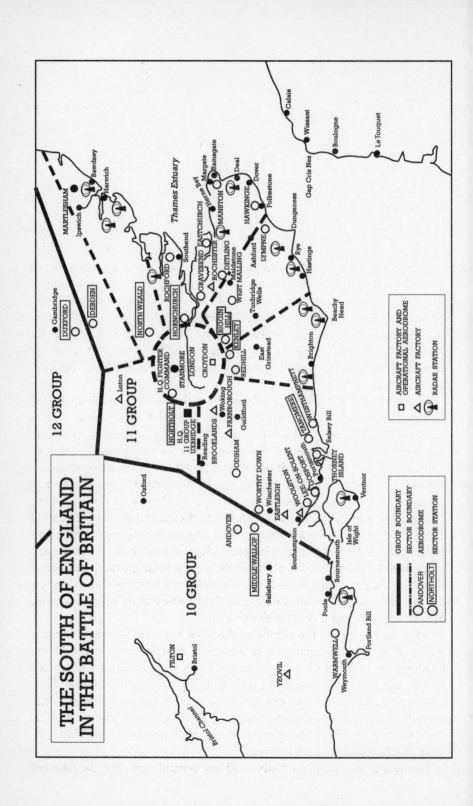

THE SOUTH OF ENGLAND IN THE BATTLE OF BRITAIN

12 GROUP

11 GROUP

10 GROUP

H.Q. FIGHTER COMMAND

STANMORE

LONDON

CROYDON

NORTHOLT

H.Q. 11 GROUP UXBRIDGE

DUXFORD

DEBDEN

NORTH WEALD

HORNCHURCH

ROCHFORD

BIGGIN HILL

KENLEY

REDHILL

BROOKLANDS

TANGMERE

WESTHAMPNETT

THORNEY ISLAND

WORTHY DOWN

EASTLEIGH

MIDDLE WALLOP

WARMWELL

YEOVIL

FILTON

Bristol

Oxford

Cambridge

Luton

Reading

Woking

Guildford

ODIHAM

FARNBOROUGH

Winchester

ANDOVER

Salisbury

Southampton

Bournemouth

Poole

Weymouth

Portland Bill

Isle of Wight

Ventnor

LEE-ON-SOLENT

WOOLSTON

GOSPORT

Portsmouth

Selsey Bill

East Grinstead

Tunbridge Wells

WEST MALLING

Maidstone

DETLING

ROCHESTER

GRAVESEND

EASTCHURCH

Herne Bay

Margate

MANSTON

Ramsgate

Deal

Dover

Folkestone

HAWKINGE

LYMPNE

Ashford

Dungeness

Rye

Hastings

Brighton

Beachy Head

Thames Estuary

Southend

MARTLESHAM

Harwich

Ipswich

Bawdsey

Calais

Wissant

Gap Cris Nez

Boulogne

Le Touquet

Bristol Channel

LEGEND

AIRCRAFT FACTORY AND OPERATIONAL AERODROME

AIRCRAFT FACTORY

RADAR STATION

GROUP BOUNDARY

SECTOR BOUNDARY

AERODROME

SECTOR STATION

ANDOVER

NORTHOLT

Preface

In 1996 the University of Edinburgh established a Centre for Second World War Studies attached to the Department of History. Designed to stimulate the study and discussion of all aspects of the history of the Second World War, the Centre also had the particular aim of breaking down the barriers between military, social and political history. It was in pursuit of this aim that we decided to organise a conference on the Battle of Britain as the foundation of a book intended to reassess established themes while opening up new ones.

Although so much had been written about the Battle – which by official British reckoning took place between 10 July and 31 October 1940 – we were eager first of all to discover the most recent thinking of the leading military historians on the subject, and to compare the views of British and German authorities. Mindful always of the human face of war we also invited two veterans of the Battle, Hans-Ekkehard Bob and Wallace Cunningham, to give their own personal recollections. Turning to the international implications, we approached historians of the United States, the Soviet Union and Japan with a request to analyse contemporary perceptions of the Battle in Washington, Moscow and Tokyo. With the aim of exploring the role of the Battle in British popular culture, we invited literary and cultural historians to discuss children's fiction, pilots' memoirs, feature film, public commemoration, and the conservation of historic sites. We have also added a chapter of our own.

At an early stage in the editing of this book we were fortunate to come across a remarkable documentary source: a complete set of the letters written by a young RAF pilot to his mother and father during the Battle of Britain. They were made available to us by their author, Nigel Rose, who very kindly agreed to our proposal to reprint them. All the other contributions to this book owe much to hindsight: the letters of Nigel Rose were written by a young man who did not know what would happen next or whether he would survive.

Our thanks as editors go firstly to all our contributors. For the financial assistance which made the conference possible we are grateful to Rolls-Royce, the Bank of Scotland, the Faculty of Arts Research Fund and the University of Edinburgh Development Fund. For additional help we are also grateful to the following: Ian Beckett, Bill Bond, Brian Bond, Horst Boog, Terry Cole, Sebastian Cox, Len Deighton, Alison Dick, Frances Dow, Brian Easdale, John Erickson, Jürgen Förster, Ronnie Galloway, Clive Gee, Tony Goodman, Sharon Lee, Michael Lynch, Gus Maclean, Anne McKelvie, David McWinnie, Andrew Newby, Andrew Skinner, David Stafford, George O. Sutherland, Judy Wakeling, and Wing-Commander John Young.

Finally we are greatly indebted to Will Sulkin and Jörg Hensgen of Pimlico for all their encouragement and guidance in the preparation of this book.

For kind permission to reproduce illustrations, the editors, authors and publishers wish to thank the following: Hulton Getty (1–5); Wallace Cunningham (6); Hans-Ekkehard Bob (7); Jonathan Littlejohn (8); Nigel Rose (9); Hodder and Stoughton Limited (11); Michael Fahie (12); RKO/The Kobal Collection (13); Rank/The Kobal Collection (14); United Artists/The Kobal Collection (15–17); Public Record Office (AIR 28/419) (18); English Heritage (19–20); Dean and Chapter of Westminster (21); Jeremy A. Crang (22).

Every effort has been made to trace and contact copyright holders. The publishers will be pleased to correct any mistakes or omissions in future editions.

Paul Addison
Jeremy A. Crang

Centre for Second World War Studies
Department of History
University of Edinburgh

High Flight

Oh, I have slipped the surly bonds of Earth,
And danced the skies on laughter-silvered wings:
Sunward I've climbed and joined the tumbling mirth
Of sun-split clouds – and done a hundred things
You have not dreamed of – wheeled and soared and swung
High in the sunlit silence. Hov'ring there,
I've chased the shouting wind along and flung
My eager craft through footless halls of air.
Up, up the long delirious, burning blue
I've topped the wind-swept heights with easy grace,
Where never lark, or even eagle flew;
And while with silent lifting mind I've trod
The high untrespassed sanctity of Space,
Put out my hand, and touched the face of God.

John Gillespie MacGee

BRIAN BOND

Introduction

As a small boy I can just recall the dramatic events in the summer of 1940. Living some forty miles west of London I did not witness any 'dog fights', but well remember German bombers jettisoning their loads in the fields along the Thames valley near Marlow. An even more vivid impression was made on me by the hectic improvisations to resist invasion: tank traps, pillboxes, signposts removed or blacked out and fields strewn with old farm equipment to make glider landings more hazardous. These were exciting times, indeed more exciting than any event in the second half of the century, but what exactly was the 'Battle of Britain' and what was to be its historical and legendary significance? Was an attempted German invasion narrowly averted, as was generally believed at the time? Was this a triumph for the gallant outnumbered defenders against overwhelming odds? And was there even indeed an agreed beginning and end to the Battle?

These and many other issues are discussed in this stimulating and wide-ranging volume, which includes not only historical reappraisals from both sides, but also participants' recollections and contemporary letters, foreign assessments and the creation of the heroic myth or legend of the Battle through the media of newsreels, films, fighter pilots' own or 'ghosted' memoirs and – a more unusual angle – juvenile literature. There are also contributions on the various ways in which the Battle has been commemorated, and on the progress of schemes to preserve its physical legacy such as the fighter sector bases, control centres and radar stations.

The chronology and epic status of the Battle of Britain were quickly established at home, notably through the media of newsreels, but also by a remarkable essay in near-contemporary history. In March 1941 HMSO published (anonymously) Hilary St George Saunders's thirty-two-page booklet *The Battle of Britain*, which sold 300,000 copies on the day of publication and perhaps as many as fifteen million in all. Saunders stressed the glamour of the Royal Air Force and the valiant sacrifices of its young pilots – 'the Few'. In a graphic yet restrained style he provided a remarkably fair and accurate account of the British side; though without of course mentioning radar or the details of the control and communications system which had made the successful defence possible. But he was necessarily far less informative about the German side; nor could he assess the contribution of the Battle to the broader development of the war. His greatest achievement was surely to imbue the British people with belief in the Churchillian slogan that this had been their 'finest hour', while at the same time conveying a sense of the island's heroic resistance and assured survival in the United States.

Although the RAF had much earlier warning than the Luftwaffe that it might have to play the leading role in the defence of Britain – indeed this had been its top priority since the mid-1930s – neither service was well prepared for the actual battle in the late summer of 1940.

The Luftwaffe, as Klaus A. Maier stresses, was badly suited for this strategic mission since its recent and very successful experience had involved the close tactical support of ground operations. In 1939 a report by General Felmy, commanding Luftflotte 2, concluded that a strategic air offensive against Britain could not be launched before 1942, when his force would possess long-range bombers. If war with Britain occurred before this time, he advocated a pure terror-bombing offensive against London and other cities.

The German conquest of Norway, the Low Countries and France radically improved the Luftwaffe's geo-strategic position, but since Hitler expected Britain to make peace he issued no planning directive in the critical weeks after Dunkirk. At the end of June, still assuming that Britain's defeat was only a matter of time, General Jodl recommended a limited air offensive to eliminate the RAF and its aircraft industry to prevent further raids against Germany. A landing was only to be carried out as the final blow when Britain's war economy had been paralysed and her air force destroyed. Only on 16 July did Hitler issue a directive for the all-out attack on Britain culminating in invasion, but in succeeding days his service leaders, especially Admiral Raeder, cast doubt on the feasibility of amphibious operations, and Hitler himself allowed that other plans might be necessary. As early as 31 July, at his Berghof conference, Hitler gave clear operational instructions for an offensive against the Soviet Union. A week later Goebbels confided to his diary that although the main air assault on Britain was about to begin, 'Invasion [is] not planned.' Goering was optimistic that his Luftwaffe could knock out Britain in daylight attacks, but never took any interest in a landing operation. Thus Germany began her first independent strategic air offensive with hastily improvised plans and an incredibly tight schedule, given that after mid-September adverse weather was likely to rule out a Channel crossing.

Germany's strategic dilemmas and inadequate practical preparations, due largely to Hitler's procrastination, were little understood across the Channel, where, as Malcolm Smith shows, the island's vulnerability to air attack was causing profound anxiety. At the outbreak of war Fighter Command had only thirty-five squadrons for home defence – a front line of about 420 aircraft with a further 300 in reserve. Against them the Air Staff reckoned that the Luftwaffe could muster 1,650 medium-range bombers; an exaggeration but still the disparity was alarming. Germany's conquests in the spring of 1940 transformed the British situation for the worse, giving the enemy bases from northern Norway to the Bay of Biscay, reducing her bombers' range, and permitting single-engined and twin-engined fighters to escort the bombers in large numbers.

Fighter Command had lost heavily in the Battle of France, but at least the return of its survivors raised the front-line strength to more than 700, the majority of them Hurricanes or Spitfires. Still, the calculation of probable losses against a sustained offensive looked daunting: Fighter Command might lose virtually its entire front-line force every five weeks with the aircraft industry targeted to prevent re-equipment. On the credit side, fighter production exceeded 400 a month for the first time in June 1940 and this output was maintained for the rest of the year. The worst problem, however, seemed to lie in the supply of pilots, in view of the heavy losses in France and the expansion of Fighter Command. The size of the peacetime RAF had been too small to provide a pool of trained pilots to man a 700-aircraft force, and it would take at least eighteen months to build up an adequate reserve. Smith detects 'a slight smell of panic about this', but shortage of pilots was indeed to pose an acute problem at the height of the Battle. On the eve of the Battle, in July 1940, Air Marshal Dowding had sufficient pilots to put between 600 and 700 fighters in the air against an attacking force of more than 1,000 bombers, over 300 dive-bombers, 800 single-engined and 250 twin-engined fighters. On this calculation, and leaving aside the unproven factor of Britain's radar defences, Churchill's rhetoric about a battle against the odds does not seem exaggerated.

From the German viewpoint, however, Horst Boog's account suggests that the whole enterprise was a rash undertaking. He also proposes a different chronology from standard British histories, with the first main battle stage from 8 August until 5 September involving an attempt to reduce Britain's fighter defences in preparation for a possible invasion; and a second general phase from 6 September until May 1941 which consisted of a general bombing operation against the economy and civilian morale. Thus, in the German table of events, 15 September holds no special place as the turning point in the Battle. Boog develops further the point that the Luftwaffe's leaders, including General Hans Jeschonnek, the Chief of Staff, were sceptical from the start about an invasion attempt and instead issued orders for an attack on the enemy air force, its ground organisation and armament industry as a precondition for a successful air war against merchant shipping and the war economy. But Goering, though also sceptical about an invasion attempt, was obliged to forbid attacks on southern coastal ports because they might be needed by the German landing forces. Hitler's directive issued on 1 August ordered the Luftwaffe to be prepared to play a full part in a projected invasion (Operation Sealion), but, as Boog shows, the Luftwaffe had loosened its commitment to such an operation even before 13 August by attempting to attack a variety of targets not directly related to securing the crossing of the Channel.

He contends that, despite unexpectedly heavy losses, the Luftwaffe enjoyed considerable success against Fighter Command and its airfields until Hitler, provoked by the British bombing of Berlin, ordered a drastic change of strategy on 7 September in favour of concentration on the destruction of London and other cities. This proved to be a self-inflicted blow or 'own goal' which gave a critical advantage to the defenders. This judgement is supported by the pilots' accounts from both sides in this volume. Ten days later Sealion was postponed, and in effect abandoned, because the Luftwaffe could not establish air superiority.

Boog sees the main reasons for German failure as: poor Intelligence, especially as regards the radar system and its value to the defenders; shortage of trained pilots; the inferior performance of German fighters (the Me 110) or their misuse as escorts to slow bombers (the Me 109); and the bombers' inadequate loads, ranges and accuracy. In its first, experimental independent mission the Luftwaffe was found to have greatly overestimated the effects of bombing. Failure to achieve any of its objectives dealt a severe blow to the Luftwaffe's prestige and had fatal indirect consequences, one of which was that Jeschonnek welcomed the planned campaign against the Soviet Union because he believed that the Luftwaffe would repeat its earlier triumphs in close co-operation with the army.

As for the British view, Sebastian Cox stresses that in late August and early September 11 Group came perilously close to collapse with six of the seven sector stations extensively damaged. Pilot losses of 120 per week could not have been sustained. But the strain on both pilots and aircraft was greatly eased by the German decision to switch the weight of attack on to London. These attacks were much easier for Fighter Command to counter and virtually ensured that the Luftwaffe would lose the Battle. He argues that Beaverbrook's claims to have played a decisive role by speeding up the production of aircraft were inflated and that much credit should go to such unsung heroes as Sir Wilfrid Freeman and Lord Swinton. On the celebrated 'big wing' controversy, Cox states that Keith Park's assessment was tactically correct and criticises Sir Hugh Dowding for not resolving the dispute between 11 and 12 Groups. He also suggests that the Air Council had sound reasons for the dismissal of Dowding in November 1940.

As we should expect, the Soviet Union, the United States and Japan viewed – and still view – the Battle of Britain from very different perspectives, and none has shown a scholarly historical interest in its operations comparable to that of the main protagonists. As Sergei Kudryashov shows,

Soviet newspapers and periodicals covered the campaign in detail and with a neutral stance: *Pravda*, for example, printed more than 300 factual reports in 1940 and 1941 (before Operation Barbarossa). The Soviet Union was also receiving military intelligence from its sources in the United Kingdom while Maisky, the Soviet ambassador, reported conversations with such leading figures as Lord Beaverbrook, the Minister of Aircraft Production, and Sir Archibald Sinclair, the Secretary for Air. After 1945 objective interest in the Battle of Britain rapidly fell victim to the Cold War. A popular interpretation was that Hitler's attack on Britain was an exercise in deception since his real enemy throughout was the Soviet Union. Hitler could have defeated Britain but chose not to: 'the road to London went via Moscow'. It was the Soviet Union which had saved Britain. With the thaw in the Cold War Soviet historians paid more attention to British resistance, but tended to focus on the Anglo–German conflict in general, and the air war in particular, before Barbarossa. Political correctness dictated that sympathy towards the RAF and the British people should be combined with sharp criticism of the political elite for its appeasement of Hitler.

The end of the Cold War has not as yet brought any marked change in Russian approaches to the Battle of Britain; indeed a recent official history of the Great Patriotic War does not even mention it as an important event. At the very least, the opening of Soviet archives should soon lead to a renewal of interest in the connection between the Battle of Britain and Barbarossa. As the author fairly concludes, 'We will never know how Hitler would have responded had British resistance been less obstinate and resolute. The fact of the matter is that Britain did not give up and Hitler was eventually trapped in a war on two fronts while Stalin got a valuable ally.'

Richard P. Hallion, in his detailed and wide-ranging account of American reactions, places the subject firmly in the contexts of American domestic politics and inter-service rivalries. He states boldly that the perceived German failure greatly encouraged the pro-British interventionist lobby, set the stage for Anglo-American military co-operation and planning, and launched the United States on the road to rearmament. These trends may be clear in the longer term, but in 1940 isolationism remained strong and a year after the Battle of Britain effectively ended (i.e. in mid-September 1941), the United States seemed almost as far as ever from armed intervention.

In a crucial respect American service leaders found it very difficult to profit from the British experience because their own strategic position was so different. Their home territory seemed virtually invulnerable to a serious attack, with the corollary that their own operational strategy was strongly orientated towards the offensive. For this reason, Hallion suggests, American planners may have missed lessons from the British defence system, based on radar, which might have prevented the disaster at Pearl Harbor.

However, the Battle of Britain was a godsend to the US Army Air Corps as proving the value of a powerful, independent air force. Had Dowding not enjoyed considerable influence with the War Cabinet and a large measure of independence from Bomber Command, not to mention from the other two services, it is possible that Fighter Command's reserves would have been used up, to no effect, in the Battle of France. Conversely, one of the main reasons for the Luftwaffe's failure was judged to be that for too long its organisation and doctrine had been subordinated to the needs of the German army. The Luftwaffe, in short, was not a genuine strategic force, but basically 'an army corps commander's supporting arm writ large'. The vision of an independent American air force was eventually realised in 1947.

Theodore F. Cook shows that although the Battle of Britain was thoroughly reported by the Japanese attachés in London, the Tripartite Pact with Germany and Italy in September 1940 meant that accounts of the RAF's victories over the Luftwaffe were not well received in Tokyo. The failure of the Germans to launch an invasion of Britain did, at least, discourage thoughts of a Japanese invasion of Hong Kong and the Malay peninsula in the summer of 1940. In the longer term, Britain's survival reduced Japan's chances of attaining her objectives in the Pacific, and eventually her homeland was exposed to air attacks. But these lessons were hidden from her leaders in 1940.

The book also includes the recollections of a Luftwaffe and an RAF veteran, and the previously unpublished letters of a young British pilot to his parents. Their accounts serve to show the difficulty of recalling the details of combat, so fast and confused were these encounters. Wallace Cunningham, the Scottish ace whose dry sense of humour can be savoured, mentions, for example, that his squadron of Spitfires was equipped with two 20-mm Hispano Cannon, which were immensely destructive but held only sixty rounds – six seconds' firing if there were no stoppages. He and the other British pilot represented here, Nigel Rose, refer frequently to the frustration caused by their guns jamming.

Hans-Ekkehard Bob joined the Luftwaffe in 1936 and flew various types of Me 109s in some 2,000 sorties, more than half of them combat missions. He recalls no feelings of hostility towards British pilots during the battles in 1940 and was puzzled as to why the two nations were at war. Unlike his superiors, Bob considered an invasion of Britain feasible because there were only a few British fighter planes left in the sky. He blames Goering for strategic errors which pushed the Luftwaffe on to the defensive at a very early stage. He recalls that, in contrast to the myth of idyllic weather, flying conditions were often bad, and he is critical of the tactics which so handicapped the German fighters. Forced to fly at the bombers' slow speed, 'we wobbled along like limping ducks'. He and his comrades were shocked by the effectiveness of the enemy's radar system. He was not conscious at the time that Eagle Day, 13 August, was of any special significance – it was just another hazardous day in the campaign. He does, however, recall that he thought the switch to the bombing of London on 7 September was a fatal error; but he is mistaken in believing that British aviation production had been 'ruined' by that date. Herr Bob's conclusion that 'war makes neither winners nor conquerors, only losers' perhaps owes more to contemporary reflections than to feelings on either side of the Channel in 1940. The Luftwaffe's failure to overcome Britain's defences was only a serious setback, but the eventual, indirect outcome was a very definite defeat for Germany.

Wallace Cunningham's droll, laconic and modest recollections are usefully supplemented by extracts from squadron combat reports which reveal some details of his distinguished record. Flying with 19 Squadron from Duxford, he comments on the report for 3 September: 'This was an unhappy occasion. We were late on arrival and North Weald was caught with aircraft on the ground refuelling . . . We had some victories but did not prevent the bombing. Moreover, the majority of cannons did not fire their complement.' Four days later the Duxford Wing flew its first offensive patrol with three squadrons and encountered an enemy force of twenty bombers escorted by fifty fighters. While allowing that the 'big wing' strategy, favoured by Leigh-Mallory in 12 Group, had its merits, Cunningham doubts whether letting the Wing increase in squadrons was always the best way of intercepting enemy formations. On 19 September, for example, the squadrons were scrambled three times, on the first two occasions without success. The Duxford Wing illustrates the international composition of Fighter Command: 242 Squadron was Canadian, 310 Czech, and 19 contained Czechs, New Zealanders, Canadians, South Africans, Rhodesians, English and three Scots.

Cunningham wisely concludes with reflections on the fallibility of memory: 'old men's memories do a lot of editing'. But he believes he and his comrades were conscious of their privilege and responsibility in defending the country: it was dangerous, exciting and fulfilling. He experienced no sense of finality or victory in September 1940; on the contrary, night operations in the succeeding Blitz were even more demanding, frustrating and hazardous.

Nigel Rose is another surviving Spitfire pilot, whose regular letters to his parents capture the offhand, authentic experience of young pilots at the time. Rose now views the letters as surprisingly immature for a twenty-two-year-old – more like the chatter of a sixteen-year-old caught reading *Biggles* under the blankets with a fading torch! Interestingly, he rates himself as a good pilot but a mediocre fighter because he lacked sufficient aggression. He also notes in retrospect an amazing lack of discretion in his letters regarding security.

From mid-August Rose flew from a station near Tangmere, which he saw heavily bombed by Junkers 87s. On 16 August he encountered about '50 Jerries and I had my baptism of firing'. He believes he 'got his man'. 'It was terrifically exciting and I'm darned if I can remember what happened at the time.' Like Cunningham, he expresses shame and frustration in being forced to return with unfired guns. By 5 September he admitted to being 'a wee bit tired'. The previous day his flight had tackled about twenty Me 110s some fifteen miles out to sea from Beachy Head. 'It was colossal fun, and we played around for about ten minutes.' Later in the letter he added, 'Boy! This certainly is the life!' A week later his plane was shot up and he was slightly wounded due to a brief lapse of concentration. He resumed flying in October and records that he fired in error at a Spitfire and was himself the target of 'friendly' AA fire. Finally, on 8 December he mentions that there was a glut of pilots so that it was hard to get a flight, whereas at the height of the Battle there had been a serious shortage.

There can be very few people alive today whose notions of what constitutes the Battle of Britain have been formed entirely, or even mainly, from personal experience or knowledge of historical sources. Films, newsreels, memoirs and a variety of imaginative literature have contributed to our sense of what it must have been like, whether experienced from the cockpit, as a spectator on the ground, or from the comfort of an armchair.

Owen Dudley Edwards contributes a fascinating insight into one of the less obvious imaginative sources – juvenile literature – taking as one of his themes 'The Battle of Britain was won on the playing fields of Greyfriars'. His starting point is the demise of many of the most popular juvenile papers on the eve of the Battle due to the paper shortage, which was exacerbated by the Nazi conquest of Norway. All but two of Lord Camrose's extensive 'stable', including the *Magnet* and the *Gem*, were sacrificed. But the prodigious output of the journalist Frank Richards had already influenced the *mentalités* of the 200,000 annual readers of the *Gem* and *Magnet* who were young enough to fight or experience the Battle of Britain. In May 1940 Richards had vividly anticipated the Battle with the attack of a 'Hun raider' on a Channel trawler. Harry Wharton, Johnny Bull and their pals were ecstatic witnesses of the action and all wanted to join the RAF.

But this was only a late, prophetic episode in a genre of air adventure stories which had proliferated, especially from the pen of Captain W.E. Johns, creator of Biggles, since the 1920s. Consequently, *Magnet* readers fought the Battle of Britain with a stock of ideas and attitudes which would stand them in good stead. They knew, for example, that they should not take authority seriously, but not openly flout it. They knew they should not expect rationality, or be surprised by injustice. They understood the value of laughter and comradeship; above all they were confident of victory. Indeed, in Dudley Edwards's memorable phrases: 'Their training deprived them of the means of envisaging defeat. Lord Camrose had killed them all on the eve of the Battle of Britain. So they went out and won it.'

The essay discusses the influence of the Chalet School series by Elinor Brent-Dyer, which stressed that even in the midst of war moral purposes must be kept to the fore. Thus it was vital to discriminate between the Nazis and good Germans. Even before it was fought, she had imaginatively placed the Battle of Britain in the moral context of the defence of Jews and of all other true religions. Richmal Crompton's William Brown also makes an appearance, usually creating mischief and mayhem, but in one fable supposedly representing the virtues of England against the evils of Nazism. Dudley Edwards concludes with a discussion of the work of Captain W.E. Johns, the writer of juvenile literature on air adventure and air warfare *par excellence*. Johns was obliged to bring his hero, Biggles, into the Second World War and he enters the Battle of Britain in a volume of short stories entitled *Spitfire Parade*, but, Dudley Edwards suggests, he could not break free from his own experience in 1914–18. Consequently, 'Biggles made the Battle of Britain an event in the First World War.' Far more remarkable, he argues, was the creation by Johns of a prototype feminist heroine, Worrals, a pilot who takes part in combat and shoots down an enemy aircraft.

What was air combat in the Battle of Britain really like and how wide is the gulf between myth and reality? Under the apt sub-heading of 'Writing in the Sky', Angus Calder explores these questions through an analysis of three influential books: Richard Hillary's *The Last Enemy* (1942), Douglas Bader's memoirs (written up by Paul Brickhill) in *Reach for the Sky* (1954), and Peter Townsend's essay in historical objectivity, *Duel of Eagles* (1970). All contain vivid descriptions of dogfights, but Calder is sceptical about their accuracy and tone. We are convinced by these and similar accounts because we have known instinctively that this is how things must have been since we saw the first films or newsreels or read about air warfare in childhood. Hillary and his fellow pilots were beneficiaries of ancient traditions of romance and chivalry updated to 'knights of the air' in the First World War and given a powerful boost in 1940 as a 'duel of eagles' or the gallant 'few' defenders against the many (ungallant) attackers. RAF pilots were also comfortably associated with imperial heroism. Calder cannot accept this version as history: in air combat in 1940 there were only three options – kill, be killed or run away. Even 'leftish literary intellectuals' were seduced by the romance of the air, as shown by their acceptance of Hillary's highly imaginative and contrived book as authentic. Though lacking the vivid descriptions of combat in the books discussed by Calder, the contributions of Cunningham, Rose and Bob in this volume convey a more accurate idea of 'what it was really like'.

Tony Aldgate pursues the same theme of the necessary gap between reality and media presentation in his account of the treatment of the Battle of Britain in films between the Second World War and 1969. Film, he reminds us, 'is not some unadulterated reflection of historical truth captured faithfully by the camera'. Quite the contrary, the factual history of the Battle has been largely marginalised in favour of creating or cultivating its legend. Aldgate cites a British newsreel of October 1940 entitled 'All in a Fighter's Day's Work' whose tone and language closely resembles that of a sporting fixture (one could easily substitute 'taking wickets' or 'bagging pheasants' for destroying Messerschmitts), and ends with the modest, well-mannered pilots enjoying a cup of tea. At precisely the same time the American series the *March of Time* presented a much more rhetorical and jazzed-up version. British films soon emulated the Americans' style, not least in celebrating the Battle of Britain as a morale-boosting victory. *Dangerous Moonlight* (1941) and *The First of the Few* (1942) made lasting contributions to the legend, which, to some degree, have influenced all filmgoers. We know that they are in many respects inaccurate and unhistorical: yet we want to believe them. By the late 1960s, when *Battle of Britain* was filmed, a more informative, questioning and anti-heroic account was called for. Much more emphasis was now placed on the wrangles between senior commanders, the important contribution of women, the significance of radar and the value of plastic surgery in rebuilding terribly disfigured pilots' faces and bodies. Despite numerous factual errors the film constitutes 'as rich a source on the subject as historians are likely to find' in that medium.

1940, as Adrian Gregory remarks, was a 'memorable' year and one would like to believe that, sixty years on, most adult Britons – and many children – will have a general knowledge of the dramatic series of events from Dunkirk to the Blitz with the Battle of Britain at the centre. Yet Battle of Britain Day, 15 September, has never come close to matching 11 November, Armistice Day, in the national consciousness. Although the bulk of Gregory's paper is devoted to showing in detail how the Battle has been commemorated, both in tangible ways and ceremonially, he remains puzzled that it has not received a higher profile or aroused the intense devotion that might have been expected. After all, as he remarks with pardonable exaggeration, it was a significant victory, 'among the two or three truly important British successes in any major war'. Various explanations are offered. Although the Battle was overwhelmingly a triumph for Fighter Command, Bomber Command and the other branches of the service were far from inactive during the critical months of 1940. Gregory suggests that there was a preference for the commemoration of the RAF as a whole rather than just Fighter Command. Also the romantic emphasis on the 'few', which was so much a feature of propaganda at the time, in the longer term made the Battle of Britain harder to portray and commemorate as a national achievement. It could further be argued that this success occurred too early in the war and was more of a deliverance from invasion than a victory or even a guarantee of future victory. There was no clear and decisive break between the Battle of Britain and the Blitz; things got worse rather than better and it would take another year at least before the threat of invasion could finally be discounted.

Students of history, and especially military history, have become increasingly concerned to preserve physical evidence of the past as commemorative monuments, as components of our 'heritage' and, above all, for educational purposes. As Jeremy Lake and John Schofield remark in their contribution on conservation, it is easy to make the case for famous sites associated with the Battle of Britain, such as the fighter sector stations at Kenley or Biggin Hill which clearly contribute to our understanding of the Battle. But is a link with the Battle sufficient justification for preserving an otherwise undistinguished site or building? The authors explain the rigorously selective criteria for statutory protection. Rarity alone may be sufficient to ensure preservation. For example, only sixty-one heavy anti-aircraft gunsites out of nearly 1,000 survive in anything like their original form. The Chain Home radar mast which survives at Stenigot in Lincolnshire is a unique example of its type and has recently been listed. Sector airfields such as Biggin Hill, Kenley, North Weald and Debden, though much changed by wartime damage and post-war developments, all display interesting features. Debden, for example, 'has retained much of its 1930s character with much of the flying field and perimeter still intact'. Tangmere, whose near-total destruction on 16 August was witnessed by Nigel Rose, keeps its deserted and ruined control tower 'as a lonely icon on the edge of the original flying field'. Duxford, one of the best-preserved examples of a Second World War airfield in Britain, is now famous as the home of one of Europe's leading aviation museums. The underground operations room at RAF Uxbridge, the 'nerve centre' of 11 Group's operations in 1940, has survived and its famous 'tote board' and plotting table have recently been restored. Lake and Schofield conclude their survey by stressing that, in addition to the obvious importance of these sites and buildings as memorials of the defiant defence of Britain in 1940, they also merit preservation in relation to the history of technology and warfare.

In a stimulating and original survey, Paul Addison and Jeremy Crang examine the national dimensions of what was truly 'a battle of many nations'. Although London and south-eastern England bore the brunt of the Battle, many other areas experienced the anxiety caused by frequent air alarms and random raids if not prolonged periods of intensive bombing. Most British citizens seem to have felt involved in what was widely believed to be the prelude to a German invasion and a threat to national survival. Wales and Scotland both counted as components of the 'strategic heartland' in terms of extensive beach defences. An enhanced sense of national unity was movingly evident in donations to the Spitfire Fund, with a small Welsh village raising the sum of £5,000 which was officially stated to be the cost of a single aircraft. This essay also shows that all regions of the United Kingdom contributed to the total of just under 3,000 combat fliers who qualify for membership of the 'few'. From a sample of 1,027 pilots whose birthplace has been established, thirteen came from Northern Ireland, thirty from Wales and eighty-five from Scotland.

The imperial contribution included some of the best and bravest pilots: among the top ten aces were two New Zealanders and an Australian. New Zealand also of course provided Keith Park, commander of 11 Group, which endured the most concentrated and prolonged attacks. In addition, although the United States remained neutral, American public opinion was seen to respond positively to Britain's gallant resistance. The British government, for its part, dispensed with the oath of allegiance to the King to facilitate the entry of American pilots into the RAF.

The authors make the important point that Britain not only received help *from* Europe (notably in the form of 145 Polish and 88 Czech pilots), but also avowedly fought in part *for* the continent; victory in 1940 would mark the first step in the struggle to liberate Nazi-occupied Europe. The Battle of Britain may consequently be viewed as a triumph for an independent island fortress at the heart of a world-wide empire, but also as showing that Britain's future was inextricably linked with that of Western Europe.

In his clear and judicious summing up, Richard Overy reminds us that in 1940 'neither side invested the air conflict with the weight of historical significance that it has borne in the sixty years since it was fought'. Without seeking in any way to debunk the British defensive achievement, it now seems reasonable to suggest that the German operational performance was better than might have been expected, given the handicaps placed on the Luftwaffe by Hitler and its own High Command. A German victory, contrary to the British myth, would have been 'against the odds'. Even had the Luftwaffe attained command of the air over south-eastern England it is far from certain that an invasion would have succeeded.

'There is no reason to believe that Hitler was not serious about the invasion plan,' Overy concludes, but the schedule was very tight. Hitler made up his mind only as circumstances unfolded and it became clear well before mid-September that the necessary command in the air over southern England and the Channel would not be achieved. Hitler and his service chiefs knew that it would be disastrous to attempt invasion and to fail. By the end of 1940 it seemed clear, even to pessimists like Harold Nicolson, that Britain had managed to avoid losing the war, but it was far from obvious how it could actually be won and what modest role Britain could play. Nevertheless, for the besieged and battered population the Battle of Britain became the symbol of defiance and as such remained 'a necessary battle for British self-esteem and international credibility'.

PART ONE

BEFORE THE BATTLE

KLAUS A. MAIER

The Luftwaffe

Preparations and Assumptions, 1933–9

With Reichsmarschall Hermann Goering as Air Minister and Commander-in-Chief of the Luftwaffe, the connection between the Luftwaffe and the Nazi regime is a striking one. It might therefore be supposed that German air doctrine was dominated by the Nazi ideology of a 'total war'. But Nazi Germany never built up a strategic air force comparable to British Bomber Command or the US Army Air Forces. Due partly to technological difficulties and poor production management, but mainly to Nazi foreign policy, the role of the Luftwaffe was a tactical one.[1]

During the second half of the 1930s Hitler's aggressive foreign policy underwent a fundamental change. He had originally hoped to conquer *Lebensraum* (living space) for the German people in the east, either in alliance with Britain or at least with her standing aside. He now realised that the British government was trying to halt his drive to the east by containing Nazi foreign policy within a general European peace settlement. From that time on Hitler's ambitions faced the risk of a major European war against Britain and her allies; this is also undoubtedly the reason why Hitler, refusing to give up his long-cherished *Lebensraum* dream, had to mobilise German resources as fast as possible. He had to wage a succession of short wars before the Western powers were sufficiently prepared to intervene successfully. Timing became all important.

Hitler's Blitzkrieg concept, which he once described as 'applying military force and thereby taking big risks', became the guiding rule for further German air armament. In April 1937 Goering ordered a final stop to the development of all four-engined bombers. Because he calculated that the German aircraft industry could produce two and a half twin-engined bombers for every one four-engined aircraft, Goering gave priority to quantity over quality. He thus committed the Luftwaffe to a medium-range air force which eventually proved ill adapted to a strategic air offensive against Britain.

Hitler's decision to intervene in the Spanish Civil War on the side of

General Franco was welcomed by Goering as an opportunity to test his Luftwaffe under combat conditions. Owing to Franco's lack of heavy weapons, the Legion Condor was engaged mainly in close air support operations. Under its Chief of Staff and last commander, Wolfram Freiherr von Richthofen, the Legion developed a very effective tactical method for this sort of action, but it was also engaged in strategic air operations. According to a report written during the summer of 1938 the Legion had attacked the following objectives: the enemy air force; units of war production; government quarters and the civilian population; supplies and transportation; troops in transit and those in the front line. As for the attacks on civilians, it was reported that the population had been impressed and terrorised by successive air attacks. In general, the reports ascribed the collapse of morale to the lack of discipline and organisation among Spanish workers.[2] The destruction of the small town of Guernica in April 1937 is even now considered by many to be a classic case of terror-bombing.

This widespread fear of the German air menace prevented the British political and military leadership from making a clear-headed analysis and realistic evaluation of the Luftwaffe's real striking power in a strategic air war. It thus had a fatal effect on British foreign policy, above all during the Czech crisis in the autumn of 1938. On 29 September of that year, when the crisis was at its peak, the military intelligence section of the British War Office (MI5) circulated a warning that at the very moment that Britain declared war on Germany, the Luftwaffe would attack London.[3] Chamberlain shared this view, justifying the policy which led to the bloodless British defeat at Munich by reference to the German air threat.[4]

In May 1939 the intelligence section of the Luftwaffe General Staff believed that the Third Reich was the only state that had advanced to a conception of total air war in both offensive and defensive respects. Following on from this, the intelligence section pointed out that during the Czech crisis the Luftwaffe had been able to exert enormous political pressure; thus it did not have to prove its real striking power in actual combat. It was also believed that the Western powers, because of their democratic constitutions and parliamentary systems, were less flexible in their political and military decision-making processes than the authoritarian German Führer state. This prejudice led to the hazardous prophecy that although the Western powers were bound by treaties and promises to Eastern Europe, a conflict in this region could be localised.[5]

A three-day staff manoeuvre by Luftflotte 2, which was earmarked for wartime air operations against Britain, gave clear indications of the technical and tactical shortcomings of the Luftwaffe for such operations. The fleet commmander, General Felmy, criticised chiefly the slow progress in tactical training caused by the rapid expansion of the Luftwaffe. His report concluded that a strategic air offensive against Britain could not be launched until 1942, when the Luftwaffe would possess long-range bombers or when the Wehrmacht had captured forward air bases in the Netherlands or France. But if war with Britain should occur before this time, Felmy wanted the Luftwaffe to attack London and other British population centres in a pure terror-bombing offensive.

Felmy's anticipation of the decisive results of such an offensive, like the anticipation of the intelligence section, rested upon experience gained during the Czech crisis. The digging of slit trenches in public parks and the handing out of gas masks in London in September 1938 was seen by Felmy as an indication of a high degree of war hysteria in Britain – in contrast to the situation in Germany. He proposed to exploit this hysteria in case of war.[6] The operations section of the Luftwaffe General Staff was less optimistic about the political results to be obtained by terror-bombing London alone, but it too hoped that the continuous bombing of industrial centres, even by small units, would eventually lead to a collapse of morale in large areas of Britain.

On 22 August 1939 Hitler told his Wehrmacht commanders that the attack on Poland would be solely a matter of nerve. He said, 'I have always taken big risks. And also now I run a big risk.'[7] Four days later he wrote to Mussolini: 'As neither France nor Britain can achieve any decisive successes in the West, and as Germany, as a result of the agreement with Russia, will have all her forces free in the East after the defeat of Poland, and as air supremacy is undoubtedly on our side, I do not shrink from solving the Eastern question even at the risk of complications in the West.'[8]

When Hitler initiated hostilities in September 1939, he had at his disposal a Luftwaffe that had become the force best suited for his Blitzkrieg strategy of short continental campaigns. On 3 September 1939 Britain and France declared war on Germany; as a deterrent force the Luftwaffe had failed.

At first, however, Hitler found this situation quite acceptable, as the Western powers did not launch a major attack and the Wehrmacht was able to subdue Poland quickly. While the last military resistance in Warsaw and Modlin collapsed under the ruthless attacks of the Luftwaffe, most of the German units which had taken part in the Polish campaign were already being transferred to the west.

Apart from the need to maintain the fighting strength of the Luftwaffe for the decisive battle with the Western powers, Hitler's hope of a 'reversal of alliances' led him to prosecute the air war against Britain with great restraint, though stepping it up by degrees. The German air commands were ordered to leave the responsibility for initiating air attacks clearly to Britain and France.

Prelude to the Battle of Britain: October 1939–July 1940

In October 1939 Hitler decided, against the opposition of the army leaders, to attack in the west at the earliest possible opportunity. On 9 October he explained his ideas to the commanders-in-chief in a long memorandum.[9] Basing his arguments on the assertions that the military utilisation of German national strength (*Volkskraft*) had reached a level 'which no efforts can improve significantly, in the short term at any rate', and that the increase in German military strength to be expected in the next few years could be matched, not indeed by France but probably by the British, Hitler pressed for quick exploitation of current German superiority now that the successful campaign in Poland had given Germany the possibility, which for decades she had longed for in vain, of fighting a war on a single front. Time was very probably working for the Western powers. Among the resulting dangers for Germany, Hitler described the disruption of production in the Ruhr by air attacks as the 'most serious and greatest danger'; a halt in production there could not be compensated for elsewhere, and 'sooner or later' would inevitably lead to the collapse of Germany's war economy and her defensive strength.

When the German attack in the west began on 10 May 1940 after numerous postponements, caused mostly by the weather, the Luftwaffe had about 1,180 bombers, 341 dive-bombers, 970 fighters, and 270 heavy fighters ready for action.[10] Although the Allies should have been warned by reports of the use of the Luftwaffe in Poland, the Luftwaffe succeeded in surprising their air units on the ground as well as their air command centres. As no persistent Allied attacks on the Ruhr took place, most of the fighter units assigned to defend it were transferred to the operations area and used to achieve air supremacy there and to support the army. As had already happened in the case of Warsaw, the Luftwaffe was used without regard to civilian casualties. When strong resistance in Rotterdam threatened to delay the quick occupation of Holland, Goering ordered a concentrated air attack on the city on 13 May to force an early capitulation.

After the defeat of France the Luftwaffe was in a very favourable geographical position for operations against Britain, but in spite of the ideas developed by Luftflotte 2 in 1938 it did not have any overall tactical plan. Such a plan appeared unnecessary because of the general expectation that Britain would agree to terms after the German victory over France. In his memorandum of 30 June 1940[11] on continuing the war against Britain, General Alfred Jodl, Chief of the Operations Staff of the German Armed Forces Supreme Command, referred to attacks on the British homeland and expanding the war to peripheral areas as measures which, in his opinion, should be used, 'if political means do not produce the desired results'. In the war against the British homeland, which he preferred, he distinguished between three possibilities: first, a 'siege' – an air and naval war against imports and exports, the British air force, and all sources of strength of the British war economy; second, a 'terror attack' against British population centres; third, a landing with the aim of occupying Britain.

Basing his arguments on the mistaken assessment that final victory over Britain was only a question of time, and that Germany was free to choose a form of military action that would 'spare her strength and avoid risks', Jodl recommended the elimination of the British air force as the first and most important aim: 'The war against the British air force must be the very first task in order to reduce and finally put a stop to the destruction of the foundations of our war economy.' For this purpose the RAF had to be defeated over the parts of Britain within the combat range of German heavy fighters (Me 110), or at least forced to withdraw to bases in central Britain. This would make it possible to 'destroy the entire southern part of Britain with its armaments industry and greatly reduce the effectiveness of British bombers against the western parts of Germany'. Eliminating the aircraft industry concentrated around London and Birmingham would make it impossible for the RAF to replace its losses. This would mean 'the end of Britain's ability to carry out military actions against Germany'. The destruction of the British aircraft industry should be complemented by a simultaneous campaign against supply depots and exports and imports, at sea and in the ports: 'Combined with propaganda and occasional terror attacks – to be represented as retaliation – this accelerating decline in the food supply of the country will paralyse and finally break the will of the people to resist and thus force their government to capitulate.' In Jodl's opinion a landing should only be carried out 'to deal a death-blow to Britain when her war economy has been paralysed and her air force destroyed, if it should still be necessary'. For Jodl, German air supremacy was therefore an essential condition of a landing.

For a short period after the defeat of France Hitler had confidently expected that Britain would leave the war.[12] Even before the conclusion of the fighting in France, he had given orders for a reduction in the size of the army in favour of the Luftwaffe and the Kriegsmarine. On 13 July the question of greatest concern to Hitler was 'why Britain is still unwilling to make peace'. General Franz Halder, Chief of the Army General Staff, noted in his diary: 'He believes, as we do, that the answer to this question is that Britain is still placing her hopes in Russia. He therefore expects that it will be necessary to force Britain to make peace.'[13]

Three days later, on 16 July, Hitler issued Directive no. 16, on preparations for an invasion of England,[14] in which he announced his decision to prepare and, if necessary, to carry out such an operation. But in conferences with the commanders-in-chief of the Wehrmacht services on 21 July Hitler repeated doubts about a landing operation: 'If it is not certain that preparations can be completed by the beginning of September, other plans must be considered.'[15] Among these plans was an attack on the Soviet Union, the last *Festlanddegen* (continental rapier) Britain could hope for. Strategic considerations coincided with his decision to return to the priority of the eastern front.[16] On 28 July, only a few weeks after he had ordered a reduction in the army, Hitler told General Fromm, Chief of Army Armaments and Commander of the Replacement Army, to increase the wartime army to 180 divisions by 1 May 1941.[17] At the Berghof conference on 31 July Hitler ordered preparations for a campaign against the Soviet Union and gave clear operational instructions. Much importance was given to deception. According to Halder's diary, deception had to be organised in Spain, North Africa and England.[18]

An entry in Goebbels's diary on 7 August is more specific:

> Main assault against England is planned to start immediately. With Luftwaffe and long-range artillery. One first taste for London. We shall probe how strong England's air fleet still is or feels. Their fighter force is said to be still quite intact. If our losses are normal then the action will continue. If not, new ways will be looked for. Invasion not planned. But we shall talk about it in our propaganda in a hidden way, to confuse the enemy.[19]

Goering never took any interest in a landing operation. He wanted the Luftwaffe to conduct an independent strategic air war against Britain,[20] in which his aircraft, according to a very optimistic assessment by the Chief of Intelligence to the Luftwaffe General Staff, could go over to decisive daylight operations 'owing to the inadequate air defences of the island'.[21]

When the Battle of Britain began, a strategic air war, not an invasion, was *ante portas Britanniae*.

Notes and References

1 See the author's detailed examination, 'Total War and Operational Air Warfare', in K. Maier et al., *Germany and the Second World War*, vol. 2, *Germany's Initial Conquests in Europe* (Oxford, 1991), pp. 31–59.
2 Bundesarchiv-Militärarchiv (BA-MA), RL 7/57.
3 F.H. Hinsley et al., *British Intelligence in the Second World War: Its Influence on Strategy and Operations*, vol. 1 (London, 1979), p. 82.
4 U. Bialer, *The Shadow of the Bomber: The Fear of Air Attack and British Politics, 1932–1939* (London, 1980), p. 157.
5 BA-MA, RL 2/535.
6 BA-MA, RL 7/42.
7 *Akten zur Deutschen Auswärtigen Politik 1918–1945 (ADAP)*, Series D: *1937–1945*, VII, no. 192.
8 *ADAP*, D, VII, no. 307.
9 *Trial of Major War Criminals by the International Military Tribunal Sitting at*

Nuremberg, Germany, 42 vols (Nuremberg, 1947–9), vol. 37, p. 466 ff, 'Denkschrift und Richtlinien über die Führung des Krieges im Westen', 9 Oct. 1939.

10 BA-MA, RL 2 III/707.

11 *Trial of Major War Criminals*, vol. 28, p. 30 ff.

12 See Maier, 'The Battle of Britain', in Maier et al., *Germany's Initial Conquests*, pp. 374–5.

13 T.N. Dupuy (ed.), *The Halder Diaries, 1939–42* (Boulder, Colorado, 1975), vol. 1, p. 506 (translation amended).

14 H.R. Trevor-Roper (ed.), *Hitler's War Directives, 1939–45* (London, 1964), no. 16.

15 'Führer Conferences on Naval Affairs, 1939–45', *Brassey's Naval Annual* (Portsmouth, 1948), pp. 119–20.

16 For Hitler's decision to turn east in July 1940 see J. Föster, 'Hitler's Wendung nach Osten. Die deutsche Kriegspolitik 1940–1', in B. Wegner (ed.), *Zwei Wege nach Moskau* (Munich, 1991), p. 113 ff.

17 B. Kroener, 'Der "Erfrorene Blitzkrieg". Strategische Planungen der deutschen Führung gegen die Sowjetunion und die Ursachen ihres Scheiterns', in Wegner (ed.), *Zwei Wege nach Moskau*, p. 133 ff.

18 Charles B. Burdick and Hans-Adolf Jacobsen (eds.), *The Halder War Diary, 1939–42* (Novato, California, 1988), p. 245.

19 R. Reuth (ed.), *Goebbels Tagebücher* (Munich, 1992), p. 1,461.

20 Maier, 'The Battle of Britain', pp. 385–6.

21 Quoted in D. Wood and D. Dempster, *The Narrow Margin* (London, 1961), p. 109.

MALCOLM SMITH

The RAF

The preparation of the RAF for the Battle of Britain can be divided into three different phases, each with distinctive problems. During the first phase, both the foundation of the RAF in 1918, and its continuation as an independent force into the peace, were highly contentious. The new force was immediately faced with the opposition of the established armed forces to its very existence and, in the period of financial retrenchment that followed the war, found survival very difficult. The significance of this period for the Battle was that it was during these years that the basic strategic principles of the new force were laid down.

The second phase was the period of rearmament in the 1930s. There were severe diplomatic and practical problems to be faced in rearmament, not helped by the fact that the Air Ministry stuck rigidly to the most fundamental of RAF strategic principles, that of the efficacy of the bomber. Only very late in rearmament did government decide that fighter defence must be given priority, although, as we shall see, it was only relatively late in this period that the technology actually developed to question the belief that the bomber would always get through.

The third phase was the early stage of the European war, up to and including the Battle of France, in which major new strategic problems were caused for Fighter Command by German victories in Scandinavia, the Low Countries and France.

Birth and Retrenchment

Air war had developed rapidly during the First World War, but this had not provided irrefutable evidence to lay the foundation for the future for air power that Trenchard was to propound in the ten years after the war ended. The RAF had been formed in the belief that bombers offered a way, quite literally, of leaping over the trench deadlock and attacking those vulnerable centres of production, as well as the civilian will to war, the destruction of which would leave the men in uniform nothing to fight with or for.[1] This was a very common belief among airmen both in Europe and in North America. What had happened in 1917 in Russia and in 1918 in Germany seemed to suggest that in total warfare the economy of a nation and its will to war were not only legitimate targets but, with the advent of the bomber, vulnerable ones as well.

The difference between British and other airmen was that the British had an independent air force formed on that very principle, whereas airmen in other countries were constrained by the strategic orthodoxies of armies or navies, in which they still served. The furious opposition of the older services to the new force in Britain helped to push the airmen into the kind of apocalyptic utterances on air power that became familiar in the 1920s. There was an even greater difference between British and other air forces when it came to the application of the principle of the air offensive. Uniquely, the British airmen claimed that in order to achieve the breakdown of the enemy economy and society, it was unnecessary to defeat the enemy air force. They claimed that the advantages open to attacking bombers were manifest: the vast cubic airspace available, which would make it nigh impossible for defenders to guess the direction of attack or even the target; and the stable gun platform available to the larger aircraft if defending fighters should find them in the first place. These advantages meant, as Stanley Baldwin later famously put it, that the bomber would always get through.[2] This being so, there was simply no need to target the enemy air force. The implications were that close fighter defence was largely a waste of time and that its provision should be confined only to the most significant of national targets.

In the period of financial retrenchment which, naturally enough following the First World War, affected all the armed forces in Britain, this argument was used in two ways. First, it was used to make the case for the continuation of the RAF as a separate service; air power had an independent and possibly decisive role to play in peacetime as a war-stopping deterrent, and a possibly decisive winning role to play if the deterrent failed. Second, it underpinned the case that, in equipping the force, as large as possible a proportion of national resources should go on bombers and as small a share as absolutely necessary should go on close fighter defence. Trenchard initially put the ratio at two bombers for every fighter.[3] This was arbitrary, to say the least, and was difficult to square with experience, limited though that was. General E.B. Ashmore had commanded the air defences of London at the end of the First World War and, in *Air Defence*, argued that a combination of fighters, lights and anti-aircraft gunnery could certainly mount a viable counter.[4] The Air Staff felt that, although Ashmore's ideas might hold for the rudimentary aircraft and the small scale of attack available in the First World War, they would not apply in the case of a determined mass attack by the faster and longer-ranged bombers now in the developmental pipeline. But, even given the terms of Trenchardian reference, establishing a ratio between bombers and fighters had nothing to do with the real question, which was that of defending vital centres. Such vital targets could be listed, did not change in number or size very often, and the fighters needed to defend them could be calculated on the basis of the strategic configuration of the targets and the capabilities of the enemy air force. The number of fighters needed had very little to do with the number of bombers. It certainly was not clear from First World War evidence that Trenchard's ratio applied to air attack, let alone air defence. As commander of the Independent Air Force in France in 1918, Trenchard had found that he needed to maintain a relentless counter-force strategy to allow his bomber force to get through.[5] Perhaps Trenchard did not mean anything too precise in his two-to-one ratio. It was meant to emphasise the danger of relying on close defence and the prime importance, in his view, of counter-attack, as technological advance would always favour the bomber. Nevertheless, this two-to-one ratio was one with which the nation was saddled for virtually all the interwar period. Here one should note a quite fundamental distinction between the role of the fighters in the Luftwaffe and in the RAF. Luftwaffe fighters would be called upon to perform many different functions in integrated operations of fighters and bombers. In the RAF, before the Second World War, the fighter had one function only, the air defence of Great Britain. Very little consideration was given to any offensive role for the fighter, even as escorts for attacking bombers.

It was also argued that Britain was particularly vulnerable to air attack. The Channel, which traditionally had guaranteed British safety from European invasion, had now become a liability because it provided cover for air attack. In the case of a British attack on France or Germany, bombers would have to make deep penetration raids before reaching Paris or Berlin. In Britain's case, bombers could appear without warning over the English south coast or the Thames estuary and be devastating London within minutes of making landfall. For the RAF, this only reinforced the case for bombers. If the possibility of a bolt from the blue could not be offset by a fighter force, then war had to be averted or, if deterrence failed, fought by a large bomber force capable of massive retaliation. This was 'a matter of faith' to the Air Staff of the interwar period, as John Slessor later admitted.[6]

This was all rather academic in the 1920s when there was no enemy in sight in Europe, no money to spend on armaments, and when the RAF spent the bulk of its time policing the Empire – hardly a job either for heavy bombers or for high-performance interceptors. But these ideas and fears structured the framework of air defence which Fighter Command was to inherit and work within in the 1930s. The Steel-Bartholomew plan of 1923 was designed to defend London against the only remotely possible air threat of the time, France. The scheme envisaged eight fighter squadrons, each assigned a sector round the southern and eastern perimeter of the capital, then eastwards as far as Devizes and north to Duxford. In the brief period in 1923 when Intelligence worried that France might be planning an expansion of its air strength, Trenchard convinced the Salisbury Committee that the disparity between French and British air figures in itself constituted a menace. The result was the fifty-two squadron scheme, to establish the RAF at home with a front line of 394 bombers and 204 fighters, roughly two to one along the lines of the Trenchardian dictum.[7] These 204 fighters would be organised in seventeen squadrons, fourteen of which would defend in the Fighting Area, namely the sectors established by Steel–Bartholomew but now expanded westwards to the Bristol Channel and north to Lincolnshire. The three remaining fighter squadrons would be stationed on the south coast, at Hawkinge, Tangmere, and on the Solent, as a thin first line of defence. The assumption was that bombers would have to be fought inland, so that some bombers would almost certainly reach what might be vital targets before they were challenged. In an age when it was considered that a bomber simply had to drop its bombs on target to achieve its mission, this was a dangerous admission. An Observer Corps would be set up, to provide as much information as possible about incoming aircraft. Anti-aircraft ground defence, virtually non-existent since 1918, was to be provided for in an inner and outer artillery zone for London, comprising 192 guns. At the same time a new command was set up, Air Defence of Great Britain (ADGB), to oversee the whole organisation. In fact, there was very little integration in this command structure. Executive control of the fighter squadrons was delegated to the commander of the Fighting Area, and the AA guns and lights would get their orders through the army. The implication, at least, was that the defensive operations of fighters and AA would be merely ancillary. The real concern of the Commander-in-Chief of ADGB should be with bomber operations.

The scheme was due to be completed in 1928. In practice, the apparent threat from France soon dissipated. Retrenchment, and then preparations for the Geneva Disarmament Conference, delayed the scheme. By 1932 the ADGB establishment stood at 42 squadrons against the 52 authorised. Most of their equipment was obsolete. In the case of AA, there were only guns, lights and men to man two of the ten sectors authorised. Only four of the fourteen Observer Corps centres had formed.[8]

Rearmament

Rearmament began in Britain with the setting up of the Defence Requirements Committee in November 1933. Initially, the DRC was much more worried by what had already happened in the Far East than with what might happen in Europe: Hitler had only just come to power, after all, and though he might be vociferous at Geneva, Germany was as yet a military threat to no one. The threat of a new German air force was to dominate the direction of rearmament from 1934 on, however, once Germany had walked out of the Disarmament Conference. Once Hitler claimed already to have air parity with Britain, in 1935, there began a hectic race to regain and maintain numerical parity with whatever the Germans said was their front-line air strength. In effect, this meant bomber strength. Not only were fighters likely to be pretty useless as a defence in war compared with a bomber counter-strike, according to established RAF ideas, but fighters would not provide a deterrent to Hitler in peacetime. If Hitler threatened to bomb Prague, a British threat to defend London in retaliation was unlikely to provoke a change of heart in Berlin. Though proposed fighter strength increased in each of the four air rearmament schemes authorised between 1934 and 1937, proposed bomber strength increased very much more, either just below or above the two-to-one ratio. Scheme A of 1934, for instance, proposed 500 bombers against 336 fighters, Scheme C of 1935 proposed 800 bombers against 420 fighters, while Scheme F of 1936 proposed over 1,000 bombers without increasing the Scheme C fighter force.[9]

The new threat from Germany obviously required ADGB to change front. The Reorientation Committee reported in 1935 in favour of continuing the policy of providing a continuous defence zone, which had been suggested by the Steel-Bartholomew plan in 1923 and confirmed by the fifty-two squadron scheme. Clearly, an air threat from the North Sea rather than the Channel would bring the industrial areas of the north of England within range of attack. This meant that though the defensive line in the west could be curtailed, it would have to be considerably increased to the north. The Reorientation Committee concluded that a continuous fighting zone should be provided from the Solent, to ring London and to continue up to Teesside. Major ports in front of this line would be defended separately. This would require twenty-five squadrons of fighters against ADGB's seventeen. It would also require more than twice as many AA guns and nearly four times as many lights. The growing front-line strength of the RAF at home was now deemed too unwieldy for a unified command, so that the ADGB organisation was split in 1936 into a number of separate Commands, the most significant of which for our purposes were Bomber Command and Fighter Command. This confirmed the lack of integration of bomber and fighter forces implicit in the ADGB structure. It says something for the relative importance the Air Ministry attached to the two Commands that the former Commander-in-Chief ADGB, Air Chief Marshal Sir John Steel, took over Bomber Command, while Fighter Command was entrusted to a man many at the top of the Air Ministry thought to be dour, somewhat unimaginative and past his sell-by date, Air Chief Marshal Sir Hugh Dowding.

Dowding was not the most light-hearted of men – hence his nickname of 'Stuffy' – and he had about him a greyness that was out of line with the youthful orientation of what in the 1930s was called 'air-mindedness'. This is not to suggest that Dowding's was entirely a negative appointment as far as the Air Ministry was concerned. His biographer argued that, given his seniority in the service, Dowding had a right to feel that he might have been given a post that would prepare him for succession to the position of Chief of the Air Staff.[10] Fighter Command, in short, was not at that time considered to be a particularly prestigious appointment, definitely second best to Bomber Command. Dowding may not have been flashy, or terribly imaginative, but he was careful, thorough and thoughtful. This was just as well, for, at this time, and with breathless haste, the possibility of providing a more effective close air defence than hitherto thought likely began to emerge. It emerged through two almost simultaneous technical developments: radar (Radio Direction Finding as it was at first known); and new interceptor fighters, which could outpace, outmanoeuvre and outgun any bomber. The application of these developments needed not so much an inspirational leader as one with gravitas, which Dowding had in plenty. Moreover, Dowding's recent experience as the man responsible for research and development at the Air Ministry clearly fitted him to oversee the major developments of the next few years.

It is not necessary to go into the detail of either technical development; they are already well known. It needs to be emphasised, however, how late these developments were in the preparation for the Battle. The very basic principle that lay behind RDF was only demonstrated at the beginning of 1935. Only one station was in existence by the summer of 1937, and it had yet to be demonstrated at that point that the equipment could give really accurate indications not simply of the existence of approaching aircraft (that much at least was clear), but, rather more usefully, their range, height, direction and numbers. When it became clear that the Chain Home system would not accurately detect aircraft below 3,000 ft, a new system had to be developed to catch the low fliers.[11] Of course, one would not want to underestimate the significance of radar, but it must be remembered that it was at the very cutting edge of technology at the time. It was just as much 'a matter of faith' to believe, in 1937 and 1938, that the air defence problem had been solved at a stroke as it was to believe in the bomber. Basil Collier called radar the 'Oracle of Fighter Command'.[12] The real point about radar, however, as in the case of classical oracles, was that its message was opaque: it needed to be interpreted and, again like the classical oracles, interpretation was a matter of intuition and experience, a hunch rather than a science. Radar could provide early warning, if interpreted correctly. New fighters could maximise the use of this information and gain time to cope with a German bomber force which Intelligence suggested was growing exponentially. Fighters using a low-wing cantilever monoplane design to maximise speed, climb and manoeuvrability were developed to Air Ministry specification F1/35, the specification itself being a response to what the annual Schneider Trophy competition had shown to be possible. There were those in the Air Ministry in 1935 who were prepared to accept the Hurricane and Spitfire for maximum production even before the prototype stage. That was thought too great a risk to take, however, and Hurricanes did not appear in numbers in Fighter Command strength until 1938. As for the Spitfire, Fighter Command only had three in the front line by the time of Munich and one of them had broken down.[13]

Dowding had been involved in both these projects before moving to Fighter Command. He now set about organising the Command to make maximum use of both of them with an information system which would give the fighters the best chance of disrupting bomber attacks before they hit their targets. Most importantly radar, if it worked and if it were not itself disrupted by bomber attack, freed the British air defence from the need virtually to withdraw from the coastal areas and prepare to meet the bombers inland – a tactical necessity basic to air defence schemes since Steel-Bartholomew. It now became possible to consider meeting the bombers even before they hit the coast and to base a major part of Fighter Command's front line as far forward as the southern coast. This was the role to be taken by 11 Group in the Battle of Britain, a major role of 12 Group to their north being to protect 11 Group's airfields while they were in the air.

While these technological developments and Dowding's organisation of Fighter Command were beginning to give Britain a chance of mounting a credible air defence, political events were taking place which were to give fuller priority to them. By late 1937 the newly appointed Minister for the Co-ordination of Defence, Sir Thomas Inskip, had become convinced that priority for bombers was no longer viable. Not only did it seem, from Intelligence estimates, that Britain had definitely lost the race to retain bomber parity with the Luftwaffe, it also appeared that Britain could not sustain indefinitely this pace of rearmament without severe economic and financial disruption. Sir Thomas concluded that Britain's best chance, if war were to come, was to face Germany with the threat of a long war.[14] This meant conserving Britain's economic resources and providing a defence for the home country, behind which the staying power for a long war could be built up. Though Inskip did not immediately see this implication, and it was to be months before the decision was actually taken, nevertheless, in practice, this meant priority for Fighter Command. When, and only when, Britain had acquired security at home, priority would again be allotted to bombers to attack German staying power.

The Air Staff railed long and loud against this new priority for fighters. It struck directly at everything they had been preaching about air power since the birth of the RAF. Given the international situation in early 1938, however, and given the Intelligence estimates of German air strength and intentions, they could no longer argue that the RAF was likely to deter Germany. They had to accept the fact that they might have to fight, and to fight against the odds. But with the prospect of no bombing force being available to reduce the German air attack, even greater weight was put on Fighter Command by the new priorities. The increasing range available to German bombers had led the Reorientation Committee to recommend and have accepted a scheme which would extend the defended zone to the Scottish borders and provide extra cover for the Midlands. They reckoned that the thirty fighter squadrons authorised in 1936 should be increased to forty-five, and that the number of guns and lights authorised should be doubled. The aircraft industry had by this time been organised into a Shadow Factory scheme. This allowed the most valuable factory space in the country to be used to produce the most important new aircraft, irrespective of whether the producing firm had designed the aircraft or not. In time this promoted a major leap in production, of Spitfires for example, but a change in priority authorised by government only in 1938 could not work through overnight.

A sobering balance sheet was drawn up at the time of Munich. In September 1938 Fighter Command had twenty-nine squadrons mobilisable against the forty-five recommended by the Reorientation Committee; only five of these were equipped with Hurricanes and even they could not operate at altitude. Fighter reserves amounted to only 40 per cent of front-line strength. The radar network provided only partial cover for eastern England and the telecommunication system that linked radar, Fighter Command HQ and the fighter sectors had hardly even been started.[15] In the aftermath of Munich, the Air Ministry launched a scheme to provide fifty fighter squadrons by 1942, with the immediate emphasis on the production of the biggest possible front line by the spring of 1939. Full reserves for that front line would not be available until the spring of 1940. Emphasis was to be on the Spitfire and the Hurricane, with the Blenheim filling the production gaps. Immediately, however, the demands on fighter production were increased still further by the new needs of the other services. The Admiralty's decision to use both Scapa Flow and Rosyth as bases for the Home Fleet increased the number of home defence fighter squadrons needed from fifty to fifty-three. The decision to double the British Expeditionary Force to be sent to the

Continent in the event of war, taken in the spring of 1939, increased demands still further. Apart from the Advanced Air Striking Force, to be composed of Bomber Command squadrons, the BEF would require an Air Component of reconnaissance squadrons but also of four fighter squadrons. Originally, these four squadrons were to be Blenheims but, in a fit of honesty he probably lived to regret, Dowding admitted that Blenheims would be ill-fitted to the role of battlefield fighters. So the Air Staff decided to send precious Hurricanes instead, to be taken out of home defence strength. The decision on the BEF also had very serious effects on the supply of AA equipment for home defence, which were not to be remedied before the Battle.[16]

So, in the summer of 1939, Dowding could contemplate an eventual force of fifty-seven squadrons, five of which were assigned to trade protection or Northern Ireland and could not realistically be seen as part of the home defence force *per se*. A further two squadrons were allotted to the defence of Scapa Flow, but could presumably be diverted *in extremis*. Another four squadrons were allotted to the Air Component, and therefore only tangentially part of a home defence scheme. This would leave forty-six squadrons with no other function than home defence. In fact, at the outbreak of war, Fighter Command mobilised thirty-nine squadrons, four of which would go to the Air Component, leaving thirty-five for home defence, with no coverage as yet for either trade or naval base protection. These thirty-nine squadrons consisted of sixteen squadrons of Hurricanes (including four for the Air Component), ten squadrons of Spitfires, seven of Blenheims, and six still equipped with Gladiators, Gauntlet or Hind. That was a front line of 468 or 420, depending on how one counts the Air Component squadrons, with a reserve of about 300 aircraft. There were a further 140 front-line fighters of various categories not assigned or trained for a home defence role. Against them, the Air Staff reckoned, stood a Luftwaffe of 1,650 medium-range bombers. In fact, the real figure for the Luftwaffe was just over 1,100 serviceable medium-range bombers, but the disparity was still alarming.[17]

Why this pre-war failure? Should we apportion blame? In 1939 the Luftwaffe was only six years old and the RAF was twenty-one. Surely they should have been in a better relative position? Recently there has been some tendency among historians to a post-revisionism on interwar international affairs. Revisionists in the 1970s and the 1980s rejected the crude anti-appeasement historians of previous years. They dwelt instead on the raft of practical problems facing the appeasers and their rearmament policy. There is a newer school, however, represented by R.A.C. Parker in particular.[18] While accepting the practical problems outlined by the revisionists, the post-revisionists suggest that Chamberlain and his government failed in the most fundamental duty of any government, to provide proper defence. Further, they argue that while they should not be blamed for trying to avoid war, the appeasers by their actions or inaction made that war more difficult to fight when it came. It might be pointed out that, in the case of the RAF at least, the government had little choice but to accept the professional Air Staff opinion that bombers were more important than fighters, and that Great Britain was deemed peculiarly vulnerable to air attack. The attempt to aid appeasement by securing parity in front-line bomber strength with Germany was at least a rational response to this problem. Sir Thomas Inskip was a brave man if he thought that the problems of defence against air attack had been solved by untested new technology. There are also positive as well as negative defences to be made. Radar was developed at astonishing speed in the last years of peace. The Shadow Factory scheme, a major intrusion in private industry in a liberal-capitalist state in peacetime, was beginning to feed through into the front line superbly designed fighters, a match for any in the world. With the important exception of the provision of pilots, all the major decisions necessary to secure the country in the Battle of Britain had been taken. Luckily, there were to be another nine months to implement those decisions.

The Phoney War, Scandinavia and the Battle of France

Dowding's hope was that the squadrons earmarked for the Air Component would not leave the country until the home defence force had reached the full fifty-three squadrons allotted. In fact, not only did he lose those four, but six more squadrons were put on alert for Air Component duty, and two of these left for France early in the war. Dowding began a series of protests about this whittling down of his force. The Air Ministry responded positively by creating new squadrons for Fighter Command, but these had to be worked up. Dowding got fifty-one of his fifty-three squadrons by the end of the year, but only two-thirds of his force was fully trained. There is nimble arithmetic involved here, but what seems to have happened is that Dowding had wangled himself two extra squadrons over and above the fifty-two squadron scheme devised in 1939, at the cost of losing six fully worked-up squadrons to France. The Air Ministry was prepared to concede this much to him because they were now predicting that the Luftwaffe would have over 2,000 bombers by the late summer of 1940, and 3,000 by the following spring. The Director of Home Operations at the Air Ministry was recommending the formation of twenty-seven new fighter squadrons to deal with this. Although the supply of fighters from the factories was improving, it was difficult to see how it could cope with such an increased demand.

Dowding further complained that the trade protection squadrons, when they were formed, were given to Coastal Command rather than to him.

Dowding was on less sure ground here, since there is no evidence that he had reckoned on these squadrons as part of the home defence force as such. He was anyway able to secure their release from Coastal Command during the Battle, to protect his flanks. Fighter Command's role in assisting Coastal and the Royal Navy in convoy duty in 1939 and early 1940 – an average of 1,500 sorties a month in the first six months of the war – provided important practical training for working up efficiency. Air fights on these duties, though there were not enough of them to come to real conclusions, resulted in casualties which favoured the defenders three to one.[19]

The Scandinavian campaign did not impinge too directly on Fighter Command, but it did of course raise the prospect of attack from Norway. More importantly, Scandinavia had a moral effect on the Command, an increased sense of pressure and responsibility. If the Royal Navy could not stop the Germans mounting a seaborne invasion just a few hundred miles away, how much easier seemed a hop across the English Channel if Fighter Command faltered in its bid to hold the skies. Much worse was to follow, of course. All pre-war plans for the air defence of Great Britain had been framed on the assumption that air attack would be launched from within pre-war German frontiers or, at worst, from the Low Countries. The fall of Holland, Belgium and France not only meant that the range for German bombers was reduced. It also meant that Fighter Command now had to add to the enemy front line the shorter-ranged dive-bombers, as well as the single-engined and twin-engined fighter force, which would now be able to escort the bombers in numbers. It also meant that Dowding could be outflanked in the west, bringing a whole new dimension of threat to the industrial Midlands and Lancashire.

When the German invasion began in May, the remaining four squadrons earmarked for France at the beginning of the war were duly despatched, leaving Dowding with forty-three fully worked-up squadrons, two of which were at that time due to go to Scandinavia. Early reverses in France led to the despatch of over thirty more fighters and, by the 14th, the French were calling for a further ten squadrons to be sent over. Dowding's response was that the air defence of Great Britain simply could not afford that weakening. Since, anyway, what was being contemplated was counter-attack rather than defence, bombers were needed rather than fighters. The implication was that it was time to test Bomber Command's Advanced Air Striking Force, the eighteen bomber squadrons in France which had not yet been committed, not to further weaken the home defence. This might well bring air reprisals on Britain, Dowding conceded, but his fighters would be much better employed defending against such reprisals over Britain, enjoying the benefits of the early warning and control systems of Fighter Command, than in unfamiliar skies over France. On 15 May Dowding attended the War Cabinet and impressed them with his arguments about the impact of the fighter losses in France for the immediate security of Great Britain. It was agreed not to send the fighters that Reynaud had asked for and to despatch Bomber Command to the Ruhr instead. Two days later, however, the situation in France had deteriorated to the extent that the War Cabinet agreed that a supreme effort must be made. Eight half-squadrons of fighters were sent out, leaving Fighter Command at home with just thirty-six. On the same day Churchill, in Paris, asked for six more squadrons to be sent. Actually, this was wholly impracticable because of the congestion of aerodromes in France, quite apart from the fact that this would denude Fighter Command of all of its remaining full Hurricane squadrons. The War Cabinet decided instead to send the Hurricanes to Kent and operate them over France in daylight, returning to Britain at night. At the same time, they ordered Bomber Command to give up its strategic attack and go for German troop and supply movements instead.

At this point, Dowding issued his famous warning letter, which ended:

> I believe that, if an adequate fighter force is kept in this country, if the fleet remains in being, and if Home Forces are suitably organised to resist invasion, we should be able to carry on the war single-handed for some time, if not indefinitely. But if the Home Defence Force is drained away in desperate attempts to remedy the situation in France, defeat in France will involve the final, complete and irremediable defeat of this country.[20]

On the 19th Churchill ruled that no more fighters should leave the country, but it was already clear that further major fighter operations in France would still be necessary, if only to get the BEF back home.

The withdrawal from Dunkirk was the tactical responsibility of 11 Group, where Air Vice-Marshal Keith Park had recently taken over command. Though Park's squadrons had already been involved over the Low Countries, this was to be the first major encounter between the Luftwaffe and the home-based force. But Dunkirk could not be seen by Dowding as an opportunity for a decisive showdown, in spite of the obvious importance of giving cover for the withdrawal. Dunkirk was at maximum range for the single-seater fighters which had done so well in France. The twin-engined fighters, however, had been severely mauled in the recent fighting and could not be so exposed again, especially without the radar warning and control available flying nearer home. To have provided continuous cover in strength over Dunkirk would have required Dowding to concentrate virtually his entire single-engined force in the few aerodromes from which they could have reached the evacuation area. This would have exposed other parts of the home country dangerously. As it was, Park could only offer either weak two-squadron patrols, which were ineffective but which covered the beaches almost continuously, or stronger four-squadron patrols, which were more effective but roused the ire of soldiers and sailors by leaving the beaches exposed for long periods.

Fighter Command strength had now been swelled by the arrival home of the squadrons serving in France. Front-line strength was now over 700 aircraft, 600 of them Hurricanes or Spitfires. The reserve stood at 250, and there were another 700 aircraft in training units or under repair. Fighter Command raised a daily average of 300 sorties a day over Dunkirk; not many, it might be said, but the fighters had already had a bad time in France and, as far as Britain was concerned, there was an even more significant battle yet to be fought. The Air Ministry believed that they had destroyed 260 aircraft for the loss of just over 100. In fact, the Luftwaffe had lost not much more than 100 aircraft in the Dunkirk evacuation[21] – evidence enough, as was the campaign in France and the Low Countries, that without the ground control organisation to help them, Fighter Command equipment was only just a match for the Luftwaffe.

The first real taste of war showed how significant aircraft production figures were to be. The large increases in aircraft production in the first six months of war had allowed Fighter Command to reach towards its authorised size; but that was with virtually no fighting. Over 400 fighters were lost during the first three weeks of May, another 100 at Dunkirk, which was the equivalent of the entire production for the previous two months. In the kind of sustained offensive on the home country expected from the Luftwaffe at the time, on the basis of such a loss rate, it was possible that Fighter Command would lose virtually its entire front line every five weeks, and virtually certain that the aircraft industry would be targeted to prevent re-equipment. During June, however, fighter production went to over 400 a month for the first time, and was sustained at that level for the rest of the year. Even this might not be enough, given the estimates of German strength, and given the need to extend the flanks of Fighter Command westward and strengthen the defence against attack from Scandinavia. In addition, twelve new radar stations were immediately commissioned to be ready by early July.

Meanwhile the Director of Home Operations, Air Commodore Stevenson, was calculating that 120 squadrons would soon be needed. That was an impossible target in the circumstances, he admitted, but he urged the formation of ten new squadrons immediately, and ten more as soon as possible. Industry could probably have produced these, but whether they could be maintained in the Battle was dubious. Now preparation came up against another problem that had been threatening throughout, the supply of pilots. The losses in France and the expansion of Fighter Command to meet the new strategic problem in the west and north put great pressure on the training establishment, but the problem was in fact more deep-seated than that. The size of the peacetime RAF had been simply too small to provide a pool of trained pilots to man a 700-aircraft force, even with the volunteer reserve and the auxiliary air force to back it. Recruitment of pilots had already been at the point of crisis for a year.[22] It would take at least eighteen months of war to build up the training establishment, including the Operational Training Units which would finally solve Fighter Command's problems. As it was, the outcome of Stevenson's worries was that four aircraft were added to the normal front-line strength of twelve in thirty-six Fighter Command squadrons, to be used in a crisis by any trained pilot who did not have an aircraft – those recalled from leave, for example. There was a slight smell of panic about this. Sixty-eight pilots were transferred from Royal Naval Air Service squadrons in June, but they did not even cover the number of pilots lost over Dunkirk in four days.

As 10 July 1940 dawned, no one in the know in Britain could have any grounds for complacency about what was to happen. The Air Ministry had consistently though not deliberately overestimated the losses they had caused the Luftwaffe – but then they had consistently overestimated the size of the Luftwaffe as a whole, so the one may have cancelled out the other. The losses in the air fighting so far appear to have been much more even than the British airmen suspected at the time, and could not have been maintained if they had continued to be the norm in the Battle. There was some evidence, from the early fighting over convoys, that the home radar and the fighter control system could produce a kill ratio much more favourable to the defenders. Such encounters had involved only small groups of enemy aircraft, however. What might happen when massed bombers, protected by escorts at least over part of their journey, attacked not convoys but the very organisation of Fighter Command itself including, presumably, the radar system on which the whole structure depended? Dowding had fifty-eight squadrons available on 10 July, four of which were forming or re-equipping and therefore non-operational for the moment.[23] The fifty-eight included nineteen of Spitfires and thirty-one of Hurricanes. The remaining Defiants and Blenheims were of questionable value in day fighting. He had 1,250 pilots, which meant that he could probably put 600 aircraft in the air. If he could find more pilots he could put up to 700 aircraft in the air. The radar and reporting system was nearly complete for the southerly and easterly approaches, but very weak in the west and in Scotland. Anti-aircraft ground defence was equipped with less than half the heavy artillery pieces considered necessary before the war had even started. Against Fighter Command stood over 1,100 medium-range bombers, over 300 dive-bombers, 800 single-engined and 250 twin-engined fighters. There was no RAF strike force capable of making any real impact on German air potential through counter-attack. Not everybody in the Air Ministry was even convinced that Dowding was the right man for the job. Indeed, if Dowding was right to believe that Fighter Command could win, then the Air Staff was simply wrong about the basics of air power. Meanwhile, the Luftwaffe was only just over twenty miles from the British coast. The only certainty facing Fighter Command on 10 July 1940 was that the next few months were unpredictable.

Notes and References

1 See M. Cooper, *The Birth of Independent Air Power* (London, 1986).
2 *House of Commons Debates*, 10 Nov. 1932, vol. 270, col. 632.
3 See, for example, Public Record Office (PRO) AIR 9/12, Air Staff memo, Air Tactics, undated; PRO AIR 19/49, Note, J. Slessor to Private Secretary to Secretary of State, 31 Jan. 1939. For a fuller explanation of the development of the RAF doctrine of war, see M. Smith, '"A Matter of Faith": British Strategic Air Doctrine Between the Wars', *Journal of Contemporary History*, 15 (1980), pp. 423–42.
4 E.B. Ashmore, *Air Defence* (London, 1929).
5 H.A. Jones, *The War in the Air*, vol. 6 (London, 1937), p. 138.
6 J. Slessor, *The Central Blue* (London, 1956), p. 212.
7 PRO AIR 8/67, Conclusions of Cabinet meeting, 20 June 1923.
8 Memo by the Secretary of State for Air to accompany the Air Estimates, 23 Feb. 1932, *Great Britain Command Papers*, Cmd 4026.
9 M. Smith, *British Air Strategy Between the Wars* (Oxford, 1984).
10 R. Wright, *Dowding and the Battle of Britain* (London, 1969); see also B. Collier, *Leader of the Few* (London, 1957).
11 R. Watson Watt, *Three Steps to Victory* (London, 1957).
12 B. Collier, *The Defence of the United Kingdom* (London, 1957).
13 PRO AIR 8/218, COS 773, Strength of the RAF, Monthly Returns; PRO CAB 53/41, The Czechoslovak Crisis, Report by the Chiefs of Staff, 25 Sept. 1938.
14 PRO CAB 24/273, CP 316 (37), Report by Sir Thomas Inskip, Defence Expenditure in Future Years, 15 Dec. 1937. The new priorities were accepted by Cabinet in Jan. 1938; see Smith, *British Air Strategy*, ch. 6.
15 PRO AIR 6/55, Air Ministry Report on the Lessons of the Emergency, 23 Oct. 1938.
16 PRO CAB 53/49, COS 912, Memorandum by Chief of the Air Staff, Possibility of the Despatch of Additional Fighters and AA Guns to France, 13 May 1939.
17 Collier, *Defence of the United Kingdom*; H. Schliephake, *The Birth of the Luftwaffe* (London, 1971).
18 R.A.C. Parker, *Chamberlain and Appeasement* (London, 1993).
19 Collier, *Defence of the United Kingdom*, pp. 90–1.
20 Ibid., p. 110.
21 Ibid., pp. 113–17.
22 PRO AIR 6/39, Note by Air Marshal Portal, The Problem of Expansion and the Availability of Personnel, 1 Feb. 1939.
23 Collier, *Defence of the United Kingdom*, ch. 9.

PART TWO

THE BATTLE

HORST BOOG

The Luftwaffe's Assault

Various chronologies of the Battle of Britain have been set out by Churchill, Dowding, Galland, Kesselring and others. A particularly useful one is the operational schedule established for the German side more than forty years ago by the Swiss historian Theo Weber. He distinguishes between an initial contact phase and two main battle phases. The initial phase lasted from early July until 7 August 1940. In this period the Luftwaffe flew fighter patrols, photo and armed reconnaissance missions and carried out dive bomber attacks on British shipping and ports in the Channel area as directed by Luftflotten 2 and 3. The first main battle phase, which ran from 8 August until 5 September, involved, above all, an attempt to reduce British fighter defences in preparation for a contemplated invasion. Its first part began with attacks on fighter bases and radar stations, as well as on other fighter-related targets, with the aim of wearing down the fighter force. These included the great air battles of Eagle Day, 13 August. The second part was characterised by an intensification of raids against fighter airfields in south-east England.

The second main battle phase ran from 6 September until 10 May 1941. This involved a general bombing operation against the British economy and targets of military relevance, as well as some retaliation bombing. It began with a strategic air offensive, mainly directed against targets in London, and developed into a night bombing campaign across the country. Although I will confine myself to the period from 10 July to 31 October 1940, which are the official British dates for the Battle of Britain, in a few instances I will have to look beyond these limits. 15 September, the turning point of the Battle in the British view, does not occur as such in the German table of events.[1]

Confused Objectives

The scheme just delineated conveys the impression of a clear-cut plan
behind the operations of the Luftwaffe. Was this really so? The rather
dilatory fashion in which the Luftwaffe conducted its activities reflects,
on the contrary, much uncertainty and indecision as to how to proceed.
The German leadership was pretty much at a loss as to what to do next after
the rapid defeat of France, which had not been foreseen. The Luftwaffe
had to establish a ground organisation for an air war against the British
Isles of an uncertain type, and had to recover from the heavy losses
incurred during the French campaign. The losses numbered 3,008 men
of the flying units, of whom almost two-thirds had been killed or taken
prisoner, and 2,073 aircraft, 1,401 of which were destroyed. These included
250 single-engined and 121 twin-engined fighters, plus 477 bombers and
123 dive-bombers. Altogether the aircraft destroyed equalled 26 per cent
of the actual Luftwaffe strength of 4 May 1940 and about 18 per cent of
its single-engined fighter strength.[2]

Hitler still hoped to come to terms with Britain diplomatically. He
hated the British for not agreeing to his terms, but admired them at
the same time. Various methods of defeating Britain indirectly were thus
contemplated. These ranged from cutting the lifeline of the British Empire
by blockading the eastern and western entrances to the Mediterranean, to
the establishment of an anti-British continental bloc – like Napoleon –
extending from German-occupied Europe via Russia to Japan.[3] Another
option was to eliminate the Soviet Union as the only potential ally left to
the British on the continent by a Blitz campaign before the United States
would be ready for open military support of Britain.[4] This idea, rather than
the invasion of Britain, was soon to dominate Hitler's thinking.[5] Before
the end of July 1940 he reversed his armament policy from the industrial
preparation of an air and sea war against Britain to that of a land war
against the Soviet Union.[6]

Goering, the Commander-in-Chief of the Luftwaffe, seeing that Hitler
had become uncertain about his plans against Britain, was not interested
in a landing operation and stretched out clandestine 'peace-feelers'.[7] He
also took a long leave from his duties. It was not until 21 July that he first
called a meeting of his senior commanders to discuss the all-important
question of how to gain air superiority in preparation for an invasion.[8]

Mainly as a result of the navy's doubts about the feasibility of a landing
– the preparation for which could not be completed before the middle of
September – Hitler directed on 31 July that 15 September be considered
the deadline for all pertinent preparations. He decreed that eight to
fourteen days after the beginning of the big air battle, which was to be
launched on 5 August, he would make up his mind and finally decide
whether the invasion would take place in 1940.[9]

There were, then, many uncertainties. How, in this atmosphere, could a plan for an air offensive in support of an invasion be developed?[10] On 25 June General Hans Jeschonnek, Chief of the Luftwaffe General Staff, had declined to comment on a proposal from General Jodl, Chief of the Operations Staff of the German Armed Forces Supreme Command, regarding the Luftwaffe's part in a possible landing operation, since, in his opinion, Hitler did not intend to cross the Channel.[11] A Luftwaffe High Command directive of 30 June concerning the air war against Britain did not mention a landing, but a host of targets for air attack.[12] During the assembly phase the Luftwaffe was to conduct reconnaissance and training flights as well as nuisance raids with small forces against industrial and air force targets. Having reached a state of readiness for the big air offensive, it was to attack the enemy air force, its ground organisation and the air armament industry as a precondition for a successful air war against merchant shipping and the war economy. Ports, cargo vessels and warships protecting merchant shipping were to be destroyed. Also on 30 June Jodl himself suggested, besides the initial attack on the RAF, the elimination of the air armament industry in the London and Birmingham areas and the simultaneous destruction of warehouses, depots and imports and exports either at the ports or at sea: landing operations were only considered as a *coup de grâce*, should that still be necessary. A similar view was expressed in the directive of the Armed Forces Staff of 2 July, in which landing operations were only mentioned as a possibility.[13] Hitler's directive no. 16 of 16 July was not much different in substance.[14] On 21 July he even mentioned 'other plans' if the preparations for an invasion could not be completed in time.[15]

Nevertheless, on the same day, Goering, hinting at landing operations in which he did not believe, forbade attacks on targets such as ports along the southern coast of England, because they could be needed as ports for supplies and disembarkation. Mine-laying was also forbidden in the area. He advised his commanders to avoid unnecessary losses until the beginning of the main air operations. As major targets, he mentioned British convoys and naval forces. Targets further inland were to be attacked by individual bombers only in order to train crews for night attacks on petrol, oil and lubrication dumps, and ammunition and air armament factories. During the main air offensive air superiority was to be gained over the enemy fighter and AA forces and the observation and reporting net paralysed. It was crucial that the British fighters were defeated. This was to ensure that the bombers could attack the RAF ground organisation under 'easier conditions'. Luftflotten and Fliegerkorps were to submit detailed tactical plans for these operations. He reserved for himself the decision about the opening of the attacks on the air armament industry, especially on the aero-engine factories, and announced a final battle to grind down the enemy by employing fighter bombers.[16] On 30 July he was informed by the Armed Forces Staff about Hitler's order to prepare for the main air offensive so that it could be launched twelve hours after it was ordered.

But the Luftwaffe was not yet ready. Goering was shocked when, on 1 August, Field Marshals Kesselring and Sperrle (commanders of Luftflotten 2 and 3) reported that only 700 bombers were serviceable in their two air fleets. 'Is this my Luftwaffe?' he enquired sadly.[17] He himself had not yet made up his mind about the tactical plans and suggestions which had been submitted by his commanders. Fliegerkorps I had, for instance, proposed to gain air superiority by destroying the enemy air force and aero-engine industry; then it would protect the Channel crossing of the navy and ground troops by attacking the enemy fleet and bomber force and providing close air support for the army; and it would further strangle Britain by destroying harbours, stocks of provisions and interrupting overseas supplies. Indiscriminate bombing as a reprisal might also be necessary. This was almost an entire catalogue of possible air operations. Fliegerkorps II was aware that the short range of the Me 109 single-engined fighters would not carry them beyond the northern outskirts of London. In recognition of the importance of the capital, it proposed an attack on military and industrial targets in greater London with the intention of drawing in British fighters from bases beyond German fighter range and engaging them in a battle of attrition. The bombers would operate in full strength only after the fighter defences had been considerably weakened.[18]

Fliegerkorps II's plan, though less Utopian than that of Fliegerkorps I, was not accepted because Hitler had forbidden attacks on targets in the London area. In view of his preoccupation with the idea of a campaign against Soviet Russia it is quite possible that he did not wish to provoke RAF raids on Berlin while fighting in the east. Goering was attracted by a somewhat different approach. The British fighters were to be worn down in the air and on the ground by concentric attacks moving progressively, and in three phases, towards London, which was itself exempted from attack. In the first five days the target zone was to be the area of 150 to 100 km around the London city limits. The bombers would next concentrate for three days on targets 100 to 50 km from London. They would then move on to within 50 km of the capital's boundaries for a further five days. After a fortnight of bombing and air battles it was hoped that the invasion could be launched.[19]

Meanwhile, Hitler had issued his directive no. 17 of 1 August dealing with the conduct of the air and sea war against England. Both were to be carried out more intensely than before in order 'to produce the necessary conditions for the final reduction of England'. The Luftwaffe was to destroy the RAF, as extensively and quickly as possible, by attacking, firstly, its flying formations and ground and supply organisation, and then the aircraft industry and the factories producing anti-aircraft guns and equipment. After having achieved air superiority, the bombing attacks were to be extended against harbours, in particular those for the provision of food supplies, and against food-storage depots further inland. Ports and installations needed for the German landing operations were to be left untouched. In addition to these tasks, Hitler demanded that the Luftwaffe preserve its strength 'to take part in full force' in Operation Sealion. Terror raids were forbidden unless ordered as reprisals.[20]

On 2 August Goering issued his 'Eagle Attack' directive to Luftflotte 3 in north-western France, Luftflotte 2 in northern France and Belgium, and Luftflotte 5 in Norway and Denmark. Again, it contained rather broad objectives, such as the establishment of air superiority and the crippling of British naval strength, preceded and accompanied by attacks on airfields, ports and factories. There was no mention yet of the importance of radar and ground control stations.[21] On 3 August Luftflotten 2 and 3 were instructed by Jeschonnek to eliminate the radar stations along the coast as a prelude to the intensified air offensive, the beginning of which had to be postponed several times because the three to four days of fine weather needed for the opening strike were not forthcoming.

On 6 August the air fleet commanders, in conference with Goering at Karinhall, must have been concerned to hear him talk about the possibility of prematurely breaking off Eagle Attack should the German losses be too high, and of presenting it as a one-off act of reprisal to the world's public.[22] This might have been connected with the above-mentioned 'peace feelers', which he tried to extend to Britain through the director of the Royal Dutch Airline, KLM; but it also reflected his own uncertainty about the success of the whole undertaking.[23] A detailed plan had only been worked out for the first day of the attack: subsequent operations would be dependent on the situation as it unfolded.[24] For Kesselring an invasion was only necessary because of the short ranges of the German fighters. Goebbels, the Minister for Propaganda, noted in his diary that an invasion was not planned, ordered the German press not to play down the British capacity for resistance, thought about 'other ways' to win the war, and soon contemplated the possibility that the conflict would drag on into the winter.[25] Jodl, who believed that the Luftwaffe could create favourable conditions for a landing operation, indicated that there were other possibilities to defeat Britain, among them the submarine war and the seizure of Egypt and Gibraltar.[26] Indeed, Hitler sent General von Richthofen, commander of Fliegerkorps VIII on the Channel coast, where he was urgently needed, to Spain for negotiations.[27] Before the opening of the main air offensive on 13 August the Luftwaffe had thus loosened its commitment to the landing operation.[28] It was attempting to attack too many targets not directly related to securing the crossing of the Channel. One is reminded of the preparation for the French campaign. Discontented with its designated role as an army support force, the Luftwaffe secured operational tasks which gave it greater independence from the army. It seems here, too, that it wanted to fight its own independent air war instead of being used only as the heavy artillery of the army.[29]

This attitude can be explained by the fact that the Luftwaffe considered fighting an independent strategic air war as its *raison d'être*. But while it had invested much time in the development of the theory of independent bombing, it had no practical experience in the conduct of a strategic air campaign. Like other air forces, it overestimated the effects of bombing. The Battle of Britain was the first large-scale, strategic bombing offensive in history, and when the RAF and the US Army Air Forces started their bombing offensives they also needed time and experience to get a grasp on the phenomenon. These factors, combined with the uncertainty and half-heartedness of the highest political and military leaders about their strategic plans, might explain why there was so much diversity of objectives and expectation about accomplishing everything within such a short time.

The disengagement of the air war from the intentions of the other services was boosted by one incident: the erroneous dropping of several bombs on London by a few German bombers on the night of 24 August in contravention of Hitler's orders. Some writers describe it as an intentional attack by major bomber forces.[30] I rely on Harvey Tress, who shows convincingly that it was an error by a few German bomber crews.[31] The official British historian of the Battle of Britain, Sir Basil Collier, gives a similar explanation.[32] Churchill, however, exploited the incident and ordered the bombing of Berlin, which, he assumed, would infuriate Hitler and induce him to mount reprisal attacks on London, where a sophisticated and effective air defence system was waiting for the Luftwaffe. Churchill had earlier reached a similar decision on 15 May 1940. After the German breakthrough near Sedan he ordered the bombing of targets in Germany east of the Rhine and thus began the RAF's strategic bombing offensive against Germany – almost three months before the Luftwaffe launched its attack against Britain. The purpose behind Churchill's order was to relieve the western front in France by diverting German fighters to the defence of Germany and encouraging bombers to attack London, where they would be expected.[33] Now he tried again. As he had calculated, Hitler lifted the restrictions concerning the British capital and ordered a reprisal attack on the city for 7 September. From then on the Luftwaffe concentrated on strategic targets in London and other cities which had nothing to do with an invasion.

Instead of pressing harder to gain air superiority over the British fighter force, the Luftwaffe actually relieved it by the change of objectives. Events moved in favour of the British defences. One of the reasons why the emphasis in target selection could be changed so easily was the fact that the Luftwaffe's Intelligence Department, against the advice of its Signal Intelligence, simply deducted British aircraft losses from strength figures which were, for a number of reasons, too low.[34] It thus came to the conclusion that Fighter Command was already very weak in early September and that the few remaining fighters could be done away with over London. The attacks turned out to be a large, self-inflicted blow against the Luftwaffe.

On 17 September the air offensive was tentatively separated from landing operations by the temporary postponement of Operation Sealion because the Luftwaffe could not establish air superiority. Hitler had already indicated this three days earlier – before what became known as Battle of Britain Day.[35] Goering remarked at this time that Sealion should in no way disturb or impede air operations.[36] On 12 October Sealion was postponed until the spring of 1941 – practically indefinitely. The selection of bombing targets now became completely divorced from landing operations. In September a division of labour had already taken place between Luftflotten 2 and 3, the former concentrating on daylight attacks, while the latter switched over to night attacks. The Luftwaffe thus admitted that day bombing, in the long run, was too costly. Before it switched over entirely to night bombing in November, fighters were for a time, and much to the annoyance of the pilots, employed as fighter-bombers.

By 5 December Hitler had lost confidence in the Luftwaffe's ability to wear down British industry and the economy.[37] Great hopes were now placed on the moral and material attrition of the British by night bombing. This night-bombing campaign was carried out with the intention of deceiving the world about Hitler's preparations against the Soviet Union – which did not escape ULTRA – and was broken off about six weeks before the onslaught in the east on 22 June 1941.[38] In April its intensity had to be reduced because many flying units were needed for the campaign in the Balkans. In retrospect, the Luftwaffe's targeting in Britain, especially after 7 September, only makes sense if one assumes that the main objective was to hold down the RAF for as long as the supposedly short war against the Soviets was being fought. Adolf Galland, the Luftwaffe ace, doubted whether the Luftwaffe High Command really had a clear concept of what it was trying to do.[39]

The Reasons for Failure

But there were other reasons for the failure of the German air offensive against Britain. One of them was faulty Intelligence. Luftwaffe Intelligence suffered from a strong belief in the effectiveness of strategic bombing and overestimated its own capabilities while underestimating those of the enemy. There was an ideological conviction of the superiority of German society over its decaying 'liberal' British counterpart: spirit and heroism over materialism and money-making.[40] The old German First World War propaganda of 'heroes' versus 'shopkeepers' was revived. The Luftwaffe was considered capable of achieving a decisive success against the RAF. In a Luftwaffe Intelligence assessment of 16 July 1940 the German air force was rated 'clearly superior' to the RAF, although, at least as far as fighters were concerned, the Spitfire had proved to be a match for the Me 109 over Dunkirk. Fighter Command's strength, it was thought, would decline once the intensified battle had started. The British aircraft repair facilities and the radar system were totally disregarded in this report. On 7 August Colonel Beppo Schmid, the Chief of Luftwaffe Intelligence, informed the air fleets and corps that the British radar net would tie the RAF fighters to their ground stations and prevent rapid concentrations at decisive points of the Battle. He also predicted its breakdown during mass assaults.[41] It was the false assessment of the role of the radar stations in the radar-directed fighter defence system that encouraged German commanders to leave them untouched after a few seemingly futile raids during the first days of the Battle. During these raids the lattice-work towers could not be destroyed and one station, which was considered to have been eliminated, continued to operate. That this was feigned traffic was not known at the time. It was also believed that the operations rooms of the radar stations were located underground, where they could not be hit, while, in reality, they were mostly located above ground.[42] Thirty years ago I talked to General Paul Deichmann about the problem. During the Battle of Britain he was Chief of Staff of Fliegerkorps II. He told me that trying to hit the radar stations and their operations rooms had been like searching for needles in a haystack and was therefore abandoned. It was further believed that the repair of electronic equipment was too easy in a country as technologically developed as Britain. Had the Germans concentrated on the development of radar defences, instead of radio-navigational aids for their bombers in conformity with their offensive air doctrine before the war, they might have come to a more thorough appreciation of the value of radar.

Another grave error of German Intelligence was the underestimation of British fighter production. Assessments relied too much on agent 'Ostro', the Luftwaffe's only source of information at the time.[43] Ostro's figures for 1940 were, on average, 50 per cent too low. He reported that in June 225 fighters had been produced, when 446 had been built. He calculated

250 in October when the number was 469. The corresponding German production figures were 164 and 200. Even Ostro's low figures should have been no reason for German overconfidence. The comparatively weak German fighter force was matched by a low output of fighter pilots from the training schools. At the beginning of the war there had been a shortage of single-engined fighter pilots amounting to 17 per cent of establishment. Both were consequences of the secondary role of the fighter arm in German air war doctrine. The Luftwaffe was geared for the offensive and more offensive than defensive aircraft were produced. In practice there was never more than one pilot per fighter plane. The actual fighter strength of the three air fleets deployed in late July 1940 was about 900 single-engined and 280 twin-engined aircraft. On the eve of Eagle Attack the Luftwaffe deployed about 730 single-engined and 200 twin-engined fighters against Britain which were serviceable. [44] Given the ratio of one pilot to one fighter, the number of German single-engined fighter pilots on the British front was no higher than 66 per cent of Fighter Command's pilot strength, decreasing during the Battle to something over 50 per cent by 2 November.[45]

As for German signal Intelligence – the results of which often proved to be correct – this was not held in high esteem by commanders because it usually did not support their optimistic scenarios. ULTRA mainly furnished the British with order of battle, state of serviceability and post-battle information, rather than advance information on operations.[46] This was certainly not as decisive for the outcome of the Battle as is sometimes believed.

The Luftwaffe was further disadvantaged by its aircraft. In a Luftwaffe–RAF comparison of 10 August 1940, Colonel-General Ernst Udet, Director-General for Air Armament, praised the qualities of the Me 110 twin-engined escort fighter and the offensive armament of German fighters in comparison with the British fighters, equipped with 'only' eight wing-mounted machine-guns.[47] A few days later, Galland, with his newly gained combat experience, asked Goering to equip his Geschwader with Spitfires.[48] The Me 110s were no match for the British fighters and had to fly defensive circles when attacked by them or needed fighter protection themselves. They suffered severe losses on 15 August and had to be withdrawn from the Battle to be used as night fighters or as destroyers in ground-support missions elsewhere. The Ju 87 dive-bombers also had to be taken out of the Battle a few days after Eagle Attack because they were too slow, very vulnerable when pulling up after a dive and also needed their own fighter protection. The short range of the Me 109 single-engined fighter was to be the main impediment to the German air offensive. With the long approach across the Channel, this substantially curtailed its combat time in the battle zone and thus its effectiveness, as well as stripping the bombers of their fighter escort north of London (providing another reason for the resort to night bombing). All these factors, combined with the inadequate defensive armament and bomb-loading capacity of the only available twin-engined medium bombers, were serious obstacles to a successful independent bombing offensive. Many commanders were aware of these problems and raised warnings, but they were not heeded. It is still not clear why drop tanks were not fitted to the single-engined fighters to extend their operational radius, as had been done in the Spanish Civil War. It seemed that an attempt was being made to conduct a strategic bombing offensive by tactical means – a strategy that up until then had been successful, but only in limited continental campaigns. Fighter commander Theo Osterkamp termed it 'romantic' air warfare.[49]

The first big German attacks on Eagle Day and 15 and 18 August revealed all the shortcomings of the Luftwaffe.[50] Many non-Fighter Command airfields were raided and important aircraft factories not recognised. Since radio communication between fighter and bomber formations in flight was impossible, the units already airborne missed each other or had to wait for the rendezvous while valuable fuel was wasted. Tactical command having been left to the air fleets there was, in the absence of a central tactical direction, a lack of adequate co-ordination. The timing of the operations of the individual air fleets left much to be desired and many opportunities to make surprise attacks on enemy fighters refuelling and rearming on the ground were not exploited. Needless to say, bomber losses were high because they could not be escorted by fighters all the way to and from the targets, while Goering's order that single-engined fighters should protect bombers, twin-engined escort fighters and dive-bombers robbed the Me 109s of their best feature – free chase. German fighter strength was totally inadequate to protect the bombers. On 15 August, when the Luftwaffe attacked across the North Sea, it was very surprised to be met by so many British fighters in northern and central England, which was an area supposedly depleted of fighters. German losses far and away exceeded those of the British. From 8 August to 6 September Fighter Command lost 480 fighters in total, 124 being damaged. The Luftwaffe lost 743 aircraft with 208 damaged. Casualties during this period on the British side amounted to 186 men killed and 163 wounded; on the German side they numbered 1,367 killed or missing and 281 wounded.[51] Goering's replacement of older fighter commanders with younger men did not change the situation. Indeed, the high officer casualties resulted in his order that there should be no more than one officer in a bomber or escort fighter crew. Goering put all the blame for the failure of the offensive on his fighter pilots and threatened to dissolve the fighter arm.[52] But the fighters did their best and they continued to fight throughout the war with no rotation. The high German losses were also the result of the fact that the fighting took place over enemy territory, the North Sea and the Channel – a handicap which Luftwaffe Intelligence had overlooked in its assessments. The Luftwaffe's sea rescue service, although very efficient, could not make up for this.

Bombing Policy and Terror Attacks

Some remarks should be made here about the Luftwaffe's bombing policy and especially its image as a terror arm, which dates back to war propaganda on both sides; a view which is upheld by younger German historians for the first years of the war.[53] It still does not seem to be generally known that Luftwaffe doctrine considered indiscriminate bombing as an exception to the rule, only justified in order to force an enemy to abstain from unlawful actions.[54] This does not mean that terror attacks were not contemplated as an application of air power: this was also done by most other air forces. But before the war the Luftwaffe General Staff rejected proposals for indiscriminate bombing. At the beginning of the Battle of Britain bomber crews were instructed to hit prescribed targets of military or economic relevance and avoid collateral damage as far as possible. Crews had to bring their bombs back if they did not find their targets. RAF Bomber Command attacking Germany acted likewise in this period. Besides humanitarian considerations, the Luftwaffe was not geared for area attacks, but rather for bombing pinpoint targets. This is why dive-bombing capacity was required even for the four-engined bombers in development and why the Stuka dive-bomber was developed. The idea of maximum destruction with a minimum of means was also at the forefront of the development of radio-navigational aids for the bombers. The training flights of bombers so equipped during the early part of the Battle gave British Intelligence, as R.V. Jones describes, the chance of finding out how the Knickebein 'X' and 'Y' beam systems worked and how they could be interfered with before they were applied on a larger scale during the night offensive.[55]

A characteristic feature of the German air offensive in 1940 was the so-called *Zerstörangriffe*. These were pinpoint attacks on important bottleneck targets by highly skilled individual bomber crews. The monthly bombing charts prepared by the Luftwaffe Air Historical Branch reveal that, during the months of August to October 1940, 2,403 attacks of this pinpoint type were carried out.[56] This approach is further substantiated by the fact that although the Germans had known since the Spanish Civil War that cities could best be destroyed by the use of incendiary bombs, only 4.7 per cent of the total bomb tonnage dropped on England in these three months was incendiaries.[57] Sir Arthur Harris wrote in his memoirs that the Germans missed their chance to set British cities ablaze.[58] This painstaking German needle-stitch approach to strategic bombing was unrealistic at the time and the pinpoint targets were in fact seldom hit. Nevertheless, it indicates the intention of German bombing policy in those early war years.

This is confirmed by a number of historians,[59] as well as by a British Air Chief Marshal who asked me recently how the Germans could drop their bombs with such relative accuracy during the Battle, which he experienced as a boy.

It is well known that Hitler's reaction to the first British bombs on Berlin was his public threat on 4 September 1940 to 'erase' British cities. Ten days later, however, he directed the Chief of the Luftwaffe General Staff, who now proposed indiscriminate bombing, to continue to bomb targets of military and economic importance as long as there were some available and not to begin terror-bombing.[60] This did not prevent Hitler, the Luftwaffe General Staff, its Intelligence Department, and the so-called 'England Committee', from contemplating whether attacks on workers' quarters in London would incite the common people against their ruling class and force the government to make peace. Another idea was to bomb the homes of the middle classes, whose political influence was considered to be greater. But even in February 1941, in directive no. 23, Hitler forbade terror attacks and in early March 1942 he cancelled such an attack on London.[61] Since Hitler was no benefactor of humanity, it may be assumed that the main reason behind this policy was his desire not to provoke indiscriminate bombing of German cities while he was fighting Russia.

As for the Luftwaffe, precision bombing was unattainable given the technological standards of the time and the influence of combat conditions on the bomber crews, and this resulted in unavoidable collateral damage on civilian quarters. This was rationalised as a means of paralysing the morale of the civilian population, especially after bombing had become even less accurate during the night offensive. Moreover, the instrument of reprisal first used to justify a few city attacks soon degenerated into a pretext for further nightly city bombings. It was only after the incendiary bombings of the German cities of Lübeck and Rostock in March and April 1942 that Hitler changed his mind and ordered intentional terror attacks on British towns, the so-called Baedeker raids. But, in practice, the bombing operations of both sides already bore traits of an indiscriminate nature.

Basil Collier described the bombing policy pursued by the Luftwaffe in the following terms: 'Although the plan adopted by the Luftwaffe early in September had mentioned attacks on the population of large cities, detailed records of the raids made during the autumn and winter of 1940–1941 do not suggest that indiscriminate bombing of civilians was intended. The points of aim selected were largely factories and docks.'[62] General Arnold, the Chief of Staff of the US Army Air Forces, who was in Britain shortly before the German air offensive ended in May 1941, wrote in his memoirs that a map of the city of London in the room of Sir Archibald Sinclair (the Secretary of State for Air) showed that although German bombs had been dropped all over London, they landed in most cases close to railway stations, switching points, power houses, transformers, bridges, docks, warehouses and factories.[63] The more desperate and ideological the war became, the more the restraints on bombing were dropped: on the British side, at the very latest, with the Air Staff directive of 14 February 1942; on the German side with the above-mentioned Baedeker raids and later with the V weapons.

The fact that the Luftwaffe, after considerable losses, achieved none of its objectives – whatever these might have been – in the Battle of Britain and broke it off prematurely had a number of consequences. Its forces in the campaign against the Soviet Union in 1941 were numerically weaker than they had been in the attack on France in 1940 and the myth of the invincibility of the German air force was destroyed. This blow to German prestige, along with the attack in the east, encouraged resistance movements in the German-occupied countries. The United States – further encouraged by the Royal Navy's attacks on the French fleet – became convinced that Britain would fight on and deserved support. Spain was now no longer willing – if she ever had been – to enter the war on the German side. Jeschonnek, fatally, welcomed the planned campaign against the Soviet Union because he was convinced that the best way for the Luftwaffe to reap success was not through independent strategic bombing, which had failed, but in close co-operation with the army, where it had won strategic victories through tactical methods in the past. This confirmed Hitler's intention to wage a two-front war, although the decision was taken before the outcome of the Battle of Britain was clear. Russia became the Verdun of the Luftwaffe because it was too big for a 'tactical strategy'. Britain now became the basis for the Allied air offensive against Germany and the stepping stone for the invasion of the Continent in 1944, both of which decided the war.

Notes and References

1 Theo Weber, *Die Luftschlacht um England* (Wiesbaden, 1956), pp. 99–107. For other detailed accounts of the Battle of Britain see, for example, Len Deighton, *Fighter: The True Story of the Battle of Britain* (London, 1977); Klaus Maier et al., *Das Deutsche Reich und der Zweite Weltkrieg*, vol. 2, *Die Errichtung der Hegemonie auf dem europäischen Kontinent* (Stuttgart, 1979), pp. 375–408; Francis K. Mason, *Battle Over Britain* (London, 1969); Basil Collier, *The Defence of the United Kingdom* (London, 1957), pp. 147–281; *Sunday Telegraph, Battle of Britain*, parts 1–3 (16–18 June 1990); Udo Volkmann, *Die Britische Luftverteidigung und die Abwehr der Deutschen Luftangriffe während der 'Luftschlacht um England' bis zum Juni 1941* (Osnabrück, 1982).

2 Bundesarchiv-Militärarchiv (BA-MA), RL 2 III/705–7, Einsatzbereitschaft der Fliegenden Verbände, Luftwaffe General Staff, 6th Department.

3 Andreas Hillgruber, *Hitler's Strategie. Politik und Kriegführung 1940–1941* (Frankfurt am Main, 1965), pp. 144–277.

4 Horst Boog et al., *Das Deutsche Reich und der Zweite Weltkrieg*, vol. 4, *Der Angriff auf die Sowjetunion* (Stuttgart, 1983), pp. 3–18.

5 Jürgen Förster, 'Der Historische Ort des Unternehmens "Barbarossa"', in Wolfgang Michalka (ed.), *Der Zweite Weltkrieg* (Munich, 1990), pp. 626–40.

6 Bernhard Kroener et al., *Das Deutsche Reich und der Zweite Weltkrieg*, vol. 5.1, *Organisation und Mobilisierung des Deutschen Machtbereichs, Erster Halbband, Kriegsverwaltung, Wirtschaft und Personelle Ressourcen 1939–1941* (Stuttgart, 1988), pp. 502–22, 787–8.

7 Weber, *Luftschlacht*, p. 89; David Irving, *Göring* (Hamburg, 1987), p. 440; Bernd Martin, *Friedensinitiativen und Machtpolitik im Zweiten Weltkrieg 1939–1942* (Düsseldorf, 1964), p. 323 ff.

8 David Irving, *Die Tragödie der Deutschen Luftwaffe. Aus den Akten und Erinnerungen von Feldmarschall Milch* (Frankfurt am Main, Berlin and Wien, 1970), p. 159; Maier et al., *Das Deutsche Reich und der Zweite Weltkrieg*, vol. 2, p. 379.

9 Hans-Adolf Jacobsen (ed.), *Kriegstagebuch (war diary) des Oberkommandos der Wehrmacht (OKW) Wehrmachtführungsstab*, vol. 1, *1 August 1940–31 December 1941*, (Frankfurt am Main, 1965), pp. 3–5.

10 Weber, *Luftschlacht*, pp. 33–4.

11 Maier et al., *Das Deutsche Reich und der Zweite Weltkrieg*, vol. 2, p. 379.

12 Ibid.

13 Karl Klee, *Dokumente zum Unternehmen 'Seelöwe'. Die geplante Deutsche Landung in England 1940* (Göttingen, 1959), p. 301.

14 Walther Hubatsch (ed.), *Hitler's Weisungen für die Kriegführung 1939–1945* (Munich, 1965), pp. 71–4.

15 Gerhard Wagner (ed.), *Lagevorträge des Oberbefehlshabers der Kriegsmarine vor Hitler 1939–1945* (Munich, 1972), p. 120; Franz Halder, *Genereloberst Halder, Kriegstagebuch. Tägliche Aufzeichnungen des Chefs des Generalstabes des Heeres 1939–1942*, vol. 2 (Stuttgart, 1963), entry for 22 July 1940.

16 BA-MA, RL 2 II/30.

17 Horst Boog, 'The Luftwaffe and the Battle of Britain', in Henry Probert and Sebastian Cox (eds.), *The Battle Re-thought* (Shrewsbury, 1991), p. 21.

18 Karl Klee, 'Die Luftschlacht um England 1940', in Hans-Adolf Jacobsen and Jürgen Rohwer (eds.), *Entscheidungsschlachten des Zweiten Weltkrieges* (Frankfurt am Main, 1960), p. 72; Militärgeschichtliches Forschungsamt, Rohden collection, film no. 2; BA-MA, RL 2 IV/33, Luftkrieg gegen England 1940–1941, Weisungen und Befehle; Jacobsen (ed.), *Kriegstagebuch OKW*, vol. 1, p. 11.

19 BA-MA, RL 2 II/30; Theo Osterkamp, *Durch Höhen und Tiefen jagt ein Herz* (Heidelberg, 1952), p. 325; Maier et al., *Das Deutsche Reich und der Zweite Weltkrieg*, vol. 2, p. 380.

20 Hubatsch (ed.), *Hitler's Weisungen*, p. 75 ff.; Maier et al., *Das Deutsche Reich und der Zweite Weltkrieg*, vol. 2, p. 378.

21 Irving, *Tragödie*, p. 161; Klee, 'Luftschlacht', p. 74; BA-MA, RL 2 II/30.

22 Jacobsen (ed.), *Kriegstagebuch OKW*, vol. 1, p. 11; Irving, *Tragödie*, p. 161; BA-MA, RL 2 II/30.

23 See note 9 above and Irving, *Tragödie*, p. 164.

24 Jacobsen, *Kriegstagebuch OKW*, vol. 1, p. 11.

25 Elke Fröhlich (ed.), *Die Tagebücher von Joseph Goebbels. Sämtliche Fragmente*, part 1, vol. 4, *1 January 1940–8 July 1941* (Munich and New York, 1987), pp. 269, 301.

26 Jacobsen (ed.), *Kriegstagebuch OKW*, vol. 1, p. 31.

27 BA-MA, N 671/6, Persönliches Kriegstagebuch des Generalfeldmarschalls Dr. Ing. Wolfram von Richthofen, 24 July 1940.

28 Albert Kesselring, *Soldat bis zum letzten Tag* (Bonn, 1953), p. 92.

29 BA-MA, Lw 3/1, Helm Speidel, Der Einsatz der Operativen Luftwaffe im Westfeldzug 1939–1940, p. 146.

30 Mason, *Battle Over Britain*, pp. 358–9; Maier et al., *Das Deutsche Reich und der Zweite Weltkrieg*, vol. 2, p. 386.

31 Harvey B. Tress, 'Churchill, the First Berlin Raids and the Blitz: A New Interpretation', *Militärgeschichtliche Mitteilungen*, 32 (1982), p. 66.

32 Collier, *Defence of the United Kingdom*, p. 207.

33 John Terraine, *The Right of the Line* (London, 1989), p. 135 ff.

34 Horst Boog, 'German Air Intelligence in the Second World War', *Intelligence and National Security*, 5 (1990), p. 371; BA-MA, N 179/46, personal diary of Field Marshal Erhard Milch, 6 Sept. 1940.

35 Jacobsen (ed.), *Kriegstagebuch OKW*, vol. 1, p. 76.

36 Maier et al., *Das Deutsche Reich und der Zweite Weltkrieg*, vol. 2, p. 389.

37 Jacobsen (ed.), *Kriegstagebuch OKW*, vol. 1, pp. 76, 82, 121, 205–6; Maier et al., *Das Deutsche Reich und der Zweite Weltkrieg*, vol. 2, p. 404.

38 In the spring of 1941, after a mission briefing against England, Goering told Galland in strict confidence that the whole thing was just a bluff to hide Germany's real intentions against the Soviet Union. Adolf Galland, *Die Ersten und die Letzten. Die Jagdflieger im Zweiten Weltkrieg* (Darmstadt, 1953), p. 122; F. H. Hinsley, *British Intelligence in the Second World War: Its Influence on Strategy and Operations*, vol. 1 (London, 1979), pp. 429–83.

39 Galland, *Jagdflieger*, p. 81.

40 BA-MA, RL 2/356, GL no. 740/40 g. Kdos., 10 Aug. 1940, p. 52 ff; Horst Boog, *Die Deutsche Luftwaffenführung. Führungsprobleme-Spitzengliederung-Generalstabsausbildung* (Stuttgart, 1982), p. 98.

41 Boog, 'German Air Intelligence', p. 362.

42 Paul Deichmann, *Der Chef im Hintergrund. Ein Leben als Soldat von der Preussischen Armee bis zur Bundeswehr* (Oldenburg, 1978), pp. 118–20.

43 On Ostro see Boog, *Luftwaffenführung*, pp. 105–9; Boog, 'German Air Intelligence', pp. 370–3; F.H. Hinsley and C.A.G. Simkins, *British Intelligence in the Second World War*, vol. 4, *Security and Counter-Intelligence* (London, 1990), pp. 199, 256, 279; Michael Howard, *British Intelligence in the Second World War*, vol. 5, *Strategic Deception* (London, 1990), pp. 177, 180; C.G. McKay, 'MI5 on Ostro: a New Document from the Archives', *Intelligence and National Security*, 12 (1997), pp. 178–84.

44 Weber, *Luftschlacht*, pp. 80–5; Volkmann, *Britische Luftverteidigung*, p. 137; BA-MA, RL 2 III/708 and 709; Collier, *Defence of the United Kingdom*, pp. 463–7. On Eagle Day the Luftwaffe, as it was deployed against England, comprised 1,370 medium and 406 dive bombers, and 813 single- and 319 twin-engined fighters (2,908 aircraft). Of these, 998, 316, 702 and 261 respectively were serviceable (2,277 aircraft). The total strength of the Luftwaffe on 10 August 1940 was 4,670 aircraft. There are some numerical differences between sources.

45 Volkmann, *Britische Luftverteidigung*, p. 180; Sir Charles Webster and Noble Frankland, *The Strategic Air Offensive Against Germany* 1939–45, vol. 4 (London, 1961), p. 501.

46 Hinsley, *British Intelligence*, vol. 1, pp. 176–2.

47 BA-MA, RL 2/356, GL no. 740/40 g. Kdos., 10 Aug. 1940, p. 52; Boog, 'German Air Intelligence', p. 362.

48 Galland, *Jagdflieger*, p. 97.

49 Osterkamp, *Durch Höhen und Tiefen*, p. 281.

54 · *The Burning Blue*

50 Horst Boog, 'Eagle Attack', *Sunday Telegraph* (17 June 1990), pp. 6–9; Boog, 'Black Thursday', ibid., pp. 8–9.
51 Volkmann, *Britische Luftverteidigung*, pp. 177, 185.
52 Galland, *Jagdflieger*, p. 111.
53 Horst Boog, 'The Luftwaffe and Indiscriminate Bombing up to 1942', in Horst Boog (ed.), *The Conduct of the Air War in the Second World War* (Oxford, 1992), pp. 373–404.
54 Luftwaffendruckvorschrift no. 16 (L. Dv. 16), 'Luftkriegführung', paras 186–93.
55 R.V. Jones, *Most Secret War* (London, 1978), pp. 92–105, 135–45.
56 BA-MA, RL 2 IV/33.
57 Maier et al., *Das Deutsche Reich und der Zweite Weltkrieg*, vol. 2, p. 407.
58 Arthur T. Harris, *Bomber Offensive* (London, 1947), p. 83.
59 See, for example, James S. Corum, *The Luftwaffe: Creating the Operational Air War, 1918–1940* (Kansas, 1997), pp. 8–11; Paul Crook, 'Science and War: Radical Scientists and the Tizard-Cherwell Area Bombing Debate in Britain', *War and Society*, 12 (1994), p. 70; Geoffrey Best, *Humanity in Warfare: The Modern History of the International Law of Armed Conflicts* (London, 1988), p. 278; Jeffrey W. Legro, *Co-operation Under Fire: Restraint and Escalation in World War II* (Ithaca and London, 1995), p. 157.
60 Halder, *Kriegstagebuch*, vol. 2, pp. 99–100; Boog, *Luftwaffenführung*, pp. 103–5.
61 Hubatsch (ed.), *Hitler's Weisungen*, pp. 118–21; BA-MA, RL 3/60, Reichsmarschall-conference of 21 Mar. 1942, p. 5181.
62 Collier, *Defence of the United Kingdom*, p. 261.
63 Henry H. Arnold, *Global Mission* (New York, 1949), pp. 227–8.

SEBASTIAN COX

The RAF's Response

The official British dates of the Battle of Britain are 10 July to 31 October 1940. Such dates are, in one sense, entirely artificial: in air warfare offensive and defensive actions are not always so well defined, in chronological or geographical terms, as in land warfare. Official dates, therefore, are designed to provide a clear beginning and end to the Battle for administrative purposes such as writing official dispatches and determining medal allocations. Many German authorities would favour a start date for the Battle somewhat later, around the second week in August, and would include the night Blitz, taking the campaign through to May 1941. This chapter, however, will concentrate very largely on the fighting in July, August and the first half of September.

The Opening Phases

Let us start with the events of 10 July, which were fairly typical of the fighting that month. The Luftwaffe was not at that stage engaging in any very serious challenge to Fighter Command, but was intent on maintaining some pressure and beginning to establish some superiority over the English Channel, if only as a preliminary to moving operations inland. Meanwhile the Royal Navy and the British maritime authorities continued to direct coastal shipping convoys along the south coast through the Straits of Dover and up the east coast, despite the very vigorous opposition previously displayed by the Luftwaffe in Norway and at Dunkirk. On 10 July a convoy was sailing peaceably through the Channel under the protection of six Hurricanes from Biggin Hill when it was attacked by some twenty Dorniers escorted by thirty Me 110s and twenty Me 109s. Over the next thirty minutes elements of four more fighter squadrons from Fighter Command joined in the fight, including Hurricanes of 56 Squadron based at North Weald, north of the Thames, but operating from Manston at the eastern tip of Kent, and other squadrons from other sectors in Fighter

Command. In the ensuing combat the German air force lost four fighters and the RAF just one, a Hurricane of 111 Squadron which lost a wing after hitting a bomber. One small ship from the convoy was sunk. Also on 10 July seventy German bombers attacked Swansea and Falmouth, killing thirty people and damaging shipping, a power station, and railway lines. The Royal Ordnance factory at Pembrey in south Wales was hit, as was the airfield at Martlesham Heath. In all, during the day, the RAF lost six fighters in exchange for thirteen German aircraft. The pattern of escorted attack on south-coast convoys and ports was to become an established one for the following month or so.[1]

Certain aspects of these early engagements were to become familiar as the Battle progressed. First the Me 110s rapidly formed defensive circles, thus revealing their own vulnerability and hence ineffectiveness as escorts. Fighter aircraft flying in circles contributed nothing to the security of their charges. Second, we may note the flexibility of the defence, with fighters from several adjoining sectors joining the fight over the convoy within half an hour, not to mention the forward deployment of 56 Squadron to Manston from north of the Thames. Third, what was apparent was the rather insouciant approach of the Luftwaffe, which, had it seriously wished to sink the convoy, could surely have despatched more than twenty bombers. The final significant feature was the drain on Fighter Command's resources represented by the defensive commitment to protecting south- and east-coast convoys.

The decision to protect such routes was in fact a pre-war one. At a meeting of the Committee of Imperial Defence (CID) in March 1939 the Minister of Transport, Dr Leslie Burgin, had submitted a memorandum in which he had expressed the opinion that the diversion of all shipping from the east- to the west-coast ports in the event of war was impracticable. The matter had not been completely resolved at the CID meeting, but there was little doubt that some convoys would pass along the south and east coasts in wartime and that the trade would need protection against air attack. It was subsequently concluded that each convoy between Southampton and the Firth of Forth would require active air escort: it could not be protected simply on a reactive basis by Fighter Command. But this requirement meant the provision of an additional four squadrons of sixteen aircraft each, at a time when aircraft were in very short supply.[2]

By July 1940 the additional four squadrons were, needless to say, only present on paper, and the provision had in any case been postulated without considering the presence of German aircraft, including fighters, in the Low Countries. On 3 July, a week before the opening of the Battle, Air Chief Marshal Sir Hugh Dowding, Commander-in-Chief of Fighter Command, had asked that the convoys be re-routed around the north of Scotland,[3] but as late as the beginning of August the Air Ministry had told him to meet the German attacks on shipping with larger formations and superior forces.

Some historians have argued that much more of this traffic should have been unloaded in west-coast ports for onward transmission by rail. This view may not entirely reflect the problems of port and rail congestion which would have arisen, but it does reflect the dismay with which many air historians regard the general unreality which pervaded some circles over the question of coastal convoys.[4] In this regard we may note without further comment that, despite the losses suffered by the convoys and the defending fighters, as late as 9 August Churchill himself was arguing that convoys should still sail because they acted as 'bait' for the Luftwaffe.

The attacks on shipping and occasional forays against southern ports occupied the Luftwaffe until mid-August. During this period Hitler and the Luftwaffe High Command engaged in fairly desultory and far from focused planning for extending the Battle. Hitler did not issue directive no. 17, ordering the final conquest of England, until 1 August. It postulated a rapid defeat of the RAF and an invasion on 15 September.[5] Goering's own directive for the defeat of the RAF was issued the following day and it too foresaw a rapid victory, in much the same manner as the French and Polish air forces had been overwhelmed.[6] Neither of these two, however, had possessed a fully functioning command and control organisation linked to radar and adequate numbers of high-performance monoplane fighters. The Luftwaffe was soon to discover that its mounting losses during July would multiply once it began to penetrate further inland. What is more, the RAF had put to good use the time granted it by Hitler and Goering's insouciance and indecision. Whereas on 30 June Dowding had 587 fighters and 1,200 pilots available for operations, by 3 August the figures had improved to 708 and 1,400 respectively and three additional fighter squadrons had formed during the month.[7] Bad weather further delayed the Luftwaffe's planned assault, code-named *Adlertag* – Eagle Day – and it was finally set for 13 August. Luftwaffe High Command issued the operations order on the 12th and, in preparation for the big assault on the following day, the Luftwaffe mounted its first attacks in strength on radar stations and coastal airfields. Commencing at 09.00 on the 12th, six radar stations were attacked, though only one, Ventnor on the Isle of Wight, was put out of action for more than twenty-four hours. Attacks were also made on the airfields at Hawkinge, Manston and Lympne. Both Hawkinge and Manston were operational by the following day.[8]

Adlertag itself was not to prove quite the triumph that the corpulent Reichsmarschall had envisaged. The day started badly when, typically, Goering decided to postpone the morning's attacks until the afternoon when better weather had been forecast. With his usual impeccable timing, however, Goering did not issue the order until the aircraft were already airborne, and the Luftwaffe's communications network proved unequal to the task of recalling all the formations in time. Kampfgeschwader II's bombers thus continued their mission when their escort had turned back, whilst conversely KG 54's bombers went home but their escorting Me 110s continued to Portland. Both missions suffered at the hands of Fighter Command.

In the afternoon the attacks were better organised and several airfields were struck. At the end of a day of heavy fighting, however, the RAF had lost thirteen aircraft from 700 sorties, whereas the Germans had flown nearly 1,500 sorties and lost forty-five aircraft, including numbers of the vulnerable Ju 87s. *Adlertag*, apart from showing that the RAF was not going to prove quite so easy to deal with as the Luftwaffe's previous victims, also demonstrated two of the Luftwaffe's fundamental weaknesses: over-confident commanders and poor Intelligence. The Germans claimed that they had destroyed seventy Hurricanes and Spitfires and eighteen Blenheims, an exaggeration of 700 per cent. Several of the airfields which came under attack did not belong to Fighter Command and Luftwaffe Intelligence identified aircraft types such as Demons, which were not even present in the south of England. They credited Tangmere with a total of fifty-five Hurricanes and Spitfires. Keith Park, the commander of 11 Group, would have been delighted had that been true.[9]

One result of the poor Intelligence was to persuade the Luftwaffe High Command that Luftflotte 5 could attack the north of Britain from Scandinavia unhindered, as it was assumed that the heavy scale of opposition must mean that the northern defences were denuded of fighters. How wrong they were. Luftflotte 5's attack was picked up on 15 August by the northern Chain Home radar stations some ninety miles off the Firth of Forth, and there was plenty of time for the 13 Group fighter controller to marshal his forces, which he did to good effect. Altogether six squadrons of Hurricanes and Spitfires attacked the Luftflotte 5 formation bringing down sixteen bombers and seven Me 110s, about 20 per cent of the attacking force. Luftflotte 5 took no further effective part in the Battle.[10]

Further south, however, Fighter Command did not have things all its own way. Whilst the Luftflotte 5 raids had been picked up far out at sea flying on a steady course towards the coast, thus giving the defence plenty of time, this simply did not occur in 11 Group. The Chain Home stations on the south coast would generally pick up German raids assembling over the Pas de Calais or the Cotentin peninsula, which would give about twenty minutes' warning time. Detection at that range was, nevertheless, uncertain and inaccurate. However, assuming the radar operator was convinced that he had an identifiable plot, it would then be 'told' through to Fighter Command's filter room at Bentley Priory, Stanmore. There it would hopefully be combined with plots from other Chain Home stations, which would give the filter officer some confidence in the plot. The raid would then be given a number and be 'told' through to the operations room next door, where it would appear for the first time on the operations room table. This process had probably absorbed about four minutes. It took thirteen or fourteen minutes for a Spitfire squadron to climb to 20,000 feet. A Hurricane squadron took three minutes longer. It took five to six minutes to fly the distance between Cap Gris Nez and Dover.[11] We can see therefore that the decision time for an 11 Group controller was extremely short if he was to have his aircraft in a position to intercept. It is little wonder that Manston and Hawkinge, at the eastern extremity of Kent, were to suffer so severely at the hands of the Luftwaffe.

The Climax of the Battle

A day of heavy fighting on Sunday 18 August marked the Luftwaffe's concerted attempt to fulfil its master's objective of destroying Fighter Command within a week. 11 Group's airfields suffered accordingly, though once more the Luftwaffe was ill served by Intelligence or targeting, or both, since Coastal Command and naval air stations at Thorney Island and Ford were heavily attacked. The Luftwaffe succeeded in destroying a number of obsolete Shark torpedo bombers. They also suffered, losing seventy-one aircraft, of which thirty-seven were bombers and eleven were Me 109s. The RAF lost twenty-seven fighters and ten pilots. Over the next five days the poor weather, which habitually interferes with the cricket season at that time of year, prevented the Luftwaffe from mounting any concerted attacks.

At the time both the British and the Germans put out exaggerated claims for the number of enemy aircraft destroyed. The difference between the British and the Germans was twofold. First, the British at least had some method of checking many of the claims because the aircraft, apart from those which came down in the Channel, should have come down on land under their control: the Germans had no such advantage. Second, the British, and especially the Intelligence organisations, were seriously interested in trying to establish whether the claims were accurate or not. There was, indeed, a thorough investigation into the validity of the statistics, with minutes exchanged right up to Churchill. This was stimulated in large measure by the dawning realisation that there was a mismatch, with 596 enemy aircraft claimed as definitely destroyed between 8 and 18 August, but wreckage being identified for only 104.[12] Fighter Command, partly for reasons of pilot morale, tended to argue that the claims were accurate, while others in the government contended that there were not enough wrecked planes on the ground to support them. On the German side, Colonel Beppo Schmid, the Chief of Luftwaffe Intelligence, was less concerned about whether the claims were accurate and sycophantically was inclined to tell Goering what he wanted to hear. Gradually as the war went on the claims made by the RAF became more realistic, but even this did not stop Fighter Command pilots so overclaiming during the offensive sweeps of 1942 that the RAF thought it was winning a battle of attrition which in fact it was losing, and losing badly.[13]

The two weeks from 24 August to 7 September were the climax of the Battle and brought 11 Group perilously close to collapse. This phase saw the Luftwaffe mount a concerted attack on Fighter Command's southern defences. Despite having lost 127 medium bombers and forty Ju 87s between 10 and 23 August, which caused the latter to be withdrawn from operations over Britain, the Luftwaffe proved itself perfectly capable of wrecking Fighter Command's sector airfields when it chose to do so. Between 4 August and 7 September six of the seven sector stations in 11 Group were extensively damaged. In this period the operations rooms at Kenley and Biggin Hill had to be transferred to nearby emergency facilities which were not so well equipped. The sector operations rooms were located on the stations themselves, and although they were protected by banks of earth and sandbags against blast and splinter damage they were not hardened or underground, so there was no protection against a direct hit. The final link in Fighter Command's command and control communications chain was thus exposed. We remember all those Battle of Britain films in which the telephone rings at the squadron dispersal. It was likely to be the sector operations room on the other end giving the order from Group to scramble. If the operations room was a smoking ruin, or the telephone lines had been cut by near misses, the phone did not ring. Park later wrote that in the period from 28 August to 5 September the damage to his sector stations and communications infrastructure had a serious effect on the efficiency of his tactical handling of the squadrons.[14]

It was not only Fighter Command's infrastructure that began to feel the strain: the pressure on the squadrons was also intense. During August the training machine produced 260 fighter pilots, but the Command lost 304 killed or wounded. This was despite a reduction in the Operational Training Unit course from four to two weeks, with pilots going into combat with as little as ten hours on Spitfires and never having fired the guns on the fighter at all. During the fortnight from 24 August to 6 September the Command lost 103 pilots killed or missing and 128 wounded, an effective loss of 120 pilots per week from a fighting strength of around 1,000.[15] Desperate measures were required. Bomber and coastal squadrons and the Fleet Air Arm were combed for volunteers, even though some of them had been combed out already. Dowding also introduced a system of grading squadrons class A, B or C. Class A squadrons were to be maintained constantly at a strength of sixteen operational pilots, with classes B and C at lesser strengths. Each day Bentley Priory would inform 10, 12 and 13 Groups of the number of operational pilots required for posting to 11 Group to sustain its class A squadrons.[16] Dowding had thus been forced by the pressure applied by the Luftwaffe to abandon his policy of rotating complete squadrons in and out of the front line and away into the comparatively quiet areas in the north. The change, therefore, did nothing to relieve the pressure on the very tired pilots of 11 Group, quite the reverse in fact, since effectively most of them were there to stay.

The supply of aircraft, surprisingly, proved less of a problem. Fighter Command had 570 serviceable Hurricanes and Spitfires available on the morning of 10 July, 610 on 6 September and 626 on 31 October. For most of the Battle the combined output of industry and the estimable civilian repair organisation proved sufficient to replace Fighter Command's losses. Nevertheless, the situation was never entirely comfortable. In the intensive fighting of the last week of August and the first week of September, Dowding lost 295 Hurricanes and Spitfires destroyed and 171 badly damaged, whereas gross output of the new aircraft and rebuilds was only 269. The reserves ready for issue in the aircraft storage units therefore declined in this phase, and, as with the pilots, had the Luftwaffe been able to maintain this level of attrition – and the Battle of Britain was effectively a battle of attrition – the supply of aircraft would have become critical. Furthermore, the problems of aircraft supply were not so susceptible to the short-term expedient measures which tided Fighter Command over its pilot crisis. That said, we should note that the Germans had their own problems in this regard, and that the British production of single-engined fighters was double that of Germany during the Battle.[17] The strength of the German fighter force in August had, indeed, declined to 69 per cent of its level before the Battle of France.[18]

On the subject of production much was made, not least by his own newspapers, of Lord Beaverbrook's supposedly miraculous impact following his appointment as Minister of Aircraft Production in May 1940. We should note, however, that the building of high-performance monoplane fighters is a capital intensive business. There is no doubt that Beaverbrook's high-profile propaganda activities, including his appeal for aluminium pots and pans from housewives, did have short-term effects in improving morale and focusing attention on the importance of an all-out effort. But it is very doubtful whether such measures produced more than a small percentage increase in production, and increases of this nature are seldom sustainable over the medium to long term.

Instead the crucial element in the increase in production which occurred following Beaverbrook's appointment was the fact that the large purpose-built Shadow Factory at Castle Bromwich near Birmingham came on line. The difference that Beaverbrook did make was in terms of the factory's management. Using the wide-ranging powers granted to him by Churchill, which had not previously been available to the Air Ministry production department, Beaverbrook was able to transfer the management of Castle Bromwich from Lord Nuffield's hands to Vickers. Vickers brought in production expertise from Supermarine which enabled the factory to start producing Spitfires in quantity. It was, nevertheless, to the foresight of those who decided before the war to build and equip the factory that much of the credit belongs: in particular, Lord Swinton, the then Air Minister, and Air Chief Marshal Sir Wilfrid Freeman, the Air Member for Development and Production. The wisdom of their decision in 1938 to develop the factory was underlined when on 26 September 1940 the Luftwaffe comprehensively wrecked the only other significant Spitfire production facility, Supermarine's own factory at Woolston, Southampton, reducing the plant's output of Spitfires by 50 per cent for the next six months.[19]

Some historians have discussed the option of a 'northern bastion' – a withdrawal by Fighter Command to a line north of the Thames – as an alternative if the German assault on 11 Group had continued at the intensity of late August and early September. It is very doubtful if this was ever a viable proposition since it would have meant abandoning most of the British army, which was concentrated in the southern counties facing a putative assault across the English Channel. Such a suggestion would surely have provoked a vigorous reaction from the Chief of the Imperial General Staff, amongst others. The ports of Plymouth, Southampton and Portsmouth, and the associated naval dockyards, would probably have become untenable, and many of the aircraft factories would have been greatly exposed, including Westland's at Yeovil, Hawker's at Kingston, Supermarine's at Southampton, and the Bristol aircraft and engine factories around Filton. Crucially, it would also have meant the effective loss of all the Chain Home stations, which were on the coast and looked outwards to sea. This would have opened up large gaps in the early warning system, and aircraft could not have been put up on a reactive basis from airfields north of the Thames. Standing patrols, which required six times the number of aircraft, would have been needed. There was a plan to provide alternative airfields further inland for each sector in Fighter Command, but this was an arrangement designed to take effect when airfields came under threat from invading forces, rather than as a result of enemy air action.[20]

While Fighter Command engaged the Luftwaffe, Bomber Command concentrated mainly on the destruction of the invasion barges. Although there was no integrated air campaign, the role of Bomber Command was important both directly and indirectly. In direct terms, between 10 and 13 per cent of the invasion barges were sunk[21] – a not insignificant proportion if you consider what effect a similar scale of loss would have had on the Allied cross-Channel invasion fleet of 1944. More indirectly, the policy of attacking the invasion barges prevented Bomber Command from carrying out its pre-war plans to attack German airfields, thus reducing the weight of the Luftwaffe's attack on Britain. The invasion barges were seen at the time as a more important target. Since Bomber Command could only have attacked the airfields at night, a tactic that would not have been very effective, it was right to give priority to the anti-barge campaign.

Victory for Fighter Command

In September 1940 the strain imposed by the shortages of pilots and aircraft was eased by the decision of the German High Command to switch the weight of the attack away from Fighter Command and on to London. The results from Fighter Command's point of view were more than just the relief of the enormous pressure which had been imposed on the defence. The attacks on London were actually much easier for Fighter Command to counter. The German belief was that London was so vital that Fighter Command's remaining strength, including the squadrons in the north, would be drawn into a climactic battle over the capital that would ensure German air superiority and might achieve the knock-out blow.

In fact, the move effectively ensured that the Luftwaffe would lose the Battle. First, it removed the pressure which had been applied to Fighter Command's larynx over the previous month. Second, and equally important, it was a fatal miscalculation to believe that greater numbers of fighter squadrons could be drawn into combat over London and destroyed. The sector airfields were so vital to Fighter Command that Park had already committed all his resources to defending them, and had also, on occasions, drawn on reinforcements from 10 and 12 Groups to help with the task. In attacking London the Luftwaffe did not draw in more fighter squadrons, but it did allow the RAF to concentrate its defending forces more effectively while simultaneously increasing the problems of the attacking formations. The German mass attacks on London – over 300 bombers and 600 fighters on the afternoon of 7 September in one attack – were easier to see and to track, both on radar and visually. The intentions of the Luftwaffe were now obvious at a very much earlier stage in a raid than they had been before, and the 11 Group and Fighter Command controllers' problem of discerning German intentions early enough to counter them, without subsequently being caught in the wrong position by a feint, was largely removed.

Furthermore, since the Luftwaffe had to penetrate further inland to reach their target, 11 Group now had sufficient time to assemble some of its defending fighters into pairs or even wings of three squadrons. The reinforcing squadrons from 12 Group, including the famous Duxford 'big wing', were also able to intervene more effectively over London and the Thames than they had been able to over Kent and the southern counties. The Me 109s, moreover, were now operating at the extremity of their range and were further constrained by Goering's instructions to stay close to the bombers. They thus became much less effective in shooting down British fighters. In sum, the Luftwaffe's change in strategy allowed Fighter Command to recover its balance. It concentrated the defending fighter squadrons and made them more effective, while simultaneously reducing the effectiveness of the Luftwaffe's own attacks and making them less capable of achieving the strategic aim of air superiority. After the switch to London there was little doubt on the British side that the RAF could at least avoid defeat if the Luftwaffe strategy remained the same.

Big Wings, Night Air Defence and Command Changes

The main theatre of the Battle continued to be 11 Group's area, under the command of Park, with 12 Group, under Trafford Leigh-Mallory, acting as a ready reserve. Inspired, however, by the aggressive ideas of Douglas Bader, who was commanding a Hurricane squadron in 12 Group, Leigh-Mallory was experimenting with a new tactic: the massing of a number of squadrons into a 'big wing', intended to match the large formations in which the Luftwaffe were attacking. Owing to the fact that the squadrons had first to rendezvous over Duxford, some of them were now taking longer to go into action than they would have done as separate squadrons. Park was furious when some of his airfields were bombed before 12 Group arrived to protect them, and a bitter dispute broke out between the two group commanders. Giving his side of the story in a newspaper article after the war, Park wrote:

> On a few dozen occasions when I had sent every available squadron of No 11 Group to engage the main enemy attack as far forward as possible, I called on No 12 Group to send a couple of squadrons to defend a fighter airfield or other vital targets which were threatened by outflanking and small bomber raids. Instead of sending two squadrons quickly to protect the vital target, No 12 Group delayed while they despatched a large Wing of four or five squadrons which wasted valuable time . . . consequently they invariably arrived too late to prevent the enemy bombing the target.
>
> On scores of days I called on No 10 Group on my right for a few squadrons to protect some vital target. Never on any occasion can I remember this group failing to send its squadrons promptly to the place requested, thus saving thousands of civilian lives and also the naval dockyards of Portsmouth, the port of Southampton, and aircraft factories.[22]

There is an element of exaggeration in this account, which succeeded in implying that 10 Group were consistently paragons of virtue whilst 12 Group were rogues whose selfish actions cost many lives. Furthermore, Leigh-Mallory died in an air crash in 1944 and was thus prevented from putting his own views on record.[23]

My own view is that much of the dispute has become distorted by the passage of time and the battles of biographers and memoir writers. It is thus sometimes alleged that the Air Staff was intent on introducing 'big wings' in 11 Group, but much of the time this was not true. The Air Staff recognised that in 11 Group a 'big wing' could not be assembled in time. The 12 Group and Air Staff view was, however, that as a reinforcement for 11 Group, 'big wings' coming from 12 Group in the north were a good idea. In this I think they underestimated the command and control problems involved in handling the 'big wings'.

There can be little doubt that Leigh-Mallory tended not to send his squadrons over 11 Group airfields as promptly as requested by Park, if indeed they ever went where they were requested to, and 12 Group's commander undoubtedly deserves much of the criticism he has received for that. But the major criticism ought to be focused on Dowding. He was told more than once – and he had an extremely efficient and astute Senior Air Staff Officer in Douglas Evill, who knew exactly what was going on – that there was a dispute between 11 and 12 Groups. It is therefore my opinion that Dowding as the Commander-in-Chief ought to have sorted out the problem between his two subordinates, and ought to have done so much earlier. Nor was Park entirely blameless. He could at times take a rather proprietorial attitude to the Battle, and regard it as being fought entirely by 11 Group with a little bit of assistance from outside when needed. Nevertheless, there can be no doubt that tactically Park was absolutely right, and had Leigh-Mallory been in command of 11 Group he would have had to modify his own ideas quickly or he would have lost the Battle.

During the final phase of the Battle the Luftwaffe switched to fighter-bomber attacks and night raids on cities. The fighter-bomber attacks were very difficult to counter. They came in fast in small formations, and often very low, thus compounding all the problems of detecting them. They did not achieve much in the way of strategic results since all they did was undertake casual raids on such places as Hastings, or shoot up a few trains on the Southern Railway, but they had to be opposed. One of the few methods of opposing them was to mount standing patrols, but this was wasteful of flying hours, fatiguing for the pilots, and in the end not very effective since interception still required a large slice of luck.

Fighter Command did not at first have any real success in opposing the night offensive. The contributions of the Balloon Command and the army's Anti-Aircraft Command were probably as significant. Airborne interception radar – AI – was in its infancy. The early AI sets were mounted in Blenheims and were extremely unreliable. They had a very short range and were susceptible to damp. The operators sat in extremely cramped cockpits which were never designed to accommodate these sets, and were required to interpret a series of what might best be described as squiggles on a small cathode-ray tube. It was difficult enough to interpret the returns on the larger display of a Chain Home radar set on the ground, but attempting to do it in the air on the smaller AI sets whilst being bounced around inside a freezing cold aircraft at night was almost impossible.

The eventual solution was to introduce Ground Control Interception – GCI. In order to do this Fighter Command had to decentralise filtering and do away with the big filter room at Bentley Priory, where all the plots from the Chain Home stations had been coming in. Since radar picked up all sorts of things, from rain clouds to flocks of Canada geese, it was the job of the filter officer to distinguish these spurious plots from those of incoming aircraft, and no plot would go down on the operations room table unless there was a fair degree of confidence that it was genuine. Ground Control Interception consisted essentially of one radar station controlling one night fighter in an orbit around the local area. The radar picked up the night bomber and vectored the single fighter from the radar vector. When the fighter got within a mile or so of the bomber it would hope to detect the bomber with its own AI radar. In order to achieve this, however, filtering had to be decentralised and handed over to the fighter groups. Dowding was opposed to this and fought it: eventually it had to be imposed on him.[24]

Contrary to the account in Robert Wright's biography of Dowding,[25] the Commander-in-Chief's dismissal in November 1940 was not the result of his failure to support the 'big wing' tactics of Bader and Leigh-Mallory. He was removed for a number of reasons, of which the most important was his judgement on the question of night air defence. Partly instigated, and strongly supported, by Beaverbrook, the Air Council had carried out an investigation into night air defence during the summer. A high-powered committee under Marshal of the RAF, Sir John Salmond, had looked at the problem and produced a series of recommendations which the Air Council had sent to Dowding. He in turn sent back a response in which he disagreed with or rejected most of the points made. He was, therefore, seriously at issue with the Air Council on this crucial question and, in my opinion, he was wrong on almost every count.

Another factor in his removal was his involvement in direct discussions and correspondence with Churchill over such matters as decentralised filtering. For an operational commander to discuss with higher authority, behind the backs of the Air Staff, topics on which he disagreed with them was not calculated to endear him to them, irrespective of the merits of the case. When, therefore, Sir Charles Portal succeeded Sir Cyril Newall as Chief of Air Staff towards the end of the Battle, it was inevitable that Dowding would have to go. He was much older and more senior than the new CAS and the younger man naturally wanted a team sympathetic to his own ideas.

Dowding was warned, in a personal interview with Sir Archibald Sinclair, the Secretary of State for Air, that he would be moving. After that interview, but before he was due to leave, the Luftwaffe blitzed Coventry on 14 November in a night attack in which Fighter Command flew 119 sorties but failed to intercept any of the 437 German aircraft which took part in the raid.[26] The following day Dowding received a telephone call from Sinclair to say that he must now go at once.

In December Dowding's successor, Air Marshal William Sholto Douglas, who had been a proponent of the 'big wing' tactics while Deputy Chief of the Air Staff during the Battle, replaced Park as commander of 11 Group with Leigh-Mallory. This has fuelled suggestions by some historians that the removal of Dowding and Park was part of a plot, instigated by Douglas and Leigh-Mallory and aided by the adjutant of Bader's squadron, the MP Peter Macdonald. This is frankly nonsense. Park went because, quite rightly, Douglas wanted someone at 11 Group who was in tune with his own thinking. While Douglas might not have been correct in his views on how the Battle should have been fought, he had every right to appoint his own team once he took over. This was hard on Park, but demonstrably did not affect his subsequent career.

As for Dowding, he was removed because he was at loggerheads with the Air Council over night defence and was thought to be resistant to change. Although his failure to squash the dispute between his two senior group commanders cannot have helped his case, his performance in the daytime battle did not represent the major reason for his dismissal. This makes a sad end to the story of the Battle of Britain, but it is difficult not to have sympathy with those officers on the Air Staff who were struggling to cope with the myriad problems and threats facing them in those dark days. To have a very senior officer such as Dowding, who was perceived to be intent on going his own way irrespective of the views of the Air Council, was hardly a recipe for future success. Dowding himself believed that he should have been appointed as the CAS before the war, and might well have harboured thoughts of taking over from Newall in 1940. It was, however, a role to which he would have been entirely unsuited and, in marked contrast to Portal, almost certainly a dismal failure.[27]

Notes and References

1 Details of fighting and losses are from Public Record Office (PRO) AIR 41/15, Air Historical Branch narrative, *The Air Defence of Great Britain*, vol. 2, *The Battle of Britain*. See also Derek Wood and Derek Dempster, *The Narrow Margin*, rev. ed. (London, 1989), pp. 172–3; Richard Hough and Denis Richards, *The Battle of Britain: The Jubilee History* (London, 1989), pp. 122–7; Francis K. Mason, *Battle Over Britain* (London, 1969), pp. 156–9. For daily losses, including those from non-combat causes, see Winston G. Ramsey (ed.), *The Battle of Britain Then and Now*, 5th ed. (London, 1989).
2 PRO AIR 41/14, Air Historical Branch narrative, *The Air Defence of Great Britain*, vol. 1, *The Growth of Fighter Command*, pp. 79–80.
3 PRO AIR 41/15, p. 33.
4 Regarding the problems of unloading and distribution, see the official history: R. J. Hammond, *Food* (London, 1952), especially chs 9 and 16.
5 Hugh Trevor-Roper, *Hitler's War Directives, 1939–1945* (London, 1964), pp. 37–8.
6 On Goering's orders and directives before *Adlertag*, see Wood and Dempster, *Narrow Margin*, pp. 220–30.

7 PRO AIR 41/15, p. 81; Wood and Dempster, *Narrow Margin*, p. 264.

8 PRO AIR 41/15, pp. 110–36; Wood and Dempster, *Narrow Margin*, pp. 272–3; Mason, *Battle*, pp. 230–4.

9 Wood and Dempster, *Narrow Margin*, pp. 274–5.

10 Ibid., pp. 280–1; Mason, *Battle*, pp. 252–6.

11 Basil Collier, *The Defence of the United Kingdom* (London, 1957), p. 168.

12 PRO AIR 41/15, pp. 225–6.

13 On Intelligence in the Battle, see Sebastian Cox, 'A Comparative Analysis of RAF and Luftwaffe Intelligence in the Battle of Britain 1940', in Michael I. Handel (ed.), *Intelligence and Military Operations* (London, 1990). This essay first appeared in *Intelligence and National Security*, 5 (1990). On the RAF's later problems with claims, see the author's chapter on RAF Intelligence in Horst Boog (ed.), *The Conduct of the Air War in the Second World War* (Oxford, 1992).

14 PRO AIR 10/5556, Air Historical Branch narrative, *Signals*, vol. 5, *Fighter Control and Interception*, pp. 42, 47–8.

15 PRO AIR 14/15, pp. 395–7.

16 Ibid., pp. 399–400.

17 Sebastian Ritchie, *Industry and Air Power: The Expansion of British Aircraft Production, 1935–41* (London, 1997), p. 226. This is the most comprehensive and impressive work on the question of British aircraft production before and during the Battle.

18 R.J. Overy, *Goering: The Iron Man* (London, 1984), p. 171.

19 Ritchie, *Industry and Air Power*, especially ch. 7.

20 PRO AIR 41/15, p. 232.

21 Collier, *Defence*, pp. 227–8.

22 Quoted in Alexander McKee, *Strike from the Sky: The Story of the Battle of Britain* (London, 1989), p. 244. Park was writing in the *New Zealand Herald* (9 Sept. 1952). His views on the Battle, and those of his many champions, are well represented in Vincent Orange, *Sir Keith Park* (London, 1984), especially chs 10, 11.

23 The only biography of Leigh-Mallory is slight and unconvincing. See Bill Newton Dunlop, *Big Wing: The Biography of Air Chief Marshal Sir Trafford Leigh-Mallory* (Shrewsbury, 1992). The author of the biography is Leigh-Mallory's great nephew.

24 PRO AIR 10/5556, pp. 52–4.

25 Robert Wright, *Dowding and the Battle of Britain* (London, 1969). Similar views have been expressed by, among others, Len Deighton in *Fighter: The True Story of the Battle of Britain* (London, 1972) and Orange in *Sir Keith Park*.

26 PRO AIR 10/5556, pp. 131–2.

27 On the military and political complexities surrounding Dowding's dismissal, see the author's revised paper delivered to the University of London's Institute of Historical Research military history seminar, 28 Feb. 1989.

PART THREE

THE VIEW FROM AFAR

SERGEI KUDRYASHOV

The Soviet Perspective

Right up to the final days of the USSR, Soviet historians paid very special attention to the history of the Second World War. As a result, Russian-language libraries alone contain more than 25,000 books on various aspects of the subject, not to speak of numerous articles and reviews. Though a great part of this literature deals with events and developments on the eastern front, its western counterpart has also received impressively thorough coverage.

The Soviet response to the Battle of Britain can be divided into a number of phases. First, there was the war itself, during which initial Soviet perceptions were embodied in a large number of official publications. This was followed by the Cold War, up to Stalin's death in March 1953. These were years of severe political confrontation with the West, which made a strong impact on Soviet military writing and left a legacy of which there is some trace even today. The third period, which lasted for almost forty years, can generally be characterised by the appearance of serious academic research and discussion.

The War Years

The fierce fighting in the skies over Britain started almost a year after Stalin had signed a non-aggression pact with Hitler. In addition to strategic and tactical gains, one of the major implications of the pact was an immediate shift in Soviet propaganda, which began to blame recent potential allies for every imaginable crime, including the outbreak of war in Europe. The pact had made Stalin one of the most important and influential European figures. On the brink of a new war, as he no doubt thought, he had swiftly and smartly outwitted the unreliable Western powers, who had neglected Soviet security interests at Munich. Now came the time for revenge. Hostile remarks by Molotov, the Foreign Affairs Minister, added more fire to the anti-Western campaign in September–November 1939.

But after a not very successful war against Finland and a surprising German victory over France, the tone of Moscow's propaganda calmed down significantly. From June 1940 the Soviet press embarked on speculations over the fate of Britain and the prospects of a possible German invasion. *Krasnaya Zvezda* ('Red Star'),[1] an official paper of the Russian military, took the German threat to the United Kingdom very seriously, predicting coastal fighting in the immediate future. Whilst Colonel V. Popov, a military journalist, paid tribute to Britain, he thought that twenty-five to thirty divisions would not be enough effectively to prevent the landing.[2] Three days later the paper reprinted an article from the *Spectator* on the same subject.[3] After that every issue of *Krasnaya Zvezda* informed its readers about the military confrontation between Germany and Britain. It reproduced news reports from German and British agencies, published speeches by Churchill and Hitler, and provided other useful material from European sources, but at the same time refrained from the slightest hint of partiality, criticism or propaganda cliché. This stood in sharp contrast to the previous Moscow propaganda line. Such a 'neutral' approach could be explained within the framework of Stalin's strategy in Europe in the summer of 1940.

The Soviet deal with Hitler, regardless of propaganda declarations, had been based on the assumption that the war in the west would last for some time, thereby enabling Stalin to strengthen his position and be well prepared to confront Hitler and his allies. But the astonishing success of the Wehrmacht severely undermined those expectations. Meeting Sir Stafford Cripps on 1 July 1940, Stalin referred to Britain as the last core of resistance to the new equilibrium in Europe.[4] Whilst he continued to appease Hitler, the attitude of his propaganda machine towards the British military effort suggested a hope that England would not surrender to the Nazis.

On 2 August 1940 *Krasnaya Zvezda* published an extensive analysis by its military expert, Colonel N. Zhuravlev. Having examined the available data, he came to the conclusion that both Germany and England faced a period of long and stubborn fighting. He praised the RAF and concluded that there was 'no doubt that the total outcome of the Anglo–German war to a great degree will depend on who is going to win the air war'.[5] On 12 August *Pravda* printed a similar message, excluding the possibility of a quick victory for either side.[6]

Both papers kept their readers well informed about the Anglo–German war. Between 1 August 1940 and 22 June 1941 *Pravda* printed more than 300 factual reports and *Krasnaya Zvezda* nearly 240. Whilst *Pravda* refrained from lengthy reports, *Krasnaya Zvezda* was more elaborate and published fourteen analytical articles. The air war was often described as a necessary precursor to the land campaign. The neutral tone did not change. Commentators and analysts ceased to praise either side or indulge in any sort of political speculations, leaving the content of the printed material to speak for itself. The German air war appeared to be unsuccessful: the Luftwaffe was unable to destroy England. Germany still retained the initiative, but fierce British air resistance had forced the Germans to embark on a lengthy campaign with uncertain results.[7]

In March 1941 a leading Moscow academic journal, *World Economy and Politics*, tried to summarise the results of the air war. One of the contributors, S. Vishnev, described in detail all the major developments, compared the British and German air forces and concluded that regardless of its importance the air war would not prove decisive in determining the outcome of the Anglo–German struggle. Vishnev avoided political comment, but his paper undoubtedly confirmed that Nazi Germany had failed to defeat England in the massive air campaign.[8] The same journal published other articles by serious academic analysts on different aspects of the British war effort. The conclusions were favourable to Britain, and increasingly so after the German attack on Russia in June 1941.[9]

The Soviet leadership was evidently kept well informed. Maisky, the Soviet ambassador to London, kept a close eye on the air war and sent regular dispatches to Moscow.[10] The recent release on the Internet of decrypts of Soviet signals under the VENONA project has enabled us to see examples of the type of information that was being sent from London to Moscow about the Battle of Britain:

From: London
To: Moscow
No: 784

18 July 1940

1 [It is] reported that the British are preparing the ground for a possible agreement with Germany. Today a TIMES leading article says that from an historical point of view HITLER has made progress in the unification of Europe and Britain is making a mistake if she sets herself the task of restoring the old order and status quo in Europe and at home . . .
2 The Secretary of State for Air SINCLAIR gave the MASTER of the METRO [the Soviet ambassador] the following information:
    Not a single aerodrome has been knocked out nor has a single major military objective been destroyed as a result of all the German air raids in July. Acquaintance with captured German fighter pilots and the study of shot-down materiel show that the Germans are at present using second-rate and very young fighter pilots against Britain. They have no good British maps or photographs of bombing targets. They are using photographs of targets which were used earlier for reconnaissance of the factories. He [estimated] that the Germans had lost 104 aircraft in July against the British 26. This difference in losses is said to be attributable to the better training of the British pilots and the fact that the British fighters are more manoeuvrable than the MESSERSCHMITTS. The British are working on a fighter armed with cannons. SINCLAIR considers that the Germans have

5,000–6,000 first-line aircraft and up to 14,000 in reserve; the first line is being constantly reinforced. He considers that the British will catch up the Germans in aircraft production in three months.

JEROME [André Labarthe, Director-General of French Armament and Scientific Research at General de Gaulle's headquarters], by the way, has reported that the British are now producing 1,200 aircraft a month. According to information in the press the Germans are producing 60 aircraft per day.

BARCh [possibly Simon Davidovich Kremer, Secretary to the Soviet Military Attaché]

From: London
To: Moscow
No: 896

16 August 1940

1   I was at CROYDON Aerodrome today after a German air-raid:
A. The aerodrome's control buildings were demolished.
B. The main and repair hangars were demolished.
C. A large number of dwellings were seriously damaged.
D. The main road along the aerodrome was closed, apparently because the serious damage to war materiel located [nearby].
E. Many HURRICANES were dispersed round the aerodrome.
F. A large number of LEWIS guns are dispersed in the fields opposite the aerodrome. They were not there last week.
2   The press reports that CROYDON was bombed by about 30 aircraft [at] a height of 600 metres. There have been two air-raid alerts again in LONDON today. Details [by letter].

DICK [cover name of unidentified London signatory]

From: London
To: Moscow
No: 915

20 August 1940

On 18 August the SAUSAGE-DEALERS [the Germans] bombed KENLEY Aerodrome. I was there today. I could not get on to the aerodrome since all the roads are closed and guarded by soldiers. Soldiers and machine-gun nests are dispersed round the aerodrome in bushes and trenches [these security measures might have been connected with Churchill's visit on 22 August]. Fuel tanks are concealed in bushes. Near the aerodrome there are bombed-out houses. A squadron of HURRICANES patrols in formation above the aerodrome the whole time in flights of three aircraft. Passers-by have their papers checked. There was no panic among the population during the alert.

DICK

From: London
To: Moscow
No: 1069

26 September 1940

1   BEAVERBROOK [the Minister for Aircraft Production] told the MASTER of the METRO that they were working on night air defence with the aim of enabling fighter pilots to see in the dark. He said that the position was good in regard to materiel; they had reserves and from October onwards would be receiving 750 aircraft from SAShA [the United States]. They apparently have as many bombers [as] the SAUSAGE-DEALERS. From November onwards they would begin to get Canadian pilots. On 20 September 119 British aircraft of three types bombed BERLIN. Apparently a few days ago the British once again secretly received peace [conditions] from the Germans. He says they are not bad. The basic [condition] is that the British are not to interfere in the affairs of the continent of Europe.

2   On 25 September I was in the western suburbs of LONDON. There has been slight bomb damage to the FIRESTONE Tyre Factory and the PACKARD automobile workshops in the GREAT WEST ROAD industrial area. One workshop has been damaged in the large SLOUGH complex of factories. At the same time the SAUSAGE-DEALERS are continuing to bomb housing and railway junctions in LONDON. As night falls the British increase the number of balloon barrages. About 150 can be seen from the METRO [the Soviet embassy] which means that there are not less than 600 in town. Their height is not more than 1,500–2,000 metres. A British-made mine weighing 1,300 kg and three metres long was dropped in TOOTING. Naval ratings sent from PORTSMOUTH rendered it safe.

BARCh

From: London
To: Moscow
No: 1170

16 October 1940

1 NOBILITY [unidentified cover name] has reported the following information on the SAUSAGE-DEALERS' air-raid on FILTON 10 days ago. 30
SAUSAGE-DEALER bombers and 30 fighters used a radio beam [the German
Knickerbein system] to fly from northern France; they passed over
PORTLAND straight for BRISTOL from where they turned on to the FILTON
aircraft factory. All the bombs were dropped in a ring of smoke laid above
the factory by one of the SAUSAGE-DEALERS. Three shelters were destroyed
by a direct hit, killing 81 people and injuring 300–500. The damage to
production was slight. British fighters appeared after the raid.
2 The FRIENDS [members of the British Communist Party] have reported
that all the Australian units are gradually being sent from the United
Kingdom to Palestine. Some British units stationed in Northern Ireland
are also being sent to Palestine. As a result of the bombing WOOLWICH
ARSENAL is working six hours out of twenty-four. Part of the ARSENAL
is being moved to WORCESTER. Last week the SAUSAGE-DEALERS dropped
[250] incendiary bombs on Aerodrome, 4 km from ARUNDEL, where British
bombers are also stationed now.

BRION [Colonel I.A. Sklyarov, Soviet Military and Air Attaché][11]

One can only speculate on what reports arrived at the Red Army General
Staff, where they would undoubtedly have been analysed. But if Stalin and
the Soviet military did pay attention to the air war, and if they tried to draw
some lessons from it, then why did the Soviet air force find itself almost
totally destroyed within two to three days of the initial German attack? It
looks as though the Germans studied their own experience in the Battle
of Britain much more thoroughly and effectively.

Some historians have suggested that Stalin never believed that Hitler
would dare to embark on a two-front war. Nonetheless more evidence
is needed. Stalin's personal papers and his archive are currently being
declassified and removed from the office of the Russian President to a
state archive in Moscow. This will take approximately two to three years
and we shall probably get the first answers at the beginning of the new
millennium.

The Cold War and After

Soon after hostilities ceased in Europe the history of the Second World War became the subject of heated political confrontation between Superpowers. In order to denigrate each other both sides employed historians. The Americans struck first by publishing a selection of documents from captured Nazi files, which stressed the extent of the co-operation between Germany and the USSR between 1939 and 1941.[12] Stalin swiftly replied with a lengthy historical report entitled 'Falsifiers of History', which attacked the appeasement of Hitler and the Munich agreement.[13] As a result the Battle of Britain received very little attention in Soviet post-war literature. Some authors did not even mention British resistance;[14] others included a few lines only, with the usual critique of British imperialism and the pro-Hitlerite policy of Chamberlain, and the terse, three-word statement, 'England continued fighting.'[15]

In this polarised atmosphere reflections on the British and American contributions to the war effort were inevitably slanted. One article in a leading Russian international magazine, *Novoe Vremya* ('New Time'), serves as a good illustration. An unknown journalist, M. Gus,[16] gave it a pointed title: 'The Legend of the Battle of Britain'. The author claimed that Hitler's major priority between June 1940 and June 1941 was not the defeat of Britain, but preparation for an invasion of the USSR. He alleged that militarily Hitler had the necessary resources for a successful landing operation, but from a political point of view he never considered it to be a definite plan. In contrast to Napoleon in 1805, who looked forward to beating Britain but was unable to, Hitler was able to but did not want to. According to Gus, the Battle of Britain was an exercise in deception in order to conceal the true intention of Germany towards the Soviet Union, to frighten the population of the United Kingdom and, if possible, to force the 'men of Munich' in the government to surrender by making a new deal.[17] What of the brave British pilots? The author admits that they inflicted substantial losses on the Luftwaffe, which Hitler had to take into account. Hitler now intended to give first priority to the defeat of the USSR, after which he would concentrate on defeating Britain. The road to London went via Moscow: hence it was the Soviet Union which saved Britain.[18] This version was warmly received and highly publicised in Soviet historiography.

After Stalin's death Soviet military historiography experienced a boom. Many participants in the Second World War wrote their own accounts. For three to four years the framework and general methodology remained unchanged and the hostile rhetoric of the Cold War was a necessary feature of almost every work.[19] But with the beginning of 'Khrushchev's thaw' came an understanding that the history of the Second World War had to be studied as a whole, with an analysis of all possible sources and existing debates in the historiography of both East and West.[20] An obvious ideological element remained, but henceforth the narrative of the war in Western Europe began to receive comprehensive treatment.[21] Some of the studies published then can still be regarded as first class.[22]

Soviet historians now paid more attention to the topic of British resistance.[23] The term 'Battle of Britain' was, however, rarely used. Normally they wrote of 'air strikes', 'air fighting' or 'air war'. In the Russian language the word 'battle' (*bitva*) applies to an encounter on a grandiose scale with huge losses and major consequences. Many authors, perhaps, felt uncomfortable with the term, since it could somehow diminish such well-known Red Army battles as Kursk, Stalingrad or Berlin. In the context of highly controversial debates about so-called 'decisive battles' or 'turning points' of the Second World War, the use of euphemisms and synonyms is understandable. Soviet writing often described the 'air war' in the skies over England not as a separate conflict but as an inherent part of the Anglo-German war before Operation Barbarossa. A general line expressing sympathy towards British pilots and the British people was usually combined with sharp criticism of the political elite for its pre-war appeasement of Hitler.[24]

Studies by Proektor and Leschinsky provide a balanced and well-documented picture. While elaborating on shifts of opinion and hesitations among the Nazi leaders, Proektor emphasises that the German military were preparing the campaign against Britain 'seriously and thoroughly'.[25] Leschinsky also emphasises 'the huge scale of the intended operation'. He pays particular attention to the German occupation plans.[26] Both authors are far from regarding the air war as an exercise in deception. Proektor maintains that Hitler and his generals underestimated the British ability to resist. The response of the British armed forces proved to be firm and well organised.[27] Leschinsky, in his explanation of Hitler's failure to invade the United Kingdom, puts in first place 'the determination of the British nation to fight for their motherland, and the might of the British Navy'.[28] At the same time, however, Proektor disagrees with Churchill and does not consider the Battle of Britain to have been a turning-point in the Second World War. In his judgement the major impact of the Battle was the burial (under a hail of German bombs destroying British towns) of the appeasement tendencies of the 'phoney war'.[29]

The Soviet perception of the Battle of Britain did not undergo any particular changes in the 1970s.[30] Only in the 1980s were new elements added with the Soviet invasion of Afghanistan, and when a fresh impetus was given to the Cold War by President Reagan's announcement of his 'star wars' programme and identification of the Soviet Union with the forces of evil. Since Soviet historiography was always ideologically sensitive, it immediately responded with a massive campaign against 'bourgeois falsifiers'. Thousands of books, pamphlets, essays, articles, reviews and dissertations emerged on the Soviet market between 1981 and 1986. The history of the Second World War was an excellent field for the exposure of 'Western propaganda lies'. Anti-Western critics treated almost every attempt by British or American scholars to praise the efforts of their own countries, without mentioning the contribution of the USSR, as a deliberate falsification. Not all Soviet authors were that hostile towards Western historiography and some tried to present a more balanced view, but their work stood out sharply as a minority view.[31]

The Battle of Britain was not forgotten. It continued to receive attention and some historians even started using the term, although only in quotation marks. At the same time interpretations of the Battle were modified. The old thesis of the salvation of Britain by the Soviet Union was revived and added as an essential conclusion to the analysis of the Anglo-German war in 1940.[32] In his book *War and Politics* the military historian V. Sekistov also revived the early Cold War attempt to deflate the significance of British resistance. In his view Hitler only wished to put on a show of intending to invade: he was not in fact very interested in the invasion campaign, but was obsessed by the idea of a future war with the Soviet Union. 'That is why the main essence of the period was not the Battle of Britain but preparations for war against the USSR,' he concludes.[33]

The interpretation of Hitler's plans and motives is likely to remain a subject of controversy among historians. The reason probably lies in the fact that Nazi policy itself was not always consistent or rational, though its core elements (militarism, anti-Communism, anti-Semitism) never changed. Since on various occasions Hitler made contradictory statements on the subject, one can speculate endlessly on his 'true intentions' towards Britain. However, each particular remark has to be analysed within the context of the time and Hitler's ability to rationalise his misfortunes. The Germans undeniably used the Battle of Britain to conceal their preparations against Russia, but Barbarossa was also a good excuse for their inability to defeat Britain. Moreover, the preparations made for the campaign in the east do not necessarily imply that the Battle of Britain was a minor episode of local importance. We will never know how Hitler would have responded had British resistance been less obstinate and resolute. The fact of the matter is that Britain did not give up and Hitler was eventually trapped in a war on two fronts, while Stalin gained a valuable ally.

Did the Battle somehow contribute to the initial success of Barbarossa? This interesting question is likely to be answered when all Stalin's papers and the documents of the Red Army General Staff are available to scholars. Meanwhile it looks as though the Battle did persuade Stalin, psychologically at least, that Germany had embarked on a long campaign against Britain, thus making him believe less in the numerous warnings of an imminent German attack. Unfortunately, modern Russian historians do not pay much attention to these particular aspects. Some continue to make anti-British assertions without much reflection.[34] A new *History of the Great Patriotic War* prepared by the Defence Ministry and the Russian Academy of Sciences does not even mention the Battle as an important episode. This is a step back in comparison with Soviet writings.[35] There is hope for better things to come, since a huge number of files have been recently declassified in Russia. Scholars will need time to evaluate these mountainous new sources and hopefully a balanced and impartial analysis will result.

Notes and References

1 *Pravda, Krasnaya Zvezda* and *Izvestia* were the three major newspapers in the USSR during the war. Though *Pravda* used to be the central one, they all were subordinate to the Central Committee of the Communist Party. *Krasnaya Zvezda* was also under the supervision of the Defence Ministry.

2 *Krasnaya Zvezda* (25 June 1940).

3 Ibid., (28 June 1940).

4 Martin Kitchen, *British Policy Towards the Soviet Union During the Second World War* (Houndmills, 1986), p. 34; Steven Miner, *Between Churchill and Stalin* (Chapel Hill and London, 1988), pp. 66, 135; *Documents of German Foreign Policy*, Series D, vol. 10 (Washington, 1955), p. 207; Vilnis Y. Sipols, *Tainy diplomaticheskie* (Moscow, 1997), pp. 250–5; *Diplomaticheskii Vestnik*, 21–2 (1993), pp. 74–5.

5 *Krasnaya Zvezda* (2 Aug. 1940).

6 *Pravda* (12 Aug. 1940).

7 See *Krasnaya Zvezda* (5 and 23 Sept. 1940; 8 and 17 Oct. 1940; 26 Jan. 1941); *Pravda* (22 Sept. 1940).

8 S. Vishnev, 'Vozdushnaya voina' ('The Air War'), *Mirovoe Khoziaistvo i mirovaya politika*, 3 (1941), pp. 51–65.

9 A. Gorchakov, 'Voina i ekonomika Anglii' ('War and Economy of England'), ibid., 11 (1940), pp. 26–36; L. Ivanov, 'Aktivizatsiya voiny na more' ('Naval War Becomes More Active'), ibid., 3 (1941), pp. 66–75; V. Gai, 'Prodovolstvennoe polozhenie v Anglii' ('Food Rations and Supplies in England'), ibid., 10 (1942), pp. 48–52; D. Zorina, 'Zhenschiny Anglii i voina' ('Women of England and the War'), ibid., 8 (1942); D. Shmorgoner, 'Selskoe khoziaistvo Anglii i voina' ('Agriculture of England and the War'), ibid., 2 (1942).

10 Ivan M. Maisky, *Vospominaniya sovetskogo posla* (Moscow, 1965).

11 http://www.nsa.gov:8080/docs/venona/monographs/monograph-1.html

12 See *Nazi-Soviet Relations, 1939–1941* (Washington, 1948).

13 *Falsifikatory istorii: A Historical Report* (Moscow, 1948).

14 I.V. Anisimov and G.V. Kuzmin, *Velikaya Otechestvennaya voina Sovetskogo Soyuza 1941–1945* (Moscow, 1952).

15 A. Krutikov, *Velikaya Otechestvennaya voina Sovetskogo Soyuzaí* (Moscow, 1947), pp. 19–20; E.N. Burdzhalov, *Velikaya Otechestvennaya voina Sovetskogo Soyuza 1941–1945* (Moscow, 1953), p. 5.

16 It might be a pseudonym.

17 M. Gus, 'Legenda o "Bitve za Angliyu"', *Novoe Vremya*, 26 (1949), pp. 12–17.

18 Ibid., pp. 15–17.
19 See *Ocherki istorii Velikoi Otechestvennoi Voiny* (Moscow, 1955).
20 Many Soviet publishing houses began translating Western works, for example A. Lee, *Air Power* (London, 1955), was published in Moscow in 1958.
21 See, for example, G.A. Deborin, *Vtoraya Mirovaya Voina* (Moscow, 1958); *Porazhenie germanskogo imperializma vo vtoroi mirovoi voine* (Moscow, 1960).
22 S.P. Platonov, N.G. Pavlenko and I.V. Parotkin, *Vtoraya Mirovaya voina* (Moscow, 1958).
23 A. Leonidov, 'Sudba, kotoraya gotovilas Anglii' ('The Fate Which Was Planned for England'), *Mezhdunarodnaya zhizn*, 4 (1960), pp. 91–7; also see 6 (1960), pp. 90–6; B. Fiodorov and A. Orlov, 'Operatsiya "Morskoi Lev" i oborona Anglii' ('Operation "Sea Lion" and the Defence of England'), *Voenno-Istoricheskii zhurnal*, 2 (1962), pp. 48–61.
24 See Alexander M. Nekrich, *Vneshnyaya politika Anglii v gody vtoroi mirovoi voiny* (doctoral thesis: Moscow, 1962); Nikolai N. Yakovlev, *SSHA i Angliya vo vtoroi mirovoi voine* (Moscow, 1961).
25 Dmitrii M. Proektor, *Voina v Evrope, 1939–1941* (Moscow, 1963), pp. 384–5.
26 Lev M. Leschinsky, *Operatsiya 'Morskoi Levi'* (Moscow, 1963), pp. 30–1, 37–45
27 Proektor, *Voina v Evrope*, pp. 388–9.
28 Leschinsky, *Operatsiya 'Morskoi Levi'*, p. 47.
29 Proektor, *Voina v Evrope*, pp. 389, 391–2.
30 The official Soviet *History of the Second World War* provided an accurate account of the German 'air strike' and refrained from any ideological generalisations. See *Istoriya vtoroi mirovoi voiny*, vol. 3 (Moscow, 1974), pp. 129–44.
31 Compare the serious monograph of Andrei N. Mertsalov, *V poiskah istoricheskoi istiny* (Moscow, 1984), with the simplistic and propagandist approach of Oleg A. Rzheshevsky in his *Voina i istoriya* (Moscow, 1984).
32 A.M. Samsonov, *Vtoraya mirovaya voina voiny* (Moscow, 1985), pp. 56–8; F.D. Volkov, *Za kulisami vtoroi mirovoi voina voiny* (Moscow, 1985), pp. 30–57.
33 V.A. Sekistov, *Voina i Politika* (Moscow, 1989), pp. 104–5.
34 M.A. Gareev, *Neodnoznachnye stranitsy voiny* (Moscow, 1995), pp. 42, 108.
35 *Velikaya Otechestvennaya Voina*, vol. 1 (Moscow, 1998), pp. 43–4.

RICHARD P. HALLION

The American Perspective

In the summer and early fall of 1940, Great Britain became the first nation in history to retain its freedom and independence through the use of air power.[1] In often bitter and costly fighting, British airmen kept control of the skies over southern England, shattered attacking Luftwaffe fighter and bomber formations, struck at ports and embarkation points for Hitler's planned invasion of Britain, and protected coastal supply convoys and shipping. The RAF's victory in the Battle was a seminal moment in the history of military air power and, not surprisingly, an exciting drama that drew worldwide attention. In particular, it held extraordinary interest for the world's airmen, especially those of the United States. But beyond this, it ended for ever the aura of Nazi invulnerability and military superiority, greatly encouraged the pro-British interventionist lobby within the United States, set the stage for Anglo-American military co-operation and planning and launched America on the road to rearmament.

Isolationists, Interventionists and Arms for Britain

By the summer of 1940 the United States was a nation rent by an increasingly acrimonious debate over whether or not it should remain aloof from what was happening across the Atlantic. Isolationists generally had no problems with American involvement in the affairs of the western hemisphere, and few if any with American overseas policy towards Asia. (Indeed some were ardent internationalists in Latin and Asian affairs.) But they did draw upon a strong 'go it alone' spirit reflecting scepticism and outright suspicion of involvement in European affairs that dated back roughly half a century to the agrarian reformers of the Populist Era in the early 1890s, and which had first flowered into prominence during the First World War. Not surprisingly (and despite isolationists being found among all social classes and in every geographic locale in the United States), the movement thus had its greatest support in the agrarian Middle West, in rural communities rather than urban ones.[2]

In the interwar years, isolationism gained strength, in part from such well-known factors as the Nye investigation of American munitions manufacturers and their policies, disillusionment with the League of Nations, and the domestic needs of a nation racked by the Great Depression. It found its fullest expression between 1 September 1939 and 7 December 1941, when isolationists increasingly battled with so-called internationalists (or interventionists) to win the minds of American citizens, a struggle symbolised by the 'Battle of the Committees' between the isolationist America First Committee and its interventionist rivals, the Committee to Defend America by Aiding the Allies and, later, the even more extreme Fight for Freedom.[3]

But was the United States as isolationist in philosophy and action as conventional wisdom alleges? By the time of the Battle of Britain, American aircraft, openly sold by American manufacturers to various Chinese factions and Chiang Kai-shek's Kuomintang government, and some piloted by American airmen, had already flown in Chinese skies against the Japanese for nearly a decade.[4] During the Spanish Civil War, though an arms embargo generally prevented American aircraft from participation, a number of mercenaries, adventurers and politically committed American pilots had flown in the Loyalist air arm alongside like-minded international colleagues and Soviet cadres against Franco's Spanish, German and Italian airmen.[5] Nor was Spain an isolated example. Despite the strength of the isolationist movement, US aircraft sold both before and after Hitler's invasion of Poland had been blooded in extensive and fierce combat by the late summer of 1940. A French-piloted, American-built Curtiss Hawk 75 scored France's first aerial victory in the Second World War, and the first RAF machine to engage in aerial combat with the Luftwaffe was an American-built Lockheed Hudson maritime patrol plane.

Already, by the late summer of 1940, Britain was in the process of acquiring thousands of American aircraft to fulfil a variety of roles ranging from training and air combat to strategic bombing and maritime patrol. Table 1 presents a listing of American combat aircraft in operational use with the RAF in 1939–40, delivered for service with the RAF or Royal Navy but not yet in combat, or ordered for delivery prior to the end of the Battle of Britain. It represents virtually a duplication of almost all of the contemporary 'frontline' force structure of the US Army Air Corps and US naval aviation forces:[6]

Table 1   Selected American combat aircraft in service with, delivered to, or on order for, the RAF and Royal Navy as of 30 September 1940

Aircraft Type	Status of British Service	US Service Designation
Lockheed Hudson	Operational	A-29 (USAAC)
Northrop Nomad	Delivered	A-17A (USAAC)
Boeing Flying Fortress	On Order	B-17C (USAAC)
Consolidated Catalina	Initial Delivery	PBY (USN)
Curtiss Cleveland	Delivered	SBC-4 (USN)
Curtiss Mohawk	On Order	P-36 (USAAC)
Curtiss Tomahawk	Initial Delivery	P-40 (USAAC)
Curtiss Kittyhawk	On Order	P-40D (USAAC)
Lockheed Lightning	On Order	P-38E (USAAC)
Bell Airacobra	On Order	P-39D (USAAC)
Martin Maryland	Initial Delivery	(not applicable)
Martin Baltimore	On Order	A-30 (USAAC)
Douglas Boston	On Order	A-20 (USAAC)
Consolidated Liberator	On Order	B-24 (USAAC)
Lockheed Ventura	On Order	B-34 (USAAC)
Brewster Buffalo	Initial Delivery	F2A (USN/USMC)
Grumman Martlet	On Order	F4F (USN/USMC)
Vought Chesapeake	On Order	SB2U (USN/USMC)
North American Mustang	On Order	P-51A (USAAC)
North American Mitchell	On Order	B-25 (USAAC)

Nor does this table take into account numerous other aircraft such as trainers, transports and utility types in British service, as well as general aeronautical equipment furnished from the United States, such as engines, propellers, instrumentation, tyres, tools, parts and the like. Overall, by 15 August 1940, Britain had already placed orders for 20,000 American aircraft and 42,000 engines.[7] Further, thanks both to pre-war agreement and wartime sales arrangements, American suppliers delivered sufficient quantities of performance-enhancing 100 octane fuel to England in time for use by Fighter Command during the Battle of Britain, a contribution of profound significance to the operational success of both the Spitfire and Hurricane fighters. 100 octane fuel enabled higher internal engine pressures, which dramatically boosted the performance of the Rolls-Royce Merlin pistol engine used in both aircraft. Available horsepower rose from a little over 1,000 hp on conventional 87 octane fuel, similar to that used by the Luftwaffe, to over 1,300 hp. So fuelled, the Spitfire and Hurricane enjoyed greatly enhanced climbing performance.[8]

From the outset of the Second World War, Britain's political and military leadership recognised the vital necessity of being able to purchase critically needed materials and weapons from the United States. Writing less than a decade after the Battle of Britain, Churchill recalled:

When the war exploded into hideous reality in May, 1940, we were conscious that a new era had dawned in Anglo-American relations ... We were conscious of the tremendous changes taking place in American opinion, and of the growing belief [in the US] that their fate was bound up with ours ... Very friendly signals were made to us from Washington direct, and also through Canada, encouraging our boldness and indicating that somehow or other a way would be found ... [accordingly] we placed new orders for aeroplanes, tanks, and merchant ships in every direction, and promoted the building of great new factories both in the United States and Canada.[9]

Throughout the growing crisis over the summer of 1940, as France and the Low Countries fell swiftly to the Nazis, and British troops came back bedraggled from the near-miraculous evacuation of Dunkirk, Churchill held firm to ensuring that America remained a reliable supplier of war materials to Britain. But together with his War Cabinet and senior military leaders, he realised that the unfolding crisis would break upon Britain long before the ambitious programme of American aircraft purchases could make a difference in Britain's immediate defence: in short, Britain would have to depend upon Fighter Command alone to ensure it retained air supremacy.

Though the critical immediate challenge was defeating the Luftwaffe, only slightly less critical was the securing of long-term American support for the British cause. The British ambassador to the United States, Philip Kerr, the Marquess of Lothian, was, as Churchill recalled, 'singularly gifted and influential'.[10] But arguably the Prime Minister's strongest ally in America was the President himself: Franklin Delano Roosevelt. The two men developed unshakeably strong bonds of mutual respect and affection. Of Roosevelt, Churchill subsequently wrote, 'I felt I was in contact with a very great man who was also a warm-hearted friend and the foremost champion of the high causes which we served.'[11]

Roosevelt had a profound interest in military aviation, characterised by a strong and growing faith in the power of naval and land-based aircraft, a significant attribute as Britain faced the crisis of mid-1940.[12] His thinking on the subject had been honed in the interwar years by the sharp debates between supporters and opponents of air power. By Munich he was an air-power enthusiast, thanks in part to careful tutelage from then Major General Henry H. 'Hap' Arnold, Chief of the Army Air Corps (and, as a full General, future chief of the wartime US Army Air Forces). In his postwar memoirs, Arnold recalled that, as the Munich crisis unfolded, Roosevelt called a meeting on 28 September 1938 of his senior staff, including the Secretaries of War, Navy and Treasury, the Chief of Naval Operations, and the Chief of Staff of the army: 'To the surprise, I think, of practically everyone in the room except Harry [Hopkins, presidential adviser] and myself, and to my own delight, the President came straight out for air power. Airplanes – now and lots of them! . . . A new regiment of field artillery, or new barracks at an Army post in Wyoming, or new machine tools in an ordnance arsenal, he said sharply, would not scare Hitler one blankety-blank-blank bit! What he wanted was airplanes!'[13] Roosevelt acceded to Arnold's request for an air force of 7,500 combat planes, with 2,500 training aircraft as well, including the development of long-range bombers, a long-sought Air Corps goal. Roosevelt, Arnold wrote, was 'one of the best friends the Air Force ever had . . . Many times he seemed more like a fellow airman than he did the commander-in-chief of all our Armed Forces.'[14]

On 15 May 1940, two days after German tanks, assisted by Stuka dive-bombers, had crossed the Meuse at Sedan, Churchill wrote to Roosevelt, with evident and obvious concern: 'We expect to be attacked here ourselves, both from the air and by parachute and airborne troops in the near future, and are getting ready for them. If necessary, we shall continue the war alone and we are not afraid of that.' He requested the loan of 'forty or fifty of your older destroyers', 'several hundred of the latest types of aircraft', and 'anti-aircraft equipment and ammunition'. The next day, Roosevelt responded cautiously (if generally positively) to this message, stating, 'We are now doing everything within our power to make it possible for the Allied Governments to obtain the latest types of aircraft.' Less than a week later, Churchill replied, 'Our most vital need is therefore the delivery at the earliest possible date of the largest possible number of Curtiss P-40 fighters.'[15] Over the next few weeks, Churchill stressed aircraft and destroyers as the two items vital for Britain to continue to survive.

Roosevelt and his Secretary of State, Cordell Hull, shared a single vision: 'an Allied victory was essential to the security of the United States'. Their vision was not shared by all administration staffers: Joseph Kennedy, ambassador to the Court of St James, felt strongly that both France and Britain were doomed, and recommended, as Hull recalled, 'that if we had to fight to protect our lives we should do better fighting in our own back yard'.[16] Roosevelt tried to 'scrape together every available war plane to ship to France', but to no avail: France fell too quickly. Instead, he focused on addressing America's own defence needs and keeping Britain in the fight. Over the previous year, the War Department had dithered over future aircraft purchases, with little thought or insight into its actual requirements.[17] Now foreign pressures intervened. On the recommendation of the American ambassador in Paris, William Bullitt, Cordell Hull recommended that Roosevelt ask Congress for sufficient appropriations to manufacture 50,000 aircraft a year for America's own requirements. Hull recalled that Roosevelt, upon first hearing the idea, 'was literally speechless, for 50,000 planes was ten times our current annual production'.[18] Though shocked, Roosevelt quickly assented, and went before the Congress on 16 May, asking for the 50,000 aircraft as part of a larger defence appropriation totalling nearly $1 billion. Though behind its potential rivals, the United States was, at last, off and running in the rearmament race 'with the Nation in a state of unlimited emergency'.[19]

Numerous examples can be given of Roosevelt's commitment to Churchill, who got his P-40s (and more besides) in time for them to fight in the Western Desert, though not in the Battle of Britain. Destroyers were more difficult, a 'colossal political risk' for Roosevelt.[20] Although the destroyer loan at first appeared unworkable, Roosevelt and his advisers, particularly the Secretaries of the Navy and War Departments, Frank Knox and Henry Stimson, laboured over the summer of 1940 and were able to arrange a 'destroyers for bases' deal that satisfied the requirements of wartime neutrality laws yet met Britain's need for ships. In early September, the first destroyer steamed from Boston, bound for Britain. Any criticism from the isolationist community was muted, for, as Robert Sherwood later noted, 'by the time the deal was announced, the air Battle of Britain had started and the swapping of a few old destroyers for a few dots on the map seemed a relatively trivial matter'.[21] But it had been a close thing.

Roosevelt did not hesitate to act quickly and even, at times, apparently recklessly. On 1 June 1940, for example, as France's Third Republic writhed in its final agonies, the President directed that the War and Navy Departments assess what they could immediately spare for Britain, to make up for the tremendous weapons stocks lost during the evacuation of the British Expeditionary Force from Dunkirk. By 11 June, hundreds of cannon, thousands of rifles and machine-guns, over 130 million rounds of ammunition, and assorted explosives and bombs were being loaded on to a dozen British freighters docked off New Jersey. It was a breath-taking transfer, for it stripped America's own military forces to the minimum level of support needed to maintain an army of 1,800,000, according to pre-war mobilisation plans. If nothing else, this bold stroke reveals the depth of Roosevelt's convictions and commitment and that of his senior foreign policy and defence team – including his senior adviser Harry Hopkins, Secretary of State Cordell Hull, Secretary of War Henry Stimson, Navy Secretary Knox, Treasury Secretary Henry Morgenthau Jr, Army Chief of Staff General George Marshall, Chief of Naval Operations Admiral Harold Stark, and the newly appointed Commissioner for Industrial Materials, Edward R. Stettinius Jr – to Churchill and the British nation.[22]

Roosevelt's team clearly intended to do whatever they could to help keep Britain free, even at some risk to America itself, and even, in some cases, against the advice of senior military personnel. Attempts to divert American aircraft production to Britain threatened to prevent modernisation of the Army Air Corps at a critical moment in its own rebuilding plans, and led to tension between Roosevelt and his air chief.

Hap Arnold recalled that disagreements over transfers with Roosevelt, Morgenthau and other enthusiasts of virtually unlimited aircraft deliveries, nearly cost him his position as air chief, and, in his own words, put him in the administration's 'dog house' for several months. He subsequently noted, 'It was the rosy dream of some Americans that we could save the world and ourselves by sending all our weapons abroad for other men to fight with. If this priority thus deprived our own air power of even its foundation stones, certain people seemed to take the view that it was just too bad.'[23]

As the Allied cause became more precarious, and the efforts of the Roosevelt administration and its allies to assist Britain increased almost to fever pitch, so too did the efforts of the isolationist lobby to keep America out of the war. Interventionists feared that isolationists would cripple weapons and munitions transfers, potentially fatally wounding an ally and leaving the United States to confront Hitler alone. Isolationists feared that emotionalism, playing upon traditional strong sympathy and identification with the British people, would overrule what Charles A. Lindbergh, writing after the war, defined as 'an American policy of strength and neutrality, one that would encourage European nations to take the responsibility for their own relationships and destinies. If they prostrated themselves once again in internecine war, then at least one strong Western nation would remain to protect Western civilization.'[24]

Lindbergh was the most distinguished aviator of his generation. As such, he had travelled widely before the Second World War examining the state of aviation technology, particularly that of Britain, Germany and Russia. His technical opinions carried great international weight, and, though only a Colonel in the US Army Air Corps Reserve, he spoke and interacted with the senior leadership of the world aeronautical community as an equal. After returning from Europe in April 1939 and recalled by Hap Arnold to active duty, he threw himself into the work of various government committees that dramatically reshaped and refocused American aeronautical research with a view to improving America's defence preparedness.[25]

Because of his background, Lindbergh was almost uniquely suited to play a leading – arguably the leading – role as an isolationist spokesman. As the gifted son of an independently minded, agrarian radical and progressive Congressman who had voted against American entry into the First World War, Lindbergh was neither provincial nor unsophisticated. Possessing a keen and wide-ranging mind, he was articulate, an able writer, personally courageous, and extraordinarily well connected, with numerous foreign friends in England and France. He clearly knew and understood air power, and thus could argue military issues with an assurance and forcefulness unknown among many of his isolationist colleagues and among Roosevelt policy advisers as well.

His first meeting with Roosevelt in April 1939 was outwardly courteous and even friendly, but nevertheless left him with profound misgivings. 'It is better to work together as long as we can; yet somehow I have a feeling that it may not be for long,' he wrote afterwards, and the meeting likely left similar reservations on FDR's side. Both men clearly took the other's measure, the beginning of a contest that would end in bitter mutual acrimony and vituperation. To a great degree, both before and after the Battle of Britain, the American debate on intervention was clearly encapsulated and typified by these two extraordinary men.

Roosevelt and Lindbergh shared many qualities: tenacity; single-minded devotion to their respective viewpoints; tireless work habits; strong, charismatic personalities which drew forth either passionate loyalty or scepticism and distrust from the average citizen; belief in a strong national defence establishment; and, in Roosevelt's case, a growing faith in air power that would bring his own views on its significance ever closer to those of the still-young airman. But in one important and very significant way, they differed greatly. Roosevelt was the first great communicator to be elected President. His press conferences were models of intimacy and shared bonhomie between the media and himself, and his legendary 'fireside chats' endeared him to the average citizen in the same way that Churchill's broadcasts raised the spirits and hopes of the British people. Patrician in background, nevertheless Roosevelt had – even by the standards of the present day – an uncanny ability to project messages and relate to the general public. Lindbergh, while an effective and articulate speaker, was uncomfortable with the public, treasuring his privacy to a degree that made him virtually a male equivalent to Hollywood's Greta Garbo.

Worse, he hated the press and media in general. This was his fatal flaw, an attitude which made his task in communicating the isolationist message all the more difficult: the Lindbergh–media relationship could, at best, be termed one of mutual antagonism. Throughout the entire isolationist fight, the media generally were far more favourable towards Roosevelt than the lanky airman – a situation that cannot be totally ascribed to Roosevelt's better public-speaking skills. Most media personages harboured a natural affinity for Britain, its people and institutions. Indeed, late in 1940, a leading Foreign Office official, Thomas North Whitehead, stated that it was 'quite unnecessary' for Britain to engage in overtly propagandistic outreach to American journalists since 'literally hundreds of American press and radio commentators are performing this service for us daily'.[26] Starting with this handicap, it is easy to see how Lindbergh's personal feud with the press made, from an isolationist perspective, a bad situation much, much worse.

Opinion polls revealed that a clear majority of Americans were overwhelmingly opposed to a unilateral declaration of war against the Nazis, but there was very strong sympathy for the British cause, and much support for supplying Britain with war materials. Understandably, Churchill and his

War Cabinet considered American public opinion profoundly important, if for no other reason than it was critical for the re-election of Roosevelt. In the words of William L. Langer and S. Everett Gleason, the growing clamour of the rival isolationist and interventionist camps

> made at least one invaluable contribution to the democratic process. They kept bringing to the surface the fundamental questions which the average citizen of the United States would have clearly preferred to avoid. Was the survival of Britain vital to the security of the United States of America? If so, were Americans prepared to underwrite that survival even if it involved not merely a limitless investment of the national wealth, but quite possibly, before it ended, of the lives of their sons?[27]

In the belief that there was a critical battle for American opinion to be won, the British revived and reorganised their information and publicity services in the United States.[28] In reality, however, it was not the media, or the politicians, or a mere propaganda campaign, that won the battle for the hearts and minds of Americans. The visible victory over the Luftwaffe achieved a public relations success that no amount of propaganda, however skilfully conceived and executed, could have equalled. Besides, as Warren F. Kimball has noted, there were 'continuing bonds of a common language, an intersected history, and a great deal of intellectual and cultural common ground'.[29] Furthermore the Battle resonated in a social and cultural sense with what might be termed 'frontier values' that Americans had long cherished: self-reliance, courage, resolution in the face of adversity, an unwillingness to be bullied, sympathy for the underdog.

Although American aid was not critical to the survival of Britain in the Battle, it had a part to play. If nothing else, the provision of 100 octane fuel had a 'force multiplier' effect on the RAF that cannot be ignored, and the virtually immediate delivery of surplus weapons and munitions for Britain's home defence ground forces markedly improved their combat capabilities in the weeks after Dunkirk. However, as the Germans themselves realised, any significant aid could not arrive until 1941, by which time the German authorities hoped to have Britain firmly in the Third Reich, a future that included plans for the deportation of healthy British males to the Continent, and the usual provisions for rounding up Jews and other 'non-Aryan' undesirables. What prevented this, as Francis K. Mason has simply and tellingly written, were 'just 3,080 men the equivalent of a Brigade Group, or the complement of a single capital warship' flying the products of British industry, and supported by their countrymen.[30]

Military Intelligence and Analysis

The seriousness of the European situation in the summer of 1940 caused senior American military leaders and analysts to pay very close attention to what was happening. In July 1940, in part because of the conflicting information he was receiving from American diplomatic sources on whether Britain could remain in the war, Roosevelt sent a personal envoy, the flamboyant and colourful Colonel William J. 'Wild Bill' Donovan (the future chief of the Office of Strategic Services), to make his own judgement. Donovan's portfolio included the assessment of a number of military and strategic issues, including public opinion and morale. On 14 July he flew to London and began an intensive series of visits and meetings. He observed the RAF in action, met Sir Robert Watson-Watt, the pioneer of radar, toured radar sites on the south coast, and met a range of other individuals from George VI and Churchill to George Orwell and rank-and-file soldiers, sailors and airmen. This experience convinced Donovan that the Battle of Britain could be won, and he told the US army military attaché, Colonel Raymond Lee, that the odds were '60–40' in favour of a British victory.[31]

Meanwhile a proposal by the British ambassador, Lord Lothian, that the United States send a senior American admiral to participate in initial staff conferences with the British military met with Roosevelt's enthusiastic support. He resolved to send a larger team composed of the Assistant Chief of Naval Operations, Rear Admiral Robert L. Ghormley, Brigadier General George V. Strong of the War Plans Division, and Major General Delos C. Emmons, commander of the GHQ Air Force, the strategic bombing arm of the army. They sailed to England on 6 August for an initial round of talks with the senior British military leadership, including the First Sea Lord, Admiral of the Fleet Sir Dudley Pound, the Chief of the Imperial General Staff, General Sir John Dill, and the Chief of Air Staff, Air Chief Marshal Sir Cyril Newall. Out of these talks, given the vague title of the 'Anglo-American Standardisation of Arms Committee', came a decision to continue further contacts, eventually leading to more extensive discussions over fourteen separate sessions in January through March 1941. Out of these – the 'ABC' (American-British Conversation) talks – came a series of understandings as to how the American and British military services might work together in the event that the United States 'be compelled to resort to war'. From an air-power standpoint, the ABC conversations transformed strategic thinking within the Army Air Corps as RAF representatives made clear that, if war came, the United States could use a much greater number of airfields in Britain to project a strategic bomber offensive against Hitler than previously thought. Thus informed, Air Corps planners were encouraged that a strategic bomber offensive option against Germany was a very practical probability. Additionally, the growing ties and obvious need for a regular process for exchanging information between the British and American militaries led naturally to the establishment of a British military mission in the United States (later designated the British Joint Staff Mission in Washington) and both a US army and navy mission in London (in addition to the existing military attaché structure), in early 1941.[32]

Meanwhile, on their return to the United States, Strong and Emmons submitted a detailed report which, if not wildly enthusiastic about Britain's chances of survival, was nevertheless optimistic: they judged morale 'high', the industrial situation 'not bad at present', the financial situation 'dubious if not definitely bad', the shipping situation 'serious' (due to lack of anti-submarine vessels and flying boats), the military situation 'fair', the air situation 'not too bad' ('Fighter Command has done magnificent work'), and the naval situation 'unfavorable' (due to lack of destroyers and a strong naval aviation arm). Overall, they concluded:

> Insofar as the defence of England is concerned, it has been for some months, is now, and probably will be for some time to come, an air war . . . The lesson from this war, as far as we are concerned, is that we must build up the striking component of our Air Force as quickly as possible. We both have the very definite feeling that sooner or later the United States will be drawn into this war.[33]

It was a very different kind of report from that which most onlookers – including military experts – would have prepared at the end of June 1940.

The Donovan and Ghormley–Strong–Emmons visits were high-level missions assessing issues of grand strategy, shared co-operation and the like. But there was another level of interest that involved more detailed examination of what was happening from the viewpoint of military science and 'lessons learned'. This was an area of particular interest to the US Army Air Corps and, especially, to its chief, General Arnold. Arnold, who had been taught to fly by the Wright brothers, was one of a band of airmen – all disciples of 'Billy' Mitchell – who believed that air power had revolutionised warfare and were working to create a long-range and, ultimately, independent air force inspired, in great measure, by the creation of the RAF.[34] He had followed events in Spain, China and then Europe with great interest. For example, in a lecture on the Sino-Japanese war at the Army War College in October 1937, Arnold warned students and faculty, 'Japan has shown unmistakably that she knows how to employ her air force.'[35]

Arnold had a coterie of excellent officers to call up for observer duty. Following Hitler's invasion of Poland he despatched them to Europe to learn as much as they could about Allied and Nazi air power. The best known of the teams that he sent to Europe was that of Colonel Carl 'Tooey' Spaatz, Lieutenant Colonel Frank O'Dwyer 'Monk' Hunter, Major George C. Kenney and Captain Benjamin S. Kelsey. Each were classic examples of long-serving officers whose rank (thanks to slow pre-war promotions) bore little relationship to either their experience or their influence. Spaatz, a First World War fighter pilot, was Chief of Plans for the Air Corps, and, in the Second World War, would command the US strategic bombing effort in Europe in 1944–5; Hunter, a flamboyant fighter ace from the First World War, was one of the Air Corps' leading fighter experts, and would eventually head VIII Fighter Command; Kenney, a Canadian by birth and another First World War fighter pilot, would become, as Douglas MacArthur's air chief, one of the war's most successful combat commanders; Kelsey, a noted fighter test pilot who had pioneered 'blind flying' in 1929 with famed aviator James H. 'Jimmy' Doolittle, went on to a distinguished wartime career in fighter operations and aircraft maintenance engineering management.

After the fall of France, Spaatz, Kelsey and Hunter moved on to the United Kingdom, where they embarked on an extensive series of meetings, tours and inspections, with virtually total co-operation from the RAF.[36] Though Kelsey had to leave after a month, Spaatz and Hunter remained in place, visiting over the next two months a variety of training and operational stations, and meeting senior RAF officials. Spaatz developed close ties – and ultimately a strong friendship – with 'Jack' Slessor, and the two dined together frequently. Initially Spaatz and Hunter spent their time getting familiar with what had occurred during the lightning-swift German assault across Europe. Gradually, however, they looked in more detail at a variety of issues, ranging from the technical effectiveness of certain kinds of equipment to questions of command and control, and relations between air and land forces.[37]

It did not take long to see which was the better air force. At the end of July Spaatz wrote to Arnold describing the Luftwaffe's 'lousy' bombing performance:

Juicy targets are available all over the islands and planes regularly make their appearance usually at night but the damage done scarcely warrants the effort. Whether they are holding back their mass of well-trained crews for an aerial blitzkrieg or whether they have no well-trained crews is not definitely apparent. However I am beginning to believe that the German Air Force was too hastily constructed and is beginning to be mastered by the smaller but much better trained (apparently at least) RAF. The fights over the English Channel during the past few weeks indicate that smaller numbers of British fighters inflict serious losses on German bombers protected by Me 109s and Me 110s, the latter in most instances outnumbering the British fighters brought into the action.

He commented favourably on night bomber operations by Vickers Wellingtons, and relayed comments from Hunter that future fighters needed more potent armament than the .30-calibre weapons then in widespread use. Hunter recommended eight .50-calibre machine-guns as best (as was subsequently followed by Republic designers for the P-47, then under development). Spaatz concluded his letter by noting:

> Unless [the Germans] attempt to take England [in August] I am inclined to believe it will have been indefinitely postponed. Unless the Germans have more up their sleeve than they have shown so far their chance of success in destroying the RAF is not particularly good. In air combat German losses in daylight raids will be huge. In night attacks the accuracy of their bombing is of a very low order. A tremendous effort using all planes regardless of loss and with prodigious use of gas might be successful, but if not it would be the beginning of the end for the German air supremacy.[38]

As the Battle went on into August, Spaatz was very impressed with how effectively the RAF marshalled its forces to confront the Luftwaffe; a visit to the fighter operations control room of RAF No. 11 Group caused him to recommend adaptation of a similar installation at Panama and Hawaii.[39]

The team studied the various aircraft used by the RAF and talked to both pilots and ground crew to determine relative effectiveness. The Spitfire and Hurricane drew high praise. Hunter flew a 'Spit' at Biggin Hill, noting that 'the controls were superior to any fighter I have ever flown . . . the stick forces were light and the airplane responded snappily to any change of controls'.[40] A sadder case was the Boulton-Paul Defiant, a single-engined two-seater fighter having four machine-guns in a single dorsal turret behind the pilot, but otherwise no forward-firing armament. Defiants had done well at Dunkirk, where German fighter pilots had mistaken them for Hurricanes, attacked from the rear, and paid the price for their lack of recognition. But in the Battle of Britain, the Me 109 pilots, now wiser, easily mastered them.

By the end of August, during which the Luftwaffe flung itself in full fury against the RAF, Spaatz and his colleagues had formed stronger impressions. On 27 August Spaatz noted that the Luftwaffe had withdrawn the Stuka from service, a clear indication of the vulnerability of dive-bombers to fighter attack. With characteristic wit, reflecting on relations between the RAF and the British army, Spaatz observed, 'It takes close co-ordination with the Army to obtain the maximum misuse of air power.' That same day, he wrote to Arnold:

> Several points of air tactics and equipment have become increasingly emphasized in the minds of RAF officers we have contacted as well as to ourselves. They are:

A well dispersed air force is a most difficult target to destroy on the ground . . .

Large formations of bombers escorted by fighters are very unwieldy. The fighters do not insure immunity from attack by hostile fighters on the bombers . . .

I have gathered the distinct impression that dive bombers are [only] useful against a force which has no fighter protection and no AA defense to speak of . . .

The importance of fire power cannot be overemphasized.

The blitzkrieg for this season will probably have spent itself by the middle of September and I shall be satisfied to cease being a high class spy. I must say the RAF have been splendid and could not have been more cooperative in letting us into their operations.

Spaatz left London for home on 9 September, spending ten days in Lisbon en route. By this time he no longer had any doubts about who would win the Battle of Britain. The English, he concluded, had developed 'real air power' whereas the Germans so far had only developed 'a mass of air [power] geared to the Army and lost when confronted with properly applied effort'.[41]

Among the other eighteen passengers on board the flight from Lisbon to New York on 19 September were Generals Emmons and Strong and a certain Lieutenant Commander Genda Minoru, the departing assistant air attaché at the Japanese embassy in Britain, who had served in London since March 1939. It is not known – and is probably unlikely, given the state of American-Japanese relations – whether the four men talked, aside, perhaps, from a perfunctory hello.

On 1 October, with the Battle in its final stages, Arnold dispatched a large Air Corps observer contingent throughout Britain, spearheaded by Major General James E. Chaney, the commanding general of Air Defence Command.[42] Accompanied by Captain Gordon P. Saville, Chaney flew from New York on 8 October, landing in Lisbon the next day and then proceeding to London. During the following weeks they visited more than twenty different types of location, returning home on 23 November. Chaney's detailed and comprehensive report still provides a remarkably thorough picture of the Battle, and an insightful portrait of the RAF.[43]

'To date', Chaney noted, 'the Germans have been definitely defeated in day fighting and have been forced to indiscriminate night bombing.' He commented in particular on the importance of the radar early warning sites and the ground observer corps, which enabled the RAF 'to make 100 fighter planes and 100 fighter pilots do the work of many times that number' because they could be vectored into a favourable position to attack incoming strikes. Chaney noted also the close integration between Fighter Command and AA Command, and the value of barrage balloons in protecting critical points.[44] Visiting the Royal Aircraft Establishment at Farnborough, he inspected a captured Me 109, a design which he thought had 'reached its peak of development'. This was not entirely accurate – the Me 109E of the Battle of Britain gave way swiftly to the more powerful and heavily armed Me 109F and Me 109G of the later war years, culminating in the Me 109K, which soldiered on to war's end – but in another sense Chaney was correct, for by late 1940 the Me 109 was clearly due for replacement. Surprisingly, Chaney gave very high marks to the Me 110, calling it 'by far the most formidable and outstanding of the German planes that have been used in any quantity to date'. He overvalued its speed and armament, and failed to appreciate its terrible vulnerability to fighter attack. But he was right about the Ju 87, which he judged to be 'very obsolete in many ways', and was far more impressed by its later brother, the twin-engined Ju 88 light bomber.[45]

He concluded with a variety of strong recommendations, including the procurement of advanced radar and countermeasures systems, radar-equipped night fighters, and advanced high-altitude day fighters with powerful multi-machine-gun or light cannon armament. He urged that bombers be equipped with far greater defensive fire power than they currently possessed and called for anti-aircraft artillery capable of firing to 40,000 feet. He also proposed the establishment of a civil defence organisation and the nucleus of a Women's Auxiliary Corps. Virtually all these recommendations were, in fact, implemented.[46] Overall, America was to benefit tremendously, during the course of the Second World War, from exposure to British science, technology and special knowledge.

The Consequences of Victory

The realities of German bombers over London, and the images of their attacks, forced the American people to choose whether to let Britain fight on alone, with its own resources, or fight with aid from the United States. However well meaning and sincere isolationists such as Nye and Lindbergh were, their views on limiting arms transfers to Britain increasingly did not resonate with the majority of Americans. Thus, the Battle secured a reliable long-term line of supplies and support from America. But it went well beyond this with the passage of the Lend-Lease Act, which constituted an important step towards the United States assuming outright belligerent status. As Secretary of War Stimson noted in the summer of 1941:

> In effect by this law Congress established between us and the nations fighting Hitler, the chief of which was Great Britain, a relation which was not substantially dissimilar to that which would have existed had their fighting forces been our own expeditionary fighting forces and we their base or arsenal. For the purpose of making these purchases the Staff and procurement officers of our Army virtually became the procurement

officers for those nations, selecting the manufacturers, making the contracts, and seeing to the deliveries.[47]

The Battle likewise accelerated the Roosevelt administration's growing tendency to tie American defence more closely to that of Britain, setting the stage for increasingly close military co-operation and even combined operations so that, by the time Japan attacked Hawaii, the United States was effectively already in an undeclared war, with 'shoot on sight' rules of engagement.

It is difficult to separate the Battle of Britain from the war in general as an accelerator of American rearmament. But the rearmament impulse blazed into full fury only as France fell and the United States confronted the alarming prospect of a Nazi Germany not only dominant on the Continent, but ensconced in what many Americans regarded as their mother country, Britain itself. In particular, the Battle acted as a powerful stimulant to American military aviation. It encouraged development of new manufacturing plants and research establishments; expansion of training of aircrews, mechanics and military personnel in general; development of new technologies such as radar; and development of more advanced and appropriate warplanes, such as the North American NA-73 and the Northrop P-61 Black Widow nightfighter.

The significance of the Battle for Asia and the Pacific as well should not be underestimated. In his desperate message for help to Roosevelt on 15 May 1940, Churchill wrote, 'I am looking to you to keep that Japanese dog quiet in the Pacific.'[48] In July, in a bid to curb Japanese militarism, the United States embargoed exports of aviation fuel and lubricants to Japan. Then Japan began pressuring the Vichy French government to permit a Japanese military occupation of Indo-China. Further, Germany, Italy and Japan were in negotiation to form a tripartite political, economic and military alliance, an ominous sign. In a telephone call to Treasury Secretary Morgenthau, on 6 September, Secretary of State Hull, with characteristic bluntness, stressed the significance of the Battle beyond Europe and his own unease: 'This whole darn thing is hanging in the balance. If the British go down, then the Japs [*sic*] will probably spread out over all the Pacific just like wild men. If the British hold on, why we'll be able to restrain them [the Japanese] and put on additional impediments to them and a loan to China.'[49]

Of course, Hull was not entirely correct, for the British success in the Battle at best only postponed Japanese aggression. But it was a critically important delay and thus, in the short term, he was undoubtedly accurate. A British defeat clearly would have accelerated the pace of Japanese aggression as Japanese militants sought to exploit it in much the same fashion that they had capitalised in Indo-China upon the Nazi defeat of France. Hull recollected after the war:

Those were months when it seemed to me Western civilization hung in the balance. Night after night I tossed in bed, pondering the effect on this country if Hitler should conquer Britain. Despite Britain's magnificent resistance, I had to envisage the possibility that Hitler's superior military machine might overcome her, and that we would then be faced simultaneously in the Atlantic with the combined remaining portions of the German, French, and Italian fleets, and in the Pacific with the Japanese fleet, while Nazi and Fascist agents in Latin America undermined our neighbors to the south.[50]

A Nazi victory over the RAF in the Battle of Britain, followed by the almost certain collapse of British resistance, would seriously have compounded Roosevelt's problems and perhaps led to an even earlier outbreak of the Japanese-American Pacific war. That this did not happen must also be counted a part of the victory of the RAF.

Lessons Learned and Lessons Ignored

The consequences of the observer missions to Britain were mixed. A tremendous number of technical insights were gained on every conceivable issue, from keeping guns and ammunition belts from freezing at altitude to the merits of how to organise a fighter control station. But other potential lessons were missed, a reminder that observers of any sort – and military observers in particular – have to be very careful about the prism they choose to look through when assessing an organisation, a country or a battle. American observers viewed the Battle of Britain from the perspective of future high-altitude four-engined strategic bomber operations, using the Norden bomb-sight for precision attacks. Such was the vision of future war to which the Army Air Corps leadership had aspired since the earliest days of Billy Mitchell's bombing trials.[51]

Thus Air Corps observers were inclined to view the Battle as a short-range, imprecise, medium-bomber campaign, in almost direct contrast to their ideal. This conception lingered long after the Battle. Major General Haywood S. Hansell Jr, the principal planner of AWPD-1, the strategic air warfare plan around which the USAAF built its air campaign against Hitler, commented:

> U.S. observers had naturally watched the Battle of Britain with keen interest. They sensed, as did the British, that the fate of the nation hung in the balance. They sought with intense interest to determine what lessons were to be learned from the first modern air war. But for all its ferocity, the Battle of Britain could not duplicate the sort of air battle that the American air planners had in mind. As a result concrete 'lessons' simply did not materialize. True, both German and British bombers proved vulnerable to

fighters, but then they were medium bombers, poorly armed and flying at relatively low altitude . . . the experience seemed inconclusive.[52]

Writing after the war, the former commander of the American Volunteer Group (the legendary 'Flying Tigers') in China, Claire Lee Chennault, recollected a visit he made to Air Corps headquarters in 1941 while on a mission to purchase aircraft and create a volunteer force of skilled fighter pilots to defend Chinese cities from Japanese attack:

Although Air Corps headquarters was interested only in the European War, I detected no evidence that its top planners had absorbed any of the lessons of the Battle of Britain where the eight-gunned Spitfire and Hurricane fighters proved more than a match for German bombers unescorted or with fighter escort stretched beyond its effective range. By the time the American daylight bombing offensive against Germany got under way in the summer of 1942, the Chinese over Nanking, the British over London, and the A.V.G. over Rangoon had thoroughly proved the failure of unescorted day bombers against determined fighter attacks. Yet American heavy bombers were sent over Europe unescorted by defensive fighters for over a year in an attempt to prove this fallacious doctrine of [Giulio] Douhet.[53]

Drawing partly on his own pre-war thinking about fighter tactics, and partly on the lessons of the Battle of Britain, Chennault strove to emulate the success of the RAF over southern England. During the fighting over Burma (and later China), he used a crude but effective warning network, consisting at first of ground observers only, but later incorporating British-furnished radar as well, to alert the Tigers to incoming air raids, their strength, composition, direction and altitude.

As a rule, analysts of the Battle were more accurate and reliable assessing technical information than operational or doctrinal information. For example, virtually all recognised the vulnerability of the Luftwaffe's Heinkels, Dorniers and Junkers bombers to RAF fighters, but then failed to connect this to the vulnerability of unescorted B-17 and B-24 bombers to interception by German fighters in 1943. They also missed the potential significance of the single-engined, single-seater, long-range escort fighter equipped with drop tanks. Escort fighters were seen either as technologically impossible or as necessarily large multi-engined aircraft. To advocates of large bomber formations relying upon interlocking fields of fire they seemed to be quite unnecessary. The vision of swarms of P-38s, P-47s and P-51s – or British Spitfires, Typhoons and, later, Tempests – cruising deep into Germany and then jettisoning showers of drop tanks like so many silver minnows before charging into mass Nazi fighter formations was not one visible to the planners of 1940–3, whether American, British or German. When, for example, Goering first heard that

American P-47s had flown deep into German territory with drop tanks, he refused to believe it.[54]

Had just one major lesson of the Battle been taken to heart, fighter and bomber operations by the Eighth Air Force in 1942–3 might have proven far more productive. The Luftwaffe tied Messerschmitt fighter escorts too closely to bombers in the name of 'protecting' the bombers; thus they crippled their ability to conduct the kind of roving sweeps ahead and around German bombers that would have been most useful in eliminating intercepting British fighters. Yet when the Eighth Air Force went to war against the Luftwaffe in 1942–3, its fighter forces followed the same operational philosophy. As a result, Army Air Forces' fighter kills against the Luftwaffe stagnated, even as bomber losses remained unacceptably high. All this changed in 1944, when Major General Jimmy Doolittle took over Eighth Air Force. Visiting the headquarters of VIII Fighter Command in January 1944, he saw a sign that read 'The first duty of the Eighth Air Force fighters is to bring the bombers back alive.' Doolittle immediately ordered it taken down and replaced with one reading: 'The first duty of the Eighth Air Force fighters is to destroy German fighters.'[55] It marked the death knell of the Luftwaffe fighter force: in the five months between then and D-Day, the Luftwaffe lost 2,262 of its fighter pilots.[56]

There was another opportunity missed: the incorporation of the lessons learned from Britain's integrated air defence system into American overseas crisis locations such as Panama, the Philippines and Hawaii. And therein lies an intriguing possibility – how this one lesson, properly appreciated and applied, might have dramatically influenced the outcome of the attack on Pearl Harbor by Genda's airmen.

Two of the great Battle of Britain commanders – Park and Dowding – left Fighter Command within weeks of the high point of the Battle. Park went first to Training Command, then to Malta, where this gifted New Zealander defended the island against concentrated air attack as brilliantly as he had south-east England. Dowding, his active career as a senior leader over despite his extraordinary success in defending his country, left for an inspection tour of the United States.[57] While he was there he met Roosevelt and Hopkins and spoke widely on the subject of air power, discussing the failure of the Luftwaffe in the Battle of Britain, hinting at the existence of radar, praising the quality of American planes (particularly the Martin Maryland, Consolidated Catalina, Douglas DB-7 and Lockheed Hudson), and advocating greater standardisation of American and British equipment.[58]

If there was one subject Dowding knew well, it was air defence, but during the four months he spent in United States, in the words of one Air Corps planner, 'Dowding's expertise was never truly drawn upon'.[59] During his stay, however, Dowding visited the Army's Air Defense School at Mitchel Field, Long Island, where, on 4 April 1941, in the presence of Major General Delos Emmons, he was briefed by a team of four officers who had studied the air defence requirements for the Hawaiian islands. The team recognised that Oahu was the vital centre, as 'practically all vital installations' were located there. A plan existed for eight radar stations (three fixed SCR-271 and five mobile SCR-270) to provide a circular airspace exclusion zone around the island of over eighty miles. But the team concluded, given the British experience in the Battle of Britain, that two more radars (one fixed and one mobile) were needed, and that different locations should be sought, so that the size of individual sectors could be reduced, and greater detection ranges of 200 miles be achieved. Further, they recommended adding no less than fourteen shorter-range SCR 268 sets (ten on Oahu alone, near fighter fields) for more precise range, elevation and azimuth bearings. These radars were to be connected via land-lines and radio to a central Aircraft Warning Service control centre at Fort Shafter, and the information displayed on four sector-control boards as well as a plotting table.[60]

However ambitious such planning was, the reality differed greatly. By the time of the Pearl Harbor attack on 7 December 1941, the radar system installed on the islands could, on paper, perform the same role as Britain's impressive Chain Home system. But in truth it was plagued by numerous problems. For example, the total complement of planned radars never materialised. The three fixed SCR-271s had arrived in the summer of 1941, but were still in storage when bombs and torpedoes were detonating up and down Battleship Row, as the buildings to house them were still under construction. The five deployed truck-mounted mobile SCR-270 sets (one was still undergoing assembly when Pearl Harbor was struck) could detect aircraft at ranges between 30 and 130 miles, but not above or below this band, and only at high altitude. Low-altitude flights were undetectable due to siting errors, and, additionally, there was an as-yet-unknown totally blank sector north of Molokai. The comprehensive communication system likewise was non-existent and the centralised fighter control station at Fort Shafter was barely functional. Sets had not been calibrated, operators were poorly trained, key personnel were not well motivated, and the overall army commander, General Walter Short, had decreed that the sets be turned on only periodically and shut down altogether at seven a.m.[61]

So it was that a little after six a.m. on the morning of 7 December, when all five Signal Corps sites picked up individual targets – the Japanese scouting force ahead of the first strike package, including one scout plane that they tracked completely across the island – and passed them to the information centre, nothing was done. And at seven a.m. all the stations, save one, shut down on time! Even then, all was not lost. One site – at Opana, on the south-western tip of Oahu – remained on, because a transport van was late to pick up the crew and the two men kept the set on for training practice. That site, several minutes later, detected the Japanese strike. Several more minutes were lost simply trying to call the information centre and get someone to answer, and when they did, at approximately seven-twenty a.m., the officer in charge (ill-trained himself) dismissed the warning as either naval aircraft offshore (they were, only not American!) or an incoming flight of B-17 bombers expected from the USA. Thirty-five minutes later Pearl Harbor was in flames.[62]

The Japanese had put into practice the lessons learned during the Battle of Britain by their assistant air attaché in London, Genda Minoru. A zealous advocate of air power, Genda returned to Japan to formulate the plan for an air assault on Pearl Harbor.[63] Of his Battle of Britain experiences, he was later to write:

> One of the lessons I learned was that the domination of the enemy air by mighty fighters was imperative for inflicting a fatal aerial blow upon the opponent. One of the main reasons for the Nazis' failure to give a thorough aerial blow upon the British mainland was their lack of this idea . . . Another impressive lesson I learned was that the Nazis' use of air forces en masse, in one wave or in successive waves, evidently proved very effective in spite of their inferior abilities . . . With these precious lessons in mind, I returned to Japan . . . to see how Japanese naval aviation had progressed in the respects mentioned above . . . It was my firm belief, learned from battle lessons in the China Incident and the European War, that a destructive blow could not be inflicted unless mass strength was used in an aerial attack.[64]

From Air Corps to Air Force, 1940–7

Perhaps the single most valuable lesson for the US Army Air Corps from the Battle of Britain was the validation of the concept of a powerful, independent air force. Had Britain not had an RAF in 1940, but a Royal Flying Corps, it is hard to imagine how it would have won the Battle of Britain. Certainly, Dowding would have been far less able to keep his fighters in reserve for the upcoming 'home match' and there is a strong possibility that Fighter Command's critical resources would have been thrown away in France, leaving Britain to confront a weakened Luftwaffe with the remnants of a fighter force: Messerschmitts versus Gladiators, with the outcome not in doubt. Conversely, as Spaatz and other observers noted, one of the major reasons the Luftwaffe lost the Battle was that it had for far too long pinned its structure to the needs of the German army. It was not, therefore, a genuine strategic force, but, basically, an army corps commander's supporting arm writ large. The outcome of the Battle of Britain, thus not surprisingly, further stiffened the will of those in the Army Air Corps who had a vision of a separate service.

But it did more than this: it transformed the thinking of American political leaders regarding air power, and though they were not yet ready to create an independent air force, they were, nevertheless, ready to give the army's air service – for the moment at least – an extraordinary amount of self-determination. In his annual report for 1941, Secretary of War Stimson reflected this 'neither slave nor free' status of American air power:

> We are trying to give the organization of our own air force the full benefit of the lessons which have been thus learned. An air force should have the freedom through independent experimentation and research to develop new forms of aircraft which will embody the latest improvements in the manufacturing art as well as the power to procure for its own force such new types of planes. It should also have the freedom to plan for their effective use and to select and train the special personnel – pilots, bombardiers, navigators, observers, and mechanics – necessary to operate the planes. It should have the power to create an air staff to plan air strategy and effective cooperation with ground and naval forces, and it should have the power to insure the permanence of the technique which it thus creates by the training and creation of an adequate permanent force of regular officers.[65]

Thanks to Roosevelt's decision during the Munich crisis of September 1938 to expand American air power, the Army Air Corps, by the time of the Battle, was already well on its way to independence. Thanks to the Battle of Britain, that quest was made to seem more reasonable and desirable by the example of a highly professional independent air force decisively defeating its nation's enemies in lofty battle. Hence the reorganisation of the army, in March 1942, to incorporate three great commands: Army Air Forces, Army Ground Forces, and Army Services of Supply, with each of their chiefs (Hap Arnold, Lieutenant General Lesley J. McNair, and Major General Brehon D. Somervell) reporting to Army Chief of Staff General George C. Marshall, and, more importantly perhaps, Hap Arnold sitting as a member of both the Joint and Combined Chiefs of Staff.[66]

In July 1943 General Marshall and the War Department doctrinally codified this *de facto* independent status by adopting Field Manual FM 100–20. All in upper-case type it boldly stated: 'LAND POWER AND AIR POWER ARE CO-EQUAL AND INTERDEPENDENT FORCES; NEITHER IS AN AUXILIARY OF THE OTHER.'[67] The Normandy experience of 1944 further solidified the claim of the Army Air Force to a separate existence. Dwight Eisenhower, who was already a supporter of air power, became after Normandy a wholehearted and enthusiastic supporter of an independent air force.[68]

The result was the eventual creation, at the recommendation of Eisenhower and others, of the United States Air Force as a separate service in 1947. Due, in great measure, to the wartime example and sacrifice of America's airmen, its ultimate establishment, under the National Security Act of 1947, went remarkably smoothly. But it must be recognised that if America today possesses an air force capable of furnishing global reach and global power, this is due in part to the value of an independent air arm as demonstrated to American decision-makers by the Battle of Britain.

Notes and References

1 I wish to acknowledge the assistance of colleagues in the Air Force History and Museums Program who suggested sources and offered much stimulating thought, including Colonel Christine Jaremko, Mr Herman Wolk, Mr William Heimdahl, Mr Jacob Neufeld, Dr Richard Davis, Ms Mary Lee Jefferson, Dr Frederick Shaw, Dr Diane Putney, Mr Sheldon Goldberg, Ms Yvonne Kinkaid, Dr Daniel Mortensen, Dr Walton Moody and Dr Jeffery Underwood. Further, I wish to acknowledge fruitful and productive discussions with Professors Wayne Cole and Keith Olson of the Department of History, University of Maryland, Mr Sebastian Cox, Director of the Air Historical Branch of the Ministry of Defence, and Professor Eric Grove of the University of Hull. My debt to them all is great.

2 The best examinations of the isolationist movement are the various studies (cited subsequently) by Professor Wayne S. Cole of the University of Maryland. I wish to acknowledge Professor Cole's influence upon my thinking, and I have drawn heavily upon his works in my argument in this paper.

3 For an overview of the isolationist-interventionist struggle, see William L. Langer and S. Everett Gleason, *The Challenge of Isolation*, vol. 1, *The World Crisis of 1937–40* (New York, 1952), vol. 2, *The Undeclared War, 1940–41* (New York, 1953); see also Wayne S. Cole, *America First: The Battle Against Intervention* (Madison, 1953); *Senator Gerald P. Nye and American Foreign Relations* (Minneapolis, 1962); *Charles A. Lindbergh and the Battle Against American Intervention in World War II* (New York, 1974); *Roosevelt and the Isolationists* (Lincoln, Nebraska, 1983).

4 Ray Wagner, *Prelude to Pearl Harbor: The Air War in China, 1937–1941* (San Diego, 1991).

5 A small number of American-designed aircraft were flown in Spain; indeed sometimes the same type of aircraft flew for both sides.

6 Ray Wagner, *American Combat Planes* (Garden City, New York, 1982 ed.).

7 H. H. Arnold, *Global Mission* (Blue Ridge Summit, Pennsylvania, 1989 ed.), p. 197.

8 For a good viewpoint of the significance of 100 octane fuel from a fighter and test pilot's perspective, see Jeffrey Quill's comments in Appendix XII, '100 Octane Fuel', in Richard Hough and Denis Richards, *The Battle of Britain: The Greatest Air Battle of World War II* (New York, 1989), p. 387.

9 Winston S. Churchill, *The Second World War*, vol. 2, *Their Finest Hour* (first published Boston, 1949; New York, 1962 ed.), p. 474.

10 Ibid., p. 343.

11 Ibid., p. 20; on Roosevelt and his relationship with Churchill, and the Roosevelt

administration and foreign policy, see Francis L. Loewenheim, Harold D. Langley and Manfred Jonas (eds.), *Roosevelt and Churchill: Their Secret Wartime Correspondence* (New York, 1975); James MacGregor Burns, *Roosevelt: The Soldier of Freedom* (New York, 1970); Eric Larrabee, *Commander-in-Chief: Franklin Delano Roosevelt, His Lieutenants, and Their War* (New York, 1987); Waldo Heinrichs, *Threshold of War: Franklin D. Roosevelt and American Entry into World War II* (New York, 1988); Frederick W. Marks III, *Wind Over Sand: The Diplomacy of Franklin Roosevelt* (Athens, Georgia, 1988); Warren F. Kimball, *The Juggler: Franklin Roosevelt as Wartime Statesman* (Princeton, 1991); Warren F. Kimball, *Churchill and Roosevelt at War: The War They Fought and the Peace They Hoped to Make* (New York,1994).

12 Jeffery S. Underwood, *The Wings of Democracy: The Influences of Air Power on the Roosevelt Administration, 1933–1941* (College Station, Texas, 1991).

13 Arnold, *Global Mission*, p. 177.

14 Ibid., pp. 179, 548–9.

15 Loewenheim et al., *Roosevelt and Churchill*, pp. 94–5, Churchill to Roosevelt, 15 May 1940; pp. 95–6, Roosevelt to Churchill, 16 May 1940; p. 97, Churchill to Roosevelt, 20 May 1940.

16 Cordell Hull, *The Memoirs of Cordell Hull*, vol. 1 (New York, 1948), p. 766.

17 I.B. Holley Jr, *Buying Aircraft: Materiel Procurement for the Army Air Forces* (Washington, DC, 1989 ed.), pp. 209, 221–8.

18 Hull, *Memoirs*, p. 767.

19 General George C. Marshall, *Biennial Report of the Chief of Staff of the United States Army, July 1, 1939, to June 30, 1941, to the Secretary of War* (Washington, DC, 1941), p. 1.

20 James MacGregor Burns, *Roosevelt: The Lion and the Fox* (New York, 1956), p. 441.

21 Robert E. Sherwood, *Roosevelt and Hopkins: An Intimate History* (New York, 1948), p. 176.

22 Churchill, *Their Finest Hour*, pp. 122–3.

23 Arnold, *Global Mission*, p. 196; see also pp. 184–94; see also James Lea Cate and E. Kathleen Williams, 'The Air Corps Prepares for War, 1939–1941', in Wesley Frank Craven and James Lea Cate (eds.), *Plans and Early Operations: January 1939 to August 1942* (Washington, DC, first published 1948; 1983 ed).

24 Charles A. Lindbergh, *Autobiography of Values* (New York, 1977), p. 187.

25 *The Wartime Journals of Charles A. Lindbergh* (New York, 1970), pp. 183–257.

26 Cole, *Lindbergh*, pp. 168–9.

27 Langer and Gleason, *Undeclared War*, p. 201.

28 For a discussion of all of these groups, see Nicholas John Cull, *Selling War: The British Propaganda Campaign Against American 'Neutrality' in World War II* (New York, 1995). While overall a useful source, I believe that Cull's book credits many of these organisations with far more influence than they actually had.

29 Kimball, *Churchill and Roosevelt*, p. 193.

30 Francis K. Mason, *Battle Over Britain: A History of the German Air Assaults on Great Britain 1917–1918 and July to December 1940* (Garden City, New York, 1969), p. 488

31 F.H. Hinsley, E.E. Thomas, C.F.G. Ransom and R.C. Knight, *British Intelligence in the Second World War: Its Influence on Strategy and Operations*, vol. 1 (London, 1979), p. 312; Richard Dunlop, *Donovan: America's Master Spy* (Chicago, 1982), pp. 203–20.

32 Mark Skinner Watson, *Chief of Staff: Prewar Plans and Preparations* (Washington, DC, 1950), pp. 113–15, 369–86; Haywood S. Hansell Jr, *The Strategic Air War Against Germany and Japan: A Memoir* (Washington, DC, 1986), pp. 27–8.

33 Archives of the Air Force History Support Office (HSO), Bolling Air Force Base, Washington, DC, Emmons and Strong to COS, US Army, 25 Sept. 1940.

34 Maurer S. Maurer, *Aviation in the US Army, 1919–1939* (Washington, DC, 1987); DeWitt S. Copp, *A Few Great Captains: The Men and Events That Shaped the Development of US Air Power* (Garden City, New York, 1980).

35 Excerpts from a lecture by H.H. Arnold, in 'Notes on the Chinese War', War Plans Division, Army War College, 27 Dec. 1940, a typescript compilation by Byron Q. Jones in the library of the US Army Military History Institute, Carlisle Barracks, Pennsylvania.

36 Richard Davis, *Carl Spaatz and the Air War in Europe* (Washington, DC, 1993), p. 43

37 Spaatz submitted a total of 29 reports via the Office of the Military Attaché from London to the Assistant COS, G-2. Copies of many (but not all) of these reports are in the HSO archives. See also Carl Spaatz, 'Leaves from My Battle of Britain Diary', in *Air Power Historian*, 4 (1957), p. 66.

38 Spaatz Papers, Manuscript Division, Library of Congress, Spaatz to Arnold, 31 July 1940 (copy in HSO archives).

39 HSO archives, Spaatz and Hunter to Military Intelligence Division, 'Organization Headquarters Fighter Group', 31 Aug. 1940.

40 Ibid., Hunter to Military Intelligence Division, 'Visit to Fighter Station', 4 Oct. 1940.

41 Spaatz Papers, Manuscript Division, Library of Congress, Spaatz to Arnold, 27 Aug. 1940 (copy in HSO archives); Spaatz, 'Leaves', p. 75.

42 HSO archives, S.J. Thurman et al., 'SPOBS: The Special Observer Group Prior to the Activation of the European Theater of Operations', Historical Section, European Theater of Operations, Oct. 1944, pp. 2–3; cat. no. 502.01, microfilm roll A5042, fr. 1041

43 HSO archives, J. E. Chaney to the Assistant COS, G-2, 'Observations on Trip to England', 15 Dec. 1940, attached as Appendix 30 to the USAAF, 'History of the Air Defense Command, 1940–41', 26 Feb. 1940 to 2 June 1941, cat. no. 410.01, microfilm roll A4000, fr. 004.

44 Ibid., pp. 1–14.

45 Ibid., pp. 15–16.

46 Ibid., pp. 20–45.

47 Henry L. Stimson, *Report of the Secretary of War to the President, 1941* (Washington, DC, 1941), p. 7.

48 Loewenheim et al., *Roosevelt and Churchill*, p. 95, Churchill to Roosevelt, 15 May 1940.

49 Langer and Gleason, *Undeclared War*, p. 18.

50 Hull, *Memoirs*, p. 863.

51 Stephen L. McFarland, *America's Pursuit of Precision Bombing, 1910–1945* (Washington, DC, 1995), pp. 89–104.

52 Haywood S. Hansell, *The Air Plan That Defeated Hitler* (Atlanta, 1972), p. 55.

53 Claire Lee Chennault with Robert Hotz, *Way of a Fighter: The Memoirs of Claire Lee Chennault* (New York, 1949), pp. 94–5.

54 Stephen L. McFarland and Wesley Phillips Newton, *To Command the Sky:*

The Battle for Air Superiority over Germany, 1942–1944 (Washington, DC, 1991), p. 114.

55 Ibid., pp. 160–1.

56 For an excellent discussion of this see Williamson Murray, *Luftwaffe* (Baltimore, 1985).

57 Basil Collier, *Leader of the Few: The Authorized Biography of Air Chief Marshal the Lord Dowding of Bentley Priory* (London, 1957), pp. 228–33; Robin Wright, *Dowding and the Battle of Britain* (London, 1969), pp. 260–1.

58 See, for example, the following *New York Times* articles: 'Standardized Plane is Dowding Aim Here' (30 Dec. 1940); 'Dowding Promises Night Bombing Curb' (31 Dec. 1940); 'Much Expected from U.S. Planes: RAF Officer Praises Their Role' (1 Jan. 1941); 'British Believed to Have New Plane Detector to Enable Fighters to Combat Night Bombers' (2 Jan. 1941); and 'Dowding to Confer on Plane-Building' (6 Jan. 1941).

59 William R. Burt, *Adventures with Warlords: Insight into Key Events of World War II* (New York, 1994), pp. 250–3.

60 'Preliminary Plans for the Air Defense of the Hawaiian Islands', 5 Apr. 1941, reprinted as Appendix M in Burt, *Adventures with Warlords*, pp. 250–3.

61 Roberta Wohlstetter, *Pearl Harbor: Warning and Decision* (Stanford, 1962), pp. 6–12; Leatrice R. Arakaki and John R. Kuborn, *7 December 1941: The Air Force Story* (Hickam AFB, Hawaii, 1991), pp. 11–16, 69–72.

62 Wohlstetter, *Pearl Harbor*, pp. 10–12; Arakaki and Kuborn, *7 December 1941*, pp. 71–2.

63 *New York Times* (21 Sept. 1940); Gordon W. Prange with Donald M. Goldstein and Katherine V. Dillon, *At Dawn We Slept: The Untold Story of Pearl Harbor* (New York, 1981), pp. 20–6.

64 Minoru Genda with Masataka Chihaya, 'How the Japanese Task Force Idea Materialized', in Donald M. Goldstein and Katherine V. Dillon (eds.), *The Pearl Harbor Papers: Inside the Japanese Plans* (Washington, DC, 1993), pp 8–9, 11.

65 Stimson, *Report*, pp. 7–8.

66 R. Earl McClendon, *Autonomy for the Air Arm* (Washington, DC, 1996), p. 97.

67 Richard P. Hallion, *Strike from the Sky: A History of Battlefield Air Attack, 1911–1945* (Washington, DC, 1989), pp. 171–5; US War Department, Field Manual FM 100-20, 'Command and Employment of Air Power', Washington, DC, GPO, 21 July 1943, pp. 1, 10–11.

68 John S.D. Eisenhower, *Strictly Personal* (Garden City, New York, 1974), p. 72; Herman S. Wolk, *Towards Independence: The Emergence of the US Air Force, 1945–1947* (Washington, DC, 1996), p. 4.

THEODORE F. COOK

The Japanese Perspective

In 1939 Japan was a nation already at war. Despite impressive victories in the first year of the 'China Incident', the conflict between Japan and China which broke out in 1937, China had not capitulated. Japanese difficulties in bringing about a conclusion to operations in China tied down almost one million fighting men and brought the nation's economy to the brink of exhaustion. This led many observers to believe that Japan was incapable of securing a victory and that it was only a matter of time before its efforts collapsed. Such beliefs in Britain were certainly fed by China's propaganda apparatus, but they harboured the kernel of truth that Japan could not win if China did not accept defeat.

At the same time, Japan seemed embarked on an overly bold and unsuccessful effort to stare down the Soviet Union along the extended border between the two countries. In 1938 a clash between Soviet and Japanese forces at Changkufeng produced a stalemate. The following year the situation became graver when war broke out at Nomonhan on the border of Mongolia. This blazed from May to September, during which time there were over 20,000 Japanese casualties, including 8,000 dead.[1]

Japanese-British relations during this period have been the subject of a number of recent works.[2] Although there were long-standing ties between Britain and Japan, and there was much respect within Japan for Britain's history and accomplishments, relations between the two countries had deteriorated in the interwar period. Shigemitsu Mamoru, Japan's ambassador in London from 1938 to 1941, saw the deterioration as a product of Britain's decision in the late 1920s to adopt a policy of co-operation with Chiang Kai-shek, while at the same time maintaining its own dominant imperial position. As Antony Best has pointed out, 'much resentment was caused by the British making moral criticisms of Japan's China policy when Britain remained at the centre of the world's largest empire and was using quotas to restrict the amount of Japanese cotton textile goods entering its colonies'. In the summer of 1939, as Europe veered towards war, Shigemitsu was particularly concerned over the efforts that Britain seemed to be making to prepare its public for confrontation with Japan over China.[3]

In the meantime, the dynamism in international relations promised by Hitler's New Order had proved appealing to the Japanese military authorities and in 1936 Japan had signed up to the Anti-Comintern pact. Yoshida Shigeru, Shigemitsu's predecessor in London who would later serve as Japan's most important Prime Minister in the post-war occupation era, argued, however, that this could only lead to disaster:

> First of all, the Japanese military is overestimating the actual military power of Nazi Germany. Having been beaten so badly by the Allied forces in the First World War, and having lost in addition all territories abroad, no matter how great the German race may be, Germany could not have recovered in a matter of twenty years to the point of being able to fight on an equal basis against Great Britain, France, and thus the United States. On the other hand, Great Britain and the United States have vast territories and abundant resources throughout the world. In addition, the fundamental political and economic strength they have cultivated over the course of the years is certainly not to be regarded lightly.
>
> The military may say that a pact with the Axis side is merely a matter of ideology, that is, simply preventing communism. But to make such a pact clearly indicates that Japan is siding with the Axis, and in the future this will inevitably develop further into something political and military. When that happens, then should the Axis side, which is advancing calling for the destruction of the status quo, cause a war, there is a danger that as the tide moves Japan may fall into a situation of having to fight against Great Britain and the United States.
>
> At present the powers are divided into two camps, but it is absolutely not the time for Japan to seek to join the Axis side. Viewing the present international situation, I think it is wise for Japan to have diplomatic *flexibility*, but if we are to take sides, then I would choose the Anglo-American side over Germany and Italy. I positively believe that this is the road to be taken for the future of Japan.[4]

With Hitler's invasion of Poland in September 1939, it remained to be seen if a European war would develop into a world war and whether Yoshida's views would prove prescient.

Watching the War in Europe

The Japanese military attaché's office in London was one of the key sites from which Japanese representatives could observe the war in Europe. It became a focal point for Japanese efforts to understand and interpret the course of the battles. The men who worked there found themselves caught up in Britain's fight for survival and their own country's growing attachment to Hitler's Germany.

Although few of the formal records for this period have survived, historians are fortunate to have the outline of a memoir by one man who experienced it all. Major Nakano Yoshio, a graduate of the Japanese military academy, was one of the assistant military attachés in Britain from December 1939 to June 1941.[5] He worked directly under the army attaché, Colonel Tatsumi Ei'ichi, who worked tirelessly to avoid war between Britain and Japan.[6] Nakano's account provides us with useful insights into the thinking and actions of the Japanese at this time.

Japanese Imperial General Headquarters often demanded analyses of the strategic situation from the attachés in Europe. After several months of war, the time seemed ripe for a round-up of information. Tatsumi and his counterpart in Berlin, Okamoto Kiyotomi, were asked for similar reports and in May 1940 they decided to meet in Brussels to exchange information. Tatsumi was given approval for the visit by the British authorities – no doubt they hoped to learn something about German troop dispositions through him – and on the evening of 9 May he met up with Okamoto in Brussels and had a pleasant dinner before returning to his hotel. Okamoto announced that along the Maginot Line it was *sajū kyūkei* (arms stacked, men at rest).

Early next morning Tatsumi was awakened, however, by the sound of explosions. He opened the shutters and saw several Belgians standing on the rooftops in their pyjamas peering up into the sky. He thought it must be a defence practice of some sort and went back to bed. He was soon re-awakened by Okamoto, pounding on his door and calling for him to wake up. The Germans had invaded Belgium. Tatsumi's first response was to berate his colleague: 'You told me it was *sajū kyūkei*.' But under the circumstances this hardly helped matters. They rushed off to the Japanese embassy and Tatsumi managed to get to Paris and from there back to London via Cherbourg.

In the meantime, the military attaché's office in London was stunned by the news of the German attack and had no way to contact its head. When Tatsumi phoned from Paris on the evening of 10 May Nakano was on night duty:

> when the call came in I was so relieved! I also was able to report the conditions of the battle I had received immediately prior to his phone call. [My information] came from a man from Domei News who often helped us in our translation, and according to this man, German forces had sliced through Belgium's Ardennes and Luxemburg and crossed into France. Sedan was said to have been occupied.

Despite his heavy workload, Churchill found time to come to lunch at the

Japanese embassy on 17 May. According to Nakano, he must have been worried about Japan's reactions and came to observe the mood. However, his self-evident authority, strong nerves and determination to be cheerful in spite of the situation in France won him respect. Indeed, Nakano admitted that 'even when I returned to Japan, and even when I was in a position of having to fight Great Britain, I did not stop admiring him'.

The military attaché's office tried to form a picture of the unfolding battle in France. The whole staff was assigned to gathering information and assessing the situation. As allies of Germany, the coastal areas were prohibited to the Japanese but the Turkish military attaché had free access and he informed them that 'countless small boats were bringing back exhausted-looking men in pitiful condition. Only a few of the men had even small arms, while most only had their uniforms. Even armoured and mechanized units had to abandon their equipment and return home.' Nakano himself went off to observe soldiers arriving at Waterloo station:

> I changed into unobtrusive clothes and observed the men as one of the passers by. I observed their equipment, their uniforms and their spirit. They looked pitiful, but even these men, who were military men who had abandoned their arms, did not even try to hide their happiness at having returned alive. I thought at that moment that Britain might in fact be extinguished.

Information on the evacuated troops was also obtained through more indirect means:

> The wife at the boarding house of assistant air attaché Imazato was a Japanese woman married to a British subject. Through this connection we asked about the condition of returning soldiers. We learned a surprising thing. The returning soldiers were kept in what was termed 'concentration camps' until their mental state had calmed down to the point where they could be released into contact with the public.

At this time Nakano and others in his office believed that the Germans would immediately attack the British mainland. Rumours swept London that German forces had landed in Scotland and that the British government or the royal family were preparing to escape to Canada.[7]

Watching the Air Battle

Japanese observers, within the restrictions of movement imposed on them by the British, reported on the events of the Battle of Britain and sought to put them in context. Nakano recalled that on 10 and 11 July accounts of sharp air battles were received. These involved British fighters intercepting German bombers over the Straits of Dover. Although only a limited number of RAF planes were put in the air, the general feeling that emerged was that they were able to defeat the numerically superior German forces.

Japan's attachés soon identified three keys to the British ability to blunt German raids, the details of which they assembled for transmission home. First, and most decisive according to Nakano, was the Spitfire. Certainly the Japanese were in no position to undertake a detailed inspection of the plane, but they drew on their own observations and the RAF's commentaries to form a picture of the aircraft's excellent rate of climb, speed and manoeuvrability, all characteristics necessary for an interceptor. The second reason cited was the emergence of co-ordinated attacks against incoming bomber formations. These exploited the weaknesses of the attackers and took advantage of the strengths of the defenders. The defence information system was reported as allowing the RAF's fighter capability to be used more effectively. The third factor highlighted was the greatly improved capability of the British to produce aircraft, especially the Spitfire, in large numbers.

The Japanese viewed the air battle over the Straits of Dover as primarily a trial of strength prior to an invasion of England. In August, when the bombing of harbour facilities and airfields was stepped up, it seemed to Nakano that a landing might be imminent:

> We expected a land battle would soon begin. At the attachés' office we began to investigate the possibilities. When I arrived there, based on my own experience disembarking in Britain, I thought that it would be impossible to land in Britain after October because of the rough seas. There was also an extreme difference between high tide and low tide. Only at high tide was [a landing] possible, while a full moon was also helpful. We felt the first possible attack date would be 15 August, and we estimated that the next possible date would be Sunday 15 September because of the confluence of high tide and full moon. Attaché Tatsumi received a special travel passport to view the battlefields from Eden, Army Minister, so he went to where he could observe the Straits of Dover on 15 August and watched throughout the night. Our office prepared for the time when the German forces would land and advance to London. We put out the Japanese sun disk flag, assembled ready-made food, and prepared our office to move with our secret code documents in case the Germans moved on London.

Although no landing took place on 15 August, large bombing raids were launched on that day. In the morning it was broadcast that Croydon airfield had been bombed, so one of Nakano's colleagues, Imazato, rushed to the scene to observe what he could. He saw that the hangars had been completely destroyed. He reported that, according to the local residents, 300 planes, including dive-bombers, had carried out a pre-dawn attack.

The concerted bombing of London began on 7 September. The Japanese soon found that they had no immunity from attack:

During the air raids of the night of the 7th, the eight-storey mansion where our army attaché's office was was hit by an incendiary bomb. At first several residents had been observing air raids, but because of the danger, all left. Only clerk Yamamoto and I were on the roof at about 9.30 in the evening. About 20 metres from me on the lawn an incendiary bomb landed and began to burn. At first it was only a little fire, sparkling. I sent Mr Yamamoto down to tell the guard. Without thinking, I myself stepped on the fire and extinguished it. It was lucky it had struck on the soft lawn portion (of the roof) because if it had hit on the hard surfaces it would have spattered oil all about and I would not have been able to put it out. Of course, it could have hit me directly. I guess I was quite lucky.

Nakano was on night duty, sleeping at the military attaché's office, when, on the night of 16 October, it was bombed for the second time:

This time a one-ton bomb crashed into the cellar of the mansion at a sharp angle from the road next to the building. It did not explode, but we thought it might have a time fuse, so all members had to leave the building immediately. I contacted military attaché Tatsumi. We evacuated, carrying our emergency food rations prepared for 15 August and our precious documents, heading to the attaché's official residence in Kensington. We then used that building as our attaché's office and the Mount Royal Hotel, facing Hyde Park, as our living accommodation. A British engineering unit removed the unexploded bomb. They first removed the fuse and then dug out the bomb itself. They were quite splendid, calm and brave. When they removed bombs one by one, they would put rope up to keep citizens from approaching, but the civilians wanted to see scary things, so they tended to crowd around. The commanders of these units were really in quite good humour and would respond to the banter of the civilians that crowded around. I was impressed by how humorous they were.

On 20 October they were bombed again:

The attaché's office was still at the official residence. Imazato and I were sleeping in the room facing the road. At that time the air raid warning sirens echoed so often that we really didn't care much and we thought that we would die when we would die, so we had not taken shelter in the air raid shelter. Then there was a sudden huge explosion. The water purification plant for Kensington had been targeted and a bomb fell across from this place in the garden. Luckily it fell amid the pear trees, dug deep into the soil and then exploded. The military attaché's residence was a one-storey building, the walls made of bricks and concrete. All the windows were blown in and the contents of the rooms were destroyed. Luckily, we were asleep, our heads next to the brick walls, so we were not injured at all.

Now we had to move again, this time the office too moved to the Mount Royal Hotel.

By the late autumn it was clear that the predictions of a German landing were inaccurate. The military attaché's office sent an analysis of the situation to the Japanese General Staff and stated that the Luftwaffe had failed to establish preconditions for an invasion: 'Daytime facility bombing of the British air force ended in failure due to the hard struggle of the British fighter command units. Germany was unable to achieve control of the air.' At the same time, it was noted, the victory in the air battles had improved the fighting spirit of the British people and, despite hardships, they were demonstrating their will to fight on: 'we estimate that an invasion of the British homeland by Germany, while not absolutely impossible, will be extremely difficult'.

The report received a cool response from the General Staff. In the light of the dazzling success of Hitler's Blitzkrieg, in September 1940 Japan had agreed a military alliance with Germany and Italy. Negative views of the German war effort were thus problematic. Okamoto, who had been promoted from military attaché in Berlin to Head of the Second Department of the General Staff, responded to Tatsumi: 'I do not believe that Hitler has given up the idea of invading the British homeland. Maybe, being bombed every day has weakened your resolve?' The attachés in London were shocked that 'even Maj.-Gen. Okamoto, it seemed, who was viewed as the coolest, and most calm person among the hot-headed attachés in Germany could make such an erratic judgement'. Tatsumi was enraged, but believed that the judgements made in London should be reported frankly to Japan, even if that risked their careers. Indeed, to the Japanese observers in London it was precisely because Japan might now find itself at war with Britain that honest assessments were needed as to why the Blitzkrieg had stalled:

> If Japan was going to fight, we had to determine what were the conditions necessary for victory. When war should be begun, or whether war should be avoided. We had to clarify this situation. Located at the very site of the battle between Britain and Germany and attacked by Germany in the very capital of Britain, we were naturally sending information that had a different perspective from the information available from the Germans who were attacking. Thus our information should be the most valuable.[8]

The failure of the Germans to launch an invasion during the Battle of Britain did, at least, discourage the more radical elements in Japan from using this 'golden opportunity' to attack Hong Kong and the Malay peninsula in the summer of 1940.[9]

Genda and the Air Battle

Lieutenant Commander Genda Minoru arrived in London as Japanese assistant naval attaché and special air attaché in March 1939. He outlined his mission in the following terms:

What I most wanted to see in Britain were the real capabilities of the British air force. To do this required detailed study of British units, but under these conditions that was beyond my capability. The only way I could really grasp the air-fighting capability of the British Fighter Command was by driving in the suburbs, or playing golf and observing the combat planes flying from nearby fields. By watching how they operated their fighter planes during training, I could estimate roughly how much ability their pilots possessed. In a sense this is extremely difficult, just watching in this manner, trying to estimate the whole capability of an entire air force, but with repetition it was possible to form an overall assessment of their abilities.

During the Battle of Britain he observed the combatants in action:

I could roughly appraise the results of air combats between British fighters and German fighters. Using these observations I was able to estimate that the capabilities of the RAF Fighter Command were much lower than that of the Imperial Japanese Navy, while those of the German Luftwaffe fighters were even lower than the British.

Such an opinion was not popular because of its implied criticism of Germany, but Genda stuck to his guns:

My conclusion was quite self-righteous and was criticised, but I was confident in it. And, when I observed the early combat engagements of the Pacific War, the results of Malaya, Burma, and the Indian Ocean actions bore out my assessment.

Genda was ordered home in September 1940 'just as the heavy German air raids began' and when 'many thought that Britain's defeat was certain'. He returned to Japan via Lisbon and New York. Although, as Richard Hallion notes in his chapter (see page 95), the American Generals Emmons and Strong shared the same flight across the Atlantic as Genda, he made no mention of any casual meetings with his fellow passengers. Nevertheless, his arrival in New York did attract significant attention in the American press even though he was only a junior attaché.

Back in Tokyo, Genda filed a report on his experiences in Britain for the naval General Staff and the Navy Ministry:

1   As for the Battle of Britain and the British air force, the Germans have an overwhelmingly large number of aircraft and are succeeding in carrying

out bombing. It is a different way of attacking from what Japan is doing on the [Chinese] continent. The way Japan is doing it is like casting a wide net, with incomplete preparations. The German way is different. For example, if they attack an air base they attack and destroy every facility including not just aircraft but also hangars and everything else. They destroy even the concrete foundations and bolts of the hangars. This kind of attack and destruction does not allow a base to be rebuilt.

2   The air war between Britain and Germany over Britain is in progress, but in my view the British will not scream out [for mercy]. The reason for this is that [the battle] is really developing to the advantage of the British in the air combat over British territory, despite the overwhelming number of German forces deployed. The two nations' fighting ability becomes the key to determining who will control the air, and I think the ability of the British Fighter Command is greater than that of the Germans. Thus the German force's air raids over the British homeland may well collapse.

3   It is generally assumed [in the Japanese navy] that aircraft and aircraft carriers are only offensive weapons. It is almost unthinkable to provide defence, but the European conflict shows otherwise. Since British aircraft are not well provided with defence, thus hit they suffer fires and pilots are lost. The German planes are well protected, with good protection for the pilots; even the fuel tanks are protected. So German planes have durability even in disadvantageous combat positions. Among the British forces, the issue of how the aircraft should be better defended is now beginning to be discussed seriously. The Imperial Japanese Navy should reflect on this point and consider adopting better protection. This can also be said about aircraft carriers. The flight deck should also be protected. The *Ark Royal* class carriers have a well-armoured deck. Of course, it is natural to defend aircraft carriers by fighter planes and anti-aircraft guns, but it is almost impossible to ensure one hundred per cent proof against attacks by aircraft.

4   Up to now, the combat situation is advantageous to the Axis side, and many assume that the Axis will win, but when the British characteristic of *nenchakusei* [literally 'viscosity' or in this context 'tenacity'] is considered, I do not believe Britain will collapse as easily as many people say. When the British ran away at Dunkirk, had Hitler invaded the British homeland, with proper preparation, Britain might well have been conquered. But now all the beaches have defensive capabilities, the seas all around are under their control and they have control of the air over the Straits and the English homeland. It is too early to assume British defeat. If this present situation continues, a British victory cannot be assumed either. The determining factor of victory in this war will come from some other factor, not yet surfaced.

In view of the military alliance with Germany, Genda's observations were unwelcome: 'They said, "If you listen to Genda, you would think the British are going to win." This contradicted the flow of the times.'

Genda was ordered on to the staff of the First Air Fleet – Japan's carrier strike force – with which he would make his reputation as a planner of the 'Hawaii Operation': the attack on Pearl Harbor. Although the lessons learnt by Genda during the Battle of Britain at the time were likely to have been less clear than his recollections made them appear, and were no doubt synthesised with his experiences in China, the importance of 'mighty fighters' and 'mass strength' in an aerial attack if a decisive blow was to be inflicted were reinforced by his analysis of the air war in 1940. In retrospect he would claim that he applied these lessons in his planning for naval operations. However, while he might have incorporated notions of concentration of force in planning the Pearl Harbor operation, it was probably more the raid on Taranto on 11 November 1940 – in which the British crippled the Italian battle fleet as it lay at anchor – which influenced his thoughts in relation to the attack. It was ironic that during the Battle of Midway – arguably one of the turning-points of the Pacific War – the Japanese would lose four aircraft carriers to the type of air attack which Genda had warned against in his Battle of Britain report.[10]

The Immediate Aftermath

The consequences of the apparent British victory in the Battle of Britain were felt almost immediately in the Far East when in October supplies to China, which had been halted in July 1940 after the fall of France and the threat of impending invasion, once again began to flow along the Burma Road. It seemed that the British were back, and while French Indo-China and the Dutch East Indies remained inviting objectives for those in Japan who sought a southern strategy, they would have to calculate once again on Britain's willingness and ability to collaborate with the United States against Japan in China and south-east Asia.

In Europe the likelihood of a German invasion of Britain seemed to recede over the winter of 1940–1 and speculation grew as to where Hitler might strike next. Many of Japan's attachés and other intelligence sources predicted that a Nazi onslaught on the Soviet Union was in the offing. However, Japan's Foreign Minister, Matsuoka Yosuke – who negotiated a non-aggression pact with the Soviet Union in April 1941 as part of a grand design to use both this agreement and the Axis Pact to force American acceptance of Japan's place in east Asia – firmly believed that Hitler still intended to invade Britain and he received the assurances of the German ambassador on this matter.[11] Lieutenant General Ōshima Hiroshi, Japan's new ambassador in Berlin, also reported that a threat to Britain still existed:

Soon after my arrival in Germany, in May 1941, I took Lt. Col. Saigo [Jūgō] and Embassy First Secretary Ushida to observe the coastal area around Amsterdam. In the ports throughout the coastal area there were many ships gathered in preparation for a landing. Further, I heard from Nishimura in Sweden that Germany had placed orders for many small boats from Sweden. Yet when I asked German officers, no one would say they were really going to do it. In Berlin there was no sign of a clear plan to conduct the landing at all. I sensed more of an active movement toward the Soviet Union. I asked Admiral Raeder, and he responded, 'Of course we are thinking about landing, but at the same time we are considering other alternatives.' As a result, I assumed that Germany was going to defeat Britain by air and submarines and that a landing would not take place. I reported this to Tokyo. Around the same time, in May or early June 1941, when I visited Italy, I heard of Hess's disappearance in Britain. I met Reichsmarschall Goering in a hotel in Italy and asked him about the invasion of Britain plans. He said, from the beginning we were thinking about it, but the navy argued that they would be able to cross the Straits by transport ships escorted by submarines, but he said that he, Goering himself, had argued for crossing in a large number of small boats, and that the [German leadership] had not been able to take a decision up to this point.

I then explained [Japan's] abundant experience in landing tactics. Goering asked me to observe Germany's preparations, so I asked specialist officer Major Sakurai of the army and accompanied several army and navy officers to observe German landing preparations on the Baltic coast. They proved quite ill-prepared as a force for large-scale operations. I did not see any eagerness among the actual units involved.

Despite this apparent half-heartedness, on the eve of the attack on the Soviet Union the ambassador had still not reconciled himself to the new strategic priorities of Germany.[12] Indeed, with the launch of Barbarossa on 22 June 1941 Japanese foreign policy was thrown into some confusion. There was some discussion of joining Hitler's war with the Soviet Union, but the military successfully argued that Japan should seize the opportunity to push south with impunity.[13]

Little attention seems to have been paid at this time to the vulnerability of Japan itself to an intensive bombing campaign. Japan's cities, described by some American strategists as mere 'paper and wood', were particularly vulnerable to air attack. Although elaborate air-raid shelters and bomb-resistant facilities were constructed in Tokyo for the senior military leadership and the Emperor, the development of air defences was not, however, accorded high priority. Several reasons can be suggested for this. The Japanese air forces had enjoyed successes during the wars with China and the Soviet Union and confidence in their abilities was high. Furthermore, until the advent of very long-range aircraft, Japan was safe from air attack if it held the continent and controlled the seas around the home islands. What was more, if anything the defeat of the Luftwaffe over the skies of Britain in 1940 demonstrated the strength of the defence in such a situation. The Japanese, it was believed, would show as much grit as the British in the face of air attack.

Japanese observers in London did their best to provide honest and accurate reports of the Battle of Britain in the summer and autumn of 1940. Their assessments of the course of the Battle were not, however, enthusiastically received by the military authorities in Japan, and the failure of Germany to bring Britain to its knees meant that when Japan embarked on war in the Pacific in December 1941 she would do so under less advantageous conditions. It was a road that would eventually lead to the mass bombing of Japan and to Tokyo in flames.

Notes and References

1   See Alvin. D. Coox, *The Anatomy of a Small War: The Soviet-Japanese Struggle for Chankufeng/Khasan* (Westport, Conn, 1977) and *Nomonhan: Japan Against Russia 1939*, 2 vols (Stanford, 1985).

2   See, for example, Antony Best, *Britain, Japan and Pearl Harbor: Avoiding War in East Asia* (London, 1995), and Kyozo Sato, *Japan and Britain at the Crossroads, 1939–1941* (Tokyo, 1986).

3   Antony Best, 'Shigemitsu Mamoru and Anglo-Japanese Relations', in Ian Nish (ed.), *Britain and Japan: Biographical Portraits* (Richmond, 1997), pp. 245–59; Antony Best, 'Shigemitsu Mamoru as Ambassador to Great Britain, 1938–1941', in Ian Nish (ed.), *Shigemitsu Studies* (London, 1990), pp. 12–13.

4   John W. Dower, *Empire and Aftermath: Yoshida Shigeru and the Japanese Experience, 1878–1954* (Cambridge, Mass, 1979), pp. 120–1.

5   Kaikōsha [Association of Former Army Officers], Tokyo, Nakano Yukio, *Dai-niji Taisen hiwa. Rondon chūzai rikugunbukan shitsu* ('Untold Story of the Second World War: The Military Attaché's Office in London') (1991). This manuscript is an early working draft of what Nakano had planned to be his memoir of his period as assistant attaché. Although ill, Nakano was working with his son on the project, but with his son's untimely death, and Nakano's own passing, the manuscript remained unfinished. Chapter 5 is entitled 'The Battle of Britain'. I am greatly indebted to Morimatsu Toshio – prolific author, Kaikōsha librarian and long-time mentor in Japanese military history – for his assistance in making Nakano's manuscript available to me.

6   Law Faculty Library, Tokyo University, Tatsumi Ei'ichi, *Tatsumi Ei'ichi kankei shiryo mokuroku* (1990).

7   Nakano, 'Untold Story', pp. 33–6.

8   Ibid., pp. 37–42.

9   Hosoya Chihiro, 'Britain and the United States in Japan's View of the International System', in Patrick Finney (ed.), *The Origins of the Second World War* (London, 1997), p. 186.

10 Genda Minoru, *Kaigun kōkutai shimatsuki. Sentō hen* ('The Beginning and the End of the Naval Air Forces: Fighters Volume') (Tokyo, 1962), pp. 9–23; Genda Minoru with Masataka Chihaya, 'How the Japanese Task Force Idea Materialized', in Donald M. Goldstein and Katherine V. Dillon (eds.), *The Pearl Harbor Papers: Inside the Japanese Plans* (Washington, DC, 1993), pp. 8–9, 11.

11 See Kase Toshikazu, 'A Failure of Diplomacy', in Haruko Taya Cook and Theodore F. Cook (eds.), *Japan at War: An Oral History* (New York, 1992), pp. 90–5; Kase Toshikazu, *Journey to the Missouri* (New Haven, 1950), pp. 38–43.
12 Oshima Hiroshi, *Moto zaidoitsu taishi rikugun chūjō Ōshima Hiroshishi yori no chō shusho* ('Hearing from former ambassador to Germany and former army Lieutenant General Ōshima Hiroshi'), part 1, 1959, pp. 23–4.
13 David Reynolds, '1940: Fulcrum of the Twentieth Century?', in Finney (ed.), *Origins*, p. 448.

PART FOUR

EXPERIENCE AND MEMORY

HANS-EKKEHARD BOB

Memories of a German Veteran

I wish to begin with some remarks on the training of German fighter pilots. Before the war the training was very thorough compared to the training during the war, which was so superficial that the pilots were basically only able to start and land their fighter planes. These badly trained pilots were hardly able to control their aircraft and they never undertook any comprehensive flight and shooting training. My own group, however, underwent intensive training which included tests and examinations in stunt flying, blind flight and flying on any aircraft type available to the Luftwaffe.

I volunteered for the Luftwaffe on 1 December 1936. In 1938, after having successfully passed through the officer academy, I went for fighter-pilot training with squadron 133 at Wiesbaden. At that time we flew Arado 68s, a wonderful biplane which was equipped with a Junkers injection motor. I was so impressed with its flying qualities that I remember this time more for the pleasures of being a pilot than a soldier. After intensive flying and shooting training we were moved to Sprottau in Silesia near Czechoslovakia as fighter squadron 133. This was the time of the occupation of the Sudetenland, which was the home of nearly three million Germans. The invasion was, however, kept a secret from us. Our task was to fly fighter escort for Ju 52 transport planes. Our planes were equipped with machine-guns, but we had neither ammunition nor ammunition belts. We were lucky that there was no shooting: we would have been in trouble.

After further training for the expanded military pilot's certificate, on 15 July 1939 I was transferred to Königsberg in east Prussia to fighter wing 21, which later became Jagdgeschwader 54. The group was equipped with Me 109 Cs and Ds. We were already flying in formation, with two planes flying together, four planes forming a flight and three flights forming a squadron. Three squadrons formed a fighter group of forty aircraft, including the planes of the staff. Our tactical flying was a result of experience in Spain. We practised flying in squads of broadly spread formations, which enabled the pilots to watch the rear space of the formation and to cover one another.

Much to our surprise, on 1 September 1939 the Polish campaign began. My first experience of fighting operations came flying escort missions for bombers. Early on we faced strong opposition from Polish PL 18 biplanes, which were quite slow but manoeuvrable.

After the Polish campaign we were transferred to the west of Germany and flew Me 109 Es. On 10 May 1940 the French campaign commenced and we began air fights with the French. During my first operation I won my first victory over a Gloster Gladiator. We also had dog-fights with Curtiss, Dewoitine and Morane fighters. We soon became aware that the Me 109 was faster than the French pursuit planes and we were able to use this against the slower, but more manoeuvrable, French planes. In a relatively short period the whole French air force was eliminated.

Another task was the supervision of the tank forces' advance towards the Channel coast. My first experience of the RAF was during the Battle of Dunkirk. At that time the RAF still flew in close chain formation: three planes flying close together followed by squadrons consisting of several chains one after the other raised in steps. This flying method probably permitted only the squadron leader to watch the horizon for enemy planes. On contact with the enemy the British pilots were rapidly confused. One of my pilots attacked a squadron of Defiants and with one burst of fire shot down three planes. With our swarm formation each pilot was able to keep the horizon in sight. These operations were a hard test for us, but we did our best to achieve air superiority.

The plan was that the British army would be exterminated by the Luftwaffe at Dunkirk and our job was to protect the bomber attacks against the British fighters. We flew fighter escorts above the bombers and had many battles with the British fighters. However, we did not succeed in preventing the British army from escaping home. The proximity of the British Isles and the great number of British boats made our task very difficult. It should be said that Hitler favoured the British and did not want to fight them. Nor could we young officers understand why we were at war with the British. When we shot down an RAF pilot in 1940 we would sit in the officers' mess and drink together. We would think, 'We are friends, we feel the same.'

Dunkirk was soon under German control. We flew explorations and took part in free hunts over the area, the Channel and the English south coast. The British fighters tended to avoid confrontation. The fact that at this time we still had at our disposal a considerable number of fighter planes ensured German air superiority. While flying in August I saw many small boats and barges in French harbours along the coast. We were all guessing what that could mean and rumours abounded. We finally came to the conclusion that a landing in England was planned. At that time we considered an invasion quite possible because the British army was in disarray and there were only a few British fighter planes left in the sky. But nothing happened and we worried about our supreme command – especially Reichsmarschall Goering.

Although it is difficult to judge these things today, from 1936 until 1940 there was great enthusiasm for Goering, who had established the German air force in such a generous way for us pilots. We had the best houses, the best airfields and, we believed, the best aircraft. But during the course of the war we recognised that several wrong decisions were taken by the supreme command of the Luftwaffe. Although we accepted his leadership, we became critical of Goering. In particular, he pushed the Luftwaffe on to the defensive at a very early stage.

In addition, the variety of German aircraft in development overstrained the aviation industry. It was not very useful to develop technically superior planes while the active pilots were still using the old constructions. Moreover, one of the best developments, the jet Me 262, with an average speed of 850 km per hour, was built too late and in too few numbers. The decisions taken by the German supreme command about aviation design and development were not very good.

During the Battle of Britain we were stationed at several airfields in the neighbourhood of Calais. My 9th squadron was posted to the field airport Quines-South. It was a big lawn area, two-thirds of which was bordered by forest in which we could park and disguise our planes and also put up tents and huts to lodge the personnel. From there we flew escort protection sorties for our bomber formations, which were attacking strategic targets in the south of England as well as convoys. In spite of the summer season, the weather conditions were very bad, so it took us a long time to fly to the gathering points for the bomber formations. We could therefore only partially accomplish our tasks. We were ordered to adapt our normally superior speed to that of the bombers and so we wobbled along like limping ducks.

As far as I know, these attacks on strategic targets, especially the aviation industry, were successful and the British fighter formations were in considerable trouble because of the lack of aircraft replacements. But in spite of this, our sorties became more and more difficult due to bad weather. During a particularly heavy sortie for escort protection we tended to fly between two cloud layers. We deemed this safe from enemy attack because above and below us was thick cloud coverage. Much to our surprise, however, we were suddenly attacked by a large Spitfire formation from the rear. At first it was incomprehensible how this formation could have attacked us in this way without being able to see us. Later we learned that the British possessed a kind of radar and were able to direct their formations to our height and direction. On our side, before we were equipped with the so-called Y-apparatus, we had to rely on dead reckoning, ground marking and instinct.

The Luftwaffe continued to undertake massive bombing attacks against military targets in order to gain air superiority for a landing in England. There have been many arguments about strategic bombing, especially with regard to the endangering or extermination of the civil population. One speaks, for example, about the terror attacks on Coventry meaning the eradication or erasing of the city. I would like to comment on this. On 2 September 1939 Hitler declared that he wished to avoid aerial attacks on civilian targets. The same day France and Britain promised to refrain from bombing civilians. On 11 May 1940, the day after becoming Prime Minister, Winston Churchill decided, with his Cabinet, to attack the German hinterland with bombers. Lord Trenchard, the father of the RAF, was also said to have supported these attacks. This began the RAF's aerial war on German cities, which culminated in the senseless bombing of the city of Dresden in February 1945. Berlin's reaction was, as you know, Hitler's threat to 'extinguish' English cities. The attack on Coventry served as a perfect opportunity for propaganda purposes. However, this so-called terror attack cannot be called that. In Coventry there were aircraft manufacturing facilities. Even Churchill had to admit that the bombing attacks on these facilities were very successful and severely crippled their ability to assemble aircraft. During the Industrial Revolution houses were built around these manufacturing sites and company owners lived in villas right next to their companies. Given the lack of accuracy of the bombs at that time it is not surprising that civilian targets close to the manufacturing sites were hit. The fact that the attacks on these sites were deemed terror attacks is, in no small degree, the work of the Minister of Propaganda – Goebbels. He wanted to use these attacks to show the German public that Germany was able to respond to the British bombings. I don't want to justify anything here: I am just trying to give you an objective account of these events.

The heavy attacks on the RAF's fighter command on 13 August were called Eagle Day. Today we know that the Luftwaffe flew nearly 1,800 missions on that day. At the time we were not conscious of this 'special day', since we flew several sorties a day on escort protection and free pursuit. We had the impression that the RAF had been considerably weakened. Although we flew up to London daily, we had few contacts with the enemy. Our fighting spirit was good. The British had an advantage, however, since they were fighting above their home territory and in an emergency they could save themselves by parachuting or making a forced landing. We, in contrast, had to endure captivity or risk a forced landing with a damaged aircraft in the open sea of the Channel. This usually meant certain death.

I remember one incident in which I had to improvise a new flying tactic. In the case of motor failure the Me 109 had a gliding angle of one to thirteen. This meant that one could achieve a distance of thirteen kilometres at a height of one kilometre. One day during the British campaign, about eighty kilometres from the French coast at a height of 4,000 metres, I was shot at in such a way that the engine's cooling system failed. Normally we would switch off the engine because of the fire hazard and turn for home, gliding. As far as I could judge, this was impossible at a height of 4,000 metres since I would only achieve fifty-two kilometres and land in the Channel. I therefore left the engine in neutral and after the temperature had cooled down I switched on the ignition, opened the throttle and climbed up as high as I could until the engine was overheated again. By repeating this procedure as often as possible I just about reached the French coast, where I made a forced landing on the beach. This procedure became known as 'to bob' across the Channel.

During six years of war I only flew the Me 109 (C, E, F and G up to G 12). I flew about 2,000 sorties, half of them combat missions. Although it was a difficult aircraft to take off and land, with my experience I was able to fly the plane to the limits of its capacity. Without exaggeration or arrogance, I should like to state that I was a match for any aircraft on any mission and at any height. Even in aerial combat at a height of 10,000 metres I was able to bank off every plane.

In August 1940 Goering sprang a surprise and made several changes to rejuvenate the command structure of the pursuit wing. At that time we still had group commanders and squadron leaders who had taken part in the First World War and who had retrained for the Luftwaffe having served in the navy, army or police. Young formation leaders with good training and experience now took over command positions. These included such well-known officers as Molders, Galland, Trautloft, Hrabak, Rall and Krupinski.

On 7 September 1940 Goering ordered a change in the bombing targets which obviously resulted from a misinterpretation of the situation. It was then an unwritten law not to bomb one another's capitals. But, presumably by accident, the RAF had bombed Berlin, which produced a lot of excitement and the supreme command retaliated and ordered the bombing of London. We fighter pilots were told that strategic targets in the London area were to be attacked: bombing civilians was out of the question. It was said that Churchill regarded this switch of targets as the turning-point of the war for Britain. The British aviation industry was so weakened by the continuous and systematic bombardments that hardly any aircraft could be produced: it was ruined. Accordingly, this change was an advantage to the aviation industry. Although the centre of London was bombed vehemently, more fighter planes could be produced. The result was that in the course of time the RAF could regain air superiority over Britain.

Sorties against England continued. In late 1940 missions became quite difficult due to bad weather conditions. However, I don't remember the German pilots losing their optimistic attitude. We noticed that the RAF formations kept away when there were German fighter squadrons in the sky. So we fighter pilots kept moving over the south of England up to London without being disturbed in any way. In order to get a rise out of the British fighters, several Me 109 squadrons were equipped with devices to drop bombs. That might have been the birth of the *Jabos* (fighter-bombers). As the squadron leader of the 9th squadron of Jagdgeschwader 54, I had to take part in a trial with a 250-kilogram bomb under the fuselage. This was believed to be very dangerous because nobody knew whether the aircraft could carry that additional weight. I was successful, however, and we then flew with bombs beneath the fuselage to attack targets in Britain. Our first target was the Tilbury Docks near London. Our bombing caused some confusion to the British. The RAF wireless communications were being intercepted and I was later informed about the contents of one such communication. The ground station shouted, 'Attack the German bomber formations.' The British formation leader responded, 'There are no bomber formations: I can only see Me 109s and these cannot drop bombs.'

In preparation for the attack on Russia fighter formations were removed. Although we knew from before the war that Hitler wanted *Lebensraum* in the east, we did not know why the squadrons were being transferred. The sorties over England died away. To draw a result from the so-called Battle of Britain is quite a difficult thing to do. Without wishing to diminish the achievements of any person, formation or institution, it is my personal opinion that the Battle ended without a decision for any party. However, I would like to salute the heroic deeds of the British fighter pilots with the words of Winston Churchill that never before had so few done so much for their country.

When I joined the Luftwaffe sixty-two years ago I had a passion for flying. It was the most important thing to me and other activities were subordinated to it. Today I am still in possession of a pilot's licence and have done approximately 10,000 flight hours. I still fly with great enthusiasm in Europe's sky with my own little sports plane: *über den Wolken muss die Freiheit wohl grenzenlos sein!* (above the clouds freedom is limitless). I should like to conclude by stating that war makes neither winners nor conquerors, only losers.

WALLACE CUNNINGHAM

Memories of a British Veteran

I might be termed an amateur ace. Although I joined the Royal Air Force Volunteer Reserve at the time of Munich, I did not get my wings until the spring of 1940 – a few months before the Battle of Britain started. The Battle was my first operational experience, as it was for many of my mates. I think I should sketch in briefly what happened between Mr Chamberlain's precious bit of paper and my getting to a squadron.

Sixty years ago, many of my age, convinced of the inevitability of war, joined the VR. For most of us flying was the attraction. We were all classed as sergeants, had no uniform, did some harmless studying at nights and flew at weekends at Prestwick flying school. Our instructors were ex-RAF gathered around a nucleus of the Mount Everest Flight – the Marquis of Douglas and Clydesdale, Macintyre, Capper and Ellison. All like characters from *Boy's Own Paper*. The Tiger Moths and Hawker Harts that we flew from a grass field were single-engined biplanes, open cockpit and with all the nostalgic smells of dope (fabric), hot oil and antiquity.

At the same time I was studying at the Royal Technical College in the last year of my diploma in mechanical engineering, which I completed in May 1939. I then went down to Kent to work with Winget, a worldwide name in civil engineering and contractors' plant (to which I returned in September 1945). The summer of 1939 was, you may know, filled with long sunny days – the better because of the imminence of war. When I left in September to complete my training at flying school I had developed a great affection for 'the garden of England' and all the friends I had rapidly gained there during the summer. I little thought that exactly one year later I would be over Kent helping to defend it.

At Shawbury, where we were kitted out, taught to salute and made fit to be seen in public, life was happy and healthy. Like most pupil pilots I wanted to be a fighter pilot and fly Spitfires. I cannot think now for what reasons, but that is what happened. I was quick on the uptake but not over bright. The winter of 1939–40 was severe with lots of snow. Shropshire and north Wales were like Switzerland. We enjoyed the dancing class in

Shrewsbury. Cross-country running was encouraged – less damaging than rugby. I led the RAF team against Shrewsbury school. Of course the lads from the Shrewsbury team were in first.

In the spring I got my wings. I was later commissioned and sent to Aston Down for two weeks to learn to fly Spitfires and be a gentleman. I was quite pleased with myself, so my girlfriend (who later became my wife) told me.

At the end of familiarisation I was posted to 19 (F) Squadron at Duxford: a plum posting. Passing through London on my rail journey to Duxford, I encountered some of our lads returning from Dunkirk. Their comments about the absence of the RAF over the beaches made me feel personally responsible for the evacuation. As I found out, 19 had been stationed for two weeks on the south-east coast operating across the Channel. The CO was shot down and made prisoner, two pilots were killed and others wounded.

Duxford, the southern sector station of 12 Group, had been 19's base for many years. It is, of course, a museum now for a variety of aircraft and still retains the officers' mess, which is used for reunions and the like. I had to become useful as soon as possible in order to become operational. This involved formation flying and dogfighting practice so that I could fly without thinking about it. It is said that this is how I drive now: wondering who is driving and waking to the fact that it's me. It also involved air firing and familiarisation with East Anglia and the Thames Estuary. Fighter pilots were not respected for their navigational ability. It was said that if the railway junction changed the points a fighter pilot became lost.

19 was the first squadron to be equipped with Spitfires, three being delivered in September 1938. The aircraft was developed from the Schneider Trophy winner and built by Vickers Supermarine. It was fast, had a good rate of climb, was manoeuvrable and was free from vices. Because of the low drag – thin wing – there was little depth to stow the armaments, so the 4 x .303 Brownings per side had to be much more widely spaced than in the Hurricane. The Hurricane, developed with less panic and reaching the squadrons some months before, had close-grouped guns giving more hitting power. At that stage of the armaments the Hurricane was the preferred aircraft against the bomber. The ratio of Hurricanes to Spitfires during the Battle was two to one. Both aircraft were equipped with the Rolls-Royce Merlin. This engine had carburettor petrol feed. The Me 109 varied in its models, but was comparable to the Spitfire. It had good armament and with the Daimler-Benz petrol-injection engine had good fighter capability. Press forward the stick in a 109 and you went straight into a power dive. Do that with a Spitfire and the engine cut out. It was necessary to flick half-roll and do the second half of a loop. The bad news for 19 was that it was the first Spitfire squadron to be

equipped with 2 x 20-mm Hispano Cannon. Their destructive capability was terrific, but they only held sixty rounds – six seconds' firing – and stoppages were frequent, so few cannon were emptied. The combat reports were continually lamenting this dangerous condition and my co-pilots and I were very frustrated that they kept on letting us down.

In early August the raids on the south-coast towns and ports had started. Portsmouth, Southampton and large convoys passing up the Channel were targets. Radar's importance became very clear, the south-coast radar stations reporting the build-up of activity on the French coast and helping to avoid wasted scrambles by the hard-pressed 10 and 11 Group squadrons. The activity was still mainly too far south to use 12 Group. I felt deprived because others were hogging the limelight.

We were, however, kept fairly busy. Four of 19 Squadron's old hands were sent up about midnight in an attempt to catch up with several bombers attacking Mildenhall bomber station. John Petrie was vectored to the correct vicinity and saw an He 111 in a searchlight. He attacked and set one of the engines on fire. The searchlight changed over to illuminate the Spitfire and the rear gunner of the doomed German bomber set Petrie's machine on fire. He bailed out with serious face and hand burns. The He crashed on the Newmarket to Royston road, the crew being killed or captured. Eric Ball followed the other He to near Colchester where, assisted by searchlights, he set the second bomber on fire and it in turn crashed near Margate with all the crew killed. This was a well-conducted operation by experienced pilots. It was very different from attacking large daylight raids, which was to come.

We also routinely escorted convoys going north from the Thames past the Dogger Banks and up past the Wash. The sandbanks held their collection of sunken ships. We often wondered if the enemy were listening to our instructions. It was important to make certain that our naval gunners knew we meant no harm – they tended to shoot first. Recognition signals – letters of the day – were not taken too seriously by the merchant navy.

Returning to Duxford after a day on convoy duty at Coltishall, 'A' Flight was given a point to intercept 'some business' near Harwich. It was my first sight of a large enemy formation. I cannot remember any of the excitement that followed. I quote from the squadron's combat reports:

16 August 1940: The Squadron on patrol at 1735 hours were given vectors to intercept an enemy formation, 35 miles east of Harwich, at 12,000 feet. The investigation proved to be 150 enemy aircraft consisting of bombers and fighter escorts. The enemy aircraft were flying southwards, the bombers in front and the escorts of 40 to 50 Me 110s behind, stepped up and a further escort of Me 109s about 1,000 to 1,500 ft above.

'A' Flight attacked in two sections of three and four respectively . . .

Pilot Officer W. Cunningham (Yellow 4) attacked an Me 110 which stall turned to the right and presented its underside as a sitting target. He fired a long burst at the Me 110, which rolled over and dived vertically through cloud. Confirmed by Flight Lieutenant Lane who saw this Me 110 still in a vertical dive as it entered cloud at 2,500 feet, and that the base of cloud was only 1,000 feet, as being out of control. Stoppage on starboard cannon after 30 rounds.[1]

In the meantime, we in 19 Squadron had been moved, complete with sleeping huts, cooking tender, PBX telephone exchange and the Welsh Regiment to guard us, to Fowlmere. This had many good features including a reduction in red tape, the main snag being that our kit was still at Duxford, where we had to go for a real bath. Arthur Blake (our Fleet Air Arm pilot known as the admiral) became messing officer and Peter Howard-Williams ran the bar. The problem for the latter was keeping the beer cool enough to prevent it going off during the warm weather: a case of 'Drink up, gentlemen.' I remember taking part in a local fête being run for the Spitfire Fund by flying round and round a village field talking to little boys on the RT at the cost of 6d each in the box. I hesitate even to think of the cost of petrol for such an exercise. But presumably it was good for local relations.

During one engagement at the end of August John Coward, who was leading Green section in 'B' Flight, was wounded and lost a foot. He was hit by an explosive bullet and during the slow parachute descent made a tourniquet with his radio lead from his helmet. He came down beside the Red Lion at Whittlesford and a young fellow of sixteen came dashing up with a pitchfork, obviously thinking he was a German. He was told to 'so and so' off and fetch a doctor. A doctor from a local AA unit turned up, but was unable to administer any morphine because the orderly corporal had gone off on leave and had taken the key to the poisons' cupboard with him. Coward was later on Churchill's staff and then an instructor at No. 55 Operational Training Unit where, incidentally, he taught the young man who had found him.

By now the attacks were concentrating on the airfields and we were getting our share north of the Thames:

3 September 1940: Eight Spitfires of the Squadron were ordered to patrol between Duxford and Debden at 20,000 feet. Operating in pairs, all aircraft were fitted with two cannons except Green Leader which had eight machine guns. The squadron was still climbing to their height of 20,000 feet, when they were warned by sector controller of the enemy approaching from the south-east and later that they were over North Weald. On reaching 20,000 feet they saw explosions and clouds of smoke from North Weald. There were 50–60 bombers at 20,000 feet, escorted by 100 fighters stretching from 20,000 to 25,000 feet, with a single fighter ahead of and above the whole formation . . .

Pilot Officer Cunningham (Yellow 2) followed his leader into the

1. Reichsmarschall Hermann Goering confers with General Hans Jeschonnek, 3 April 1940

2. Air Chief Marshal Sir Hugh Dowding, in conversation with Group Captain Douglas Bader DFC DSO at North Weald airfield soon after the end of the war in 1945

3. A few of the 'Few', 14 September 1942: (*from left to right*) S/Ldr A.C. Bartley DFC, W/Cdr D.F.B. Sheen DFC, W/Cdr R. Gleed DSO DFC, W/Cdr M. Aitken DSO DFC, W/Cdr A.G. Malan DSO DFC, S/Ldr A.C. Deere DFC, Air Chief Marshal Sir Hugh Dowding, F/Lt R.H. Hillary, F/O E.C. Henderson, WAAF, MM, W/Cdr J.A. Kent DFC AFC, W/Cdr C.B.F. Kingcome DFC, S/Ldr D.H. Watkins DFC and W/O R.H. Gretton

4. A crashed Me 109 on
show at Windsor Castle
to aid the Spitfire Fund,
3 October 1940

5. Inspecting a wrecked German
plane, 7 September 194

6. Fighter pilot Wallace Cunningham
of 19 Squadron

7. Fighter pilot Hans-Ekkehard Bob
of 9/JG 54

8. Edinburgh, 19 September 1998: Cunningham
(*left*) and Bob exchange memories of the Battle

9. Fighter pilot Nigel Rose
of 602 Squadron

10. Biggles enters the Battle

11. Worrals, the female fighter pilot

12. Pauline Gower of the Air Transport Auxiliary

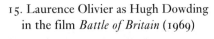

13. Sally Gray and Anton Walbrook in a scene from the film *Dangerous Moonlight* (1941)

14. Kenneth More as Douglas Bader in the film *Reach for the Sky* (1956)

15. Laurence Olivier as Hugh Dowding in the film *Battle of Britain* (1969)

16.-17. Film stills from *Battle of Britain*

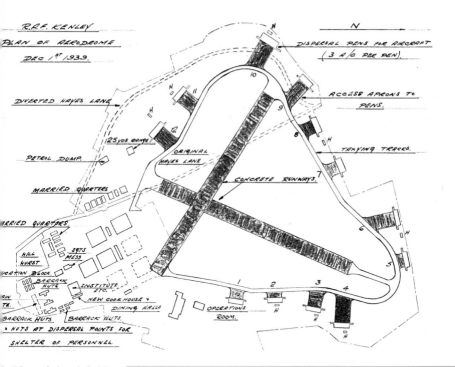

R.A.F. KENLEY
PLAN OF AERODROME
DEC 1ST 1939.

N

DISPERSAL PENS FOR AIRCRAFT
(3 A/C PER PEN).

DIVERTED HAYES LANE

ACCESS APRONS TO
PENS.

25 YDS RANGE

TAXYING TRACES.

PETROL DUMP.

ORIGINAL
HAYES LANE

CONCRETE RUNWAYS.

MARRIED QUARTERS

MARRIED QUARTERS

HILL
NURST

SGTS
MESS

UCATION BLOCK

BARRACK
HUTS

INSTITUTE
ETC.

NEW COOK HOUSE &
DINING HALLS

OPERATIONS
ROOM.

BARRACK HUTS   BARRACK HUTS.

HUTS AT DISPERSAL POINTS FOR
SHELTER OF PERSONNEL.

18. Plan of the airfield
   Kenley, December
   1939

19. The officers' mess
    at Biggin Hill

20. Pillbox on the airfield
perimeter at Debden

21. The Battle of Britain
memorial window in
Westminster Abbey

22. The White Hart at
Brasted, Kent: a favourite
haunt of the 'Few' during
the Battle of Britain

attack, but fired only 9 from port and 4 from starboard before his guns jammed.[2]

This was an unhappy occasion. We were late on arrival and North Weald was caught with aircraft on the ground refuelling. Liaison was bad, with controllers in 11 Group overloaded and tending their own aircraft. We had some victories but did not prevent the bombing. Moreover, the majority of cannons did not fire their complement. We had a visit from Sir Hugh Dowding, AOC Fighter Command. There was some quiet discussion mainly between the AOC and our CO. He accepted that the cannon aircraft should be withdrawn for the present and that we should be re-equipped with 8-machine-gun aircraft. The next day they arrived, ex-OTU junk or perhaps from the Caledonia market. On 5 September Squadron Leader Pinkham was shot down by an Me 109. He crashed and was killed at Cliffe, about one and a half miles from the factory I joined in 1939.

The COs of 242 and 310, based at Duxford, and Brian Lane, the new CO of 19 at Fowlmere, considered the problem of co-ordination of Duxford with 11 Group. A few practice flights were made and it was concluded that a scramble of the Duxford Wing would be quite uncomplicated. 242 and 310 Hurricanes would take off from Duxford and simultaneously 19 would take off from Fowlmere. There would be no joining up over the airfield. The Hurricanes with Bader's 242 leading would turn on course for the rendezvous, climbing at optimum rate. 19's Spitfires would fly on the same course to one side, aiming to be 3,000–4,000 feet above. The aim was to arrive with the Hurricanes attacking at the bomber level and the Spitfires at top cover (109's) level. The idea was soon put to the test:

7 September 1940: The day the Duxford Wing flew its first offensive patrol, consisting of 19, 242 and 310 Squadrons.

Towards five o'clock that evening, more than 300 bombers and many hundreds of fighters headed for London. The Duxford Wing was scrambled. The eight Spitfires of 19 saw a force of 20 bombers escorted by 50 fighters flying past at 15,000 feet . . .

Pilot Officer W. Cunningham (Yellow 2) attacked an Me 110 and as he broke off 'blacked out' and lost formation. He climbed and joined up with some Hurricanes. They flew east and attacked an enemy formation of 24 Heinkel 111s. He singled out one Heinkel 111, attacking from astern. The enemy aircraft set ablaze, and he attacked again from below, after which it began to lose height rapidly and crashed ten miles inland from Deal or Ramsgate. He climbed again and found three He 111s proceeding east. He attacked from astern and fired two bursts at the leader. Whitish smoke started to come from his tail but it did not lose height. Unable to continue the attack having run out of ammunition, he returned to base.[3]

Although we did not have the benefit of Kenneth More leading 242 Squadron, Douglas Bader did reasonably well as a stand-in. Perhaps he was not the most skilful of pilots, but he carried the confidence of his squadron and they followed him into the attack. He used to complain of having cold feet at high altitude. Evidently the nerve ends send a misleading message. It was said also that he was more resistant to the effects of 'g' in a tight turn. The tin legs did not provide a place for the blood to go – thus no blackout.

On the subject of Bader, he and I were later in Oflag VIB POW camp together and the pair of us were allotted a place on a tunnel – a poor effort from a latrine pit to outside the nearby barbed-wire fence and entanglement. The exit shaft fell in while we were lying in the tunnel all kitted out and ready to escape. We could not get out and we could not get back. We managed eventually to crawl back to our hut before dawn – Douglas making a noise like a knight in armour.

In the meantime, the Duxford Wing continued to intercept the attackers:

9 September 1940: The same three squadrons scrambled at 1700 hours.

Nine Spitfires of 19 saw the enemy initially as the Luftwaffe were flying north-west . . .

Pilot Officer W. Cunningham (Red 3) after attacking the main formation with no visible results, broke formation to attack some Me 110s when a stray Me 109 passed right in front of him. He took up position on its tail and fired two very long bursts. The Me 109 burst into flames and some parts of his engine flew out. Cunningham watched the destroyed Me 109 for a while and saw its pilot make no attempt to jump. On landing he found one bullet hole in the mainspar of his port wing.[4]

This was a time when the availability of aircraft and pilots was becoming precarious, as replacements were not keeping up with our losses. One day in early September, when there was a lull, Sailor Malan and I were sent to Supermarine near Southampton to visit the production units. In fact, they were a collection of subcontractors using, I remember, a laundry, a bus depot, a garage and other similar premises with mainly girl workers. Enemy attacks on that bit of the south coast were near-continuous, as was the air-raid alert. A lot of the alerts were general area warnings. It was proposed that the factories' own warden would sit on the roof and sound the alarm only when it looked truly dangerous. Sailor and I arrived at a factory, the line shafting and machines were shut down and we delivered our own line of pep talk to the girls gathered around. We then got back, with relief, to our war:

15 September 1940: The Duxford Wing were scrambled at 1122 hours and consisted of 19, 242, 302, 310 and 611 Squadrons. 242, 302 and 310 were heading south at 25,000 feet, with 19 and 611 Spitfires stepped up behind them at 26–27,000 feet. The Wing saw the enemy 3,000 feet below and down-sun. For once the Wing had position, height and numbers . . .

Pilot Officer W. Cunningham (Blue 3) broke away from his section to attack a solitary Me 110. His first attack from above and right rear quarter, set the enemy aircraft's starboard engine on fire. He broke away, turned in from the left and delivered another attack from the left hand side. He considered the Me 110 as good as destroyed and broke off the attack. The enemy aircraft was then attacked by two Hurricanes who more or less shot him from the sky . . .

The Wing landed, refuelled and was ordered up again at 1412 hours. Fifty-six aircraft had taken part in the morning's combat but only 49 were available for the afternoon . . .

Pilot Officer W. Cunningham (Yellow 3) attacked the main enemy formation, but was attacked from behind by Me 109s. Sergeant Roden was hit in this attack. After an indecisive dogfight with an Me 109, Pilot Officer Cunningham had a Hurricane come up on his tail. They then attacked an enemy formation, opening fire at 300 yards on the left hand machine. The Me 109 dived through the clouds on fire.[5]

The Duxford Wing was operating pretty much as was hoped. It was a unit with initial attack capability, able to put on a bit of a show, then break up as sections or individual aircraft. It was, moreover, a reasonable method of collecting and bringing thirty-six aircraft tidily to the point of the battle. I am, however, doubtful if a tendency to let the Wing increase in number of squadrons was always the most effective way of getting our defence force to the intercept. The Battle continued:

18 September 1940: The squadrons were scrambled three times at 0900, 1250 and 1616 hours. The first two occasions without success. On the third, they spotted AA bursts to the south-west of London, and found two enemy groups of about 20–30 bombers, but could see no escorts . . .

Flight Lieutenant Lawson (Red 1) led Red Section into an attack on nine Junkers 88s. He attacked one and could see his tracers hitting the port mainplane and engine . . .

Pilot Officer Cunningham (Red 2) followed Red Leader and attacked the same Junkers.

Sergeant Lloyd (Red 3) joined Pilot Officer Cunningham in the attack on the Ju 88 and they both continued firing until the Junkers 88 crashed in flames at Sandwich.[6]

The constitution of the Duxford Wing was a good cross-section of nationalities: 242 (Canadian), 310 (Czech) and 19 (Czechs, New Zealanders, Canadians, South Africans, Rhodesians, English and three Scots). Our friends from overseas tended to be mature and experienced pilots. In particular, the Czechs had a healthy hatred of the enemy and – despite some difficulties with the language – they also made a great contribution to the social life of the Duxford area. I recall Plzak writing to his girlfriend in Cambridge and asking, 'Jock, what is the difference between "beautiful" and "bloody fool"?' I cannot vouch for it, but a young WAAF requested an interview with her section officer to discuss a problem she had. The SO asked if she'd had a check-up and got the answer, 'No, it was a wee Glasgow laddie.'

General Janocek presented me with the Czechoslovakian Air Force Wings, of which I am very proud. I was told by the Czechs I flew with that they gave you free admittance to the underground and the brothels in Prague. That was untrue – at that time Prague did not have an underground.

The Wing undertook various patrols over south-east England and the Channel, and we became the target for attacks by small formations of Me 109s. At the end of October Blake (our popular admiral) was on search behind the Wing and was picked off. He was found near Chelmsford. We continued, however, to achieve successes:

> *15 November 1940*: The Squadron was on convoy patrol, 25 miles east of Deal at 20,000 when two condensation plumes were sighted above at 35,000 feet . . .
>
> Squadron Leader Lane (Red 1) climbed after the leading enemy aircraft and when it sighted the Spitfires approaching, turned east and dived. He ordered line astern and at 8,000 feet opened fire. He then observed an object leaving the aircraft which appeared to be a piece of cowling, at the same time a stream of coolant appeared from the port engine . . .
>
> Pilot Officer Cunningham (Red 2) saw smoke coming from the port engine of the Me 110 after Red Leader's attack. He then attacked firing three bursts and saw the starboard engine break into flames, and eventually crash into the sea. Pilot Officer Cunningham's windscreen was splintered by a bullet from the rear gunner.[7]

On this occasion the CO couldn't get his guns in line and kindly let me get my nose in. This was like hounds after a fox: a changed situation for the squadron.

About a month after the Battle of Britain had petered out, we had a visit from their Majesties King George VI and the Queen (our present Queen Mother) to Duxford sector station to present gongs. We paraded in one of the hangars and the King and Queen had lunch with us in the mess. They were happy and at ease and it was a pleasant occasion. What made us take Her Majesty to our hearts was her ability at the old pub game of shove ha'penny. It showed proper upbringing. Of course today she is our much-loved patron of the Battle of Britain Fighter Association – with her twinkling smile and her Norah Batty stockings.

It is difficult to be sure that my thoughts at the time are not what I now think I ought to have believed. Old men's memories do a lot of editing. Fighting over one's own land is, however, fulfilling and even the more juvenile enthusiasts among us became aware of the responsibility and privilege placed on us. The fighting over the convoys, ports, docks, airfields, factories and London was, despite some postponement, run to the Germans' timetable. But I do not believe there was finality at any stage and in the end the courage and steadfastness of the people of London allowed us our greatest victory.

After the Battle was over the raids continued. There were sneak attacks during the clouded winter days and full-scale blitzes at night on London, Coventry and industrial centres. These night raids were hard to combat in a single-engined fighter with the engine in your lap and an incandescent flaming exhaust manifold in each eye. Twin-engined aircraft with radar were for a time successful. In 1941 I was escorting low-level bombers at sea level across the Channel. Our job was to draw the fire – which I did. About a year after the end of the Battle of Britain I was having champagne and tomato sandwiches in a German Ack-Ack regiment's mess on the sands near Rotterdam before proceeding east under guard.

Notes and References

1 Derek Palmer, *Fighter Squadron* (Upton-upon-Severn, 1991), p. 182.
2 Ibid., pp. 186–8.
3 Ibid., p. 190.
4 Ibid., pp. 191–2.
5 Ibid., pp. 194–6.
6 Ibid., pp. 197–8.
7 Ibid., p. 203.

NIGEL ROSE

Dear Mum and Dad:
An RAF Pilot's Letters to His Parents,
June–December 1940

These letters were written by me to my parents during the Battle of Britain. I was a pilot with No. 602 City of Glasgow fighter squadron, flying Spitfire Mark 1s and stationed first at Drem in East Lothian and then at Westhampnett, a grass satellite airfield about two miles from the parent station at Tangmere, near Chichester, in Sussex.

I had joined the RAF Volunteer Reserve at the end of 1938 whilst training to be a quantity surveyor. At that time the probability of a war seemed never far away, and to join something seemed sensible and 'in'. There was no recent service background in the family (except for an uncle in the Somerset Light Infantry, who was killed at Arras in 1916).

Now, at almost sixty years' distance, the letters evoke a number of thoughts. First, they seem to be surprisingly immature in composition and content, considering I was twenty-two at the time. More like the chatter of a sixteen-year-old who has recently emerged from under the blankets after reading Biggles *with a fading torch. Undeniably, I was a late developer!*

I was, I think, a good pilot, but an indifferent fighter pilot. Partly this may have been due to the fact that postings of newly fledged pilots to Operational Training Units at the time of Dunkirk were cancelled and we were sent straight to squadrons. For some, this may not have mattered, but I realise now that in my case it did. I have to admit, too, that a strong aggressive focus was sadly never one of my strong points!

Finally, an aspect that puzzles me is that there seems to be little sign of discretion for reasons of security. I suppose that in 1940 it was not the important factor that it very soon became.

Nigel Rose
Beaumont-cum-Moze, Essex
19 July 1999

Officers' Mess
Drem
East Lothian

21 June 1940

Dear Mum and Dad,

I'm glad I was able to get in touch with you last night because I feel a little guilty about being so late with this letter.

The journey, after that triumphal send-off, progressed smoothly but rather slowly, and eventually I tumbled out onto the platform at Drem at about 7.30. A good lady with an enormous car kindly gave me a lift to the aerodrome which turned out to be a most delightful spot. The camp itself is small and pleasant, and the Officers' mess is most comfortable, and better still, there's a very pleasant type of young officer here, and they've been extremely helpful.

It's rather nice to belong to a 'Spitfire' squadron because they are fairly few and far between, and the Spitfire is still the fastest single-engine fighter I believe. I've still to make my maiden voyage, but hope to do that tomorrow. Up to now I've flown a Tiger Moth and a Magister round the countryside just to get an idea of the lie of the land.

It's quite exciting being on a 'war' station because at odd times the tannoy loudspeaker system (which can be heard all over the camp) will blare out 'Pongo Green Section patrol St. Abbs Head Angels 9' – and within two and a half minutes three Spitfires will be in the air climbing rapidly up to 9,000 feet on the look out for an enemy. More often than not the alarms are false but the excitement's there, nevertheless. My C.O., a DFC, has 2 planes to his credit and, no doubt, would have more if this was a busier part of the country. The squadron has bagged 8 so far.

I haven't had the opportunity to leave the camp yet, but I understand North Berwick is a good spot, a quiet resort, possessing a very fine swimming pool. Gullane is quite near here.

At the moment we newcomers are in a Training Flight, and we probably shan't become operational for a month or so, because there's a great deal to be learnt apart from adapting ourselves to the Spitfires.

I shall probably drop you a line again soon after the weekend,
Love, as ever

Nigel

14 July 1940

Dear Mum and Dad,

Since my last letter to you I've ventured twice across the border. On Tuesday I flew down to Acklington in our Tiger Moth, to act as Range

Officer for some practice firing, but the operation was cancelled and I returned the same afternoon. Then on Friday a party of four of us set out by train for Carlisle and brought over some new Spitfires the next morning. Moreover two or three days this week have been complete washouts with incessant heavy rain, so my training hasn't progressed very far since my last report. However I hope to get a patrol or two to do tomorrow or very shortly.

Thank you so much for the cake which is of the very popular variety, and also for the photographs – I'd forgotten there was such a colossal selection!

By the way, about the magazine question, I ought to mention that most of the British ones are of course taken in the mess, and the most acceptable from my point of view are cast off *Esquire*s and *Life*s.

There hasn't been very much excitement lately, chiefly I think because of the bad weather; but on Tuesday 'Red' Section, the section of 'A' flight to which I will be attached, bagged a Dornier, shooting it smack into the sea.

Granny has sent me numerous past copies of the *Church Times* with articles by Uncle Walter: needless to say I was a little terrified at first, but they seem to be quite interesting.

It was nice of Aunt Violet to dig out these friends of hers in Dunfermline, but that place is on the other side of the Forth opposite Edinburgh and too far to be of much use. For even when 'released' we have to be within an hour's recall.

Which brings me to the question of leave. There seems to be a vague sort of rota, so that we each take it in turns to take four days' leave. But usually, just when one's name is next on the list, somebody scraps the list and makes out a new one, and once more the prospects disappear!! The last list, now superseded, bore the appropriate caption 'Subject to alteration, cancellation, or any other bloody thing'! If by some miracle the present arrangements hold, I hope to come South in about a month, but I'll let you know more about that at a later date.

Our C.O. Sq/Ldr Pinkerton has left us for a ground job, and our new C.O. Flt/Lt (now Sq/Ldr) Johnstone is a rattling good bloke, and can't be more than 25 summers old. The station commander, incidentally, is Wing Commander Atcherley of Schneider Cup fame. He's a wonderfully versatile man, extremely popular and absolutely the right fellow to be harbour-master of a fighter station. On the whole I don't think I could have fallen in with a nicer crowd of chaps, and the atmosphere is excellent.

Cheerho!

Love as always

Nigel

PTO   By the way, Dad, thanks very much for sending me the straight-jacket literature. Actually it would be practically superfluous, because the armour-plating on a 'Spit' is something like this

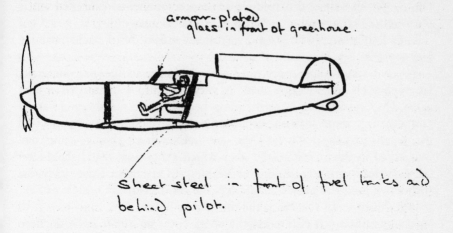

– all of which gives one pretty good protection front and rear. One shouldn't present a sideview to the enemy! How the thing flies with all this armour plating, for which it was not designed, I can't imagine! And they talk about clipping 3′ off the wingspan!

26 July 1940

Dear Mum and Dad,

Yesterday really should have been a red-letter day. For not only did two copies of *Esquire* arrive but also a letter and a couple of wizard cakes of the usual popular brand. This was obviously considered by the Fates to be too much of a good thing, for later on, in the space of about a quarter of a second, I managed to do about £3,000 worth of damage! The only intimation I had was that, after doing a landing at a satellite aerodrome near here, I heard a sharp crack as I was running along the grass. Thinking that I might have bent the flaps a little with a stone chucked up by the airscrew, I got out to inspect, and found to my consternation that there was a great gaping hole in the bottom of the fuselage. Apparently, on landing, I had run right over a dirty white marker flag and the stick had grazed the parachute-flare trap door, flicking it open. Out fell the heavy container which, still attached to the plane, thumped up and down gashing the fuselage in the process. Providentially the detonator failed to respond to the jerking.

If the remedy consisted of slopping dope on the wound and pasting on fabric very little importance would be attached to the incident, but stressed skin aircraft like Spitfires depend almost entirely on the flawlessness of the metal skin for their strength, with a result that a new fuselage is the only answer. Price, as I said, about £3,000! But far more important is the fact that fighter aircraft of this type are not exactly numerous and each one is of immense military value at the time, as you can imagine.

Hell! I suppose it's no good crying about it now, but I could certainly kick myself!

You don't know how much fun I get out of opening up your numerous letters, parcels and packages, and I'm very grateful for the magazines and cakes. Opportunities to leave the camp become scarcer and scarcer and I rarely manage more than one excursion a week. I believe I told you about the vagaries of the leave lists that are hoisted from time to time: one was issued in the middle of the week which announced that I should get six days' leave starting yesterday. Needless to say this edition was soon withdrawn, and the present one offers me six days in the middle of next month. More about that when the time draws near.

Not awfully much else to enlarge upon. I was on duty out on the flare path the other night when one of our fellows 'clobbered' a Heinkel which was held in the searchlights. He, the enemy, jettisoned three magnetic mines at a healthy distance (about five miles) from here and the explosions were terrific to watch. Absolutely wrecked an acre or two of potatoes I'm told.

I've only been up on one 'flap' since I last wrote and that was as fruitless as the rest. All the same I find I get hauled out of bed at all hours to come to 'readiness', which involves donning my 'Mae West' and sitting down in the crew room prepared to go up on a patrol. But it's a good life and I wouldn't swap it for any other.

The weather has cheered up quite a bit lately, though we still get our full share of rain and thunderstorms.

It's all rather sad about the cottage but here's hoping that we get back there again before long.

Very best love

Nigel

1 August 1940

Dear Mum and Dad,

Cranfield has written asking for my birth certificate. I wonder if you could hunt it up for me – I believe I sent it along together with my passport and school certificate when war broke out?

I was very pleased to get your letter and to hear about the new flat – you might send me some more details some time, and also I'd rather like to know how to get there in case I was shot away on leave prematurely.

Not very many 'flaps' have cropped up since I last wrote – I had two patrols one morning before breakfast, the first one starting at 4.15 and two and a quarter hours' flying was put in before the grapefruit. This morning I was hauled out of bed at 2.45, and had to trek down to the dispersal point to be at 'readiness'. My flight commander, Flt/Lt Urie, flew a 'Spit' into the ground last night and left a trail of wheels, wings, supercharger casing and twisted panels for a distance of about 100 yards. This puts my little effort in the shade, though it was very bad luck on the fellow, who is a damned good sort.

The big date as far as I'm concerned is now August 17th, but as I've explained before, no reliance must be placed on it. Anyhow, if the Jerries don't start their 'blitz' by then I shall be very much surprised.

I've written to Uncle A saying I should only be too pleased to take care of his binoculars pro tem. It's very kind of him to offer them.

Very best love

Nigel

Accidentally I put 410 on the clock yesterday. Computed at an average height of 7,000 ft this means that the aircraft was doing about 465 mph. This strikes me as being awfully fast, but the old hands here just smile condescendingly, conveying the impression that having clocked 600 there might be something to be proud about! But a mere 465, bah! snail's pace!

8 August 1940

Dear Mum and Dad,

Every now and then we are given 48 hours leave in which we are fairly safe from recall, barring, always of course, the start of a 'blitz'. Such a period was handed to me yesterday and I quite seriously thought of creaming up to town for a day and a night. But since I hope to be back in just over a week, and since the financial aspect is rather dismal for a 1st class return to London, I decided not to try it.

Very many thanks for your various letters and my birth certificate. That was absolutely wrong of you to pay the Bruce Green bill, because after all these little things are within my scope nowadays, but thanks very much indeed for doing it.

I wish I could write back and say that I'd shot down a Heinkel, but the darned things just don't materialise when my section is 'first off'. They come usually at night, and as usual when it's my turn for 'duty pilot' they turned up on time the night before last. The duty pilot has the miserable job of compromising between making the flare path and other lights dim enough to placate the Defence Officer, and at the same time bright enough to bring the wretched pilots safely to land. The airborne fellow has the first consideration and it's rather harrowing to have to turn on the floodlight when you can hear the deep desynchronised rumble of the Jerry's engines!

I sat at the controls of a Heinkel yesterday – it certainly is a very well-built plane and there's no skimping on the workmanship so I'm told.

The more I hear about the new flat the more I know I'm going to like it, and the idea of having breakfast on the balcony five floors up is most intriguing.

I'm glad to hear that you've seen Peter, and that he's looking fit. I've written to Tony to ask him to send my little motor-bike up here as it really would be very useful for nipping round the perimeter track to dispersal point, and also for popping into Edinburgh now and then. I attended a wizard little party in Edinburgh last night, at which the Intelligence Officer of 602 provided a magnum of 1929 Krug. One of the fellows in my flight, Donald Jack, has just been presented with a daughter (Penelope, Penny) and I rather believe that the flight is going to celebrate the christening in no quiet manner, which should be good fun.

Uncle Alfred has got me an introduction to Sir Hew and Lady Hamilton Dalrymple who live at Leuchie near North Berwick. I tried to contact them this afternoon, but her ladyship was out. I'm already being accused of 'castle-combing'! I spend all odd moments just now filing up a wee brass casting of a Spitfire, and it's the devil trying not to file too much off in the wrong places. I hope to have it finished by the time I come South. Roll along the 17th and heaven forbid that there's a 'blitz' before the 23rd.

Love as always

Nigel

                                                        RAF Station
                                                        Tangmere
                                                        Chichester
14 August 1940   Sussex

Dear Mum and Dad,

As we rather anticipated we've been transferred down here for a week or two to help with the good work on the coast. We moved rather hurriedly and I forgot to take any note of the new address which I believe I know. However, in case I'm wrong, I'll send this to 33a, where I'll know you'll get it sometime, if not immediately. We certainly are just about in the middle of things here, arriving yesterday afternoon in the middle of a scrap. We landed without getting involved and are now on our toes waiting for our first proper chance. Actually this isn't Tangmere itself, though for service reasons that is the address.

The journey down was very pleasant – we stopped to refuel at Church Fenton in Yorkshire, having an excellent lunch and can of beer there.

We live for the moment in a typical Sussex rectory (perhaps I'm not really qualified to call it that!) but there's that delightful smell of soap and flowers and new mown grass, and wasps in abundance. The squadron bagged two 'certains' and three unconfirmed at tea just after we arrived yesterday.

I can't think we shall have any of that dearth of Jerries that we experienced in the North – there were 512 counted in the various raids round Southampton and here yesterday! The squadron whom we are relieving has been bringing down the most fantastic numbers of Jerries and are now badly needing a rest for reforming.

Will you please tell Tony not to send my motor-bike, if he has not already sent it along to Drem.

Excuse this scrawl. Facilities aren't of the best, but I'll try to keep you up to date with the news.

By the way, is there any way of getting you quickly on the 'phone?

Love as always

Nigel

16 August 1940

Dear Mum and Dad,

I'd no sooner arrived back here at about one o'clock when a crowd of Junkers 87s dive-bombed Tangmere and just about razed the hangars to the ground. We had a magnificent view of the whole affair and it was most thrilling to watch.

This evening, six of us on patrol at 16,000 ft ran into about 50 Jerries and I had my baptism of firing. I made three attacks and on the last, I believe, I may have got my man for he went into a vertical dive and hadn't pulled out by the 10/10 clouds at 6,000 ft. It was terrifically exciting and I'm darned if I can remember what happened at the time. The others got quite a good haul I believe, and as I had a cine camera mounted in my aircraft I'm on my toes waiting for the film to be developed to know if I was aiming anywhere near the fellow!

More soon,
Love as always,
Thanks v. much for the wizard 24 hrs.

Nigel

22 August 1940

Dear Mum and Dad,

Just a midweek word or two to inform you that everything is bathed in sunshine and that I'm in fine fettle.

By rather a peculiar run of fortune, I received another 24 hours yesterday and got a lift into Southampton, where I stayed the night with the Wallers. Actually I'd been there precisely three minutes when a Ju 86 came out of the clouds and loosed off a 'stick' of bombs – some welcome, that!

Had three patrols in quick succession this afternoon, two of which seemed quite promising, but fizzled out before we could find any trace of the Hun.

Had a letter from Eve today, sanctioning the projected visit to Graffham, but, darn it, she's got herself engaged – which takes rather more than half the gilt off the gingerbread, so to speak.

Am fixing up about the trunk at Soton, and shall get it sent on to Tony.

Love as always

Nigel

Letters are all arriving pronto. To hasten things a bit more, you can now, with official sanction, put 602 Squadron in the address.

26 August 1940

Dear Mum and Dad,

Two patrols yesterday, one at 22,000 ft for 20 minutes which didn't have any results, and then in the evening the squadron was ordered off to patrol the Dorset coast at 20,000 ft together with a squadron of Hurricanes. The Controller did his job well and brought us slap into a whirling mass of 109s and 110s, and in no time at all it was a free-for-all scrap. I left the 109s alone because I was a bit afraid of going for a Hurricane by mistake, but I got in two or three cracks at the 110s at reasonably short range. The last one went down in very similar circs to the one of last Friday week, except this time there was blue-white smoke pouring from his port engine. I followed him down in a dive as far as I could, but had to pull out when I had about 420 mph on the clock (at 12,000 ft this is about 520 true air speed) and I lost sight of him. As I flattened out and turned there was a vivid red explosion on the ground more or less in the direction in which he had been diving, and I assumed that this was the 110. Actually I oughtn't to claim this, but I feel so certain that between my two little efforts I must have got at least one that I'm calling it destroyed.

The squadron's claiming 12 for yesterday's scrap. On my way back I found the top cover to No. 1 Port gun was missing – it must have blown off in the dive. My fuel tank gauge let me down, giving a reading of 18 gallons when I was still at Bournemouth, and 12 gallons when I was crossing Southampton Water, so I assumed my tank was punctured, and landed at Hamble to see what had happened.

As it turned out, it was only a faulty gauge, and I had plenty of fuel left. When they had given me a new gun cover I returned here.

You must excuse this sudden rush into print, but it's a very good safety-valve to the pent-up excitement to be able to sit down and write short notes about the action.

Incidentally two of our chaps baled out and both are safe – so, touch wood, the squadron is still intact in its personnel, although we've lost quite a lot of Spits altogether.

Hope to find a letter from you today.

Love, as always

Nigel

I hope the London raids have kept well clear.

[undated]

Dear Mum and Dad,

I suddenly awoke to the fact yesterday that it was just about a week since you last heard from me and when letters from you both arrived simultaneously I thought it was about time to get down to it.

Thanks, first of all, for the cake and the chocolates which arrived in good order and are very popular. Thanks, too, for the £5 which I return herewith. It was damned nice of you, Dad, to be so prompt about it, but my conscience hardly allows me to accept it yet!

Actually I feel pretty certain that my score is 2 at the moment, and on the strength of my combat reports the Intelligence Dept. at Tangmere has given me both. But one can't be dead certain! However, I'll have a small fortune off you before long!

I've got the cine film of my first effort back, and, as was to be expected, it's rather disappointing. There's an Me 110 floating about quite clearly, but it's rather small and looks not unlike this –

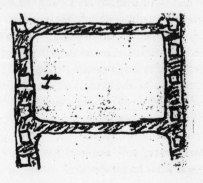

I'll bring the film along next time I come home.

Since I was home last we've had a couple of exciting incidents. About three days ago, at about 15,000 ft over Biggin Hill, we came across some 30 Hun bombers escorted by hordes of fighters. Although my flight was in an excellent position to half-roll down onto the bombers, we were ordered to keep aloft in order to keep some of the enemy fighters from coming down on 'B' flight, which had gone into the attack.

I saw lots of whirling Me 109s and Spitfires and Hurricanes, but couldn't get a grip of things at all and finally dived out of the muddle so that I could get a better idea of what was to be done. But by the time I'd pulled out I'd lost sight of the enemy, and although I flew South to try to catch up I couldn't make it! It's a wretched business returning with unfired guns!

Yesterday at midday we were patrolling Gravesend at about 10,000 ft, and when some of the chaps saw a bunch of 110s in formation, the scene seemed set for a decent scrap.

But somehow the leader lost touch, and nobody was engaged. A pity, because it was a wonderful chance.

I was given my 'released' day out of turn on Friday last, and went over to Graffham to see the Spicers. Eve had turned up on the aerodrome with a YMCA canteen during the morning, much to my surprise, and I arranged to visit them for tea. I stayed the night at the 'Angel' at Petworth.

Probably my next 'released' day will be Sunday, but I'm not sure at the moment.

Very best love, as always

Nigel

5 September 1940

Dear Mum and Dad,

Things are moving fairly fast again now, and in view of an expected climax within the next fortnight all temporary leave has been stopped, which means that I may not get up to town again for a bit.

For the last three days we've been at it pretty hard, and I for one am getting a wee bit tired. We've had several patrols at 22,000 ft over Dover, Sheppey, and we came slap over London the day before yesterday. From that height the 50 odd miles between the city and the coast looked about as far from here to the bottom of the garden, and the Channel itself might have been a widish river!

Yesterday we were directed into a raid coming in towards Beachy Head, and had an absolutely superb scrap about 15 miles out at sea.

'A' flight tackled about 20 Me 110s which immediately went into a 'defensive circle'. It was colossal fun, and we played around for about ten minutes. It's a curious thing that because you are so anxious to 'draw a bead' on the enemy you forget all about flying the aeroplane, and it's easy enough to find yourself stalled and spinning, just when you're about to press the button!

I cracked at about 8 of them altogether, and gave one quite a long burst at pretty short range. A lot of white smoke came out of his port engine and he slipped away downwards, but I couldn't see any result (Intelligence Dept. tells us – I don't know if it's likely – that the Jerry conceals smoke bombs under his engine cowling, which he ignites when sore pressed, in order to discourage the attacker from harassing him any more).

It was pathetic to see them firing deflection shots at you from a long way away – they seemed to miss by miles. The scheme is to fly round in the opposite direction to the defensive circle, and poop at one and then dash away to position yourself again.

I was so fascinated by the whole thing that I gave them the most marvellous chances, but they would insist on preserving their circle! I picked up three bullets, two in the wings and one under the engine.

Meanwhile the bombers (for there were some bombers too) were being attacked by 'B' flight, who went into them as they came inland. They got 2 and one probable.

Today, having been on our toes since 5, we've already had two patrols, both abortive. O yes! Last night, too, we chased a couple of single seater fighters off Beachy Head, but we had to let them go. Personally I didn't see them at all – there was so much oil on my windscreen due to a faulty airscrew.

Boy! This certainly is the life!

We've been having a spot of food-poisoning just lately, which has been slightly upsetting, but it seems to be passing off.

By the way, I did thank you, didn't I, for the cake and the chocolates, both of which were grand!

Nigel

When's this weather going to break! We've had continuous sunshine every day we've been here practically, and it's ideal for Jerry for his mass fighter escorted raids!

10 September 1940

Dear Mum and Dad,

I was very pleased to get your telegram this morning and to know that you had successfully dodged the bombs. Poor old London – there must be an awful lot of holes in its surface just now. But it seems to me that this is the first proper sign of Jerry's nervousness, to indiscriminately bomb the capital, and except possibly to disturb the Jewish element, I don't suppose it's done much damage to the morale – rather the opposite. I'm looking forward tremendously to hearing from you, but posts are bad nowadays, and I may have to wait a bit.

The squadron has been depleted a little since I last wrote, but we are in fine fettle, and very thankful for the rain and low cloud which shrouds us this morning.

Three of us had a very exciting chase a day or two ago when we came upon an Me Jaguar over Portsmouth at 18,000 ft. I was No. 3 in the section, and was too far back to attack the fellow when he was spotted. However he rolled on his back and dived helter skelter to sea level, and we three hared down after him. We caught him up about 5 miles south of Bembridge and the first fellow to attack set his port engine on fire. I attacked next, and although I gave him a 5 sec. burst from dead astern, it seemed to have no further effect (I don't think I've got the art of aiming properly yet – it's a difficult business, and can only be learnt by experience). Finally the third fellow went in, and he (the enemy) blew up and fell into the sea, leaving a burning patch of oil and petrol on the water.

A lot of our patrols have been over London way lately, and the squadron has had several scraps up there.

So much for now,

Very best love

Nigel

By the way, no news is always good news as far as I'm concerned, because in the event of my being wounded or otherwise incapacitated, you'd know within 4 hours.

12 September 1940

Dear Mum and Dad,

Your admonition (Dad's) not to give Jerry too many chances came just a few hours too late. As a result I'm now proudly carrying my port arm about in a sling feeling a b— fool – though not entirely depressed! However let me explain.

Yesterday we ran into the customary gaggle of Me 110s escorting bombers towards Selsey Bill. I had a crack at one of the 110s and fastened my nose onto him and, I think, holed him a bit. I got the usual white smoke out of one of his engines, and as far as I can remember, the other also seemed to be sprouting smoke. However, as I've explained before, this is no proof that the fellow has been plastered, and, anxious to make certain of him, I stuck behind him giving him quite a lot of ammo. Meanwhile I narrowly missed colliding with another 110, whose pilot wasn't looking where he was going.

Ass that I am, I forgot the proved axiom – '3 sec. burst and break away like mad' – and I followed my target straight into a circle which he and his friends were forming. It was just too easy for the 110 behind me, and he didn't lose the opportunity. With a sharp report my left tail plane became a piece of tangled metal, hit by a cannon shell, and another shell, solid, went through the fuselage on the port side, and emerged out of the starboard wing. (Of this of course I knew nothing at the time, but calculated it after seeing the plane on landing.) The Jerry then turned on his machine guns, giving me about 15 thro' the starboard wing and a dozen or so thro' the fuselage. One went thro' the air bottle, which put my guns, flaps and brakes out of commission, another slap through the wireless. The latter seemed to resent this treatment because it packed up straight away.

Something must have chased round the cockpit, because there was a hole in one of the dials, and the glass was broken in some of the others. An armour piercing bullet did its job well and pierced the armour-plate at the back, and as a result I received some small bits of metal in the left elbow, with a laceration (small) thrown in.

At first I considered the possibilities of bailing out, because the aircraft felt rather peculiar to fly, and I wasn't sure if it was controllable. However, she came out of her dive and I made off home p.d.q.

We took the arm along to the Royal West Sussex Hosp in Chi and had it x-rayed. Nothing much wrong, but quite a few wee bits of metal inside – the x-ray photograph looks something like this

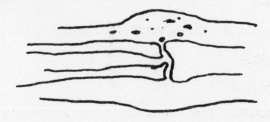

– tho' apart from the one abrasion, there are only pin-pricks to show where the bits went in! And, so far, it hardly hurts at all.

But aircraft at Fighter Command are terribly valuable now, and I'm very annoyed at cracking one up like that. Especially as a complete section of three aircraft had crashed the night before – the poor devils were sent off on patrol at dusk and they piled in coming in to land in the dark – none of them had flown Spits at night before! O God, O Montreal!

I'm afraid I shan't get any leave, although I shall try hard to get a day or two before I start flying again.

Very best love, as always

Nigel

15 September 1940

Dear Mum and Dad,

I'm afraid your warning that letters sent to 26 Grove Court might not be forwarded didn't sink in, and, on re-reading your letter concerning this, it's dawned on me at last that there are probably a couple of mine mellowing on the doormat at this very moment. And now I feel a wee bit perplexed, for almost certainly if I send this to Sheffield, it'll arrive just after you depart. Still, we'll risk it.

For the past four days I've been leading a life of leisure and boredom since I foolishly let my Spit be riddled by an Me 110, on Thursday, I think it was; and I got a slight wound on the left elbow into the bargain. It's rather like a small gunshot abrasion and doesn't hurt a bit, but I carry the limb about in a sling so that it'll get a chance to heal quickly, and the 'wounded soldier' effect is terrific.

I won't recount the incident, it's chronicled in a letter I sent to London last Thursday, and anyway isn't very interesting. I wish to goodness they'd let me fly again now, instead of waiting around feeling absolutely A1. Just possibly I shall get a day or two off on the strength of it, and if so I shall come up to town. If you're still away, I'll look in on Tony and Mickie as you suggested, and I might run down to Norwich to see June.

I went over to see the Spicers yesterday and met Eve's future husband.

I hope all goes well with you and that you haven't had too much of this bombing business.

Love as always

Nigel

3 October 1940

Dear Mum and Dad,

This morning a most enormous package arrived containing the two letters that you sent the day I arrived at the flat. I'd no idea you'd sent such comprehensive instructions, and it was rather tragic to feel that they were of no use after all. But the postcards are intact and none the worse for their journeys backwards and forwards and they'll start dribbling in shortly.

Now that I'm grounded temporarily there's even less news than usual – because, when I think of it, all I used to write about were the various sorties made from day to day. I got rather annoyed with the medical people here for being such b. fools about my arm, and in consequence I'm going up for a Board at the earliest opportunity. It's absolute agony sitting on the ground when the chaps come back from a show with Do 17s and Me 110s to their credit!

The Adjutant has been laid up for the past few days and as the Intelligence Officer has been doing some of his work, I've been helping the I.O. out with his. But, as I say, taking combat reports from the fellows after they've returned from a successful slaughter (unescorted bombers sometimes!) makes me squirm. However, I suppose, as everyone tells me, there'll be quite a respectable chunk of the war left by the time I start flying again.

I dreamt I brought down an Me 109 last night – an absolute beauty, which landed with its undercart up near the windsock on the aerodrome here – boy! was I a hero! And was I disappointed when I woke up!

I had a very pleasant stay with Tony and Mickie, and made one expedition up to town with Mickie in the course of it.

Sleeping in an improvised dormitory with both sexes was new to me, but proved quite comfortable, and except on the few occasions when Mickie lashed out over Tony's neck and smote me on the shoulder blades, I slept like a log. When the all-clear went in the mornings we would retire upstairs, and I'd get in three hours of wonderful sleep.

I set out for here on Sunday at midday, and arrived on the camp by six o'clock, which wasn't bad going really.

Thank you very much for the time at Sheffield which was grand, and although unavoidably quiet, it probably did me an awful lot of good!

Love as always

Nigel

9 October 1940

Dear Mum and Dad,

Since I last wrote to you, I've been up to Halton to have a Board at the Central Medical Establishment and was there passed fit for flying again. And now having had half-an-hour's practice this afternoon I'm back in the ranks again. Thank goodness! It really isn't worth being slightly damaged in the RAF – there's much too much fuss and bother about it all! Incidentally did you spot my name in the RAF Casualty List yesterday? I didn't realise they'd do that!

I was glad to get a letter from you when I returned this morning and to hear your plans about 'pieds-a-terre'.

Presumably it will now be safer to address letters to 36, G. S. St when I think you're going to be in London. And the Sheffield ones to the Rutland until you move into the new place. The latter sounds grand!

I spent last night in London, at the Kenilworth Hotel, and got very little sleep. That appalling swish of bombs falling not too far away was most disturbing!

I haven't got very much to shout about just now, but, no doubt, will have more in a day or two.

Love, as always

Nigel

16 October 1940

Dear Mum and Dad,

By now, I expect, you'll have switched over to the Kenwood Hotel, so I'll address this there, when it's finished. Very many thanks for the two cakes, together with your letters. The chocolate cake suffered a wee bit in transit, but that didn't detract at all from its popularity, and there's practically no trace left of it now – which is a good sign!

I've been on lots of patrols recently, but I haven't seen a Jerry yet since my return. We've had several high patrols – one at 29,000 feet over Dungeness – and flying is getting a little bit chillier than of late.

I cycled over to Graffham to see Eve the other day, and was rather taken aback to hear that banns no. 1 were to be published this Sunday, and that the wedding takes place next month. She'll then depart to Farnboro' and I shan't know a darned soul under 25 years in this part of the world! Something'll have to be done! The nights are getting longer and staying in the very dull and stuffy mess is not an attractive proposition – moreover, cinemas and beer swilling are shallow forms of entertainment, and one soon gets pretty sick of them. I think Eve herself is the most hopeful person, but I don't think the Spicers know anyone actually in Chichester itself.

I hope Mickie is feeling better. It was darned nice to get those cookies from her.

Not much this time, I'm afraid.

Love to you both

Nigel

26 October 1940

Dear Mum and Dad,

I hope this'll turn up punctually on Monday morning because I've left rather a long gap between my last letter and this.

Thanks v. much for forwarding the collars and hanks, and also for your letter which included the note from Mrs Morris. It's very flattering to feel that somebody I can scarcely remember should ask after me. I have an idea Canon M. used to look rather like Gladstone. Is that right, or am I merely imagining things?

The Spicers wrote to a Mrs Hollist Barnes who lives in Chi, and as a result I went over to tea with her on Thursday. She was a little terrifying in that she was rather concerned with my church life and asked one or two embarrassing questions about Church Parades etc. Moreover, I don't think I exactly oiled the wheels of genial conversation when I cheerfully sat down on an embroidered altar-front (her 18th I believe). I don't know whether she'll be able to introduce me to any young people round here, but it is just possible.

The Officers at Tangmere are honorary members of the local Squash Club here, and I went to one of their weekly dances last night, meeting a quite attractive girl called Pamela Anding. Things look better now!

I saw my first set of Jerries since I boobed on Sept. 11th. We were at 28,000 ft, and they at 34,000, and we didn't have a chance of catching them. I just quaked with anxiety at one point when I thought they were going to come down on us (6,000 ft below, and at such an altitude that we were waffling about in the rarefied atmosphere!). I put in over four hours flying yesterday, mostly at high altitudes, and I felt quite tired at the end of it.

Give my love to Tony and Mickie next time you see them. I shall be writing to Tony shortly I expect.

Very best love, as ever

Nigel

30 October 1940

Dear Mum and Dad,

The Intelligence Officer went on 48 hours leave yesterday, leaving me to do any combat reports should they be necessary, and remarking that if the average of the last few weeks was maintained, I should have nothing to do.

No sooner had he gone than we went up on a patrol which took us to 27,000 ft above Maidstone. We found ourselves in an absolutely wizard position to come down on the tails of about 50 Me 109s which were returning from Biggin Hill direction. I got in quite close behind a 109 and gave him the woicks and volumes of white smoke came out of him (indicating that his radiator was shot up). Then he turned away downwards and I got in another burst, when parts of his engine cowling or his cockpit cover flew off. I didn't see him crash, but I doubt whether he got very far in that condition, so I claimed a 'probable'. I went on down to Dover direction, and saw a couple of planes ahead of me which looked rather suspicious. When a lot of shooting suddenly started it struck me that the nearest one to me was possibly an Me 109 with a cannon firing backwards (this type of thing has been found). I gave him a short burst from some way away and was rather taken aback to find he was a Spitfire when he sheered off. The other was an Me 109 and the pilot had just baled out before I broke up the party. I circled round the 109's pilot and waved, but the fellow was sulky and wouldn't wave back. I don't think I damaged the Spit – it was a long shot – but it shook me a bit at the time. I came back along the coast, and beat up the cottage at Winchelsea on the way, landing here, with darned little petrol left.

Twice yesterday when on patrols at 22,000 ft or so, we've been shot at by AA fire, and it's rather disturbing to see these black blobs suddenly appearing all round the squadron.

The other day over the I.O.W. [Isle of Wight] we got mixed up in a sort of dogfight, but I never got my guns to bear at all. Twice I saw a machine converging on my beam, and was rather startled to find the wretched things firing at me! I thought they were Hurricanes! Maybe they were! Anyhow they missed.

So much for now. Sorry it's all shop – but that's about all I can write about!

Love as always

Nigel

11 November 1940

Dear Mum and Dad,

Have just had a perfect example of bad-weather flying. It was raining fairly hard when we took off and we entered cloud at about 4,000 ft, and after climbing laboriously up to 23,000, still in cloud, we gave it up as a bad job and came all the way down again. It's rather unearthly flying in this continuous mist with only other Spitfires in the formation to look at for half an hour or so.

I've had one exciting interlude since I last wrote, when the C.O. and I intercepted a Dornier over Bognor, flying just above the cumulus. The

C.O. worked it so that we dodged round a clump of cloud and swooped down on the unsuspecting Hun, and the rear gunner must have had the hell of a fright. Between us we fired about 2,000 rounds at him from fairly close range with no result. I broke away down beneath cloud and saw the Jerry coming out too. I flew parallel with him trying to get in a good position for a beam attack and left it too late and he climbed back into the cloud again. I saw quite a lot of sparks flying out of him before he disappeared finally, and I think we must have damaged him quite a lot.

Several times over Portsmouth recently we've had incomplete engagements – ie: everybody chases everybody else everywhere, and if one sees an Me 109 to fire at one is lucky. On the other hand every other aeroplane is suspected of being a 109, and 'Spitfire neck' is a common complaint afterwards. It's hectic.

I was very pleased to get your letters, but I sympathise with you about the uncertainty of your plans. I hope things will work out all right before long. I notice incidentally that your letters usually take 3 days to reach me. Are mine that long in transit?

Pamela and I went to a cocktail party at Tangmere on Friday and that proved to be quite good fun. The champagne was being slopped about rather freely (it was an effort by the Mess to get rid of a few hundred pounds!), and in a way it was quite a good thing that we had to leave fairly early for Pamela to be in by twelve o'clock! I've been able to see quite a lot of her recently though her parents keep a strict eye on her (a wise precaution I suppose in these days).

I couldn't get away for Eve's wedding, but I sent her a linen table-cloth with four napkins to match which seemed moderately sensible. I must confess to finding it very difficult to think of something suitable.

I had a letter from Peter today and he seemed to have swayed back towards his job again now that more service contracts were coming in. Perhaps it's just as well.

Very best love,
As always

Nigel

If anybody at the hotel would like a course of mud-baths, recommend this place.

3 December 1940

Dear Mum and Dad,

At one o'clock yesterday a really grand week came to a close, and I put on my Mae West again and ran up the engine of L.O.B. alias The Flying

Porpoise. (In point of fact this was all a waste of energy as there were no customers yesterday at all.) The four days at Penn Court with you were wizard – there wasn't a moment when I was at a loose end, and from Tuesday midday till Saturday morning we always seemed to be doing something entertaining. Moreover, having returned here I took Pamela to a dance on Saturday evening and spent most of Sunday at the Andings' house at Bognor. The only regret I have is that I missed seeing Peter.

I stupidly brought away the key of no. 33 (room) with me, and I sent that back yesterday.

Things have been fairly noisy here in the evenings since I came back, and last night some disgruntled Hun dropped two large bits of nonsense about half a mile away, shaking the mess to its foundations. I've now taken to wearing my tin hat when I cycle to Bognor at night as the AA is now particularly heavy, and one can hear the wee bits whistling down at intervals.

The gloves are a smashing success and the envy of the entire mess. They're exactly right for flying in and I'm very pleased with them indeed.

I was rather taken aback when I returned to find that a great friend of mine, a fellow in 'A' flight with whom I'd flown quite a lot and known well since Drem days, had been killed whilst I was away. It's rather a serious loss too, because he had the best eyes in the Squadron and always saw things years before anybody else.

I've now been made a section leader (actually Hanbury and I now lead Yellow section alternately), so my responsibility is now increased from one Spitfire to three! You're coming on, Rose!

So much for now – I'll write again at the end of the week.

Love, as always, and thanks for making my leave so successful

Nigel

8 December 1940

Dear Mum and Dad,

Thank you so much for your letters and the cakes. The ginger cake was the first to suffer and it was absolutely A.1. The other is still intact, but looks most inviting and won't survive long.

The rather unsatisfactory situation of having only 12 serviceable pilots in the squadron is now reversed, and we are now absolutely brimming over with new talent, which makes it darned difficult to get any flying at all. Of the two evils I think I rather prefer the former.

When I was about 5,000 ft above Chichester the day before yesterday, the engine of my machine decided to go on strike, and I had some rather exciting moments getting the wretched thing back to the aerodrome. After everything had been checked and found OK I took it up again and there was na' bother at all. Rummy! Some peculiar things have been happening to our aircraft in recent weeks, and there's a strong suspicion amongst the personnel that there's quite a bit of sabotage going on in the camp.

Pamela and I were being given a lift back from a dance at the Squash Club in Chi to Bognor the other night when the driver, a young subaltern, tried to get the better of a roundabout curb, failing rather miserably, and tied the steering gear of his chariot in knots. It transpired that it was essential for him to be back on duty in Southampton by 8 o'clock in the morning, and as it was then midnight we had to think up something quickly. Eventually we rang up Gage (who bought Anastasia from me), and he rattled over to Bognor with her. At 1.30 we set off for Southampton arriving there at four, and eventually we crawled into bed at 6.20. Anastasia had fits of hiccoughs periodically which made the journey rather irksome and as it was very cold and dark it was a very tiring business. It seemed funny driving through the old familiar streets again, now quiet and empty at four o'clock in the morning, and seeing gaunt skeletons of buildings and heaps of rubble as in London. We shared the driving equally and it was all we could do to keep awake!

If we are still here, I'd like it very much if you would come down here for a night somewhere round about Christmas, say three or four days before. But we can fix that up as the time draws nearer.

So much for now. Love as ever

Nigel

16 December 1940

Dear Mum,

I'm glad I managed to get into touch with you today because just at the moment our affairs are very unsettled. The Squadron was supposed to proceed to Prestwick, Ayrshire, the day before yesterday, but due to unsatisfactory weather in the guise of fog, low cloud and gales etc we are still hanging about waiting to go. We made an attempt this morning but after a mere 10 miles or so had to return.

It's all very awkward because all our kit went on Saturday and almost all of us have only the clothes we stand up in and a toothbrush. On the other hand it's rather nice having a short reprieve and I've been practically living with the Andings since the posting came through. At the last moment I was very nearly posted to 610 Sqdn who are coming South. Some of our fellows have suffered this fate, but as I came down here in August I'm destined for a 'rest' in the North.

I hope you've been having some quieter nights recently and that you find that returning to the flat was a good move.

My new address will be c/o Officers' Mess, RAF Station, Prestwick, Ayrshire. The countryside I'm told is very pretty and the climate pretty good in the winter, and the fellows seem to think it's the best 'rest' station in Scotland. As far as I'm concerned, I don't feel I need a rest at all, but the ground crews and airmen are a little fed up with this place, and as most of them are Scotties they'll probably welcome the change.

You remember that cheque for £10? Could you please repeat the dose – not for any specific reason, but because I think the balance of credit isn't too big after the Anastasia affair? I don't know whether my bank is still standing – it was in the middle of Southampton and probably sustained a certain amount of damage! As I shall probably want to draw a little money for Christmas, I'd rather like to be sure that the cheques won't bounce!

I'm meeting Pamela in Chi this afternoon for tea and then we are risking a Laurel and Hardy farce. This uncertainty about our move is rather disconcerting in that I never know when I'm saying goodbye to her!

Love, as always

Nigel

[Nigel Rose and Pamela Anding were married in 1941.]

PART FIVE

THE MAKING OF A
BRITISH LEGEND

OWEN DUDLEY EDWARDS

The Battle of Britain and Children's Literature

The Cherry Orchard

> If there is a Tchekhov among my readers, I fervently hope that the effect of the *Magnet* will be to turn him into a Bob Cherry!
>
> Frank Richards, 'Reply to George Orwell', *Horizon* (May 1940)

The Battle of Britain was won on the playing-fields of Greyfriars. But Greyfriars did not exist. A fictional public school, founded in the late sixteenth century, it was the home of Bob Cherry, Harry Wharton, Billy Bunter and other legendary characters whose adventures appeared in the pages of the *Magnet*, one of the most popular boys' weeklies of the interwar years. Its sister paper, the *Gem*, featured the exploits of Tom Merry and his friends at the equally venerable and almost as famous St Jim's.

Born on 15 February 1908, the *Magnet* continued until issue no. 1,683, 18 May 1940. By 25 May, the date of next issue duly announced as usual in its precursor, the Germans had foolishly halted their advance against the Allied troops centred on Dunkirk and the evacuation was about to start. Greyfriars was the first major literary casualty of the pending Battle of Britain.[1]

It was not the only one. The *Magnet* and the *Gem* belonged to a stable of juvenile papers published by the Amalgamated Press, proprietor William Ewert Berry, first Lord Camrose (1879–1954). A Tory press lord whose pride and joy was the *Daily Telegraph*, Camrose now took hurried stock of the printing economics of the crisis. *Modern Boy* had already been incorporated with the *Boys' Cinema*; the combined paper's last issue was also on 18 May 1940. The *Gem* had been blended into the *Triumph* after its last issue on 30 December 1939, and the *Triumph* met its personal tragedy on 25 May 1940. The *Ranger* had become the *Pilot* on 4 March 1935; after 2 April 1938 it was incorporated in *Wild West Weekly*, founded on 12 March 1938 and running for fifty issues to be incorporated in the *Thriller*, which on 9 March 1940 became the *War Thriller*: it ended on 10

May 1940. Of the boys' weeklies controlled by Camrose, his bestseller, the *Champion*, and his tabloid-cum-strip-cartoon *Film Fun* were the only two to survive. Everything had to be sacrificed to the newsprint needs of the *Daily Telegraph*, all the more now that the Nazi invasion of Norway on 9 April would curtail timber supplies for paper.[2]

The decision seems to have been precipitate. The *Champion* was by now outselling the *Magnet* among boys of twelve and thirteen, but the *Magnet* was preferred by more intellectual fourteen-year-olds, by all fifteen-year-olds and by girls of any age. The *Magnet* sold weekly in excess of 200,000 copies between 1925 and 1935, but had now fallen to 40,000; the *Gem* had held the same peak and was down to 16,000 when it merged. The *Champion*'s zenith was 150,000. *Film Fun* was outsold by the last *Magnets* for all categories except school-leaving teenage girls: the *Magnet* had nearly double its circulation among twelve-year-old boys, quadruple for thirteen- and fourteen-year-olds, nine times for fifteen-year olds.[3]

On the eve of their demise the *Magnet* and its stable-mates had been under attack from another quarter. In March 1940 Cyril Connolly published in *Horizon* George Orwell's celebrated essay on 'Boys' Weeklies'. Noting that Greyfriars and St Jim's and their leading characters had changed scarcely at all since the stories first began in the Edwardian era, Orwell (1903–50) assumed that they must be the work of many hands:

> The stories in the *Magnet* are signed 'Frank Richards' and the stories in the *Gem* 'Martin Clifford', but a series lasting thirty years could hardly be the work of the same person every week. Consequently they have to be written in a style that is easily imitated – an extraordinary artificial, repetitive style, quite different from anything else now existing in English literature.[4]

This prepared him for the *coup de grâce* when Frank Richards replied:

> Mr Orwell finds it difficult to believe that a series running for thirty years can possibly have been written by one and the same person. In the presence of such authority I speak with diffidence: and can only say that, to the best of my knowledge and belief, I am only one person, and have never been two or three.

'Frank Richards' was one of the pen-names of the author Charles Hamilton (1876–1961), who also wrote as Martin Clifford, Ralph Redway and Owen Conquest. With an output of about two million words a year, Richards (as he will be called here) wrote at various times for most of the children's papers belonging to the Amalgamated Press.[5]

Orwell saw an ideological motive behind these papers:

> *All* fiction from the novels in the mushroom libraries downwards is censored in the interests of the ruling class. And boys' fiction above all,

the blood-and-thunder stuff which nearly every boy devours at some time or other, is sodden in the worst illusions of 1910. The fact is only unimportant if one believes that what is read in childhood leaves no impression behind. Lord Camrose and his colleagues evidently believe nothing of the kind, and, after all, Lord Camrose ought to know.[6]

But Lord Camrose's readiness to junk his pap for the puerile proletariat so rapidly suggests that the *Magnet* was not, after all, given so high a priority by its proprietor. Camrose had acquired his juvenile weeklies in 1926 when the Amalgamated Press was bought by the Berry brothers from the estate of the late Lord Northcliffe, and if any conspiracy went into the making of Bob Cherry and Billy Bunter it died with that demonic and demented magnate. The creation of the generation who fought the Battle of Britain seems to have been left chiefly to Frank Richards himself, and if we are to measure the *mentalités* of the 200,000 readers of the *Gem* and the *Magnet* per year when they were old enough to learn, and young enough to fight the Battle of Britain, we may watch the dogfight between the Old Etonian novelist and journalist, founding literary sociology as a fine art, and the writer whose existence as a sole author Orwell had found it impossible to credit.[7]

Orwell attributed the longevity of the papers' success to the judicious variation of character traits and origins, ensuring that almost every boy reader could find someone to identify with:

> There is the normal, athletic, high-spirited boy (Tom Merry, Jack Blake, Frank Nugent), a slightly rowdier version of this type (Bob Cherry), a more aristocratic version (Talbot, Manners), a quieter, more studious version (Harry Wharton), and a stolid, 'bulldog' version (Johnny Bull). Then there is the reckless, dare-devil type of boy (Vernon-Smith), the definitely 'clever', studious boy (Mark Linley, Dick Penfold), and the eccentric boy who is not good at games but possesses some special talent (Skinner, Wibley). And there is the scholarship-boy (Tom Redwing), an important figure in this class of story because it makes it possible for boys from very poor homes to project themselves into the public-school atmosphere. In addition there are Australian, Irish, Welsh, Manx, Yorkshire and Lancashire boys to play upon local patriotism.[8]

The general thesis is excellent, the specifics sometimes inaccurate. The *Gem* and *Magnet* certainly made it a policy from early years to have several Irish, Scots, Welsh, Indian, Canadian, South African or other Empire representatives: it is Shakespeare's eve of Harfleur, where his odds tilted to favour his ancestral Welsh (Richards makes much of Scots' brains).[9] But reader identification went further. Jews came to St Jim's and Greyfriars and were warmly defended against bigotry (the relevant St Jim's story featured the dignified and generous Dick Julian defeating the muscle and morals of the usually likeable Monty Lowther, who then bitterly repudiates his own earlier caddishness against Jews). The Indian 'nabob' Hurree Jamset

Ram Singh talks an absurd pseudo-learned babu English, in devotion to a teacher whom he loyally believes spoke better English than do the English, but has a keener mind and more alert understanding than his white friends and is inseparably a comrade in the form leader group, 'The Famous Five'. He is also the Greyfriars crack bowler. Scholarship boys such as the former mill-worker Mark Linley of Lancashire have to fight off odious snobbish prejudice against workers: Linley even meets suspicion from those who befriend him that he may not share their taboos against lying and stealing.[10]

Orwell's critique reflected his love-hate relationship with the year 1910, symbolised in *1984* by Winston Smith's love of the old junk shop which turns out to be manned by the Thought Police. It is aggravated by *Puritanismus Orwelleanus*, the art of enjoying oneself and then analysing why one shouldn't have. He also insisted that his antiques be really old: given that the *Magnet* and *Gem* survived from Edwardian days, he maintained they had not changed: he wanted them behind the times, to be diagnosed with delighted reproach. 'The outlook inculcated by all these papers', he wrote, 'is that of a rather exceptionally stupid member of the Navy League in the year 1910.' Yet Richards as early as July–September 1936 made a violent attack on Mussolini, thickly undisguised as a circus proprietor named Muccolini and unaffectionately known as 'Mucky': he is blackmailed by Billy Bunter for spying on RAF installations, attempts his murder and is then jailed by Ferrers Locke, Richards's in-house clone of Sherlock Holmes.[11]

Richards, a little like one of his own creations, disdained to play his opponent's game by proving his innocence on a charge he did not accept as indictable. In his lengthy reply to Orwell, published in the May 1940 number of *Horizon*, he wrote:

> His most serious charge against my series is that it smacks of the year 1910: a period which Mr Orwell appears to hold in peculiar horror. Probably I am older than Mr Orwell: and I can tell him that the world went very well then. It has not been improved by the Great War, the General Strike, the outbreak of sex-chatter, by make-up or lipstick, by the present discontents, or by Mr Orwell's thoughts upon the present discontents!

But while Richards was composing his reply the *Magnet* was printing his very own overture to the Battle of Britain:

> 'Oh!' gasped Bob. 'Look!'
>
> From the clouds the black dot had shot – nearer now and larger. It was a plane – swooping down on the trawler. And as it swooped, the stuttering clatter of a machine-gun thudded through the air.
>
> 'A Hun!' breathed Harry Wharton.
>
> It was a German raider.
>
> They saw the trawler twist and turn, like a hunted animal. The German

plane roared over it, rattling out machine-gun bullets, and roared on. The juniors watched breathlessly, their hearts thumping.

'Oh, if a fellow could get at the rotters!' breathed Johnny Bull, clenching his hands.

Crack-ack-ack-ack-ack!

It came again, the enemy plane sweeping over the trawler, flying low, and raining shot.

Then suddenly Bob gave a whoop of joy.

'Look!'

He pointed.

Out of the blue shot another plane – a Spitfire.

The juniors, in wild excitement, waved their caps.

'Hurrah!' gasped Johnny Bull. 'The Hun doesn't want any – look!'

The enemy plane evidently had sighted the patrol plane shooting out to the rescue of the mine-sweeper. The rattle of fire died out, and the German plane began to climb.

'He'll get him!' breathed Bob. 'Oh! Just to see him get him!'

The Hun was climbing fast. But the Spitfire was swooping at him, and now the fighter's guns were roaring. Distant as they were, the air round the schoolboys on the cliffs rocked with sound.

'Look!' yelled Bob.

'Oh look!' gasped Nugent.

The German had climbed too late! It seemed about to disappear into the clouds when suddenly the juniors saw it turn over, and the next instant it was hurtling downward. It burst into flames as it fell – and what looked like a trail of fireworks swept down to the sea.

'Got him!' breathed Johnny Bull.

The Spitfire sailed alone in the blue.

It was climbing – climbing fast! The juniors, for a moment, wondered why. Then they saw two shapes that shot out of the clouds to the east — and a third!

The raider had not been alone! Three Messerschmitts were rushing out of the clouds at the lone Spitfire – and the Spitfire climbed and climbed, till it was a speck in the blue, and vanished in clouds. The Messerschmitts climbed and vanished; the clouds hid all that was passing; but dully, from beyond the cloud curtain, came the echo of spitting fire.

The firing died away over the sea.

The schoolboys watched till their eyes ached – but they saw no more. The fight – if it was still going on – was above the clouds, and far out to sea. For half an hour they hardly stirred – but nothing more was seen, and silence followed the sound of the guns.

'Three to one,' said Bob, at last. 'Well, one British pilot's as good as three Huns!'

'By gum!' said Wibley. 'By gum! If a fellow was a bit older—'

Wibley had forgotten, for the moment, his ambition to be an actor. Just then he wanted to be in the Air Force.[12]

As early as 1924 the *Greyfriars Herald* (the Greyfriars school magazine, edited by Harry Wharton) had run a feature supposedly from 1940 in which Flight Commander Robert Cherry, RAF, was starting out on his flight around the world, accompanied by his observer Captain Mark Linley. The identification of the principal schoolboy heroes with a future destiny as air pilots goes on from there.

The *Gem*-reading years for Battle of Britain pilots found the St Jim's stories again and again accompanied by air adventures: 'Young Thunderbolt and His Team of Butterflies', 'Hawks of the Atlantic', 'The Spy Flyers' (by Flying-Officer W. E. Johns), a series on St Frank's Airship School, 'Biggles' South Sea Adventure' (by Captain W. E. Johns), 'Mad Carew's Dawn Patrol' (continued in the *Triumph*). Many of these would be First World War stories even in the early months of the Second World War, above all Mad Carew ('"Mon Dieu, but that man can fly!" gasped a famous French general'). None, so far as we know, were by Frank Richards, though the 'Famous Five' (Harry Wharton and his friends) made occasional air journeys which they enjoyed and Billy Bunter, appropriately anti-heroically, did not. Advertisements for recruitment to the Fleet Air Arm and other air careers, or for air force publications, beamed at the reader. Model aeroplanes, make-it-yourself gliders and so on, were available, or given away.[13]

Air travel was a fantasy becoming reality in Frank Richards's lifetime, and his stories were reality becoming fantasy. Public school commentators from Orwell to Arthur Marshall complained that 'these stories are fantastically [*sic*] unlike life at a real public school', a parochial objection. The most distinguished work in English literature to deal with a secondary school is presumably James Joyce's *A Portrait of the Artist as a Young Man*, and of the millions of words which have been devoted to it, have any enquired whether the very real schools portrayed in it were public schools or not? As it happens one was, one wasn't, but nobody cares. Greyfriars was a great deal more real than any public school to far more people than could have attended one.[14]

Yet Richards's strongest card was his wit and humour. His fifty million words about Greyfriars up to 1941 constitute the funniest school stories ever written, all the more because they covertly preached life and learning. His delight in absurd classical similes was boundless, and from time to time broke all bounds. The Greyfriars boys are largely Philistine, yet time and again real or imagined crooks are threatened by them with apposite citation from Thomas Hood's 'The Dream of Eugene Aram' (especially if the suspect is masquerading as a schoolmaster). Even the illiterate Bunter cites *Tristram Shandy*, no doubt unknowingly, when the arrival of Vernon-Smith's millionaire father to confront his son's expulsion demands allusion to the old and the young Obadiah. Analogies were updated to anticipate the Battle of Britain: 'A Spitfire whizzing out to meet a Messerschmitt had nothing on Bunter, as he headed for the gallery.'[15]

Greyfriars is amusing to the readers, but to the participants it contains a good deal of hell. The authority figures vary in unfairness, but they are quick to condemn, slow to admit error, place weight on a bad record and frequently make no allowance for a good one. The exigencies of the plot may demand this, but the whole tone of the tales is of 'us' versus 'them'. Quelch may be the most just of his fellow-masters, but the victory is an easy one: and sometimes he will be less just than the Head, or the head prefect. The real injustice, though, lies with the prefects, whose worst figures (Loder, Walker, Carne, Knox at St Jim's) are endless transgressors of school regulations ready to frame younger scapegraces, and to lay on sadistic canings at far greater length than masters will inflict.

The Battle of Britain, then, was fought by *Magnet* readers who knew they should not take authority seriously, but not flout it. They knew they should not expect rationality, or be surprised by injustice. They were taught by Richards that rank mattered little, and that bastards could be found on any social level or point in the chain of higher command. They learned that humans may and usually do improve after some very rocky starts, and that patience as well as principle are necessary to make the most of relationships. They learned the value of laughter, camaraderie, nonsense, and deflation of pomposity, albeit secretly. They learned that an appearance of rigour under inspection is expected although nobody believes in it. They learned that a firm heart, a love of friends and a sense of humour could sustain through fearful odds, and one might be faithful unto death to an institution that seemed pitiless and brutal.

But the *Magnet* graduates to the Battle of Britain had learned one other vital lesson: solipsism. It was not simply that they would win when the sky seemed darkest, whether for Vernon-Smith at the witch doctor's stake or Wharton alone in a shark-laden Pacific. It was that time and again the tales turned on solipsism, however much ridiculed by narrative, schoolfellows or readers: Bunter's readiness to assume his latest lie is viable and potentially convincing, however self-contradicted; Coker's denunciation of junior boys (believing in his innocence) for having the impertinence (rightly) to blame another Fifth Former; Wharton's ability to make a train of nonexistent insult follow an imagined offence; Vernon-Smith's pursuit of depravities he despises to show his indifference to rules he fears; Johnny Bull's repetition that he told you so; which will certainly cause you to bump him if he says it again; the masters with their notions of justice and education – all are denounced as absurd, yet each in turn supplies the pivot of a story or episode, and their very idiocy has its infectious attraction.[16]

They could hardly have received a more valuable training. They needed all the laughter, and anti-pomposity, and high spirits, and *esprit de corps*, and resentment but acceptance of unjust authority Richards could give them. They needed his cheerful appearance of Philistinism sustained

by incessant hilarious literary allusions, howlers and malapropism, his
groundwork of narrative in Shakespeare and Macaulay and the Bible. They
needed a leader whose solipsism would not countenance the possibility of
the surrender pure logic so obviously demanded, and who in addition
most impressively mingled the greed of Billy Bunter, the obsessiveness of
Horace Coker, the frequently disgruntled leadership of Harry Wharton,
the rule-breaking iconoclasm of the Bounder, the superlatively noisy high
spirits of Bob Cherry: after all, Winston Churchill had been in public life
even longer than the *Magnet*.

Their training deprived them of the means of envisaging defeat. Lord
Camrose had killed them all on the eve of the Battle of Britain. So they
went out and won it.

War and Peace

> We, the girls of the Chalet School, hereby vow ourselves members
> of the Chalet School Peace League. We swear faithfully to do all we
> can to promote peace between all our countries.
>
> Elinor M. Brent-Dyer, *The Chalet School in Exile* (1940),
> ch. IV, 'The Chalet School Peace League'[17]

The Second World War began for Greyfriars School, as it did for Britain,
with annoyance and jokes about the blackout and gas masks and shelters,
although by April 1940 a Gestapo agent was illuminating a tower to give
German bombers a direct hit for the obliteration of Harry Wharton and
Co. The Second World War began for the Chalet School in the summer
of 1938 in a small town in Austria, whence several of its members had to
flee to Switzerland in disguise after protesting against the ill-treatment of
a Jewish goldsmith by a Nazi mob:

> Down the side street there came an old man with a long, grey beard,
> plainly running for his life. A shower of stones, rotten fruit and other
> missiles followed him. Stark terror was in his face, and already he was
> failing to outdistance his pursuers.
>
> 'Why, that's old Herr Goldmann, the jeweller!' cried Jo. She knew the
> old Jew well, for he usually had her watch for repairs at least once in two
> months. He was a decent old soul, kindly, charitable, and honest, and she
> liked the old man, who had taken to sending her Passover cake every year,
> and gibed gently at her misfortunes with her watch . . .
>
> 'You low cads! You cowards!' she cried. 'How dare you chase an old
> man like this? Twenty of you against one! You – you *huns*! You – Hans
> Bocher!' she added, catching sight of one young hooligan whom she knew.
> 'Last winter, when you were all starving, didn't Frau Goldmann send soup
> and coffee every day to your home? And didn't Herr Goldmann give you

a job so that you had a regular wage? And is this the way you show your gratitude? You *deserve* to starve!'

'He's a Jew! Jews have no right to live!' declared Hans Bocher sullenly. 'Give place, Fräulein Bettany, and hand over the old Jew to us! Better take care, or you'll be in trouble for this. Let him go! We'll see to him!'

Miss Wilson, deputy head of the Chalet School, rescues Herr Goldmann, and the parish priest, Vater Johann, enables her and the nine girls to escape. But the mob subsequently kills the Jews and the priest.[18]

The author, Elinor M. Brent-Dyer (1894–1969), wrote the first of her Chalet School series, *The School at the Chalet* (1925), after a holiday in the Austrian Tyrol. She was received into the Roman Catholic Church in December 1930, possibly after a summer visit to the Passion Play in Oberammergau that year: it is vividly described in *The Chalet School and Jo* (1931). The martyrdom of Vater Johann is crucial for Brent-Dyer: Austrian Roman Catholics, even priests, were not so noticeable as he in defence of the Jews after the Anschluss. But Pope Pius XI was vehement in denunciation of Nazism, even issuing his encyclical *Mit brennender Sorge* (1937) in German rather than the customary Latin: it described Hitler as 'a mad prophet possessed of repulsive arrogance', and had to be smuggled into Germany to be read in the churches.

To Brent-Dyer, therefore, the war, and specifically the Battle of Britain, was for Austria, not against it. *The Chalet School in Exile*, published in March 1940, was written to tell Britain for what – and for whom – it was fighting. The war was well and truly on as she was writing, but the contrast between her build-up of the European background and that of Frank Richards could not be more striking. The *Magnet* of 28 January 1939 had the Bounder illicitly listening to the wireless in the dormitory:

'Herr Hitler addressed a crowd of ten thousand persons this afternoon at—'

Sudden silence again.

Smithy, it seemed, was not interested in the chin-wag of the Führer . . .

'I'm getting the ten o'clock news!' said Vernon-Smith. 'The football results will be given over again – when the gabblin' ass has finished talking about Hitler and Mussolini . . .'

'In a speech at Turin this afternoon, Signor Mussolini stated that the just aspirations of the Italian people . . .'

Sudden silence again as Smithy shut off! He did not want to hear about the aspirations of the Italian people; just or unjust! All this dreary stuff was simply irritating to Smithy.

This isolationism could not have been more at variance with the Chalet School books. They seem deeply conscious of a growing English introversion and anti-European isolation, which they intend to combat. The dutiful, sometimes inspirational, Empire recruitment of personnel is deliberately, perhaps derivatively, replaced by representatives of as many European countries as possible (Russia and, oddly, Spain, are evidently not possible). The books lack a colour mix: the only non-white student, a Kashmir girl, appears in *Lavender Laughs in the Chalet School* (1943) as a result of wartime relocation (as with many girls, parental illness at a sanatorium linked to the school enlists another pupil).

Catholic writers were more cosmopolitan than the mass of Protestant counterparts in Britain, but normally their cosmopolitanism consisted of support for the European Right, sometimes traditional, sometimes totalitarian (Franco more than Mussolini, Mussolini more than Hitler): anti-Jewish attitudes were often evident in mild or toxic quantities. Brent-Dyer shows no sign of this, her most obvious Catholic bias being a preference for south Germans and Austrians over Prussians. The contrast between this and Richards's comic foreign masters is vast. Brent-Dyer makes her Austrians, Germans and French credible.

The refounding of the Chalet School in Guernsey presents her with few problems, but Hitler presented the Channel Islands with many. Jo and her friends reach England in the next book, *The Chalet School Goes to It* (October 1941), after a voyage on a private yacht machine-gunned by a U-boat and bombed by a German biplane, somewhat obstructed by a 'British fighter'. The school finds yet another home on the Anglo-Welsh southern border, but some of its anti-Nazi graduates and supporters are interned by the British. Even English pupils and teachers have to rediscover Britain in time for its Battle. A Colonel Black interrogates all the girls individually to see if anything is known of the origins of lights on the grounds. He is denounced by Jo, now married with triplets but twelve-year-old sister of the school's founder when the series began:

'He had a nerve, I must say, to go questioning the girls like that, let alone the Staff! What does he take us for? I don't believe he's an Englishman at all! He's a wretched Nazi dressed up in our uniform, going round to make people discontented with the government.'

Coming from a character only just returned to Britain after experience of Nazi Austria, it reinforces Brent-Dyer's theme: 'who are we and for what are we fighting?'[19]

The great distinction between Richards and Brent-Dyer turned on whether the Battle of Britain was fought against Germans or Nazis. For Harry Wharton and Co., as for many others, there was no appreciable distinction: they had, after all, intervened in the First World War when Vernon-Smith had almost been executed ('"Keep a stiff upper upper lip," said the Bounder. "If we've got to face it, it's no good whining. Don't let the curs have the laugh of us."'). Although their philosophy showed some maturity in the thirty years since the fifteen-year-olds had last been at war, they were still fighting Germans, now calling themselves Gestapo, or bombing from newer aircraft.[20]

Brent-Dyer had her Chalet School girls pledge their loyalty in the Peace League to their lost comrades cut off by Nazi government or conquest: she was a member of an international organisation and while the Irish Roman Catholic majority thought little enough in those terms the British Romanists, compensating for minority status, did. Miss Annersley (unlike Miss Wilson, not a Roman Catholic) tells the school:

> 'You have not, I hope, forgotten our Peace League? As things are, we can do very little for those of its members who are still in enemy country. But remember, they are Chalet School girls, who have been trained in the same ideals as you have. God alone knows what these girls may be suffering now, and there is only one thing we can do to help them. Let us do it with all our might. We mean to gain the victory; for, make no mistake, this evil thing called Nazi-ism that has reared its head above the world like a venomous snake must perish as all evil must. There are many in Germany, more in Austria, who hate it as we do.'

The Chalet School Peace League was firmly against chauvinism and allied witch hunts as part of its anti-Nazism.[21]

The Chalet School Goes to It had some advantages in evangelising a wartime audience. The series was published by Chambers of Edinburgh, a safer publishing city than London, where Cassell's, a prominent juvenile publisher, had been bombed out in recent months and others had similar fates. The book trade had suffered, children's fiction worse than most. Ironically it fared well during the Battle of Britain (221 children's titles published in June 1940 out of 1,092), but it slumped hopelessly from October 1940 (13 out of 494 in January 1941, 31 out of 793 in June 1941). People were reading more, but wartime conditions took a cruel toll. A book which got through was sold, and borrowed, with far less competition than previously. Where Greyfriars fell, the Chalet School revitalised adrenalin on the advent of war, without which it probably would not have kept going for 43 more books.[22]

Brent-Dyer's own experience as Principal of the Margaret Roper School, Herefordshire, since 1938, lends a particular authenticity to *The Chalet School Goes to It*, which is set in the same part of the world. But where Margaret Roper benefited from remoteness from bombing raids, the Chalet School needed more newsworthy copy as reading matter for survivors of the Battle of Britain. During a nearby night bombing raid ('The Hun was out to break our morale if he could, and he went at the work with all his evil might') Miss Annersley is fire-watching on the lawn while the girls sing Bunyan's 'Pilgrim' in the cellars:

As the Head stood there, anxiety on her pale face, something came hurtling down from the heavens, falling within six yards of her . . . She saw a small cylinder with a long streamer attached, and in the light of the full moon she could make out white letters on the black material of the streamer. Bending forward she saw in printed lettering the words 'Schule Chaleten'. The Chalet School! What on earth did this mean?

There is no excuse for Miss Annersley. She certainly ought not to have done any such thing. But such was her excitement, she forgot all military orders and all precautions and picked the thing up. Then, after a final glance up at the roof, for another German plane was choking its way across, she pulled at the streamer, and at once a rolled paper came out of the cylinder . . . It held two or three lines of printed script. Very simply it said, 'Chalet School, hail! The brother of two old girls greets you. They have bid him tell you they will never forget the Chalet School Peace League, and they will love you always. Their brother joins them, though he is forced into this abomination. Karl Linders.'

Emmie and Joanna Linders! Miss Annersley caught her breath as she recalled the two German girls who had been such favourites in the school where they had been for some years. She knew that their father had been taken before a tribunal more than once and threatened with the concentration camp for his political views. She had hoped that he and his family had managed to escape before the war, but it was evident that they had not, since Karl was flying in the Luftwaffe. Poor Karl! She had known him in the old days, a handsome jolly lad of fifteen or sixteen. He must be nineteen now. He had always told her how he hated Hitler and all his works, and now he was forced to do Hitler's evil work.[23]

C'est magnifique, mais ce n'était pas la guerre. It may be doubted whether any more improbable moment exists in the looniest tabloid for today's jaded appetites. The navigation problems, the security considerations, the implications had the document been picked up by Colonel Black, not to speak of braining Miss Annersley, all mark it as fabulous and fantastic. But a moment's reflection makes it clear that this is Brent-Dyer's intention. The greater the improbabilities, the more arresting the parable.

In due course Karl Linders crashes into the sea and is taken prisoner:

Joey . . . went to see him, and he told her how Emmie and Joanna were doing their best to keep the Chalet School flag flying in Nazi Germany, as well as many another Old Girl of the Chalet School, and he was able to give them news of quite a number. His parents were dead, and the two girls lived with an uncle and aunt who would be kind to them. He hoped that it might be possible for them to get out of Germany some time, but he could not see when . . . all this happened in September . . .

The concept of the Battle of Britain as the most convenient means of rescuing Germans may startle the historian: but it also supplied a unity of propaganda. The Chalet School undertook for the Second World War the work of John Buchan in the First World War. Buchan had become an official British propagandist when writing *Greenmantle*. In that book and in *Mr Standfast* Buchan tries to come to terms with the humanitarian critique of war. Cool commentator as he was, Buchan's artistic sense of human ambiguity shrank much more scientifically than his supposedly more professional fellow historians from hate-the-Hun and hang-the-Kaiser interpretations: he also knew that such rhetoric made few converts, and a near-bankrupt Britain in 1916 desperately needed converts, especially in the United States. The Kaiser appears in *Greenmantle* as a doomed figure racked by nightmares and guilt, the very sympathy with which he is presented being a much more credible vehicle of indictment. Equally some very likeable Germans appear in the story as encountered during Hannay's tour of espionage in Germany, above all the family who shelter him over Christmas. But the idea of such good people impoverished and enslaved to a ruthless war machine hardens the case against Germany. The lunatic gallantry of Karl Linders enlists a decent Germany on the British side, and uses the old convention of chivalric combat in air warfare to new purpose. *Mr Standfast* concludes with Pieter Pienaar's final victory over the great German air ace, a Manfred von Richthofen figure; but what of the Battle in 1940 when the spirit of good German air power embraces the British cause? Moreover, while Buchan knew exactly what he was doing in the midst of these apparent concessions to critics of war, Brent-Dyer is the more effective because she is not playing games. The Battle of Britain transformed her Peace League into inspirational war propaganda, all the more because she contextualised the Battle in advance, in the cause of the defence of the Jews and of all other true religions and persecuted peoples.[24]

The People's William

> '*Sleep?*' echoed William in disgust. 'I jolly well wouldn't waste an air raid *sleepin'* in it.'
>
> . . .
>
> 'Gosh,' said William excitedly. 'I can hear bombs.'
> But it was only the Bevertons arriving . . . They were both dressed in the latest in siren suits, and had obviously taken great pains with their make-up and *coiffeurs*. Mrs Beverton wore a three-stringed pearl necklace, large jade ear-rings and four bracelets. She had, moreover, used a new exotic perfume that made William cry out in genuine alarm, 'Gas! Where's my gas mask?'
>
> Richmal Crompton, 'William – The Salvage Collector', *Modern Woman* (Jan. 1941)

Richmal Crompton Lamburn (1890–1969) published her first story of the eleven-year-old William Brown in 1919, and her last appeared posthumously in 1970. The formula is Frank Richards's, but where his creations were insulated against unduly severe draughts from the real world by their fantastic boarding schools whence they emerged into exciting but highly literary foreign or domestic landscapes, William's unnamed English village was ruthessly subjected to the historical process. Crompton alone could claim to have written the history of village life in a countryside commutable from London, conveying the revolutionary impact of the wartime changes. Before the war William's elder brother Robert suffered the tortures of the damned on courting a girl whose father has a butler:

> Lieut.-Col. Pomeroy's butler was a kind-hearted man who, in private, could imitate farmyard noises almost as well as a professional, but his public manner was terrific and made Robert feel that he could see right through to his underclothes and knew them to be of inferior quality.

The Robert of 1945 would be subject to no such challenges, although his own family's more modest 'cook, housemaid and char' had by now shrunk to one domestic, if that.[25]

William's chief literary forebear is Mark Twain's Tom Sawyer. He is scapegrace, harum-scarum, the terror of a respectable family and the centre of village schoolboy escapades, indulgently referred to by his sardonic, polio-crippled creator as 'a little horror', but firmly at her side as a romantic iconoclast, despising sneaks and model children. He is self-interested but also magnificently, if catastrophically, altruistic.

The war necessarily increased the adult world's intervention in William's world and William's interference with theirs. The adult world invited William to be a big boy now and take responsibility, and had frequent occasion to regret the invitation. Above all the adult world presented William with the presence of armed forces and other war service personnel, to whom he responded enthusiastically. The revolution in the village is mirrored by the revolution in the services, notably in their attitude to William, the best case of which, in miniature, is the air force on its local aerodrome. Before the Battle of Britain, the air force is an alien, condescending intruder symbolised by the languid Wing-Commander Glover squiring William's beautiful sister Ethel, who is painfully ready to betray her world to his:

> 'It's a rotten floor, of course,' drawled Wing-Commander Glover, adjusting his monocle.
> 'Absolutely rotten,' agreed Ethel languidly, as she leant back in her chair and sipped her tea elegantly.
> 'But interesting to watch the natives.'

'Frightfully interesting,' said Ethel, trying to look as little like a native as possible.

'Some pretty frightful dancing, isn't there?'

'Frightful,' said Ethel, with an air of aloof disgust.

'An awful crowd, too.'

'Awful,' agreed Ethel, with a world-weary smile.

'Well,' said the Wing-Commander, 'shall we tread another measure or are you tired?'

'Oh no,' said Ethel, trying to strike the happy mean between readiness to tread another measure and lofty amusement at the whole affair.

The William stories do not feature the Battle of Britain itself, but its effects blaze clearly from its immediate aftermath. A story published in February 1941 brings William and his friends into RAF circles (characteristically by ambushing one of their entertainers under the illusion he is a German parachutist in drag):

> The Outlaws sat in a crowded hall surrounded by a god-like company of men in Air Force blue – men who sailed the skies and brought down German bombers as regularly and unconcernedly as you and I have marmalade for breakfast.
> That in itself would have provided one of the greatest thrills of the Outlaws' lives. But, added to this, the god-like beings were jovial and friendly. They teased Ginger about the colour of his hair. They called William Old Bill. They gave them humbugs and peardrops . . . It was the happiest day of their lives.

Two years and six months later, William 'has made many friends among the airmen' and is helping produce their RAF Benevolent Fund variety show.[26]

Crompton herself, for all her Tory origins, may have summed up her own retrospective verdict in one of her adult novels, *Westover* (1946):

> 'I always wanted to go into the old man's business,' said Derek, 'but, now I'm in it, it's all as flat as a pancake. This working *against* people gets me down . . . trying to "do" the next man instead of giving him a helping hand as one did in the war. The old man says you must have competition, and the essence of competition is to knock the next man out, and Heaven knows the old man's straight enough. It isn't that there is any funny business about it. It's that – well, when for five years you've been working *with* people – all pulling together – it sort of gets you down to have to start working *against* everyone, trying to queer their pitch. All decent chaps, too . . . Gosh!' he ended, 'I sometimes think I'd give the rest of my life to have one day of the Battle of Britain back.'[27]

Crompton's own service during the Battle of Britain was directed against its likeliest local effect: she joined the auxiliary fire service where she lived in Bromley, Kent (near the Battle of Britain airfield at Biggin Hill), working chiefly at its telephones because of her paralysed leg – which did not protect her from having to jump to salute the officious local butcher assigned as her superior. The result was 'William – the Fire-Fighter', in which the Outlaws' vendetta against the AFS Section Officer Perkins ('a youthful platinum blond, with an exaggerated idea of his own importance') eventuates in their discovery and quenching of a fire in his lodgings, evidently started by his cigarette. Crompton's Battle of Britain might demolish old class snobbery with her approval, but not for the establishment of new petty tyrants.[28]

Crompton's services to the social historian of wartime Britain may be unrivalled, and in the midst of her pitiless satire we may be laughing so hard that we miss the force of the evidence. 'William – the Salvage Collector' turns on the absurd Bevertons mismanaging an exhibition to help the Spitfire Fund, so that thanks to William's innocent intervention soldered saucepans are labelled German incendiary bombs, and fish slices as part of Dornier wings. Yet even this tells the Blitz-saturated readership that Hitler's arsenal of death can be cut down to size. And in retrospect, it seems magnificently resilient of the British to use the detritus of the Nazi weaponry in the Battle as fund-raisers for further British defence. A victor collects and re-uses weapons captured from the vanquished. An air battlefield complicated this process, but ways were found, and morale was improved by supposedly tasteful presentations of the internal organs of Messerschmitts, the respectability of which occasions masked the exultation of a Roman triumph.[29]

Crompton tells it like it is, one feels, never permitting false self-aggrandisement to flourish: and there are a few cowards dodging bomb raids and armed service, but only through William's eyes are we given a glimpse of real, momentary, terror. Without realizing it, he surprises a spy at work: 'something flashed into his face that made William – he didn't know why – want to turn and run for his life. It vanished so quickly that William thought he must have imagined it . . .' He does not run, and his uncomprehending intrusion amazes him by unmasking the spy. His other spy encounter brings its 'curious cold feeling travelling up and down his spine', yet on 'impulse' he follows the persons causing his fear and exposes them. Crompton had far more regard for her creation than to turn him into a wartime youthful saviour of the *Boy's Own Paper* variety: an iconoclast may not become an icon. But shortly after the Battle of Britain her story 'Claude Finds a Companion', a consciously dreamlike, haunting work, seems to make him the emblem of Britain in the Battle.[30]

William is selected as companion for her son by a theorist of upbringing, who construes his temporary indigestion as idealism and who then leaves the boys – William smaller than Claude – to their own devices as she dashes off on another lecture tour.

The new boy and Claude were together at the edge of the pond. The new boy was more or less coated with mud, as new boys generally were after a little frolic with Claude down by the pond. Only one thing made the spectacle different from the many similar ones Uncle Eustace had witnessed before. The new boy wasn't crying . . . This interested Uncle Eustace, and he stayed to see what would happen next. What happened next interested him still more. For the new boy had taken Claude by the collar, hauled him wriggling to the edge of the pond, and pushed him down in the mud on his face. Claude scrambled to his feet and came, bawling and yelling, back to the house . . .

Uncle Eustace moved hastily away from the window, rubbing his hands and smiling a little smile of satisfaction.

Upstairs the housekeeper received the bawling Claude and dried and changed him with barely concealed delight.

My reading of the story is that the former little companions are Austria, Czechoslovakia, Poland, Norway, Denmark, Belgium, the Netherlands and France. Uncle Eustace and the servants are covert anti-Nazi elements in Germany, the housekeeper perhaps being the Jews, given Claude's habit of kicking her shins 'hard' with his 'heavy' shoes. Claude's mother (Mrs Dayford) and her theories are Nazi ideology, her stress on Claude's manly fearlessness being Nietzscheanism, Wagnerism and so on. In Crompton's *Weatherley Parade* (1944) Nazism is kicking hard in 1937: '"The devils were kicking an old woman in one of their filthy Jew-baiting orgies, and, when Jo tried to interfere, they knocked her down and kicked her too . . . And I had to soft-soap the bastards and cringe to them. God! I wish that I'd had the guts to stick a knife into one of them!"'

'Dayford' may be an allusion to *Der Tag* and to subjugation of the English Channel. Mrs Dayford insisting that right theories are being correctly applied, when in fact smaller children are being brutally assaulted, matches the Hitlerian rationale of the beneficence of Nazi liberation. William's first precipitation into the mud is Dunkirk. His reply is the Battle of Britain. The more protracted fight which follows is the Blitz and the continuing war. And William in this story is conspicuous in smallness and skill. It is the old English self-image from Agincourt and the Armada to the Battle of Britain. Then as now it was, in the slogan of the cartoonist David Low, 'VERY WELL, ALONE'. But that is not Crompton's full message. William thinks he is fighting alone, but he does not realise his moral authority or the strength of silent support for his cause. He has the support of servants, usually his natural enemies (a second metaphor here, showing common cause of worker and bourgeois against the tyrannies seeking to overawe them). Uncle Eustace symbolises an older German wisdom, silenced, but at its heart anti-Hitler. And when Mrs Dayford returns, Claude suddenly realises he prefers William's way of life to his own. To Crompton, as to Brent-Dyer, the many who owed so much to the few included not only

Hitler's victims, but even his troops: but where Brent-Dyer saluted the reluctant enemies, Crompton's Claude meant Hitlerians of today destined to reject Hitler tomorrow – provided that William Carried On.[31]

Men Without Women?

'Wars aren't for women,' growled the C.O.

'If you said they *shouldn't* be I'd agree with you,' rapped out Worrals. 'Who started the war, anyway? Men. Take a look at the world and see what a nice mess men have made of it. No wonder they had to appeal to women to help them out.'

The C.O. moved uncomfortably. 'I was thinking of *certain* jobs,' he countered.

'What jobs?' flared Worrals. 'As far as I know there's only one job in this war that hasn't been done by women. I've never heard of a woman commanding a battleship – but maybe that's only because there are more spare admirals than ships.'

W.E. Johns, *Worrals of the Islands* (1945), ch. 1

'From this attitude of profound amazement every time a job is done successfully by girls you can judge the vanity of the male tribe, my dear. The fuss over women pilots even before the war was not so much what they did as because they were women. Such conceit!'

'Be fair,' protested Frecks. 'Men have come off the high horse quite a lot since the war started.'

'I notice they climb back on again, though, at every opportunity,' countered Worrals.

Ibid., last ch.[32]

Captain W.E. Johns (1893–1968), *the* name inseparable from the Battle of Britain, was not a captain but a second lieutenant in the Royal Flying Corps whose DH4 (55 Squadron) crashed behind German lines on 16 September 1918, killing his observer, A.E. Amey, and ending his war. He had been sent out on a bomb-throwing mission, illegal under international law of that time, and was informed by the Germans that he would be shot for it. He was still a prisoner, despite escape attempts, when he learned the war was over, on 11 November 1918. He served in the RAF until 1927, leaving as Flying Officer.[33]

Johns inaugurated his magazine *Popular Flying* in April 1932 with a story, 'The White Fokker', signed 'William Earle'.[34] It opened with a group of pilots in conversation in an RFC Squadron in France about 1917, of whom the fifth to be introduced was

Bigglesworth, popularly known as Biggles, a slight, fair-haired, good-looking lad still in his 'teens, but an acting Flight-Commander ... talking, not of wine or women as novelists would have us believe, but of a new fuse spring for a Vickers gun which would speed it up another hundred rounds a minute.

His deep-set hazel eyes were never still and held a glint of yellow fire that somehow seemed out of place in a pale face upon which the strain of war, and sight of sudden death, had already graven little lines. His hands, small and delicate as a girl's, fidgeted continually with the tunic fastening at his throat. He had killed a man not six hours before. He had killed six men during the past month – or was it a year? – he had forgotten. Time had become curiously telescoped lately. What did it matter, anyway? He knew he had to die some time and had long ago ceased to worry about it. His careless attitude suggested complete indifference, but the irritating little falsetto laugh which continually punctuated his tale betrayed the frayed conditions of his nerves.

The story and others around the same character were published in August 1932 as *The Camels Are Coming*: not very surprisingly they concluded with the likeable neurotic falling in love with a girl who proved a German spy, taking to drink, crashing and being made prisoner to discover the Armistice had just come through. Even then Johns (signing without rank) declared Biggles 'is a fictitious character, yet he could have been found in any R.F.C. mess during those great days of 1917 and 1918 when air combat had become the order of the day and air duelling was a fine art ... he represents the spirit of the R.F.C. – daring and deadly when in the air, devil-may-care and debonair when on the ground.'

This official briefing confronts us with the discrepancy in Johns's version of what he was doing, and the reality, much as though he was inviting modern literary critical techniques which violently reject contextualisation. Although Johns was a great advocate of the development and strengthening of British air power in the 1930s, he retained the uneasiness of a soldier about writing for the public while making a success of it in editing *Popular Flying*. His 'Biggles' as a character was inconsistent, as pilots facing daily death might be expected to be: he began more vulnerable, and more credible, than the authoritative figure who went on to lead a hundred books. But he was never truly alive to the extent he had been in 1917–18.[35]

Naturally Johns looked back to the RFC for Biggles's peacetime exploits, although the interwar stories often picked up moods from their widely scattered terrain, and benefit greatly from a genuine sense of entertainment. Johns may not have reached the delicious ironies of Crompton, or the happy absurdity of Richards's schoolday drama strewn with classical analogy, but there was a good working humour: the endless escapes from death not only become funny to the reader but even to the participants, as for example in *Biggles in Africa* (1936), where each chapter seems to discover a fresh zoological specimen avid to finish them off. Biggles retains enough humanity to weep in *Biggles Air Commodore* (1937), or faint in *Biggles Sweeps the Desert* (1942), but the introduction of an eager teenage disciple in Ginger reduced the necessity for Biggles's redeeming weaknesses. Johns still remained more ambiguous than he could admit. The Biggles stories breathe a covert but no less cold hostility to the higher command which had ordered Johns on missions for which he could have been court-martialled and shot.

Biggles begins the Second World War with three books set in or off Scandinavia: Johns was anxious to offset the British disasters in Norway in the popular mind.[36] Biggles then had to enter the Battle of Britain and in *Spitfire Parade – Stories of Biggles in War-time* (1941), Johns sought to do this. But, symbolically for the pattern of Battle of Britain fiction, it was far from clear in which war Biggles was fighting. The book begins with Air Commodore Raymond informing Biggles by letter that he is to command a new squadron, composed of 'star turns and officers who do not take kindly to discipline'. The first of these is a monocled idiot, Lord Bertie Lissie, almost drawn to Orwellian specifications ('he's a devil with a Spitfire and a wizard with a gun, but I'm afraid he's as mad as a hatter'): Lissie, if stiff upper lip to the point of paralysis, is amusing, rather obviously. The second character, 'Tug' Carrington, is more instructive:

'His trouble is that he has an inferiority complex – thinks people are laughing at him behind his back because he's a Cockney – and tries to hide it by a show of cheek. Added to that, the war is a personal matter with him; his parents were killed in one of the first raids on the East End. I doubt if he should have been given a commission, but it's too late to alter that now. For heaven's sake don't laugh at him or he's liable to shoot up your mess. He went through the School of Flying in ten days and left behind him a trail of broken aeroplanes and nerve-shattered instructors. I believe his flying is ghastly to watch; he's got his own ideas, and nothing will prise him off them. For the past month he's been with a Coastal Squadron, and as he was popular there he must have his points. He's all yours. Just let him go.'

Raymond's snobbery is important. Johns deferred more woodenly to aristocracy than did other writers, and his commando series, the 'Gimlet' books, reeks with it to toxic levels. But with whatever intentions, we seem back with Carrington to Orwell's demand for a 'People's War':

The new-comer walked slowly into the room and stood stiffly to attention.
'I'm Carrington, sir,' he said, with a suspicion of a Cockney accent.
'Will you please salute when you come into this office,' returned Biggles curtly.
'Regulations say you only salute when wearing a hat, sir.'

'What do you mean by coming here without a hat? Where is your hat?'

'Nailed up in Number 8 Squadron Mess, sir.'

Biggles stared at the speaker. He saw a slim, nervous-looking youth whose pale face was thin and pinched as though with hunger. His hair was short and crisply curled. It was soaking wet. Rain trickled down his face and formed a dew-drop at the end of his nose. Pale grey eyes regarded the C.O. steadily. Occasionally his jaws moved with a rolling motion.

The C.O. got up and held out his hand, rather awkwardly; he was wondering why a squadron with the reputation of Naval Eight should have kept the hat. 'Glad to see you, Carrington,' he said. He glanced at the clock. 'Why are you late?'

'I didn't know I was,' came the answer, promptly. 'Your clock is a minute fast.'

Biggles frowned. 'You're sure of that?'

'Certain. I set my watch by H.Q. time this morning – and they get it from Greenwich.'

Biggles drew a deep breath. 'I'll take your word for it,' he said stiffly. 'I hope you'll like it here.'

'I reckon so,' nodded Carrington, casually, glancing round. 'One place is much the same as another to me,' he added.

Biggles swallowed. 'This is going to be a squadron with a reputation,' he said tersely. 'I hope you'll bear it in mind.'

'Biggles Takes Over' and 'The Coming of Carrington', almost exactly sequential in time, establish the start of Biggles's squadron (666, the mark of the Beast, a possible comment on the ferocious names given to combat aircraft). Their air-combat data were doubtless archaic, but they seem written to enshrine the Battle and Carrington is a fairly credible Cockney. After that Johns threw in his hand. He followed house policy as he knew it from the *Gem*, to encourage non-English readers by recruiting Scots and Welsh pilots to the squadron. Irish neutrality leads him to settle for a volunteer Irish-American New York cop originally from Cactusville, Texas. But the arrival of Angus and trundling in of Taffy are simply Biggles adventures from the First World War published in a pulp paperback only six years earlier. The other stories are also largely cannibalisations, frequently crudely so: Richards's huge output necessitated retreading of old ground, but he did it in a chess enthusiast's reworking of variations in a master game.[37]

The sentimental prologation of Edwardianism (though not so complete as Orwell assumed) contrasts sharply with the women writers, Brent-Dyer and Crompton, who saw a new world in more than weaponry, and saw it had to be encountered with more than ridicule. Johns, only beginning his Biggles saga in 1932, *should* have been more immune to the past than the others, but was in fact much less so. In part, they knew how much of the past they needed to drop as well as to use, Richards knowing when to build on Thomas Hughes or Talbot Baines Reed, and when to branch out;

Brent-Dyer making the same decision for Bessie Marchant or Dorothea Moore; Crompton having William use his handkerchiefs to carry tadpoles or dam streams where her master, Mark Twain, made Tom Sawyer reject a handkerchief and despise boys who used one as snobs. Johns, writing air stories, had no such forebears. He was profoundly dependent on his own war, and was *sui generis* in writing from knowledge of it. He might lean on some traditional author to inspire individual works. But his war fiction had to distance itself from France in 1918 to get anywhere. Biggles made the Battle of Britain an event in the First World War.

It leads to one extraordinary conclusion. There are images of the Battle of Britain in wartime children's literature, but they are all imaginative: Harry Wharton and Co. on the cliff, Miss Annersley on the lawn, William in the air-raid shelter can visualise what they do not witness: Richards gives the clearest image of aerial combat over Britain in 1940, but essentially a prophetic one as he probably knew; Brent-Dyer gives an image of the supportive enemy through the fall of the message; Crompton separates the Dorniers (proclaimed by William) from the cows and motor-cycles (diagnosed by his father); Johns alone could see the Battle for what it was, yet he could only clothe it in what he had once known it to be. Because he was nearest to the experience of participants by profession, he was furthest from their time. At least he tried: long-standing boys' writers of air fiction such as George E. Rochester and Percy F. Westerman simply avoided it altogether. 'Tug' Carrington may be alone, but as a symbol of the actual Battle of Britain he was not bad.

What went wrong in general was that the Battle was too visible. Too many people had seen too much, yet (as Richards had warned) too little. So much experience was more than writers could fulfil for readers who might know much more about the Battle than they did. And yet the conventional Johns, fixing the Battle in archaic terms, was to prove its great revolutionary, in a concept that far outgrew its origin in fiction. It was apparently in 1940 that the Air Ministry asked Johns to invent a new character to publicise the Women's Auxiliary Air Force. Johns selected the name 'Joan Worralson', which has a strong ring of 'Johnnie' Mollison, the name by which he knew Amy Johnson. Worrals first appeared in the *Girl's Own Paper* towards the end of the Battle of Britain in October 1940.

Before Johnson's death-crash aged thirty-seven in January 1941, Worrals had already been hailed by Graham Greene, reviewing comic-book super-hero fiction: 'The spirit of these heroes is best exemplified by a heroine – Worrals, who shot down the mysterious "twin-engined monoplane with tapered wings, painted grey, with no markings" in area 21-C-2.' Worrals's feminism is explosive, and reflective of Amy Johnson's fury that so little place existed for women in public life save (in her own case) as a record-breaking freak. Johns as early as June 1934 had sympathised in *Popular Flying*: 'They are going to fly . . . make no mistake about it. The average girl flies as well as the average man . . . [ready to prove] lady aces in a national emergency.' This meant killer status, seized by Worrals in her first instalment when radio instructs all pilots to stop a spy plane 'at all costs'. Her male CO, with what seems intentional Ibsenism, reproves her: 'As one pilot to another I congratulate you on your skill and initiative – now wait a minute – but officially, I must warn you that you simply must not do this sort of thing.'[38]

A killer woman pilot as emblem for the Battle of Britain accounts for Greene's classification of Worrals with fantasy heroes. A survey in November 1941 recorded two-thirds disapproving of women being armed combatants, and Worrals does not personally kill anyone for the next three books. From the first, Nazis are presented as the extreme in male chauvinism: '"When you leave here", he said slowly, "it will be to go to a country where they know how to control impetuous young women like yourself."' But when Worrals next shoots to kill, it is against Nazis using killer women (Hitler gave Hanna Reitsch the Iron Cross 1st Class three months before that book's publication).[39]

Much British male chauvinism in and out of the services was as horrified by women flyers as by women killers, and the WAAF, while proclaiming itself 'a fighting service helping the RAF", added '(on ground only)'. It was from the Air Transport Auxiliary that Johns drew the first details of Worrals's ferry-pilot activities, but given the miserly provision of its women pilots (eight by 1 January 1940 raised to 26 in that year), it needed no recruits. Johns therefore wooed girl readers for the WAAF with ATA propaganda.[40]

And Johns's WAAF heroines were firmly based on ATA personnel. Amy Johnson kick-started Worrals: indeed Worrals as first presented is bored with the ferrying the WAAF would never have allowed her to do and yearning for adventure in ways which may have killed Amy Johnson. Worrals's Sancho Panza, 'Frecks' Lovell, has occasional moments of hysteria recalling Johnson. But the main model for Worrals quickly became Flight Commandant Pauline Gower (1910–47), who built up the ATA women almost single-handed, and recalled by one of her recruits as 'a person of great force, clear thinking, and by all standards most efficient and knowledgeable. She had the ability suddenly to become warmly human, able to joke with anyone immediately after she had told them they must do better or else.'

Gower would ultimately succeed Johns as flying feature-writer for *Girl's Own Paper*. Her sardonic feminism was in perfect Worrals tone: she would denounce the theory that 'the hand that rocked the cradle wrecked the crate'. Her *GOP* story-telling shows that she, too, believed women must be ready to kill. *Worrals of the WAAF* certainly confronted the issue at once. The first page crackles with Worrals's anger: 'Men can go off and fight, but girls – oh no.' And like Gower she uses her initiative to force projects on reluctant men, with a hint of her family links to the ruling few, to achieve egalitarian revolution from the Battle of Britain.[41]

Johns's own feminism, improbable as it might appear to casual commentators, was both deep-rooted and directly activated by the Battle. The Camrose massacre of the innocents did not hit Johns as hard as the magazine-dependent Richards, but it lost him the *Gem*, *Modern Boy* and *War Thriller*. His common-law wife Doris Leigh then made him go to a literary agent and he was directed (apparently for the first time) to *Boy's Own Paper*, which he had read in his Edwardian youth, and *Girl's Own Paper*, both sworn by the Religious Tract Society to survive for the duration of the war. His arrival moved the *BOP* from its traditional fantasy and brought the *GOP* into the war with Worrals. But the price was that he had to lie about his marital status, and Doris to pose as 'Mrs Johns' for fear the Religious Tract Society would blacklist him. So Worrals was born of the Battle of Britain and conceived in feminist rage. The thought that she was but a female Biggles misses the point: she could echo Biggles but radicalised him. Above all, Worrals can tell the higher command where they get off by faulting them on gender bigotry, where Biggles remains ultimately their victim. The hatred of lying crackling through the spy stories *Biggles Flies East* and *Biggles Defies the Swastika* offers a simple ethical dissent, appropriate for children's fiction, hinting at the underlying hostility to brass hats who demand the lies and despise the ethics. Events pointed the irony in *Biggles Defies the Swastika* written in the Blitz but all too relevant to its reprisals: '"Well, I'm here, and if I can put a spoke in the wheel of the savages who drop bombs on helpless civilians I certainly will," he mused grimly.'

Worrals reverses the normal Biggles pattern. He deplores his superiors' readiness to sacrifice him, as in real life Johns was so casually ordered to become a war criminal. She sneers at their reluctance to use her, anxious as they are to exploit her, and even finds Biggles's own Air Commodore Raymond to receive some of her choicest castigations. For W.E. Johns the Battle of Britain ensured that women's liberation could be the measure of men's liberation.[42]

But in one respect Worrals and Frecks resembled Johnson and Gower less than they did their own supposed comrades in the WAAF: during the Battle of Britain they were, respectively, eighteen and seventeen years old. It made them twenty-eight and twenty-seven for their last appearance, when Johns's feminism was clearly losing its wartime fervour. But like the Battle of their birth, they remain a revolutionary landmark for the inspiration of future generations.

Epilogue: What Children?

In December 1940 the French Catholic writer Georges Bernanos wrote from Brazil the first of his *Letters to the English*. Bernanos was of the French Right; he had also been an impassioned enemy of Franco's prostitution of the Catholic Church in his own interests and those of his Nazi and Fascist allies during the Spanish Civil War. Bernanos was a great fighter, a great hater, a great lover – in philosophical terms. Bernanos was in his way a giant: there is a vastness in his rectitude, and in his rightness, as – to be fair – there is even in his Rightness. And on the question of what the Battle of Britain had to do with children, his is the final voice. There has been much apologising for past misdeeds in history by people who know they themselves inherit little blame, but hope to inherit much favour, especially at future elections. For myself, it seems appropriate as a two-year-old during the Battle of Britain in justly neutral Ireland (for belligerent Ireland would have been crushed by a German invasion at once and Britain caught in Nazi pincers) to thank the United Kingdom of Great Britain and Northern Ireland for its conduct and courage, for saving the rest of us while saving itself. The rest is for Bernanos to say to our generation as to theirs:

> O men of England! These pages will reach you, I suppose, some time next December. Christmas is the feast of childhood. I call down the blessings of childhood on the English nation. Hurrah for your childhood! Unfortunately, we French have never taken much pains to understand the English. In the fifteenth century our ancestors called them 'Godons' [Goddamns] and followed them in the streets with cries of 'Ware tail!' because they thought that, as a punishment for their sins, they carried this devilish appendage hidden in their breeches. We never understood you English very well, though many of us did know, even then, that English children are among the loveliest in the world. A happy Christmas, then, to the children of England! We thought of you all as 'milords' with high collars and fat paunches, as men enjoying huge fortunes derived from cotton mills and West Indian sugar, as the people who had invented the pound sterling, the race-horse, and – one day, when you were feeling particularly liverish as a result of eating boiled mutton floating in a melancholy sea of potatoes – the umbrella. And now, for the last six months, day after day, you have been telling us a fairy-tale, a tale that no serious adult, no man of ability or experience, could possibly understand – a children's tale. Hurrah for you English children!
>
> No one knows better than I do that, in the course of centuries, all the great stories of the world end by becoming children's tales. But this particular one has started its life as such, has become a children's tale on the very threshold of its existence. I mean that we can recognise in it the threefold visible sign of its destiny. It has deceived the anticipation of the wise, it has made the faint-hearted eat humble-pie, it has staggered the

nitwits. Last June, all these folk, from one end of the world to the other, no matter what the colour of their skins, were shaking their heads. Never had they been so old, never had they been so proud of being old. All the figures that they had swallowed in the course of their miserable lives, as a safeguard against the highly improbable activity of their emotions, had choked their arteries, and they were stuffed tight with statistics. They were ready to prove that with the Armistice of Réthondes the war had become a mathematical impossibility; as though man had been made for mathematics and not mathematics for man. Some chuckled with satisfaction at the thought, but they were not the most dangerous, because hatred is a salt which has the property of preserving old men from corruption, at least for a moment. Others threatened us with the contagion of their pity, dissolving before our eyes, melting into impotent, vile-smelling tears. 'Alone against the world', they said. 'It is a children's story.' And that is precisely what it was – a tale for children. Hurrah for the children of England![43]

Notes and References

1 Both Orwell's essay and Frank Richards's reply are conveniently reprinted in George Orwell, *The Collected Essays, Journalism and Letters*, ed. Sonia Orwell and Ian Angus, vol. 1 (Harmondsworth, 1970), pp. 505–31, 531–40, and with greater scholarship in Peter Davidson (ed.), *The Complete Works of George Orwell*, XII: *A Patriot After All 1940–1941* (London, 1998), pp. 56–86 and see also pp. 10, 156. For later treatments of the subject see E.S. Turner, *Boys Will Be Boys* (London, 1948); W.O.G. Lofts and D.J. Adley, *The Men Behind Boys' Fiction* (London, 1970); Isabel Quigly, *The Heirs of Tom Brown* (Oxford, 1982); P.W. Musgrave, *From Brown to Bunter* (London, 1985); D.L. Kirkpatrick, *Twentieth-Century Children's Writers* (London, 1978); Mary Cadogan, *Frank Richards* (London, 1988). Many of the original *Magnet* and *Gem* series were reprinted by Howard Baker, sometimes embracing neither a full series nor a discrete chronology in the choice of items per bound volume.
2 Data assembled from the British Museum *Catalogue*.
3 A.J. Jenkinson, *What Do Boys and Girls Read?* (London, 1946), pp. 64–75, 210–23. The most obvious forebear of *Magnet* and *Gem*, *Boy's Own Paper*, survived them, being the product of the Religious Tract Society and its publishing house, Lutterworth, but in 1939 the *Magnet* was read by two to three times its readership, and *BOP*'s classic seminal school stories from Talbot Baines Reed (1852–93) had descended to lesser hands.
4 Orwell, *Collected Essays*, vol. 1, p. 507.
5 Richards in ibid., p. 534
6 Orwell in ibid., p. 531.
7 Lofts and Adley, *Men*, p. 187; Cadogan, *Richards*, pp. 154–5; Herbert A. Hinton (1888–1945), editor of *Magnet* and *Gem*, 1911–16 and 1919–21, was warmly (and hence closely) regarded by Northcliffe, to whom he was said to be related.
8 Orwell, *Collected Essays*, vol. 1, pp. 514–15.
9 See for example, *Gem* (19 June 1937): 'A Son of Scotland'.
10 Cadogan, *Richards*, pp. 79–85; see also *Gem* (18 Feb. 1939), *Magnet* (26 Oct. 1929).
11 Orwell, *Collected Essays*, vol. 1, pp. 516–18, 528.

12 Richards in ibid., p. 532; *Magnet* (13 Apr. 1940).

13 *Greyfriars Holiday Annual* (1924), p. 139; ibid., (1928), p. 27.

14 Orwell, *Collected Essays*, vol. 1, p. 509; Arthur Marshall, *Girls Will Be Girls* (London, 1974), pp. 116–17.

15 A classic instance of the Aram citation is its use by the Bounder to unmask a temporary schoolmaster, who is in fact a Scotland Yard detective, in the 'Courtfield Cracksman' series, *Magnet* (8 Dec. 1929 to 8 Mar. 1930); *Magnet* (4 Feb. 1939); *Magnet* (20 Apr. 1940)).

16 e.g. *Magnet* (24 Oct. 1931); *Magnet* (1 Oct. 1938).

17 Elinor Brent-Dyer, *The Chalet School in Exile* (Edinburgh, 1940), p. 57. This text reads 'Chalet School League', but reproduction in later stories, for example, *Lavender Laughs in the Chalet School* (Edinburgh, 1943), p. 64, is as above.

18 Brent-Dyer, *Exile*, pp. 119–20.

19 Elinor Brent-Dyer, *The Chalet School Goes to It* (Edinburgh, 1941), p. 156.

20 Cadogan, *Richards*, p. 133.

21 Brent-Dyer, *Goes to It*, p. 105.

22 Data from contemporary issues of the *Bookseller*.

23 Brent-Dyer, *Goes to It*, pp. 197–8. For Brent-Dyer's life, see Helen McClelland, *Behind the Chalet School* (London, 1996).

24 Ibid., pp. 215–16.

25 Mary Cadogan, *Richmal Crompton* (London, 1986), p. 116.

26 Richmal Crompton, 'William and the Bird Lover' (book text: 'William and the Bird Man'), *Happy Mag* (Apr. 1940), reprinted in *William and the Evacuees* (London, 1940), p. 83; 'The Outlaws and the Parachutist', *Modern Woman* (Feb. 1941), reprinted in *William Does His Bit* (London, 1941); 'William and the Brains Trust', *Modern Woman* (Aug. 1943), reprinted in *William and the Brains Trust* (London, 1945), pp. 14–16.

27 Cadogan, *Crompton*, pp. 116–17; Richmal Crompton, *Westover* (London, 1946).

28 Cadogan, *Crompton*, pp. 114–15; Richmal C. Ashbee (ed.), *William at War* (London, 1995), pp. vii–ix; Crompton, 'William – the Firefighter', *Modern Woman* (Sept. 1940).

29 Crompton, 'William – the Salvage Collector', *Modern Woman* (Jan. 1941); also 'William Helps the Spitfire Fund', *Modern Woman* (Mar. 1941).

30 'William Makes a Corner', *Modern Woman* (Dec. 1940); 'William and the Black-Out', *Happy Mag* (Feb. 1940); 'William and the Tea-Cake', *Modern Woman* (Jan. 1943); Crompton, *William and the Brains Trust*, pp. 98–101; Crompton, 'Claude Finds a Companion', *Modern Woman* (Apr. 1941).

31 *William Carries On* (1942) is the next series book-title after *William Does His Bit*, which concludes with 'Claude Finds a Companion'; David Low, *Europe at War* (Harmondsworth, 1941), p. 80 (18 June 1940); Richmal Crompton, *Weatherley Parade* (London, 1944), pp. 219–20.

32 Captain W.E. Johns, *Worrals of the Islands: A Story of War in the Pacific* (London, 1945).

33 On Johns, Peter Beresford Ellis and Piers Williams, *By Jove, Biggles!* (London, 1981), is essential. 'Captain' was a title prefixed to boys' fiction signatures by magazine editors over the previous century (Robert Louis Stevenson originally published *Treasure Island* as 'Captain George North').

34 'William Earl' were his first names.

35 For Biggles in the First World War see in particular W.E. Johns, *The Camels Are Coming* (London, 1932), *Biggles of the Camel Squadron* (London, 1934), *Biggles*

Learns to Fly (London, 1935) and *Biggles in France* (London, 1935). Johns's masterpiece, a First World War novel set in Palestine, was *Biggles Flies East* (London, 1935).

36 *Biggles in the Baltic* (London, 1940), *Biggles Sees It Through* (London, 1941), *Biggles Defies the Swastika* (London, 1941).

37 *Spitfire Parade* (London, 1941).

38 For Worrals and Amy Johnson see Mary Cadogan, *Women with Wings* (London, 1992); Graham Greene, 'The Unknown War', *Spectator* (29 Nov. 1940); Johns is quoted in Cadogan, *Wings*, pp. 161–2; W.E. Johns, *Worrals of the WAAF* (London, 1948), p. 40.

39 Johns, *WAAF*, p. 71; Joanna Bourke, *An Intimate History of Killing* (London, 1999), p. 317, but the entire chapter (pp. 306–44) is essential treatment of the issue of female homicide under official auspices.

40 Johns, 'Life in the WAAF', *Girls Own Annual*, LXII (1941), p. 25. On Gower see Lettice Curtis, *The Forgotten Pilots* (Henley-on-Thames, 1971), and Alison King, *Golden Wings* (London, 1956), both by ATA pilots, and above all Michael Fahie, *A Harvest of Memories: The Life of Pauline Gower MBE* (Peterborough, 1995).

41 Ellis and Williams, *Biggles!*, p. 189; Cadogan, *Women*, pp. 105–22, 157–74. I am grateful to the RAF veteran at our Conference who insisted that Gower rather than Johnson was the main influence on Worrals, and I am deeply honoured by my friend Mrs Catherine Koe for giving me her memories and lending me her memorabilia of Pauline Gower during their schooldays under the Sacred Heart Nuns at Tunbridge Wells.

42 On Johns's marital difficulties see Ellis and Williams, *Biggles!*, especially pp. 204–7, and on magazine publication pp. 274–9; Johns, *Swastika*, p. 61.

43 Georges Bernanos, *Plea for Liberty*, trans. Harry Lobin Binsse and Ruth Bethell (London, 1945), pp. 13–14. In the preparation of this article I must acknowledge the aid of fellow critics of old years (my parents, my sisters Mary and Ruth, my schoolboy friends Conan Rafferty, Niall Gibbons and especially Michael Gerald Little, and the Buchanan family); also Rosy Addison, Tony Aldgate, Edinburgh's Old Town Bookshop, Morag Bruford, Edinburgh University Library, my wife Bonnie Dudley Edwards, my children Sara Parvis, Leila Prescott and Michael Lee Dudley Edwards; also Catherine Koe, Jennifer Litser, Sean Mac Reamoinn, the National Library of Scotland, Patricia J. Storey and, above all, the two editors, Paul Addison and Jeremy Crang, colleagues whose research, teaching and inspiration have been invaluable over the years and whose exemplary patience with an overlong manuscript has resulted in such an admirable abridgement that what was intended as my tribute has become much more their collaboration. Anyhow, it is theirs with my love.

ANGUS CALDER

The Battle of Britain and Pilots' Memoirs

Writing in the Sky

A Battle of Britain fighter pilot might write a passionate, confused book about his experiences, publish it in 1942, see it become a bestseller, then within months die in a crash while training. That was Richard Hillary's *The Last Enemy* – perhaps the most celebrated memoir of the Battle. Or he might make his personal story part of a carefully researched survey of the Battle, beginning with its First World War antecedents, and covering the events of the summer of 1940 from many angles, with an admirable attempt at an historian's objectivity. Peter Townsend's *Duel of Eagles*, published in 1970, is that book. Or, in the aftermath of the war when his heroic stature was still taken for granted by everyone, he might let a vivid professional writer produce something between a ghost-written memoir and a fictionalised biography – this was *Reach for the Sky*, Douglas Bader's story as told by Paul Brickhill, published in 1954 and, as a notable bestseller, soon turned into a successful feature film.

But however it came out, the tale would include dogfights. Bader's third person features in my first extract:

> 'Break 'em up,' yelled Bader and swept, firing, through the front rank of the bombers. He pulled up and veered behind a big Dornier turning away left, fired and fired again. A flash burst behind the Dornier's starboard engine, and flame and black smoke spewed from it. Suddenly he was nearly ramming it and broke off. Hell, aircraft of broken formations darting everywhere in the blurred and flashing confusion. In front – 400 yards away – another Dornier seeking cloud cover between the 'cu-nims'; he was catching it rapidly when his eye caught a Spitfire diving steeply above and just ahead. It happened fast. The Spitfire pilot clearly did not see the bomber under the long cowling; he dived straight into the middle of it and the Dornier in a burst of flame split and wrapped its broken wings round the fighter. Tumbling fragments glinted above the crumpled mass as the two aircraft fell in burning embrace.[1]

Is the following Hillary or Townsend?

One after the other we peeled off in a power dive. I picked out one machine and switched my gun-button to 'Fire'. At 300 yards I had him in my sights. At 200 I opened up in a long four-second burst and saw the tracer going into his nose. Then I was pulling out, so hard that I could feel my eyes dropping through my neck. The sky was now a mass of individual dog-fights. Several of them had already been knocked down. One I hoped was mine, but on pulling up I had not been able to see the result. To my left I saw Peter Pease make a head-on attack on a Messerschmitt. They were headed straight for each other and it looked as though the fire of both was striking home. Then at the last minute the Messerschmitt pulled up, taking Peter's fire full in the belly. It rolled on its back, yellow flames pouring from the cockpit, and vanished.[2]

Townsend or Hillary?

We were still climbing, trying to reach the bombers. Keep well away from those fighters! Not easy, though, with them sitting on top of us, able to strike as they pleased. Better move out towards the sun. But a dozen Me 110s now pinned us down. Every time they dived out of their defensive circle, I called, 'Leave them alone,' and wheeled the squadron towards them to shake them off our tails.

Then the inevitable – down came the Me 109s and it was each one for himself. When my Me 109 came, firing, I whipped round and caught him doing that fatal turn across my sights. Tighten the turn, nose up a little, and I had him. The Me 109 staggered, like a pheasant shot on the wing. A big piece flew off, maybe the hood. A plume of white smoke trailed. I had a split-second impression of the pilot, seemingly inert during those last dramatic moments. Then the aircraft stalled and dived to earth near Hastings.

This time I had the feeling I had killed a man, but there was no time for remorse. If it was him this time, it could be me the next. In the mounting frenzy of battle, our hearts beat faster and our efforts became more frantic. But within, fatigue was deadening feeling, numbing the spirit. Both life and death had lost their importance. Desire sharpened to a single, savage purpose – to grab the enemy and claw him down from the sky.[3]

I let Townsend, in the third extract, run on longer because, remarkably, it is the career RAF officer, a fighter pilot since 1935, not Hillary, the intellectual, the 'long-haired boy' who joined up straight from university in 1939, who describes himself as momentarily flicked by the painful apprehension that Messerschmitts carry human beings like himself and reflects that his own purpose was 'savage'. Hillary, writing far closer to the event, describes himself as rationalising his first kill as a noble deed:

My first emotion was one of satisfaction, satisfaction at a job adequately done, at the final, logical conclusion of months of specialised training. And then I had a feeling of the essential rightness of it all. He was dead and I was alive; it could so easily have been the other way round; and that would somehow have been right too. I realised in that moment just how lucky a fighter pilot is. He has none of the personalised emotions of the soldier, handed a rifle and bayonet and told to charge. He does not even have to share the dangerous emotions of the bomber pilot who night after night must experience that childhood longing for smashing things. The fighter pilot's emotions are those of the duellist – cool, precise, impersonal. He is privileged to kill well. For if one must either kill or be killed, as now one must, it should, I feel, be done with dignity. Death should be given the setting it deserves; it should never be a pettiness; and for the fighter pilot it never can be.[4]

Townsend applies what we are prone to think as 'normal' human criteria in ethics, and mundane compassion. Hillary is arrogantly antinomian. The fighter pilot transcends normal human criteria. 'Impersonality' is a privilege.

Commenting on this passage, the American scholar Samuel Hynes, who has surveyed Battle of Britain memoirs, generalises that 'Hillary was right about one thing – in a fighter pilot's war, death is impersonal . . . it's not a man you kill but a machine.' This he perceives in those countless passages where it is 'it', a Dornier or Messerschmitt, which plummets blazing, not the persons or person in 'it'. Brickhill, writing for Bader, has a Dornier 'embrace' a Spitfire.[5] One might justify this usage by pointing out that incessant death didn't bear much talking about and pilots were notoriously laconic about even close friends who did not return from combat, but were said to have 'gone for a Burton' (beer). Or one might conclude that Townsend's adjective 'savage' expresses quite fairly the brutalisation implicit in fighter combat, and foregrounded in Derek Robinson's powerful novel *Piece of Cake*, published without public outcry and with much success in the 1980s.

Bomber planes could not be beautiful. But the main fighter planes of 1940 – especially Spitfires – had the visual appeal of clean, interesting lines while remaining human in scale, like large toys. They appealed to boys. They appealed to women. In the nature of it, several generations in Britain remembered, or grew up with, two indelible visions of the Battle of Britain. One is from the pilot's cockpit. Film camera or prose description gives us the image of the Messerschmitt attacking, as it were, ourselves, like an immense wasp. Our paranoia is the pilot's. Our relief as the enemy hurtles blazing groundwards is his. Or, from the ground, we saw, we still see, we still imagine, the spectacle of 'our boys' *duelling* (and the title of Townsend's book impresses this notion even more strongly than Hillary's sentences of intellectualisation) with equally matched adversaries above our rooftops: a gallant show, perhaps leaving behind some of those vapour trails across clear blue skies which still haunt many people whose memory falsely tells them that the weather that summer was exceptionally fine.

Whatever happened happened very quickly. A British fighter had only fourteen seconds' worth of bullets. It happened in confusion. Footballers interviewed on TV these days will often admit that they didn't know how they scored this or that goal until they saw the action replays. The discrepancy on the British side between pilots' claims for kills in 1940 and actual German planes destroyed is long proven beyond a peradventure to be based on misperceptions in the heat of battle. There are obvious reasons for assuming that the somewhat sensationalist Brickhill, and Hillary, who is self-consciously writing 'literature', are not likely to be telling us *exactly* what happened. But I think even the experienced and conscientious Townsend can hardly be trusted as an exact reporter. Dogfights happened *somewhat* as writer after writer describes them. The main plot is variable, the subplots are numerous. But we know that dogfights happened *like that* because we have known it since we first saw it on newsreel or read about it in childhood or watched certain feature films. So we believe each writer in turn. However, so far from projecting an epic vision of individual deeds of daring, the basic plot of the dogfight assimilates each pilot with every other, and every burst of combat with every other such burst. The protagonists, contrary to what Hillary affirmed, are not men with freedom to express personal quiddities, but Spitfires, Hurricanes and those Messerschmitt cowboys of the air herding dark, sluggish cattle with udders full of death: Heinkels, Dorniers. Yet because we believe it without question to be true we can comfortably associate the basic plot of the dogfight with ideas of 'chivalry', duels, 'knights of the air', derived from discourses within Western culture in general and British culture in particular, originating long before humans could fly and wildly inappropriate to what actually went on over Kent and Sussex in August and September 1940. There was in fact more scope for individual self-expression, and even for chivalry, in certain phases of infantry warfare. In the air, in a fighter, it was kill or be killed – or run away. There were only those three possibilities, unless one throws in the option to strafe or not to strafe enemy aircrew parachuting down or helpless in lifeboats in the Channel.

Fighter planes were designed for defence, but also for attack. Ordered to strafe, their pilots had no choice except possible charges of insubordination. Peter Townsend, who interleaves the Luftwaffe's experiences with that of his own RAF, muses on the role of the Messerschmitt pilots in France during the Dunkirk evacuation:

> As for us the enemy was until then a *thing*, not a person. They shot at an aircraft with no thought for the men inside it. But now they had the job of ground-strafing as well. Sensitive, highly strung Paul Temme said, 'I hated Dunkirk. It was just unadulterated killing. The beaches were jammed full

of soldiers. I went up and down at three hundred feet "hose-piping."'
Cold-blooded, point blank murder. Defenceless men, fathers, sons, and
brothers, being cruelly massacred by a twenty-four year old boy.[6]

Even in defence, the results of fighter activity might be casually murderous.
German bombers crashed on English houses, or jettisoned their bombs at
random as they fled. The great air ace Robert Stanford-Tuck (twenty-seven
confirmed kills by January 1942) was pursuing a Junkers 88 over south
Wales one evening, fired at it long range, failed to hit it, but saw its
bombs dropped. Next morning he received a call from his father that
his brother-in-law, stationed under canvas with the army in Wales, had
been killed the previous night. Tuck checked. Only one stick of bombs
had landed on Wales. Only one man, a soldier, had been killed.[7]

The Romance of the Air

There were immediate reasons why civilians should idealise the pilots of
the Battle of Britain. Also, the airmen themselves shared in a 'heritage of
discourses' involving English chivalry which provided potent pretexts for
idealisation. And both civilians and airmen were susceptible to the very
recent mystique attached to aviation itself.

To be resoundingly obvious, civilians saw that these men were fighting
to save Britain from conquest by an exceptionally brutal enemy. Sometimes
very young indeed, commonly undertrained for the job, they elicited pathos
as well as admiration. Whether all the civilian population always loved all of
them is doubtful. An RAF man venturing among London shelterers in the
autumn of 1940 was liable to get a hostile reception – why wasn't he up in
the sky out there defending the people? There is the curious case of the pilot
found still in the cockpit of his aircraft in the mid-1990s during routine civil
engineering excavations in Hove. He had crashed into this populous place
in 1940 and had literally been blotted out. One suspects that in the general
fear and commotion no civilian could be bothered to inspect the crash, let
alone rush to his aid. Now at last he has been interred in a regular way with
appropriate honours.[8] Army conscripts resented the superior sex appeal of
the 'Brylcreem Boys' of the air, and may have transmitted their prejudices
to others. But that same appeal confirmed that these were indeed the young
men of the hour, as Churchill said they were.

All literate Britons in and out of uniform were affected by interacting
myths and discourses involving heroic combat, some as old as the presumed
King Arthur, others originating as recently as 1914–18. In the context of a
truly decisive battle, these were easily sufficient to explain the mystique of
Douglas Bader, and of other aces who had not had his distinction of losing
their legs in a peacetime air accident. Fused with certain preoccupations

of the literary intelligentsia between the wars, they grounded the cult of
Richard Hillary.

It would be tedious to rehearse the oft-told tale of how, spurred by
misreadings of Walter Scott, and more accurate readings of Alfred
Tennyson, the British Victorians had saturated their culture with misty
notions of chivalry. Christian soldiers marched to war, and Sir Galahad's
strength was as the strength of ten because his heart was pure. The
iconography of the Pre-Raphaelites penetrated the school chapel and
the Sunday School and there cohabited with imperialism. Growing up
just after the Second World War, as I did, it was still impossible to
avoid the presence of such a mix in school textbooks and the minds of
the older teachers. John Mackenzie's researches have suggested that, so
far from declining and falling, imperialist ideology was still at its climax in
1939–45.[9] John Buchan's immensely popular First World War spy thriller
Mr Standfast (1919) had concluded with an exciting, if historically baseless,
episode in which the crippled Afrikaner air ace Peter Pienaar had saved the
Allied side from defeat in France in 1918 by taking on the gallant German
aviator Lensch and bringing him down at the cost of his own life. Though
Pienaar, a former big-game tracker in his fifties, hardly conformed to type,
it was easy to assimilate the 'knights of the air' with the conception of the
ideal imperial hero, gallant, young and presumed pure, invoked by so many
public and private memorials for the fallen of wars from the Crimean to
Flanders, suggested by prints in school halls representing Sir Galahad or
Spenser's Red Cross Knight.

The notion of a knightly chivalry of the air was potent throughout
Europe. Flying, as George L. Mosse, documenting this, has remarked,
signified the conquest of the sky, an intimation of eternity, which pointed
back to the pre-industrial ages, to innocence and Arcadia. In 1914–18
all pilots of whatever nationality ranked as officers, all were volunteers,
none were conscripted. While Von Richthofen had been a passionate
hunter in peacetime, the British probably went further than anyone else
in assimilating air war with the imperialist cult of team games.[10] The young
officer in Henry Newbolt's oft-quoted poem 'Vitaï Lampada' rallies the
ranks when the sands of the desert are sodden red, the Gatling's jammed
and the Colonel's dead, by invoking the spirit of the cricket field – 'Play
up, play up and play the game.' There were sacred and secular versions
of sportsmanship to be invoked in 1940 in connection with the Battle of
Britain. The famous newsvendors' placards which displayed Spitfire kills
as if they were cricket scores might suggest idealised versions of Hutton
opening the England innings against furious fast bowlers, or Compton
joyously smiting Australia's best, to name the rising young heroes of
the day. Or they might, closer to reality, suggest the changing-room
atmosphere of the fighter base, with men such as Bader stomping about
swearing at the Huns. Bader, before he lost his legs, had been tipped to

play for England at rugby football. Hillary, twixt and tween, recalls early in *The Last Enemy* the exploits of an undistinguished, unofficial rowing eight from Oxford University which turned up in Germany in 1938 to compete for General Goering's Prize Fours. Spurred on by German insults directed at their decadent race, they came through to win by the slimmest of margins. 'Looking back,' Hillary wrote, 'this race was really a surprisingly accurate pointer to the course of the war. We were quite untrained, lacked any form of organisation and were really quite hopelessly casual.'[11] British improvisation on ground and air, as Hillary misconstrued it, was superior to inflexible Luftwaffe tactics because of joyous traditions of youthful sportsmanship.

But more technically minded watchers, and later, readers, among the British public were enthralled by the very new traditions of manned flight and air warfare. The Spitfire itself was romantic enough, without invoking knightly jousts or Wally Hammond's fabled cover drive. When Neville Chamberlain flew to Munich to see Hitler in 1938, his choice of transport must have seemed to his older compatriots as disturbingly innovative as the release of Prosecutor Starr's report on President Clinton through the Internet did to such oldies in 1998. Though civil aviation had made progress before the Second World War, and transcontinental flights were available, few people in Britain had yet been in the air. Until the advent, well after the war was over, of the package holiday and the big passenger jet, flying remained outside normal experience and retained glamour, if no longer mystery.

In his famous book *Sagittarius Rising*, published in 1936, Cecil Lewis describes how in 1915 he bluffed his way into the Royal Flying Corps as a sixteen-year-old schoolboy. Barely old enough to register the fact when the Wright brothers made the first successful flight in a heavier-than-air machine at the end of 1903, Lewis could 'hardly remember a time when [he] was not air-minded'. At prep school he made gliders out of paper and studied the pages of *The Aero* and *Flight* magazines. By the age of thirteen, befriending a fellow fanatic, he was obsessed with making serious model aeroplanes:

> But, in spite of this passion for 'aeronautics' – as they were then called – it never occurred to me that I might be actively concerned in them. That I myself might fly a real full-sized aeroplane was beyond the bounds of the wildest possibility. Then came the War . . . The opportunity opened, and the onlooker became participant.

Training with the RFC in France enhanced Lewis's love of planes and flying and introduced him to the concept of the dogfight:

> Follow my leader with Patrick gave me my first taste of aerial fighting, getting your nose and your guns on the enemy's tail and sitting there till

you brought him down. It was a year later before I actually did any, but, from the first, the light fast single-seater scout [fighter] was my ambition. To be alone, to have your life in your own hands, to use your own skill, single-handed against the enemy. It was like the lists in the Middle Ages, the only sphere in modern warfare where a man saw his adversary and faced him in mortal combat, the only sphere where there was still chivalry and honour. If you won, it was your own bravery and skill, if you lost it was because you had met a better man . . .

As long as man has limbs and passions he will fight. Sport, after all, is only sublimated fight, and in such fighting, if you don't 'love' your enemy in the conventional sense of the term, you honour and respect him. Besides, there is, as everybody who has fought knows, a strong magnetic attraction between two men who are matched against one another. I have felt this magnetism, engaging an enemy scout three miles above the earth. I have wheeled and circled, watching how he flew, taking in the power and speed of his machine, seen him, fifty yards away, eyeing me, calculating, watching for an opening, each of us wary, keyed up to the last pitch of skill and endeavour. And if at last he went down, a falling rocket of smoke and flame, what a glorious and heroic death! What a brave man. *It might just as well have been me* . . .

So, if the world must fight to settle its differences, back to Hector and Achilles! Back to the lists! Let the enemy match a squadron of fighters against ours. And let the world look on! It is not as fanciful as you suppose. We may yet live to see it over London.[12]

Reading or re-reading this in 1940, one might have imagined that Lewis had been exactly prophetic. That was how journalists and speechmakers conceived the Battle of Britain – a 'duel of eagles' in the air between gallant young men of both sides.

Yet in fact the Battle wasn't like that. Nor was Achilles, if you read the *Iliad* carefully, quite the model that a humane person, after due consideration, could have proposed. Leaving his tent to avenge Patroclus, he performs as a serial killer, ruthlessly attacking a defenceless Trojan boy away from the battle. When he drags the dead Hector behind his chariot, his triumphalism disgusts all decent sentiment. Lewis was in fact a humane man, not a gung-ho warrior. His notion that wars might be decided by competing fighter squadrons represents a desire to return battle to the olden days of chivalry when supposedly champions in single combat could settle matters (an idea which harks back to times when warfare, for a settled tribal group, might have a ritual, ceremonial character). But even the air battles of the First World War contradicted Lewis's idealised vision of air combat, as his own pages show clearly enough. Formations of scores of fighters had engaged each other in confused combat. Of one tussle involving relatively few planes, Lewis remarks, 'It would be impossible to describe the actions of such a battle.'[13]

When he heard that the matchless Don Bradman of serial killers, Baron Manfred von Richthofen (eighty kills), had at last been felled, probably by ground fire as, like insensate Achilles, he flew low over the British lines in pursuit of a helpless victim whose guns had jammed, the British ace Mannock remarked, unchivalrously, 'I hope he roasted all the way down.'[14] The British decision to bury him themselves with full military honours was a rather touching attempt to assert the Arthurian view of aerial warfare, more formal than Adolf Galland's invitation to Douglas Bader, grounded and imprisoned in France, to join him for tea, with an assurance that he would not be interrogated, while the Germans were preparing to receive a replacement metal leg from England for that British Hector.[15] Mannock himself (credited with seventy-three kills) was a leader in the air already anticipating the anti-individualistic ethos of Leigh-Mallory's 'big wings' in 1940. 'Always possessed by an exemplary caution, to avoid unnecessary risks he would painstakingly manoeuvre to secure the best possible position from which an attack could be launched in strength.'[16] Albert Ball (forty-one victims), granted a posthumous VC, and a statue in his home town, Nottingham, was in contrast adored for his recklessness. Lewis, who was with him on his last sortie, summarised his ethos: 'Absolutely fearless, the odds made no difference to him. He would always attack, single out his man, and close. On several occasions he almost rammed the enemy, and often came back with his machine shot to pieces.'[17] And this Ajax didn't last very long. Meanwhile, his fellow knights of the air had meaner tasks to perform. A young American flying with the RAF wrote in his diary in August 1918, 'Yesterday we did ground strafing down south. That's my idea of a rotten way to pass the time . . . All the machine guns on the ground opened up and sprayed us with tracer and a few field guns took a crack at us, but we got through somehow and dropped our messages [bombs] and shot up everything we could see on the ground.'[18]

'Everything we could see' included people. The memoir-writing of the fighter pilots of 1940 was prefigured in descriptions from the 1914–18 war when allegedly knight-like single combat with visible honoured adversaries had been the norm. It is understandable that cricket-loving public opinion in 1940 should gratefully swallow, in days of great peril, the idea that their prime defenders were 'knights' or 'duellists' of the air. But why did leftish literary intellectuals, whose formation between the wars had involved bitter scepticism about modern mechanised combat, accept Hillary's book in 1942, as most seem to have done? And how could Hillary himself believe what he wrote?

I think the 'Romance of the Air' holds the answer. W.B. Yeats, mourning the death of his friend's son Major Robert Gregory, serving with the RFC in the First World War, had contributed, in 'An Irish Airman Foresees His Death', a short poem which many knew by heart:

> Nor law, nor duty bade me fight,
> Nor public men, nor cheering crowds,
> A lonely impulse of delight
> Drove to this tumult in the clouds;
> I balanced all, brought all to mind,
> The years to come seemed waste of breath,
> A waste of breath the years behind
> In balance with this life, this death.[19]

No one could have been less like a heroic aviator than the unphysical national bard of Ireland. Yet Yeats hit unerringly on formulations which represented the Spirit of Aviation as it developed between the wars. Cecil Lewis expresses this spirit in a notable passage. He is utterly disgusted with the carnage on the Somme: 'a sort of desperation was in the air. The battle had failed. The summer was over. The best men had gone.' He goes up alone on patrol 'one dreary grey morning' and rises above the clouds into a private heaven:

> Here it was still summer ... A hundred miles, north, south, east, west. Thirty thousand square miles of unbroken cloud-plains! No traveller in the desert, no pioneer to the poles had ever seen such an expanse of sand or snow. Only the lonely threshers of the sky, hidden from the earth, had gazed on it. Only we who went up into the high places under the shadow of wings![20]

After him into the air went the epic long-distance fliers of *entre deux guerres* – Alcock and Brown, then, solo, Lindbergh, Amy Johnson and Beryl Markham, who wrote in her memoirs, published in 1942, and extolled as a masterpiece by Ernest Hemingway, about how she learnt to fly in Kenya:

> After this era of great pilots is gone, as the era of great sea captains has gone – each nudged aside by the march of inventive genius, by steel cogs and copper discs and hair-thin wires on white faces that are dumb but speak – it will be found, I think, that all the science of flying has been captured in the breadth of an instrument board, but not the religion of it.
> One day, the stars will be as familiar to each man as the landmarks, the curves, and the hills on the road that leads to his door, and one day this will be an airborne life. But by then men will have forgotten how to fly; they will be passengers on machines whose conductors are carefully promoted to a familiarity with labelled buttons, and in whose minds knowledge of the sky and the wind and the way of weather will be extraneous as passing fiction.[21]

The French writer Antoine de Saint-Exupéry, born in 1900, a year after Lewis, had been a pioneer pilot in the early, dangerous days of airmail post, pitting himself with such legendary fliers as Jean Mermoz and Henri Guillaumet against the air over the Sahara and the peaks of the Andes. His prize-winning novel of 1931, *Vol de Nuit* ('Night Flight'), had been filmed by Hollywood, starring Clark Gable. Friendly with intellectuals in advanced Parisian literary circles, and respected by them, well-grounded in Nietzsche and Proust, he extended in his memoir, *Terre des Hommes* (1939) – a major bestseller as *Wind, Sand and Stars* in the United States and Britain – his religious sense of what flight meant: how it lifted men up and taught them wisdom which could be brought to earth and translated into fraternal action. 'No sum', he told his readers, 'could buy the night flight with its hundred thousand stars, its serenity, its few hours of sovereignty.' Writing of the almost unbelievable heroism of Guillaumet, who, not fearing death but for the sake of wife and friends, trekked back to the world of men after crash-landing in the remotest Andes, Saint-Exupéry rhapsodises: 'He is among those beings of great scope who spread their leafy branches willingly over broad horizons. To be a man is, precisely, to be responsible. It is to know shame at the sight of poverty which is not of our making . . . It is to feel, as we place our stone, that we are contributing to the building of the world.' George L. Mosse comments that though Saint-Exupéry 'professed himself a democrat, in reality [he] emphasized the metaphysical dimension of pre-industrial virtues, attacked the acquisition of material goods, and implicitly exalted an elitism just like that of the wartime pilots'.[22]

Hillary and the Lonely Impulse of Delight

Independently, the so-called 'Auden generation' of young British writers, not fliers themselves, had made the airman a favourite motif. As Sebastian Faulks points out in his interesting recent biographical study of Richard Hillary, they were haunted by the memory of an Italian anti-Fascist poet called Lauro de Bosis, who flew in a light plane from Marseille to Rome in October 1931 to drop political leaflets and never returned. 'A man', Faulks observes, 'was to make his point, alone, then die. His action should preferably be politically motivated, but there was a possibility that action itself could redeem.' It was not only in France that currents were tending towards the Existentialism so fashionable in the years immediately after the Second World War. The Anglo-Irish poet Cecil Day Lewis, not to be confused with the airman-author of *Sagittarius Rising*, hailed Auden himself in one poem as 'Wystan, lone flier, birdman' and produced a verse narrative 'singing' of two Australian war veterans called Parer and McIntosh, who flew from England back to the Antipodes in a written-off DC 9. Faulks further notes the significance for the Auden generation of T.E. Lawrence, 'of Arabia', who turned away from his army colonelship and public adulation to enlist in the RAF as a mere 'aircraftman'. Lawrence was an intellectual who questioned his own motives in those actions which had made him a hero, and became more truly heroic by renouncing public applause.[23]

Hillary was a well-read young man, certainly aware of the latest literary fashions. He was a fluent and effective writer who could certainly, had war not come, have fulfilled with success his ambition to be a journalist. He was fated to make his name by a book which combines elements very potent in 1942. First, there was his relatively straightforward narrative of the training, then the engagement in action, of a young Battle of Britain pilot. To this he added quasi-political musings, using a real comrade, Peter Pease, whose deeply English Christian idealism fascinates him, and an imaginary fellow student from Oxford, David, a conscientious objector working on the land who, after the Battle in which Peter Pease has died, has come to question his own decision and thinks he will join up for military service. In his windy concluding paragraphs, lone survivor of his fraternity of young pilots, the narrator sees that what he must do is write, about them, and for them, so as to justify 'at least in some measure, my right to fellowship with the dead, and to the friendship of those with courage and steadfastness who were still living and who would go on fighting until the ideals for which their comrades had died were stamped for ever on the future of civilisation'.[24]

These elements alone would have provided the material of a brief book of great interest, most likely, to the Ministry of Information. What made, and still makes, *The Last Enemy* seem exceptional is the heroic young killer's presence throughout the book as victim of battle, angrily unresigned to his status as martyr. The book begins with his agony. On 3 September 1940, flying out of Hornchurch, Hillary emerges from 'a blur of twisting machines and tracer bullets' to find a Messerschmitt below him; he attacks, hits the German plane – 'him' – with a two-second burst, then 'like a fool', lingers to 'finish him off' with another three-second burst. As the German spirals downward in flames, Hillary himself is hit by an assailant he does not see and his cockpit becomes 'a mass of flames'. He barely manages to parachute into the North Sea and his face and hands are horribly burnt. Later, we will learn of the painful months in which the pioneering plastic surgeon Archibald McIndoe gave him new eyelids and lips and released, though not completely, his clawed hands. There had been nothing in previous writing about war to prepare readers for this epic of medical science, in which Hillary is only one among hundreds treated.

How Hillary might have described the Battle of Britain had he survived without such mutilation we can barely guess. After the war was over, he might not have been attracted to the ideas, proto-Existentialist, or quasi-'Résistencialist' *à la* Saint-Exupéry, or merely gaseous, which most readers now will find an impediment to their pleasure in a fascinating narrative – though at least they also cut across the Mills-and-Boonish possibilities inherent in Hillary's close relationship, after she visits him in hospital, with the fiancée of his now-dead friend Peter Pease. I think it is unwarrantable of Sebastian Faulks to set Hillary's life in a triptych of 'fatal Englishmen' flanked by the tragic young painter Christopher Wood, who killed himself, and the brilliant post-war journalist Jeremy Woolfenden, who died aged thirty-one of alcoholism. It was indeed tragic that Hillary insisted on rejoining the RAF to fly after the success of his book, like Wilfred Owen gratuitously returning to the trench life which he had exposed so fiercely in his poetry and T.E. Lawrence abdicating from public admiration. Hillary was not fit to fly and his fatal crash was so predictable that it tempts thoughts about suicide. But unlike Wood and Woolfenden, Hillary had objective reasons to be confused and depressed, which would have applied whether or not he had been 'English'. A notably attractive young man – he is said to have lost his virginity at sixteen – he was now disfigured. He was doomed to represent, in public, as long as he lived, the fate of his comrades who had died in the Battle of Britain. He would not have had to be alert to the more morbid strains in Western philosophy to experience at times an intense 'death wish'. The guilt of the survivor alone has been enough to drive people mad.

A facile reading of Hillary's text makes him into an appropriate sacrificial martyr for a Just War which is also a People's War. The 'last of the long-haired boys', he seems to represent an insouciant, privileged pre-war generation of Oxbridge *jeunesse dorée* who perish in the Battle of Britain. Cynical about political ideals, he finds idealism. Arrogantly contemptuous of the masses, he finds that his fate has merged with theirs. In a brilliant but invented episode, he is caught in a London air raid and takes refuge in a pub. The next-door house is hit. Despite his painful hands, Hillary helps dig out a dead child and a middle-aged woman, whose face 'through the dirt and streaked blood' is 'the face of a thousand working women'. He gives her brandy from his flask. She reaches for her child, weeps, utters her dying words: 'Thank you, sir . . . I see they got you too.' In great distress, Hillary now realises that the Battle of Britain, as Peter Pease had 'instantly recognised', was a crusade against evil.[25] A cascade of rhetoric which surges from this fictional incident to the book's conclusion implies that the woman's death, mingling with memories of Peter, has inspired him directly to write what the reader has just read.

In fact, Hillary had read a sample to a publisher during his convalescence, but finished the book only after a trip to the United States. The Ministry of Information thought he might be useful for propaganda there and arranged his discreet attachment to the Air Mission in Washington. But his horrible appearance convinced the Embassy that they could not send him forth to inspire US factory workers. Unable to do anything useful, bar four anonymous broadcasts, the frustrated Hillary turned back to his book. In New York he met Antoine de Saint-Exupéry. This amiable, physically ungainly man, highly intelligent yet childlike, had lived in the USA in exile since 1940, well supported by his fame and spellbinding all who met him with his card tricks. He represented the Spirit of Aviation in person, and Sebastian Faulks suggests that Hillary imbibed sentiments from him which made him scorn life and insist on returning to the air. (As did Saint-Exupéry himself. Over-age, and physically hampered by old injuries sustained in air crashes, he died in 1944 flying for the Free French air force, probably shot down by a German fighter above the Mediterranean between Nice and Monaco.)[26]

Be that as it may, it is the dissonance between proto-Existentialist conceptions related to flying and the book's virtually propagandist conclusion which gives *The Last Enemy* some permanent interest. Hillary wears the mask which McIndoe has given him. He projects the antinomian, potentially arrogant, Spirit of Aviation, relates it to the personal arrogance for which he chides himself, and so exposes it to question. But, reciprocally, his self-projection as outsider calls into question vapid propagandist banalities. It is the thought-provoking inconsistency of the book which makes it valuable.

He might well question the notion of the flyer as independent knight-errant. He jauntily describes how, after his squadron of Spitfires has broken up in a series of dogfights, with plenty of ammunition left, he roams the skies, finds no Spitfires, but attaches himself as 'arse-End Charlie' to a squadron of Hurricanes. Suddenly he is raked by fire. Going down in a spin he tries to warn the Hurricanes, but his radio has been shot away. He finds the whole experience 'most amusing'.[27]

Reading this made Peter Townsend angry. In *Duel of Eagles* he describes a Hurricane patrol from Croydon in late August 1940:

> At eighteen thousand feet a lone Spitfire joined us. It was a foolish, almost criminal act. Our wave-lengths were different and thus we could not communicate. And, end-on, a Spitfire could be taken for an Me 109. 'Watch him very closely,' I called to our tailguard, our 'arse-end Charlies'.
>
> The controller's voice was faint. A blood-red, sinking sun stained the blue-grey haze. With the thin voice of the controller calling 'Bandits in your vicinity,' we turned aimlessly here and there and craned our necks, searching uneasily in the treacherous light . . .
>
> It was the 'Ace' who noticed the Spitfire had changed into an Me 109. 'Look out, Messerschmitts!' he yelled, and each of our sections slammed into a left hand turn, but not before the square wing tip of an Me 109 flashed by just above my head. Straightening out, my heart sank. To starboard, Hammy's Hurricane was heeling slowly over, wreathed in flame and smoke. Then it tipped downward into a five-mile plunge to earth. Only Nigger Marshall got in a shot at the Me 109. It dived abruptly into the haze, but its destruction was never confirmed.

Was Richard Hillary in that Spitfire? The height and position agree. It was only after he 'managed to pull himself together and go into a spin' that he thought of warning the Hurricanes – impossible anyway on his wave-length even if his radio had not been shot away. Hillary crash landed 'in the back garden of a Brigade cocktail party.' The timing agrees, too.

Whoever it was, we felt bitter about the Spitfire. Had it kept on the flank where we could see it, Hammy might never have died. 'If this Spitfire pilot can be identified, I would like these facts brought home to him, because his ... action contributed to the loss of one of my flight commanders,' I wrote in my combat report.[28]

The 'lonely impulse of delight' was, it seems, as treacherous a motivation in combat as the mythology of 'the knights of the air' is to the writing of sensible history about the Battle of Britain. Townsend emphasises that, ideally, effort was selfless and collective. And participants in aerial warfare ought to know rather more about the proper functions of an arse-end Charlie and the technology of radio communication than Hillary, it seems, had bothered to learn.

Notes and References

1 Paul Brickhill, *Reach for the Sky: The Story of Douglas Bader* (London, 1954), pp. 220–1.
2 Richard Hillary, *The Last Enemy* (London, 1942), pp. 130–1.
3 Peter Townsend, *Duel of Eagles* (London, 1970), pp. 361–2.
4 Hillary, *Last Enemy*, pp. 121–2.
5 Samuel Hynes, *The Soldier's Tale: Bearing Witness to Modern War* (London, 1998), p. 127.
6 Townsend, *Duel*, p. 229.
7 Laddie Lucas, *Out of the Blue: The Role of Luck in Air Warfare, 1917–1966* (London, 1987), pp. 100–2.
8 *The Times* (26 Oct., 3 Nov., 10 Nov., 11 Nov., 26 Nov. 1996).
9 John Mackenzie, *Propaganda and Empire* (Manchester, 1984), pp. 231–6 ff.
10 George L. Mosse, *Fallen Soldiers: Reshaping Memory of the World Wars* (New York, 1990), pp. 120–2.
11 Hillary, *Last Enemy*, p. 21.
12 Cecil Lewis, *Sagittarius Rising* (London, 1966), pp. 7–8, 45–6.
13 Ibid., p. 176.
14 Nigel Steel and Peter Hart, *Tumult in the Clouds: The British Experience of the War in the Air, 1914–1918* (London, 1997), pp. 320–2.
15 Brickhill, *Reach*, pp. 290–4.
16 Steel and Hart, *Tumult*, p. 324.
17 Lewis, *Sagittarius*, p. 73.
18 Neville Duke and Edward Lanchbery (eds.), *The Crowded Sky: An Anthology of Flight* (London, 1964), pp. 151–2.
19 W.B. Yeats, *The Poems*, ed. D. Albright (London, 1994), p. 184.
20 Lewis, *Sagittarius*, pp. 147, 149–50.

21 Beryl Markham, *West with the Night* (London, 1988), pp. 163–4.
22 Antoine de Saint-Exupéry *Wind, Sand and Stars*, trans. William Rees (London, 1995), pp. 21, 29; Mosse, *Fallen*, p. 123.
23 Sebastian Faulks, *The Fatal Englishman: Three Short Lives* (London, 1997), pp. 197–200.
24 Hillary, *Last Enemy*, p. 221.
25 Ibid., pp. 209–16.
26 Faulks, *Fatal Englishman*, pp. 163–6; see Curtis Cate, *Antoine de St-Exupéry* (Heinemann, 1970).
27 Hillary, *Last Enemy*, pp. 132–4.
28 Townsend, *Duel*, pp. 362–3.

TONY ALDGATE

The Battle of Britain on Film

At a press conference before the London première of the 1969 motion picture *Battle of Britain*, Squadron Leader 'Ginger' Lacey admitted that the film abounded in technical and factual errors. There were no less than 193 errors, all told, he candidly asserted. For a start, he pointed out that some of the Spitfires used in the production were, of necessity, later models than the ones actually in operation during 1940. They had, in fact, been acquired from a wide array of sources including aviation museums and flying clubs in Britain, the quaintly named American Preservation Society, the Confederate Air Force, and indeed the Spanish Air Force, which sold them to the film company and also, incidentally, provided pilots to fly them. By the time producer Harry Saltzman had assembled a fleet of 100 Spitfires or more, he had gathered together sufficient planes to constitute – allegedly – the world's thirty-fifth largest operational air power.

Having offered this initial clue as to the film's catalogue of errors, 'Ginger' Lacey then invited cinemagoers to identify the remaining mistakes once the film was released. 'Please don't write to me,' he asked, 'just try to spot the other 192.' Lacey had been a technical consultant on the film and one of seven British advisers in all, along with three Germans including Lieutenant General Adolf Galland. Like the other advisers he was a former Battle of Britain pilot and an expert on the historic events represented on the screen. He was, therefore, aware of the compromises over authenticity which had been made during the production of a film that was required to recoup its twelve-million-dollar budget and also show a profit.[1]

One looks in vain, as often as not, if one looks for signs of 'fidelity', 'reality' or 'authenticity' in a fiction or feature film such as *Battle of Britain*. Nor, usually, is there much more realism or veracity to be found in newsreels or documentaries of the Battle of Britain, whether made at the time or retrospectively. But this, of course, comes as no surprise to the historian. It is a truism, long since accepted but still worth repeating, that film is not some unadulterated reflection of historical truth captured faithfully by the camera. The reality is both mediated and constructed, invariably with some wider ideological, propagandist or commercial motives.[2]

So it proved with the film coverage of the Battle of Britain. From the contemporary representations of 1940 to the epic 1969 feature film and beyond, the 'factual' history of the Battle has been largely marginalised in favour of creating or cultivating its legend. What, then, constituted its particular cinematic construction at various key moments, and what motivated the film-makers in each instance?

The Wartime Cinema

As far as British propaganda was concerned, the Battle of Britain was in some respects a battle too soon. It was fought at a time when the Ministry of Information was still establishing itself and seeking to formulate policy after a rapid turnover of both ministers (Lord Macmillan, Sir John Reith and Alfred Duff Cooper) and heads of its Films Division (Sir Joseph Ball and Sir Kenneth Clark). With the appointment of Jack Beddington as the third Director of the Films Division in April 1940, however, the actuality film coverage of the momentous events that followed the end of the 'phoney war' – the fall of France, the evacuation from Dunkirk and the Battle of Britain – began to take on a semblance of order and a distinctive identity. A Gaumont British newsreel of 7 October 1940, for instance, contained a story entitled 'All in a Fighter's Day's Work', with a commentary read by E.V.H. Emmett:

> *Emmett*: At a moment's notice the pilots and planes of any fighter station in Britain are ready to take to the air. In a matter of seconds the sky defenders of the United Kingdom are away on what has now become a routine job, shooting down Nazis. We must never forget what a debt of gratitude we owe to this branch of the Royal Air Force. They have been destroying the enemy at the rate of four to one. Imagine what would have been our plight today if those figures had been reversed. A typical squadron under the Fighter Command returns home doing the 'victory roll'. On landing, the pilots report their bag to the Intelligence Officer:

> 'Hello. Well, here you are again.'
>   'Yes. We ran into a bunch of about fifty of them today.'
>   'What sort?'
>   'About thirty bombers and twenty escorting fighters, I should think.'
>   'What did you do? Did you get any?'
>   'We were on detail to the fighters, actually, up above. And I got a cert 110.'

'Nice work.'

'Saw two chaps bail out. And one of their parachutes unfortunately, or fortunately, didn't open. He crashed in the Thames estuary after that little do we had.'

'Did he hit you at all?'

'No, he didn't hit me . . . I believe we got off unscathed this time. We were over London quite a bit and I don't think the old place has changed a lot. There's plenty of balloons still left around there and I think Jerry's going to have a pretty tough time to make a real mess of it. Well, I think a cup of tea is indicated now, don't you?'

'Yes, good idea.'

This event was treated as an everyday affair and, in keeping with the domestic newsreel coverage of the day, exhibited the traditional British characteristics of modesty and restraint. If the commentator's words served fleetingly to highlight the RAF's successes, the pilots themselves were presented as temperamentally inclined to underplay their achievements. And though there was a modest attempt to generate a measure of visual excitement at the outset with shots of the squadron scrambling, it is noticeable that when the planes have safely returned and the score tally is taken, a calming cup of tea is called for and genially welcomed. This was doubtless intended as a reassuring and heartening message, reinforced when, in the midst of a contingent of Polish airmen, a benign and appealing dog appears – man's best friend and, like the pilots, unperturbed by the war. The 'live' interviews direct to camera, moreover, add significantly to the seeming naturalism of the proceedings.

Although this type of understatement typified British propaganda output, it would not suffice for the American newsreel companies, as the documentary series *March of Time* showed in a story entitled *Britain's RAF*, also released in October 1940. The commentary not only revealed the difference in the American approach to the subject but also demonstrated where the company's sympathies lay:

Commentator: In 1940's historic Battle of Britain, no branch of the RAF has seen more arduous active service than the Fighter Command. Under able Air Marshal Sir Hugh Dowding, the thousands of flyers, veterans and youngsters who pilot England's squadrons of deadly Spitfires and 400 mile an hour Hurricanes have become the dreaded nemesis of Adolf Hitler's highly touted Luftwaffe.

Day after day as waves of German squadrons head over England, the men of the Fighter Command taking to the skies are proving to all the world not only that their equipment is unsurpassed in speed and manoeuvrability but that the British flyer is superior to his Nazi enemy in skill, daring and experience . . . To the RAF fighter pilot has come rich reward for his months of nerve-racking strain, for his perilous hours of daily combat miles above the earth – the sure and heartening knowledge that day by day he and his fellow airmen are cutting down the numerical superiority of Nazi air power from its one time peak of five-to-one . . .

Today as the world watches the Battle of Britain, it sees England still mistress of the seas and, in over a solid year of war, the Royal Air Force still unconquered not only over Britain but in the Near East and Far East. As the Second World War spreads to new and distant spheres in late 1940, the outcome of the Battle of Britain and of the whole war itself may well depend on England's ability to maintain an uninterrupted flow of materiel, of machines, and, above all, of men who have been trained and who have the courage and the will to fight. [Assembled pilots sing 'There'll Always Be an England'.] Today, as war goes on, the Royal Air Force is the toast not only of the British Empire but of the whole democratic world. For never in all history have so few men rendered such great service to so many. Time marches on.

In addition, the audience were treated to 'action-packed' footage purporting to represent a dogfight off the coast of Dover. In fact, the British cameraman working for *March of Time*, Ray Elton, secured the shots when filming a training flight of Spitfires over the Bristol Channel to which he had been granted privileged access by the Ministry of Information. It was not Dover at all. But in the usual *March of Time* fashion this actuality material, along with shots of Air Chief Marshal Sir Hugh Dowding, and references to Bomber Command as well, were judiciously mixed with stock film footage and a stirring musical soundtrack in order to enhance the overall dramatic effect. In keeping with *March of Time*'s policy of re-enacting events whenever necessary, cinemagoers were treated to a fabricated interrogation scene in which a 'captured' Luftwaffe pilot explains he was surprised by the speed and efficiency of the British fighter planes before being shot down.

Although it was in effect a mini-feature film, it was intended to pass as reportage and caused something of a furore among British newsreel companies who complained bitterly that they were being denied the opportunities for filming that Ray Elton enjoyed on behalf of *March of Time*. In the opinion of one recent British historian, Michael Paris, 'this short film tried to cover too many aspects of the work of the RAF to be effective'. But the essential point about the film is that it was intended principally for American consumption and was released to cinemagoers there at a time when the United States was still ostensibly neutral. Hence the fact that *March of Time* enjoyed priority over the British newsreels at this juncture.[3]

Such efforts were succeeded in the United States by Colonel Frank Capra's fifty-minute documentary film *The Battle of Britain* (1943) for his influential *Why We Fight* series. Though released after the United States had entered the war and intended primarily for the orientation of American troops, many of the films in his series were given widespread theatrical distribution and the series was awarded an Oscar. Capra was helped throughout by British Information Services in New York, where channels were opened between his Signal Corps Special Services Film Unit and the Ministry of Information Films Division through Capra's able British assistant, Pamela Wilcox. The daughter of the eminent film producer Herbert Wilcox, she had been seconded from her work with John Grierson at the National Film Board of Canada.[4]

As a result, the Americans produced stirring stuff. But they were quickly matched by British film propaganda, not least in celebrating the Battle of Britain as a morale-boosting victory. The feature film companies, understandably, were intent on glamorising the event and nowhere more so than in *Dangerous Moonlight* (1941) and *The First of the Few* (1942). The former, in truth, used the Battle of Britain as mere backdrop to a romantic and melodramatic story in which Anton Walbrook plays a Polish composer and concert pianist who escapes from Warsaw in 1939, lives fleetingly if successfully in America where he marries a journalist (played by Sally Gray), but then decides to forsake his career, return across the Atlantic, enrol in the RAF and take part in the Battle of Britain.

Directed for RKO British Productions by the accomplished Brian Desmond Hurst, the film was especially notable for its theme music, the Warsaw Concerto, which was composed by Richard Addinsell. Though *Dangerous Moonlight* included actuality film of aerial combat, it was the love story and the evocative musical background that captivated cinemagoers. While the *Sunday Times* critic dutifully recounted that it was 'worth seeing for its authentic shots of air battles', Mass Observation respondents repeatedly maintained that the film was enjoyable first and foremost, as one 32-year-old clerk from Westcliff-on-Sea remarked, for its 'fine acting, good music'. But even in its rhapsodic or overly sentimental moments, the storyline allowed Anton Walbrook plenty of opportunity to highlight 'the conflict between love and duty, between personal desire and patriotism', and to wax lyrical about the romance of the air, the spirit of aviation and the cult of the flyer.[5]

The First of the Few was equally popular with audiences and an even bigger hit with the critics, turning out to be the most successful British film of 1942, and second only in box office terms to Hollywood's *Mrs Miniver*. Starring Leslie Howard, who also directed, it co-starred David Niven and the musical score was composed by William Walton. A somewhat fictional biopic, it told the story of R.J. Mitchell, the creator of the Spitfire, who had died in 1937, but had lived to see his celebrated fighter adopted by the Air Ministry. William Whitebait of the *New Statesman* extolled its virtues:

> *The First of the Few* has been made into something of an English occasion; and memorable it is, as a film, and patriotic in a true sense. Why don't

we at all times – in peace as well as war – make more of our modern heroes and legends? Lawrence of Arabia seems one of the obvious choices for a film director of talent. The producers of *The First of the Few* have celebrated an almost unknown name in R.J. Mitchell, the designer of the Spitfire. He sprawls on a sea-cliff and watches the streamlining of the gulls; works away from the current box-and-string ideals in flying; builds strange all-of-a-piece craft for Schneider races; and kills himself working to put his Spitfires in the air before it is too late. Leslie Howard gives one of his admirable performances in this dedicated life. Who could better convey the seclusion, amiability, dreaminess and courage required of the part? The only trouble is that in the earlier parts of the film, with a succession of new planes and Schneider races, the tension sags and Mr. Howard gives us once more a perfect portrayal of Leslie Howard. I don't mean this as too serious a criticism, because acting so accomplished brings its own delight, but it isn't till the tragic end approaches that we feel for R.J. Mitchell something of what Paul Muni once made us feel for Zola. This is a sincere, exciting, well-constructed and well-acted English film. Walton's music deserves special recommendation. His fugal movement for the assembling of parts of the Spitfire adds immensely to the most moving sequence in the film.[6]

But the cumulative effect of the film's creative and artistic endeavours was perhaps best shown in an impressive and stirring climax where, after a victorious dogfight at the height of the Battle of Britain, Niven leads his flight into silhouette against the skyline, opens his cockpit hood, looks to the heavens and says in tribute to the aircraft's designer, 'They can't take the Spitfire, Mitch, they can't take 'em.'

In the wartime context such idealised heroics were understandable enough in view of the propaganda requirements of the hour. And, of course, they helped to consolidate the legend of the Battle of Britain.

The Post-War Cinema

During the 1950s some critics professed amazement at the popularity and proliferation of the war film genre in Britain. As Leslie Mallory, the film critic of the *News Chronicle*, put it:

The most baffling attribute of the British picturegoer is his capacity for enjoying widescreen war fables which he knows to be sacrilegious pantomimes of the conflict he personally lived through ... Only an ass would object to a well-made war film which tells its story credibly. But studio after studio is clambering on the battlewagon with chunks of pseudo-reportage which are being hawked to audiences as 'true hero' tales ... Air war, as Pinewood [Studios] sees it, is Wing-Commander Kenneth More soaring through the blue with merry quip and jest.[7]

William Whitebait in the *New Statesman*, though equally lamenting the addiction to war films, was more circumspect and astute:

A dozen years after World War II we find ourselves in the really quite desperate situation of being not sick of war, but hideously in love with it. Not actively fighting, we aren't at peace. The H-bomb looms ahead, and we daren't look at it; so we creep back to the lacerating comfort of 'last time'. No old general preparing to lose the next war could dream more disastrously. And I think that war films, nearly all of which hark back emotionally as well as factually, contribute more than any other source to this daydream; because if the horror of war strikes the eye more than any other way, so does its glossing over lull fears and angers, and creates an imaginary present in which we can go on enjoying our finest hours. That is a price paid for victory.

So while we 'adventure' at Suez, in the cinemas we are still thrashing Rommel – and discovering that he was a gentleman – sweeping the Atlantic of submarines, sending the few to scatter Goering's many. The more we lose face in the world's counsels, the grander, in our excessively modest way, we swell in this illusionary mirror held up by the screen. It is less a spur to morale than a salve to wounded pride; and as art or entertainment, dreadfully dull.[8]

Lewis Gilbert's 1956 film *Reach for the Sky* exemplified the tendency towards 'true hero' tales in its account of the life and travails of the legless air ace Douglas Bader, played by Kenneth More. The film was hopelessly adulatory in tone, with Bader seen to be responsible, virtually alone, for devising and instituting the airborne tactics that were eventually employed by Air Vice-Marshal Trafford Leigh-Mallory's 'big wing' at 12 Group. The film's general air of self-congratulation, not to mention its altogether uncritical approach, were symptomatic of the cloying complacency and insularity that overcame the British cinema during the 1950s, and were redolent of a film industry in the doldrums.

By 1967, when production started on *Battle of Britain*, much had changed. The broader social and political context had altered considerably as a result of American involvement in Vietnam, the emergence of a powerful anti-war lobby, widespread student protest, and the onset of a 'cultural revolution' in Britain. War films were no longer in vogue or as popular as they had previously been at the box office. The producers of the film, Harry Saltzman amd Benjamin Fisz, were as adamant as former film-makers in celebrating the Battle of Britain as an event of legendary import, but there was now an emphasis on a measure of historical revisionism and, indeed, upon a revision in part of the war film genre. The Scottish novelist and scriptwriter James Kennaway, who died in a car crash nine months before the film opened, self-consciously fashioned his screenplay to reflect a more downbeat approach to war.[9]

The result was a film which attempted to address several key issues, sometimes contentious, which had hitherto been submerged in stereotyped cinematic conventions. Nods and gestures these attempts might have been, but they were significant in their way. The role of the Women's Auxiliary Air Force was foregrounded, for example, as also was the role of Czech and Polish fighter squadrons and, crucially, the significance of radar. There was also reference to the value of plastic surgery in rebuilding pilots' faces, bodies and lives. Bill Foxley, one of the original wartime 'guinea pigs' of the plastic surgeon Sir Archibald McIndoe, was brought into the production to play a part in an RAF plotting-room scene. Damaged and grounded pilots had often been used in this way.[10]

Where previously, in *Reach for the Sky*, Kenneth More had portrayed Douglas Bader as jauntily devising the tactics and strategy that won the Battle, cinema audiences were now given some indication of the inner wranglings over the conduct of the Battle between Leigh-Mallory, Air Vice-Marshal Park and the commander-in-chief of Fighter Command, Air Chief Marshal Dowding. Also featured were an element of conflict between the RAF's needs and the Prime Minister's wants, and a hint of dissent in the lower ranks. Of course, it helped considerably that distinguished and experienced British actors such as Laurence Olivier, Patrick Wymark and Trevor Howard lent gravitas to the proceedings in the roles of Dowding, Leigh-Mallory and Park, respectively. The overall effect of the film was also enhanced by the fine aerial photography from Skeets Kelly and John Jordan, as well as a superb musical score composed, in part, by William Walton, whose 'Battle in the Air' piece was used in a brilliantly edited sequence that served as a fitting climax to the scenes of aerial combat.

The film, however, did not do as well at the box office as was hoped or expected. There was, perhaps, too much of an obvious history lesson about it for the average cinemagoer's liking. The critics were generally lukewarm and David Wilson spoke for many of them when he wrote: 'It was obvious that a British made, American financed, late Sixties tribute to our finest hour would not turn out simply another *Reach for the Sky*; so the film is circumspect, defused, anti-heroic, with the emphasis firmly place on the battles in the air rather than the personalities on the ground.'[11] Yet even for the aviation enthusiasts the 193 errors to which 'Ginger' Lacey had referred militated against its claims to authenticity. But whatever its flaws, *Battle of Britain* is as rich a source on the subject as historians are likely to find on film. If nothing else, as the actress Susannah York explained in an interview about her scene with Bill Foxley, the burned airman, the film brought home some of the harsh realities of the Battle:

> It was the first time I had ever come really close to a man who has had his face burned and I knew there was one thing I mustn't do, and that was not look him straight in the eye. So I did that. He held out his

hand and I took it. And that was the moment, I think, when something changed gear in me. I hadn't realized that his hands had been so badly burned. I only heard afterwards about how Battle of Britain pilots used to take their gloves off to get better control of their planes, and then – when the fire started – they … Anyway, I took his hand and I realized what the whole ordeal must have been like. And then, each time we met after that, he would still hold out that deformed hand, and I would still take it, I would still look him straight in the face, and suddenly – well, suddenly he wasn't a man who was burned any more, but the nice man he is under the skin. We were suddenly in communication, and it wasn't just between a man and a woman, but between a different generation, a different kind of experience.[12]

Notes and References

1 See, for instance, the report by Margaret Hinxman, quoting Lacey and others, in 'The Few, Three Decades Later', *Sunday Telegraph* (16 June 1969); found on the microfiche collection for *Battle of Britain*, British Film Institute (BFI) Library, London. Extensive background on the film's production is also provided in Leonard Mosley, *Battle of Britain* (London, 1969).

2 The literature on 'Film and History' is now considerable, but the following sources deal, especially, with the value of film as historical evidence: J.A.S. Grenville, *Film as History* (Birmingham, 1971), and Anthony Aldgate, *Cinema and History* (London, 1979). For extensive analysis of film coverage during the Second World War see, in particular, Anthony Aldgate and Jeffrey Richards, *Britain Can Take It: The British Cinema in the Second World War*, 2nd ed. (Edinburgh, 1994), and James Chapman, *The British at War: Cinema, State and Propaganda, 1939–45* (London, 1998).

3 Michael Paris, *From the Wright Brothers to Top Gun: Aviation, Nationalism and Popular Cinema* (Manchester, 1995), p. 129. Although too easily dismissing the *March of Time* item, Paris's account deals astutely and convincingly with the subsequent film coverage of the Battle of Britain. *Britain's RAF* was released in the United States in Oct. 1940 (vol. 7, issue 2) and given a British release in Nov. 1940. For background on both the series and this story, in particular, see Raymond Fielding, *The March of Time 1935–1951* (New York, 1978), pp. 254, 339. The story was also used in a Flashback production, 'Not Quite Alone', Channel 4, 15 Oct. 1986. This included an interview with Ray Elton, in which he explained the consternation it caused among British newsreel companies. For more on the Newsreel Association's jealousy of the special treatment afforded to the *March of Time* see the excellent account by Nicholas John Cull, *Selling War: The British Propaganda Campaign Against American 'Neutrality' in World War II* (New York, 1995), p. 52.

4 This is explored at length by Anthony Aldgate, 'Creative Tensions: *Desert Victory*, the Army Film Unit and Anglo-American Rivalry, 1943–5', in Philip M. Taylor (ed.), *Britain and the Cinema in the Second World War* (Basingstoke, 1988), pp. 144–67, and Anthony Aldgate, 'National Pride and Prejudices: *Tunisian Victory*', in *Britain Can Take It*, pp. 299–325.

5 See the reactions to the film cited in Jeffrey Richards and Dorothy Sheridan

(ed.), *Mass Observation at the Movies* (London, 1987), pp. 231–2, 233, 238, 259, 271 and 288. For the *Sunday Times* review see the microfiche on *Dangerous Moonlight*, BFI Library, London. James Chapman also analyses the film in *The British at War*, pp. 197–8. For background on its production and the strained relations between Walbrook and Hurst see Stephen Bourne, *Brief Encounters: Lesbians and Gays in British Cinema 1930–1971* (London, 1996), pp. 5–55. Bourne considers the film a 'gay classic' in view of the number of gay men who worked on it: Hurst and Rodney Ackland wrote the script, the gowns were by Cecil Beaton, the music was composed by Richard Addinsell and Anton Walbrook was the leading man. There were also candid interviews with former servicemen, including Battle of Britain pilots, on the theme of homosexuality during the war in 'Sex and War', *Timewatch*, BBC, Oct. 1998.

6 *New Statesman* (29 Aug. 1942).
7 Quoted in James Chapman, 'Our Finest Hour Revisited: The Second World War in British Feature Films since 1945', *Journal of Popular British Cinema*, 1 (1998), pp. 68–9.
8 Ibid., pp. 70–1.
9 Kennaway finally shared the scriptwriting credit with William Greatorex. But his downbeat and highly individualistic approach to military subjects, perhaps born of his National Service experiences on the Rhine, had already been shown in his 1956 novel, *Tunes of Glory*, which he then turned into a screenplay for Ronald Neame's 1960 film of the same title, starring Alec Guinness and John Mills. For more on Kennaway, see Trevor Royle, *James and Jim* (Edinburgh, 1983), and Susan Kennaway's published collection of her late husband's 'diaries' and letters, along with her own account of their marriage, in James and Susan Kennaway, *The Kennaway Papers* (London, 1981).
10 The story of Sir Archibald McIndoe's pioneering plastic surgery unit at East Grinstead had figured briefly in a 1950s BBC television drama starring Peter Murray, which was loosely based upon Richard Hillary's *The Last Enemy* (1942), which describes his own harrowing experiences. It also resurfaced as the background to a 1990s ITV series, *A Perfect Hero*, scripted by Alan Prior, with Nigel Havers in the lead role and James Fox as a fictitious plastic surgeon 'Angus Meikle'. Hillary is one of the subjects studied in Sebastian Faulks, *The Fatal Englishman: Three Short Lives* (London, 1996), pp. 109–208. There is more detailed background on McIndoe in Leonard Mosley, *Faces from the Fire* (London, 1962). For the advances made in wartime plastic surgery and their impact on post-war cosmetic surgery, see Elizabeth Haiken, *Venus Envy* (Baltimore, 1997). The Ministry of Information commissioned a 26-minute colour film in 1944, *Plastic Surgery in Wartime*, which covered the work done for civilian and military casualties at one of the Ministry of Health's special plastic and facio-maxillary centres, but it did not deal specifically with Battle of Britain pilots. It was produced by the Realist Film Unit, directed by John Taylor, and photographed in Technicolor by Jack Cardiff, who discusses his work on the film in *Magic Hour: The Life of a Cameraman* (London, 1966), pp. 73–4.
11 *Monthly Film Bulletin* (Nov. 1969), p. 228.
12 Quoted in Mosley, *Battle of Britain*, p. 183.

ADRIAN GREGORY

The Commemoration of the Battle of Britain

1940 was and is 'memorable'. Few adult Britons and relatively few children would not be able to recognise its significance. The year is remembered as a connected series of dramatic events: Dunkirk, the Battle of Britain and the Blitz. The Battle of Britain stands at the centre of the sequence. It was an air battle of an unprecedented type and one that could be assimilated into the 'Island Story'. But herein lies a mystery. The Battle of Britain has been widely commemorated, but it has never been commemorated with the intensity that it arguably justifies and which might have been anticipated. 15 September – Battle of Britain Day – has, for example, never come close to matching the reverence with which 11 November – Armistice Day – was marked in the interwar years.[1] Some of the reasons for this are obvious. The First World War touched directly far greater numbers than the Battle of Britain. But this does not seem adequate reason. Revisionism notwithstanding, the Battle was a significant victory: amongst the two or three truly important British successes in any major war. Even if it did not prevent invasion, it was the first clear-cut defeat of the Third Reich and the only defeat Germany suffered between September 1939 and December 1941. As such it had an overwhelming moral importance. Moreover, while the outcome of the Battle of Britain did not guarantee victory in the war, it provided, like the Battle of Trafalgar, a measure of security from which victory could be pursued. But in contrast to the navy's celebration of Trafalgar, the Battle of Britain has never become central to the institutional memory of the RAF.

There are several roots to this problem. The founder of the RAF, Lord Trenchard, argued that it was wrong to commemorate a battle that had come to be so closely associated with one Command: Fighter Command. It also seems likely that he had difficulty coming to terms with the fact that his service's greatest achievement was a 'mere' defensive victory which consisted of ascertaining the enemy's intentions and thwarting them.

Dowding's role in the Battle was particularly problematic. The fighter chief became increasingly difficult for the regular RAF mind to fathom. An unorthodox figure, he was known to rail against the sporting, unimaginative, public-school 'hearties' who dominated the services. Furthermore, his deep interest in spiritualism and, above all, his passionate commitment to animal rights must have seemed baffling to his church-parading and fox-hunting peers.[2] His marriage to the much younger widow of a junior officer, herself a strong personality, added to his alienation. The wonder is not so much that he was dismissed in 1940 after the Battle, but that he ever rose to a significant command at all: his sheer competence being the best explanation. In his own lifetime Dowding must have appeared – bluntly – to have been a crank.

The RAF was therefore left with a dilemma. On the one hand the commemoration of the Battle of Britain was useful in terms of the publicity it generated, but on the other it was a Battle which was associated with a notorious oddball, who some thought had been treated badly by the RAF, and who retained the loyalty of the overwhelming majority of his men: his 'chicks' as he called them. The fact that Dowding almost lived to see the thirtieth anniversary of the Battle must have compounded the problem.

There was also some ambivalence on the part of the post-war government. It would be unfair to suggest that Labour was hostile to commemorating the Battle, but the mythology of the 'People's War', which had played a role in bringing the party to power, probably made it cautious about appearing to elevate it too much. The very reasons which had made the 'few' so rhetorically appealing to Churchill in 1940 – the elite to whom the 'many' owed a debt – would render them unsuitable as an image of popular struggle. The great man was also, inevitably, part of the problem. How could Labour build up the memory of a battle associated so closely with the Leader of the Opposition?

Battle of Britain Day, 1945

The first Battle of Britain commemoration in peacetime was celebrated as the war in the Far East was coming to an end. The commemoration was therefore tied to the thanksgiving week celebrations for the end of hostilities. It was to be held in two parts. 15 September, Battle of Britain Day, the day which was considered to have marked the turning-point in the Battle, fell on a Saturday and was to be marked by the opening of RAF stations for an 'at home' and a grand fly-past over London. This was to be followed on the Sunday by a service at Westminster Abbey.

The organisation of an 'at home' by the RAF represented a return to peacetime practice. Such activities had been popular in the 1930s, particularly the Hendon air display. Ninety RAF stations were opened to the public and the open days appear to have been a considerable success. They were attended by 'many hundreds of thousands' and proceeds from programme sales were donated to the RAF Benevolent Fund.

The fly-past – which is depicted in the closing scene of *Reach for the Sky* – consisted of RAF squadrons drawn from Fighter Command. The planes were current service models including the new Meteor jet fighters. *The Times*'s aeronautical correspondent noted with regret the absence of any Hurricanes, retired from squadron service in 1944. The weather conditions were poor and low-lying cloud prevented the operation from being carried out at the intended height of 4,000 feet. But this simply made the spectacle more exciting because the fly-past took place instead at 1,000 feet. The formation was led by Douglas Bader, newly returned from Colditz, and included many other veterans. The squadrons formed up over North Weald and flew in over the East End, still devastated from wartime bombing. The Prime Minister, Clement Attlee, sent a message of thanks: 'Congratulations to Fighter Command on the magnificent flight over London. All who saw it were greatly impressed by the triumphant sweep of the squadrons led by some of those who five years ago won immortal glory in the defence of our capital and in the fight for freedom for all peoples.'

The service in Westminster Abbey drew a far larger congregation than was anticipated and, in the words of *The Times*'s disgruntled correspondent, the Air Ministry had 'apparently made no arrangements for the service to be reported'. As a result his description of the proceedings is somewhat patchy. He could not, for example, hear the Dean of Winchester's sermon. The nave was occupied by men of the RAF, Dominion and Allied air services and women from the auxiliary services. Immense crowds lined the route to the Abbey and 'seemed to have increased rather than diminished after the service'. The King did not attend in person, but was represented by Air Chief Marshal Ludlow Hewitt. Clement Attlee was, however, among the congregation. The music included the national anthem and Kipling's recessional. If a specifically 'Labour' element was present in the proceedings, it was to be found in the procession, which included 'work people from the aircraft industry' as well as units from AA Command and the Home Guard. This suggests an awareness that the best way to counteract the risk of an 'elitist' commemoration was to stress that Fighter Command was the spearhead of a much larger national effort.

London was certainly the centre of the commemoration, but elsewhere there had been efforts to mark the anniversary. Expectations were not, however, always fulfilled. Kenneth Adam expressed his disappointment in *The Times* on 18 September:

Your reporter's experience in Westminster Abbey prompts me to describe the disappointment of a party attending Matins in Canterbury Cathedral yesterday. The party included my two children, both of them old enough to know something of the meaning of the anniversary, and attending a service in the Cathedral for the first time, two RAF officers who had their own reasons for thanksgiving, three Londoners all of whom narrowly escaped death in the air raids, and an American business man with a deep love for Britain. The service held was largely inaudible to those who sat at the eastern end ... The sermon was on the New Guinea Mission, a worthy cause, but not the one which we had been led to believe we were celebrating.

This criticism prompted a reply from Dean Hewlett Johnson the following day:

The evening service, which is in the sole charge of the Dean, was devoted to the Battle of Britain. Before a congregation exceedingly large, special prayers took the place of ordinary prayers and I myself preached entirely on our deliverance at the hands of the small but valiant Air Force, in which my own nephew, under 21 years of age, fought from first to last. Describing as graphically as I could what I had seen with my own eyes, I expressed my conviction that by their valiant deeds our fighters had saved Britain and saved civilization. After myself seeing the camp at Oswiecim [interestingly the Polish name for Auschwitz is used], I know the fate which would have been in store for us apart from that deliverance. Their deed saved the world from the most terrible attack ever made on the fellowship of men.

This explicit linkage of the Battle of Britain with the defeat of Nazi genocide was unusual. Although it was no doubt strongly implicit in 1945 when the memory of the liberation of the concentration camps was still fresh, the meaning of the Battle has generally been perceived as a defence of the British people against tyranny.

The Battle of Britain Chapel

Westminster Abbey also became the site of the major Battle of Britain memorial. St Paul's Cathedral had, on the surface, a far stronger association with the events of 1940: it had provided some of the most memorable images of the Blitz, indeed of the entire war, through the photography of Herbert Mason. The choice of the Abbey can, however, be explained on symbolic and practical grounds. Westminster Abbey was symbolically a national, rather than a purely 'London' cathedral, and it was already home to the Tomb of the Unknown Warrior. On practical grounds, it had an available side chapel.

The Battle of Britain Chapel, which had been built under the Tudors, was dedicated on 10 July 1947, the seventh anniversary of the official start of the Battle. It was dedicated to all the men of the RAF who had died during the period of the Battle. The principal feature of the memorial was a stained-glass window, designed by Hugh Easton, consisting of forty-eight lights, which was paid for by voluntary subscription. The lower lights of the window contained the badges of the sixty-three squadrons of Fighter Command cited in Dowding's final dispatch on the Battle. The inner panels depict the Royal Arms and the badge of the RAF. The flags of Canada, New Zealand, South Africa, Poland, Belgium and Czechoslovakia and the United States are also incorporated.

Several panels display a Christian theme. In one a Squadron Leader kneels before the Child Christ, who raises his hand in blessing. The Virgin Mary stands behind. Below, the Virgin is represented in her sorrow, with the dead Christ across her knees, a classic Pietà. This, according to the programme of unveiling, symbolises 'the mothers and widows of those who lost their lives'. Kneeling to this vision is a Flying Officer. On the opposite side of the window a Sergeant Pilot is portrayed, his head bowed before the vision of Christ crucified. This symbolises the sacrifice of the pilot himself. Above, is the vision of the resurrection as seen by a Pilot Officer, with Christ carrying the banner of the Resurrection, a banner similar to that of St George. Here, the programme explains, is 'the pilot's triumph'. At the foot of the window appear Shakespeare's words: 'We few, we happy few, we band of brothers.'

The memorial as a whole is a powerful restatement of the theme of redemptive sacrifice. Indeed, it is probably the strongest example of the synthesis between Christian and patriotic tradition of all British war memorials. Catherine Moriarty has made us aware of the pervasive Christian iconography of First World War memorials, but few go as far as this explicit association of a military event with Holy Week.[3] Whether this should be seen as the co-option of religion by patriotism, or vice versa, is a moot point. The Church of England was, however, increasingly drawing war commemoration into its control.[4]

The Roll of Honour, which was presented to the Abbey by Bruce Ingham, was written on parchment and bound in leather. It contained the names of 1,495 pilots and aircrew. These included not only 449 members of Fighter Command, but also 718 in Bomber Command, 280 in Coastal Command, 14 in other commands and 34 members of the Fleet Air Arm.

The Battle of Britain Memorial Service

With the creation of the Memorial Chapel, the commemorative service in the Abbey could be fixed in form. The programme for the Battle of Britain Sunday service in 1965, the twenty-fifth anniversary of the Battle, displayed some unusual features because of the special occasion, but it incorporated many characteristics of the regular Abbey service.

At 9.00 a.m. the RAF ushers were to arrive at the Abbey. At 9.30 the central band of the RAF, the Queen's colour squadron, the lining party, the ensign party and the RAF police were to report for duty. BBC and ITV personnel were also due to appear in order to set up their equipment. This was unusual: generally the event was not televised. At 10.00 the lining party was to take up position and at 10.10 the west door was opened to ticket holders. VIPs were to take their seats between 10.30 and 10.45. At 10.53 the newly widowed Lady Churchill was to arrive and at 10.57 the Queen.

The ensign party, escorted by twenty Battle of Britain aircrew, which was somewhat more than usual, was then to march up the centre aisle. At the Lantern aisles, the ensign party was to advance to the steps of the high altar, whilst the veterans peeled off to both sides to take their seats. At 11.05 the national anthem was to be sung and the service begin.

The Battle of Britain Memorial Flight

In the meantime, in the late 1950s the Air Ministry had begun to consider the possibility of another memorial. One suggestion was the preservation of Biggin Hill, where a museum might be established. Another was that the Battle 'should pass into the currency of the English Language in the same way as Trafalgar and Waterloo', by renaming London landmarks: one option was to name the new London Bridge 'Battle of Britain Bridge'. A further proposal was the preservation of a Spitfire and a Hurricane as a static display in central London.[5] What eventually developed was a permanent flying tribute to the Battle.

In 1957 three Spitfires and a Hurricane had been brought together as the RAF's Historic Aircraft Flight. These planes participated in the Battle of Britain fly-past over London. However, the forced landing of a Spitfire on a cricket pitch at Bromley in 1959 led to the discontinuation of the fly-past. The Flight was then mainly used at Battle of Britain open days, the number of which was falling during the 1960s.

The film *Battle of Britain* reinvigorated the Flight. The film company hired the planes and paid for the restoration of several others. One of the planes restored was Spitfire P7350, a veteran of the Battle which had entered squadron service in August 1940. A second Hurricane also joined from Hawkers. In 1969 the Flight was officially renamed the Battle of Britain Memorial Flight. During 1973 it performed at eighty air displays around the country. In 1987 the Flight reached its peak strength of seven fighters.

The Battle of Britain Fighter Association

The Battle of Britain Fighter Association (BBFA) was not formed until some time after the war. It had its origins in the fact that many men were claiming to belong to the 'few' without adequate credentials. Claims for membership of the 'few' were clearly laid out in the qualification for the Battle of Britain Clasp to the 1939–45 service medal. Those entitled to the clasp were those who had carried out a sortie with one of the qualifying fighter squadrons during the period of the Battle as defined in Dowding's final dispatch. The qualifying period was 10 July to 31 October 1940. The question of who was an official Battle of Britain pilot was reasonably clear in theory but muddy in practice. The Air Ministry failed to impose adequate checks on clasp holders and as a result there were many unqualified individuals claiming the status of veterans of the Battle. An informal meeting of veterans was held at Shepherd's Hotel in London in 1948, a favourite wartime Fighter Command haunt, to try to bring some order to the situation, but no formal organisation was established for several years.

Meanwhile, veterans of the Battle who were still in the RAF had taken to holding an annual reunion on 15 September. Dates and location are uncertain, but one such dinner was definitely organised in London for 1947.[6] These dinners were regularly attended by Dowding and Sir Keith Park, the former commander of 11 Group. With the support of a serving RAF officer, Basil Embry, by the early 1950s the venue for these reunions had been established at Fighter Command HQ, Bentley Priory, and the event had an organising committee. Documentation is scanty, but it is fairly clear that the reunions also came to include veterans retired from the service. At this time the organisation was known as the 'Battle of Britain Pilots' Reunion' and an official tie was commissioned. When Embry retired from the RAF, the dinner at Bentley Priory was replaced for a few years by an annual cocktail party at Biggin Hill, and then transferred to the RAF Club in Piccadilly.

The BBFA was formally established in March 1958. The first 'life president' was Dowding, who died in 1970. He was succeeded by Park until his death in 1975. A.R.D. MacDonell (who flew with 64 Squadron during the Battle) served as chairman from 1959 to 1978 and was succeeded by Christopher Foxley-Norris (3 Squadron). Tom Gleave (253 Squadron) was the secretary for thirty-five years. The association's patron was, and still is, the Queen Mother. The purposes of the association were to celebrate the comradeship of the veterans, to honour Dowding, and to commemorate the Battle and those who died in it. In the late 1950s the annual dinner was held at the RAF Reserves Club, but in 1960 it resumed at Bentley Priory, where it was held until 1980, when remodelling at the former HQ forced a relocation to West Drayton. It returned to Bentley Priory in the mid-1980s.

During the 1960s the routine of the annual reunion on 15 September was fairly fixed. The BBFA committee would first meet at the Air Ministry. In mid-afternoon, Dowding, accompanied by an RAF chaplain and representatives of the association, would lay a wreath at the RAF memorial on the embankment. The activity was clearly strenuous for the ageing Dowding, but his sense of duty to the memory of his 'chicks' was strong. In 1961 he was suffering from bad arthritis, but still struggled up to London.[7] The BBFA would then assemble at Bentley Priory at 6.30 p.m. At 7.30 the association would hold its AGM and at 8.15 dinner would commence.[8] The event was usually attended by 120–200 veterans, which was roughly half the membership.

At the reunion in 1963 the question of dates was discussed. MacDonell was strongly of the view that the convention of meeting on 15 September should be strictly observed, but he agreed to canvass the membership after some put forward the view that a weekend reunion would be preferable. A questionnaire was included with the regular BBFA newsletter. Of the 140 members who responded, 105 were in favour of retaining 15 September for the meeting and only 25 were in favour of changing the date to the Saturday preceding Battle of Britain Sunday.[9]

1965 marked the silver anniversary of the Battle and the BBFA turned its thoughts towards a more permanent commemoration. The impetus for this came in fact from outside the association. In the autumn of 1964 a Mr Sandom and Mr Strathearn contacted the association to canvass support for the creation of a 'Battle of Britain Trust Fund'. Strathearn worked in advertising and public relations and drew up a putative glossy pamphlet for the fund: 'Of course we all spare an occasional thought for THE FEW. But more than an occasional thought is needed. Few they were, but always just that one too many for the bereaved – their mourning parents, their widows, their children yet unborn. We invite you to help repay that debt.'[10] The fund was to be used for a chapel and museum at Biggin Hill and for a 'living memorial' in the form of youth scholarships in aeronautics.

The motives of these two men are hard to fathom: they might well have been genuinely grateful members of the public who wished to honour the men of Fighter Command. The BBFA, Air Ministry and the Royal Air Force Association (RAFA) were, however, deeply suspicious of their proposals, some representatives suspecting a commercial scam. More to the point, the proposals looked likely to cut across established service charities. A meeting was held under the aegis of the RAFA in December 1964 to co-ordinate a response. It was resolved to contact Sandom and Strathearn in order to 'stop or delay the launching of the appeal'. If this failed, authorisation was given for the issue of a joint statement by the RAFA, the Air Ministry and the BBFA distancing the organisations from the appeal.[11] This apparently saw off the proposal,[12] but the association took the precaution of registering the title 'Battle of Britain Trust Fund' to pre-empt any similar ideas.

This outside initiative did, however, prompt a certain amount of reflection on what the BBFA itself planned to do for the anniversary. Gleave discussed the idea of a memorial with Dowding, who favoured the foundation of a Battle of Britain Memorial Home for Airmen. In a letter to the RAF Benevolent Fund, Gleave supported this idea on the grounds that 'few people nowadays have much interest in any form of memorial which does not produce some tangible practical return for the money', but added that such a project might 'cut across the objects of other institutions or associations' and subsidise 'what is in fact the responsibility of the state'.[13]

In the event, the new initiatives in 1965 were organised outside the BBFA and consisted of celebrations. On 20 September the City of London held a Battle of Britain reception at the Guildhall. The Honourable Artillery Company attended in full dress uniform and a Spitfire was placed on a dais in the hall. Ten days later the RAFA organised a Battle of Britain ball at the Dorchester. It was a lively affair: 1,500 guests consumed 900 bottles of champagne and 500 bottles of wine. Among those who attended were the Prime Minister, Harold Wilson, and the Leader of the Opposition, Edward Heath.[14] Unfortunately, Lord Dowding was unable to attend: he slipped leaving his club for the reception and broke his thigh.

The anniversary inspired grateful tributes to those who had fought in the Battle. The BBFA was sent an unsolicited poem from a Raymond Candy, who had served as a fireman during the Blitz:

> A quarter of a century has gone
> Since Britain and Freedom stood alone
> And 'the Few of' the Royal Air Force
> Put the Luftwaffe totally off its course . . .
>
> For weeks Hitler's Luftwaffe made
> London subject to raid after raid
> And it did also make the most
> Of bombing the South East Coast . . .
>
> Wave after Wave of bombers came over
> The North Sea and the strait of Dover
> But the 'few' their resources did revive
> and destroyed one hundred and eighty five.

Gleave thanked the author cordially and filed the poem away.[15]

1969 saw a disruption to the normal commemorative schedule due to the première of *Battle of Britain*. The film had been made with the support of BBFA and was a major commemorative event in its own right. As a result, the association was prepared to break with precedent and rearrange its commemorative activities around the opening of the film. At the London première the BBFA received pride of place and its members were seated in the centre stalls around Dowding. This was to be one of his last public engagements.

The central event of 1970 was the memorial service for the BBFA's president. The service was held at Westminster Abbey on 12 March. 3,000 people attended and Gleave had the honour of carrying the casket to the table by the Abbey memorial. The BBFA annual reunions continued and, for a few years, there was also a regular get-together at Shepherd's Hotel. The early 1970s, however, perhaps marked the apex of the 'social' commemoration of the Battle: the advancing age of the veterans made attendance more difficult over the succeeding years.

The Dowding Statue

An appropriate memorial was not raised to Dowding until eighteen years after his death. There were several reasons for this. The Second World War left a paucity of monumental commemoration, partly as a reaction to those erected in tribute to the dubious commanders of the First World War. It is also likely that Lady Dowding's insistence that the only appropriate memorial to her late husband would be an animal sanctuary resulted in delay. Furthermore, there were bureaucratic obstacles to be overcome. These were not due to active hostility: the project was never politically controversial in the way that the 'Bomber' Harris statue would prove to be. They were more in the shape of administrative red tape.

The BBFA first began seriously to raise money for a statue in 1983. By 1987 it had pledges for £10,000 from its members and had received planning permission from Westminster Council for the Aldwych site. In May, however, the Department of the Environment contacted the Fine Art Commission, which oversaw the erection of statues in the capital. The Commission objected on the grounds that it had not been consulted. The prime objector appears to have been Norman St John Stevas. The situation was not helped by the comments of David Backhouse. He was one of the two sculptors asked to submit a proposal, but had been defeated by Faith Winter. Eventually, after the matter had been debated in the House of Lords, the Department of the Environment waived its objections, which seem to have been more procedural than substantive. An important influence in this respect was an article by Gavin Stamp in the *Spectator* on 24 October

1987, which bemoaned the failure of the nation to acknowledge its debt to Dowding.

Fund-raising continued and more than £60,000 was eventually raised. This sum covered the cost of construction, unveiling and a cleaning allowance. The statue was unveiled by the Queen Mother on 30 October 1988. It had narrowly been beaten into existence by a memorial to Dowding in Tunbridge Wells, which had been the project of his stepson David Whiting.[16]

The Custodians of the Battle

The RAF and the BBFA have been the major custodians of the memory of the Battle of Britain. It seems likely that the relatively low profile of the Battle in public commemoration is related to the attitudes of these bodies. Although the BBFA has done a good deal to perpetuate the broad memory of the Battle, it has devoted much of its energy to establishing the credentials of fighter aircrew who claim to have been participants in the Battle of Britain. Moreover, there is substantial correspondence in the association's archive which indicates that Tom Gleave was required to explain tactfully to ground crew of 1940 that while their work was fully appreciated by the aircrew, the BBFA was an aircrew association and they were not therefore eligible for membership. Most of the association's activity has thus been involved with the task of authenticating, and preserving the exclusivity of, the 'few', and with providing a social forum for veterans. This has sometimes run at cross purposes to the pedagogic task of developing popular commemoration.

The relationship between the BBFA and the RAF has also played a role. MacDonell, for example, the long-serving chairman of the association, was a serving RAF officer until the 1960s. This brought certain advantages in terms of the BBFA's central tasks of establishing aircrew credentials and the organisation of social functions. It also meant, however, that the BBFA was generally content to allow the RAF a free hand in defining the commemoration of the Battle.

The RAF might have entertained certain doubts about Dowding's idiosyncrasies, but also did not want to elevate the Battle of Britain above its other contributions to the war effort. Whilst it was recognised that the bravery of the fighter pilots should be acknowledged, this was not to be at the expense of the other arms of the service. More aircrew, for instance, died in Bomber Command than in Fighter Command, even in 1940, and it was perfectly reasonable for the RAF to wish to avoid the appearance of slighting that sacrifice.

The ultimate solution to this institutional dilemma was to allow the commemoration of the Battle to stand symbolically for all the sacrifices of the RAF during the war. This required some careful retuning of commemoration. The best example of this was the incorporation, in 1973, of a Lancaster bomber into the Battle of Britain Memorial Flight. At first glance it seems incongruous to include an aircraft which first flew operationally in 1942. But it was a gesture that allowed the sacrifices of the bomber crews a place in the legend.

Public interest in the Battle is still strong. In 1996 the Battle of Britain Historical Society was launched with the support of a remarkable number of celebrities, including Len Deighton, Melvyn Bragg, Richard Briers, Michael Winner, Ian Hislop, Clive Anderson, Paul McCartney, Bobby Charlton and Henry Cooper. The society, which publishes a regular newsletter, *Scramble!*, seeks to perpetuate the memory of the Battle, especially among children and young people, with the aim of passing on the torch to the next generation.

Notes and References

I am grateful to John Young and the BBFA for allowing me access to their records.

1 Adrian Gregory, *The Silence of Memory: Armistice Day, 1919–1946* (Oxford, 1994).
2 H. Kean, *Animal Rights* (London, 1998), pp. 197–8.
3 C. Moriarty, 'Christian Iconography and First World War Memorials', *Imperial War Museum Review*, 6 (1994), pp. 63–75.
4 Gregory, *Silence*, pp. 215–21.
5 Battle of Britain Fighter Association (BBFA), misc. files, box 12, draft minute of Air Ministry meeting, 24 Nov. 1959.
6 Information from John Young, including F.E. Rossier's photograph of 1947 reunion; BBFA, Gleave papers, box 1, typescript 'Introducing the Battle of Britain Fighter Association', 1958.
7 BBFA, Gleave papers, box 2, *Newsletter*, no. 10.
8 BBFA, Gleave papers, box 2, arrangements for 15 Sept. 1962.
9 BBFA, Gleave papers, box 2, *Newsletter*, no. 15.
10 BBFA, Gleave papers, box 2, 'Battle of Britain Trust Fund Mission Statement'.
11 BBFA, Gleave papers, box 2, minutes of RAFA meeting, 10 Dec. 1964.
12 BBFA, Gleave papers, box 2, letter from Air Ministry to Sandon, n.d.
13 BBFA, Gleave papers, box 2, letter from Gleave to Air Vice-Marshal Whitley, 4 Apr. 1965.
14 BBFA, Gleave papers, press clippings, 24 Sept. 1965.
15 BBFA, Gleave papers, box 2, Candy poem.
16 BBFA, 'Dowding Statue' file.

JEREMY LAKE AND JOHN SCHOFIELD

Conservation and the Battle of Britain

When Richard Hillary, in the process of recovering from terrible injuries sustained as a fighter pilot during the Battle of Britain, sat down to write *The Last Enemy*, his thoughts turned from the story of men, machines and the camaraderie of arms to a growing sense of loss. His fictitious final chapter, an account of the death of a working-class woman in the Blitz, touched on the essential paradox of this battle.[1] This was that although the heroic 'few' and their machines were rightly eulogised as 'knights of the air' through art, music and film, the summer of 1940 witnessed the realisation that civilians were not immune to 'the new impersonality of warfare [which] turned killing and maiming into the remote consequence of pushing a button or moving a lever'.[2] 100 civilian deaths in June air raids rose to 300 in July and 1,150 in August. The grim tally between 3 and 11 September was 1,211, including 976 in the London area.[3] Whilst none of the civilians subjected to aerial bombing in 1940 could have foreseen the full scale of the horrors that were to lie in store for the civilian populations of the combatant countries of the Second World War, many would have been aware that the location of airfields and anti-aircraft sites in and around the great urban areas manifested a significant shift in the conduct of warfare.

The sites associated with the Battle of Britain reflect to varying degrees both the popular image of the battle, embodied in the heroism and sacrifice of the combatants, and the all-embracing nature of 'total war'. Famous place names such as Biggin Hill and Kenley, therefore, have a dual historical and cultural significance which in our view makes them worthy of conservation.[4]

Attitudes towards this heritage are, of course, inextricably linked to its complexity and associations. The bomb-shaped memorial erected in 1935 'in protest against war in the air' outside Sylvia Pankhurst's home at Redbridge in London manifested a growing realisation that, despite the liberating potential of air technology, air power had turned civilians into military targets.[5] The image in the mind's eye of the mass destruction of civilian populations, and of names such as Guernica, Dresden and

Hiroshima, challenges our very notion of heritage. The protection of historic buildings; through listing under the Town and Country Planning Act of 1944 was, in fact, the outcome of a heightened awareness of the potential destruction of a nation's culture which aerial bombing brought in its wake.[6]

We now recognise that the horror and 'hot emotions' associated with some sites of the more recent past should not preclude their preservation, and indeed that they embody society's 'duty of memory'.[7] Illustrative of this is the identification for protection immediately after the Second World War of the concentration camp at the Camp du Struthof, at Nazweiler in Alsace, and the debate which followed the archaeological recovery in 1987 of the Gestapo headquarters' basement in Berlin, now conserved as 'a place where terror was planned and administered'.[8] In a different sense, the ruins of Coventry Cathedral and the Atomic Bomb Dome at Hiroshima symbolise the devastating effects of war, the resilience of the communities directly affected by it, and the resurgence of economic, social and cultural fortunes.

In contrast to the popular interest in the materiel of twentieth-century conflict, including the military aircraft which attract thousands to museum sites, it has only recently been possible to consider more dispassionately the historical role and importance of the sites and buildings which made up Britain's defensive and operational infrastructure. The range and variety of structures involved is enormous, a direct reflection of the changing nature of external threats and the new and varied countermeasures built in response to them. These have had a profound effect on the landscape, from the construction of airfields, radar sites and anti-aircraft batteries, to the thousands of structures and earthworks associated with the anti-invasion defences erected throughout Britain in the summer of 1940. Prominent amongst sites opened to the public are the tunnels associated with the Dunkirk evacuations at Dover Castle, and the Imperial War Museum sites at Duxford airfield and the Cabinet War Rooms in Whitehall. Recognition of the importance of the last, constructed in 1938 as the 'central shelter for government and military strategists' during the Second World War, underlay the announcement in parliament in 1948 that it should be preserved as a historic site, although it was not until 1981 that the decision was taken to open it to the general public.[9]

Local authorities and communities also recognise the value of such sites. Hence the involvement of Hackney Borough Council in the reopening of an air-raid shelter, built in Rossendale Street in 1938.[10] Similarly, veterans and various private trusts and societies have participated in the conservation of the 1940 Emergency Coast Battery at Battery Gardens in Brixham (Devon) and the establishment of privately run museums at the Battle of Britain airfields of Hawkinge (Kent), Tangmere (West Sussex) and

North Weald (Essex). Organisations such as the Fortress Study Group and the Airfield Research Group have stimulated the study and recording of twentieth-century military sites, and volunteers working for the Defence of Britain Project, initiated by the Fortress Study Group and the Council for British Archaeology in 1995, have undertaken a leading role in the systematic survey and recording of such sites.[11] Similar work is now being undertaken throughout Europe.[12]

English Heritage is the government's statutory adviser on all matters concerning the conservation of the historic environment in England. Its statutory duties are, first, to secure the preservation of ancient monuments and historic buildings; second, to promote the preservation and enhance the character and appearance of Conservation Areas; and, third, to promote the public's enjoyment, and knowledge, of ancient monuments and historic buildings. In fact the terms 'ancient' and 'historic' are both something of a misnomer, as the scope of this legislation ranges from prehistory to the recent past.

English Heritage's survey of twentieth-century military remains embraces all three of these statutory duties, but with more emphasis on the first and third: protection and understanding. In modern conservation practice sustainability is the key, and this requires a sound understanding and characterisation of the historic resources. Prior to our national survey there had been no systematic review of sites, their typology, national distribution, vulnerability and rates of survival. Without such information decisions about the preservation of individual structures could not be made on the basis of an informed judgement.

In 1994 English Heritage's Monuments Protection Programme (MPP) commissioned a survey from the Council for British Archaeology, undertaken by Dr Colin Dobinson, which aimed to provide an overview for eleven classes of monument, and a further study of military airfields for English Heritage's listing team, using material held in the Public Record Office.[13] This material survives in staggering quantities, ranging from Cabinet papers to the daily records of military units and service and civilian departments. In the following two sections we describe the outcomes in terms of the types of monument and building relevant to the Battle of Britain, and reflect on the strategies necessary for their conservation.

The Landscape of War

Much of the infrastructure of the RAF in the summer of 1940 had been deployed with a very different type of air war in mind. In contrast to the post-1933 Luftwaffe, the interwar RAF envisaged future wars as being fought from fixed and secure bases built in permanent materials. The first phase of this scheme, the principles of which were established by the Salisbury Committee of 1923,[14] took place under the guiding hand of General Sir Hugh Trenchard, who formed the RAF as the world's first independent strategic air force. His scheme involved the construction of offensive bomber bases in East Anglia and Oxfordshire, sited behind an 'aircraft fighting zone' some fifteen miles deep and stretching round London from Duxford near Cambridge to Salisbury Plain. It was the creation of this zone which accounted for the rebuilding of several First World War bases around London: Biggin Hill (1914), Northolt (1915), North Weald (1916), Kenley (1917) and Tangmere (1918), and the refurbishment of the satellite stations at Hawkinge (1915) and Martlesham Heath (1917).[15] Although political and financial factors prevented the completion of Trenchard's scheme, the collapse of the Geneva disarmament talks prompted the government to embark after 1934 on its largest interwar expansion of the air force. This accounted for the construction of a number of new fighter airfields which were later to play an important role in the Battle, including the 11 Group sector stations at Debden (1937) and Middle Wallop (April 1940), and Biggin Hill's satellite at West Malling (June 1940).[16]

The result was the construction of more than fifty new permanent stations between 1923 and 1939 and the extensive rebuilding of those retained after 1918, representing an unprecedented peacetime investment, far exceeding in real terms even the coastal fortifications built under Palmerston's administration in the 1860s.[17] Standardised designs for every aspect of airfield operations proliferated, from bomb storage, simulated training, motor transport and storage to accommodation for all ranks, cinemas and barbers' shops.[18] The design of Trenchard's stations displayed a stark utilitarian architecture which – apart from the Garden City inspiration for station married quarters – owed much to the army background of the designers, who worked from the office of the Air Ministry's Directorate of Works and Buildings. But it was the need to provide for dispersal in the event of air attack which made airfield planning markedly different from the more condensed layouts of naval or army barracks. This is exemplified, for example, in Trenchard's requirement for the crescent, as opposed to previously linear, arrangement of hangars, and the designs for officers' quarters, which dispersed the mess, recreation rooms and accommodation in order to obviate the risk of a single run of bombs destroying an entire complex and its occupants.

The expansion of RAF bases also had to take account of public concerns over the likely impact on local communities and the environment. This was the context in which the Prime Minister, Ramsay MacDonald, instructed the Royal Fine Arts Commission to become involved in airfield design. A process of consultation with the Air Ministry was initiated with visits by three distinguished architects, Sir Edwin Lutyens, Sir Reginald Blomfield and Giles Gilbert Scott, and a leading authority on planning, Professor

S.D. Adshead, to Upper Heyford and Abingdon in November 1931. This resulted in the creation in 1934 of the new post of architectural adviser to the Director of Works and Buildings, and the submission of many of the early building designs to the Royal Fine Arts Commission for their approval. Subsequently, much of this liaison work with the Air Ministry was handled personally by Lutyens.[19] The buildings erected during the expansion of the 1930s were, as a consequence, more carefully proportioned than their predecessors, a clear distinction being drawn between neo-Georgian for domestic buildings and more stridently modern styles for technical buildings. From 1938 new buildings and stations, including Middle Wallop and West Malling, made increasing use of concrete and flat roofs in order to speed up the building process and counter the effects of incendiary bombs. Decontamination centres, with their encircling blast walls, appeared on bases from 1937, and were built with the fear of gas attack in mind.[20]

In 1936 Air Chief Marshal Sir Hugh Dowding was appointed commander-in-chief of Fighter Command and proceeded to put in place an additional infrastructure that ensured the survival of Fighter Command in 1940. Vital to the new system of command and control were the Chain Home radar stations, the first five of which became operational in 1938; Observer Corps posts linked by telephone and teleprinter to the Filter Room at Fighter Command Headquarters at Bentley Priory, Stanmore; the operations rooms, which controlled the Groups into which Dowding had subdivided his command; and finally, within each Group, the operations rooms on the principal sector airfields, which controlled the fighter squadrons.

Also of critical importance to the operation of Dowding's airfields, and especially the sector stations, was their ability to disperse and shelter aircraft from attack, ensure serviceable landing and take-off areas, and control movement. The need for dispersal led to the establishment from 1936 of satellite landing grounds and the adoption in 1938 of the principle that the stationing of aircraft around the perimeter could be an effective means of preventing a knock-out blow.[21] The development of radio communication, and the introduction in 1938 of the strip principle – the organisation of the flying field into different zones for take-off, landing and taxiing – brought with them an acceptance that movement on the airfield needed to be controlled from a single centre. Hence the increasingly sophisticated designs for control towers, which evolved from the tower design of 1934 to the Art Deco horizontality of the watch office, with meteorological section, in 1939.[22]

There was also increasing recognition that the wet clay of the vital sector airfields built around London – Biggin Hill, North Weald, Northolt and Kenley – could pose a serious obstacle to effective air defence. The wet winter of 1936–7 had led Dowding to warn that '[if] our fighter aerodromes were out of action for half a day it might have the most serious consequences'.[23] In March 1939 the Air Ministry eventually agreed to Dowding's proposals for all-weather runways and perimeter tracks to dispersals.[24] In the following month it was agreed that fighter stations should have dispersals for three squadrons of twelve aircraft each, after which fighter pens with blast-shelter walls and internal air-raid shelters were erected on key fighter airfields.

Additional to the airfields and radar stations under Dowding's operational command were anti-aircraft and searchlight batteries, acting in unison with barrage balloons. The heavy anti-aircraft gunsites were often substantial constructions including emplacements, living quarters and technical and operational buildings. There were three types of heavy anti-aircraft gunsite: those for static weapons (mainly 4.5 and 3.7 inch); those for 3.7-inch mobile guns; and those accommodating 5.25-inch weapons. At least seven formal designs are known to have been issued for 4.5- and 3.7-inch emplacements down to 1945. Some 980 heavy anti-aircraft gunsites were constructed during the Second World War, mostly positioned close to naval bases, major towns and munition factories. Decoy sites, conceived as an additional means of airfield defence by the Air Ministry in the wake of the Munich crisis, were also constructed to divert the enemy bombers away from their main targets.

It would be easy to forget that, while critical battles for command of the skies were raging overhead during the summer of 1940, a vast effort was being made to construct anti-invasion defences.[25] The home defence strategy of General Sir Edmund Ironside, Commander-in-Chief of Home Forces, was based on maintaining a 'coastal crust' of beach defences, combined with static defended lines extending inland over a wide area of the country. Their purpose was to contain the advance of an enemy from the coast or an inland airborne landing by the use of obstacles and troops on the ground, thus allowing time for relief by a mobile reserve. The pivot was the GHQ line, employing most of the existing anti-tank guns in association with anti-tank obstacles, and following, where possible, topographical and man-made features such as rivers, canals and railway embankments. It was designed to shield London and the principal production centres in the Midlands, and was supplemented by a series of command, corps and divisional stop-lines to confine, break up and delay a German advance from the coast. These stop-lines included pillboxes for anti-tank guns or light machine-guns, normally combined with roadblocks and weapon positions in the form of trenches and pits. Where there were no natural or man-made obstacles, massive anti-tank ditches were dug. Strongpoints were concentrated at strategic points to create 'anti-tank islands' or 'hedgehogs'.

This policy of fixed lines of obstruction and defence was countermanded in August by Ironside's successor, General Sir Alan Brooke. Greater emphasis was then given to mobility rather than to static defence, which some senior officers regarded as fostering a 'siege mentality'. In October, by which time over 14,000 pillboxes had been constructed along stop-lines, Brooke ordered that the dwindling supply of cement be concentrated on the completion of beach defences. Fortifications came to be concentrated on nodal points, supplemented after 1941 by new anti-tank weapons such as the spigot mortar. The actual threat of invasion was lessened by Hitler's advance into the Soviet Union from June 1941, and in February 1942 Home Forces forbade the construction of pillboxes. All told, some 20,000 pillboxes had been constructed, together with hundreds of miles of anti-tank ditches and obstacles.

Finally we come to the many crash sites resulting from the Battle. It is not possible to give a precise figure for the number of military aircraft lost over Britain, or within its territorial waters, during the Second World War. Over 1,000 wartime crashes are estimated in Suffolk and 767 in Lincolnshire.[26] The number of aircraft lost at sea is particularly difficult to gauge, but the log of the Skegness lifeboat is one useful source, recording sixty-one occasions on which the boat was called to aircraft crashes.[27] These crash sites have been the subject of much work over the years by aviation archaeologists, excavating them under licence from the Ministry of Defence, and some of the aircraft recovered have been restored.[28] A Hawker Hurricane recovered from Walton on the Naze in 1973 is now displayed at the RAF Museum, Hendon, while a Messerschmitt 109 was taken from the sea off Dymchurch, Kent, in 1976.[29]

Material Remains and Their Protection

Before we turn to a more detailed discussion of some of the Battle of Britain sites and buildings which remain, it is necessary to review briefly some of the options available for their preservation.[30] It has to be decided which elements of the historic environment are to be preserved as found, which can be subject to limited change, and which can be exchanged for other benefits. Where statutory protection is appropriate, the form of protection selected is designed to encourage the type of management that will best ensure the site or structure's long-term future. Scheduling, for example, can be used under the terms of the 1979 Ancient Monuments and Archaeological Areas Act. Here the preferred option is the retention of sites as monuments not in day-to-day use. Listing, by contrast, will be more appropriate where the continuing or new use of built structures is both desirable and feasible.[31] In recommending sites for scheduling or buildings for listing, the role of English Heritage is advisory, and each recommendation made to the Department for Culture, Media and Sport must be compelling and demonstrate the site's *national importance* (in the case of scheduling) or the structure's *special interest* (in the case of listing).

In applying the rigorously selective criteria for statutory protection, the historic significance of a site or building needs to be taken into account, as does its condition relative to other sites of its type, its suitability to be adapted for other uses, and its vulnerability. Rarity alone may be sufficient to underpin selection. Of the 980 heavy anti-aircraft gunsites built, only sixty-one survive in anything like their original form and all are thus strong candidates for protection. The Chain Home radar mast which remains at Stenigot in Lincolnshire is a uniquely complete example of its type and has recently been listed. Group value is also an important criterion and relates to sites where defences survive in their original configuration, to clusters of buildings which are particularly well preserved and to the strategic significance of particular areas.

Where statutory protection is not appropriate, English Heritage provides advice in the form of planning guidance. The government has issued instructions that archaeological remains should be recorded in advance of redevelopment or removal. Similar instructions have been drawn up in relation to historic buildings in order to protect the fabric of the landscape.[32] The views of local communities and interest groups also need to be considered. Conservation Areas, designated by local authorities, can play a significant role in conserving important sites.

Of all the sites connected with the Battle, none has greater resonance in the popular imagination than the sector airfields which bore the brunt of the Luftwaffe onslaught. In the words of Churchill, they were the bases 'on whose organisation and combination the whole fighting power of our Air Force at this moment depended'.[33] 11 Group, commanded by Air Vice-Marshal Keith Park, occupied the front line of the Battle. Its 'nerve centre' at Uxbridge and sector stations at Kenley, Northolt, North Weald, Biggin Hill, Tangmere, Debden and Hornchurch took some of the most sustained attacks of the Battle, especially between 24 August and 6 September when these airfields became some of the Luftwaffe's prime targets.

Biggin Hill is commonly regarded as the most significant of 11 Group's sector stations: more enemy aircraft were destroyed by squadrons based there than at any other station during the war. Following its use during the First World War, work on rebuilding the station in permanent fabric began in 1929, with several buildings bearing the datestones of 1930 and 1931: the Air Estimates for 1933–4 reveal that £190,000 had been allocated for this purpose. The airfield also witnessed pioneering air-to-air and ground-to-air experiments in radio communication and, from 1936, it was used as a laboratory for the Fighter Direction Organisation, which linked radar to aircraft.[34] The autumn of 1939 saw the construction of a tarmac runway, measuring 4,800 by 150 feet, and in June 1940 the completion of twelve fighter pens positioned beside the new perimeter track.

The parts of the site which are now missing were destroyed in the Luftwaffe raids of 1940. The raid of 30 August resulted in severe damage to the barracks, WAAF quarters, workshops and stores. The following day the Sector Operations Room took a direct hit and the hangars were badly damaged. On 6 September, after further raids had rendered much of the base unusable, the last remaining hangar was destroyed on the orders of the base commander.[35]

The surviving buildings on the so-called North Camp site are largely representative of the designs associated with Trenchard's expansion scheme. The barracks and station headquarters have all survived remarkably well. Of the buildings which have undergone some alteration, commonly in the form of replacement doors and windows, the most historically important are the station sick quarters, dating from 1930, with a decontamination annexe added later, and the institute building. Other buildings, such as the motor transport sheds and workshops, also survive.

Across the road, which divides the site, stand the married quarters, typically planned and designed on Garden City principles and now restored to an excellent standard as private housing. Also to be seen is the officers' mess, a finely detailed neo-Georgian composition now restored as a house and situated next to the telephone exchange centre which played a crucial role during the Battle. Although documentation has not yet been traced, it is very probable that the mess was one of the buildings designed in partnership with the Royal Fine Arts Commission during the winter of 1934, the great attention paid to its composition owing much to the fact that Biggin Hill's proximity to London made it the subject of frequent visits by officers from other air forces.[36]

The airfield has retained two fighter pens, which are still in use for light aircraft, the rear wall of a third and a centrally sited Picket Hamilton fort. To the east side near one of the blast pens there still survives a modest weatherboarded hut, of Air Ministry Sectional B-type design, resited and now wedged between two recently built warehouses. This was the dispersal hut, familiar from wartime photography, as the building in and around which pilots rested before being given the order to 'scramble'.

After Biggin Hill, the sector station to have retained most of its original built fabric is Northolt in west London. The airfield has been subject to considerable post-war development, but many designs of the 1920s have survived from its rebuilding as a fighter station under Trenchard, including the officers' mess of 1923 and the original four barracks blocks. Also to be seen are two hangars, the station workshops and the operations room, and a single pillbox.[37]

Kenley also retains a few of its buildings. The officers' mess, prominently sited on the west side of the aerodrome and still displaying the scars of the devastating Luftwaffe raid of 18 August 1940, now stands as the most impressive surviving building dating from the rebuilding of the station between 1931 and 1933. Less prominent are the sergeants' mess and the workshops, sold to developers by the Ministry of Defence in 1999 but still standing. Kenley, however, can boast the most complete surviving fighter airfield associated with the Battle of Britain. A large part of Kenley Common, still managed by the Corporation of London, was converted for use as an aerodrome for the Royal Flying Corps in 1917 and enlarged through an Act of Parliament in 1939. The 800-yard runways and perimeter tracks were completed in 1939, and extended by a further 200 yards in 1943. All twelve fighter pens under construction in April 1940 have survived.[38]

Although the airfield at North Weald was remodelled for jet fighters in the 1950s and only one hangar, two watch offices and the officers' mess have survived in a complete state from the 1920s, it has the most complete set of fighter pens after Kenley.[39] Debden has retained much of its 1930s character, the best surviving example of which is the operations block. Much of the flying field and defensive perimeter are still intact.

As for the other sector stations, only fragments now remain of Tangmere, where the raid of 16 August 1940 caused great damage and destruction. The deserted and ruinous control tower survives as a lonely icon on the edge of the original flying field, now in agricultural use.[40] Very little also remains of Hornchurch, though glimpses of it are still to be seen in *The Lion Has Wings*, Michael Powell's propaganda film of 1939. Havering Borough Council has developed what is left of the airfield as a country park, with a fighter pen and some gun posts and pillboxes integrated into a walk around the former perimeter. The former married quarters and officers' mess are now set amongst more recent developments.[41]

Not much is left of satellite stations such as Manston and Hawkinge. At West Malling, however, the anti-aircraft/observation tower on the airfield's perimeter has been retained as a landmark at the entrance to a new housing development and there are plans to convert the control tower into a community centre. The former officers' mess currently serves as the offices of Tonbridge and Malling District Council.

Duxford, the most southerly airfield of 12 Group under the command of Air Vice-Marshal Trafford Leigh-Mallory, is one of the best-preserved examples of an interwar military airfield in Britain, with fabric representative of both expansion periods. It was one of only forty-five stations retained for the RAF after 1918, first as a Flying Training School and then as a fighter station for 19 Squadron. Duxford, which became famous for its association with the 'big wing' tactics of Douglas Bader, was subsequently chosen as one of the locations for the film *Battle of Britain*, one scene from which involved the destruction of one of its wartime hangars. It was also the subject of a public inquiry in 1976 when Sir Douglas Bader argued for the retention of the entire airfield in opposition to the construction of the M11 motorway across the eastern boundary of the site. It is now the home of one of Europe's leading aviation museums, run by the Imperial War Museum.[42]

The other aspect of the Battle that has usually attracted great public interest is the system of command and control. Pre-eminent among the surviving Chain Home radar stations is Bawdsey, the site of a large Victorian house close to the Deben estuary, where from 1936 Robert Watson-Watt and his team carried out the key experimental work that was to form the basis of Britain's air defence system. A measure of the site's importance was the attention paid to its protection against attack in the summer of 1940, clearly visible today, for example, in the ring of pillboxes on its landward side. The site is still dominated by the transmitter mast, whose height enabled the transmission of long wavelength signals, and this is now the lone and slightly truncated survivor of the original group of four transmitter masts, their position marked on the ground by large concrete anchor blocks. The tower, the receiver block and the transmitter block – the last, remarkably, retaining its original switchgear – are still to be seen.[43]

The Observer Corps have not left any distinctive sites from the Battle of Britain period: their posts were not given permanent structures until the reorganisation of the service in 1942 and, besides the construction of dugouts, huts and shelters on an ad hoc basis in 1940, were chiefly recognisable by the telegraph poles which linked them to the Fighter Command system.[44] Some excellent examples remain, however, of the operations rooms, which represented a critically important link in the chain of command. Among them is the underground operations room, manned by Dowding and his team in 1940, at Bentley Priory, Stanmore, the late-eighteenth-century mansion which served as the headquarters of Fighter Command. The room was later remodelled during the Cold War period.

The underground operations room at RAF Uxbridge, built in 1938, which became the strategic centre of 11 Group's operations during the summer of 1940, has survived complete with its original air filtration system and power supply. It was here, on 15 September 1940, that Churchill witnessed Air Vice-Marshal Keith Park deploying the squadrons of 11 Group. The plotting room has now been restored by the Ministry of Defence to match Churchill's detailed description, complete with its 'tote board' and plotting table.[45]

Debden provides a particularly good example of an operations room at a sector station in 11 Group, comprising a protected roof design of 1937 and surrounding blast walls of reinforced concrete.[46] Duxford, by contrast, incorporates the best surviving example of a 1924 design, which resembles a rectangular, hipped-roof bungalow protected by blast walls made of earth. The operations room at Northolt, though externally altered by new windows and the removal of its blast wall, has retained its original internal plan, with a shuttered opening providing communication between the direction-finding room to its right, where the cross-bearings from the fighter pilots' radio telephones were translated into a map position, and the plotting room.

Whilst these sites and buildings deserve protection for their place in the history of national defence and their evocation of a heroic stand against all odds, they also deserve consideration for their importance to our understanding of the history of technology and warfare. English Heritage's aim is therefore to broaden awareness of the wider historic significance and educational potential of these sites, in order that ill-considered demolition and alteration should be prevented. It will then be possible to preserve them for the benefit of a wide constituency of interests, from historians and archaeologists to school groups and local communities.

Notes and References

The authors would like to thank Vince Holyoak for advice on aircraft crash sites. We should also record that much of the information on airfields was provided by Paul Francis and Colin Dobinson, in separate projects commissioned by English Heritage, and that information on all other types of twentieth-century military site stems from work by Colin Dobinson and Mike Anderton. We are also indebted to Roger Bowdler of English Heritage for sight of his unpublished reports on Kenley, Biggin Hill and Hornchurch.

1 Richard Hillary, *The Last Enemy* (London, 1942; Pimlico ed., 1997), pp. 174–6.
2 Eric Hobsbawm, *Age of Extremes: The Short Twentieth Century* (London, 1994), p. 50.
3 Henry Pelling, *Britain and the Second World War* (Glasgow, 1970), p. 97; Peter Hennessy, *Never Again: Britain, 1945–1951* (London, 1992), p. 31.
4 For a summary of English Heritage's approach, see C.S. Dobinson, J. Lake and A.J. Schofield, 'Monuments of War: Defining England's 20th-Century Defence Heritage', *Antiquity*, 71 (1997), pp. 288–99; also see English Heritage, *Monuments of War: The Evaluation, Recording and Management of Twentieth-Century Military Sites* (London, 1998).
5 This monument, in the shape of a small stone bomb on a square plinth, was erected on land owned by Sylvia Pankhurst outside 587 High Road, Woodford Green, London. It is now listed at grade II, principally on the grounds of its historical value.
6 Andrew Saint, 'How Listing Happened', in Michael Hunter (ed.), *Preserving the Past* (London, 1996), pp. 115–34.
7 See David Uzzell, 'The Hot Interpretation of the Cold War', in *Monuments of War*.
8 Reinhard Rurrup (ed.), *Topography of Terror: Gestapo, SS and Reichssicherheitshauptamt on the Prinz-Albrecht Terrain* (Berlin, 1998). For protected sites in France, most notably the Junkers Aircraft Factory, Struthof, and the internment

camp at Aix-en-Provence, see Bernard Toulier and Paul Smith, *Mille monuments du XXe siècle en France* (Paris, 1998).

9 Imperial War Museum, *The Cabinet War Rooms* (London, 1996).

10 This has now been listed at grade II, having retained many of its original fittings such as the air-filter units and the electric generator, driven by the pedals of a twin bicycle frame.

11 Andrew Saunders, 'The Defence of Britain Project', in *Monuments of War*, pp. 7–9. For a description of field remains, see Bernard Lowry (ed.), *Twentieth-Century Defences in Britain: An Introductory Guide* (York, 1995).

12 An example of such surveying and recording is Johannes Bruns's work on airfield sites in Germany.

13 The categories of site covered by the Monuments Protection Programme are as follows: anti-aircraft artillery, 1914–46; anti-invasion defences, 1939–45; bombing decoys, 1939–45; Operation Diver sites, 1944–45; Operation Overlord embarkation sites, 1942–45; coast artillery, 1900–56; civil defence, 1939–45; airfield ground defences, 1939–45; radar (with acoustic detection), 1937–45; Cold War sites, 1947–69. The scope and methodology of the survey is summarised in Colin Dobinson, 'Twentieth-Century Fortifications in England: the MPP approach', in *Monuments of War*, pp. 2–6. The listing team's survey of airfields has assessed surviving sites and associated documentation. See Jeremy Lake and Paul Francis, 'Thematic Reviews: Military Aviation Sites and Structures', in *Monuments of War*, pp. 13–17.

14 Colin Dobinson, 'Twentieth-Century Fortifications in England', vol. 9, 'Airfield Themes' (unpublished report for English Heritage, 1997), p. 25.

15 Ibid., pp. 31, 34, 39, 41.

16 Ibid., pp. 113–14. Middle Wallop was transferred to 10 Group during the Battle.

17 Even in 1932, 45 per cent of the armed services' procurement expenditure was absorbed by the RAF.

18 See Paul Francis, *British Military Airfield Architecture* (Sparkford, 1996).

19 Dobinson, 'Twentieth-Century Fortifications', pp. 136–7.

20 Francis, *British Military*, pp. 186–193.

21 Dobinson, 'Twentieth-Century Fortifications', pp.107–8.

22 Francis, *British Military*, pp. 118–24.

23 Dowding, quoted in Dobinson, 'Twentieth-Century Fortifications', p. 155. The RFC had used cinders to combat waterlogging at Northolt in 1916. See David J. Smith, *Britain's Military Airfields* (Wellingborough, 1989), pp. 11, 19.

24 The airfields chosen for runways, in order of priority, were Kenley, Biggin Hill, Church Fenton (the main sector station for the north of England), Debden, Northolt, Tangmere, Turnhouse and Hendon. See Dobinson, 'Twentieth-Century Fortifications', pp. 166–8.

25 See Colin Dobinson, 'Twentieth-Century Fortifications in England', vol. 2, 'Anti-invasion Defences of World War II' (unpublished report for English Heritage, 1996).

26 See I. McLachlan, *Final Flights: Dramatic Wartime Incidents Revealed by Aviation Archaeology* (Sparkford, 1989).

27 S. Finn, *Lincolnshire at War, 1939–45* (Brayford, 1973), pp. 113–14.

28 All crash sites are protected under the terms of the 1986 Protection of Military Remains Act, which makes it an offence to 'tamper with, damage, move or unearth the remains of any designated military aircraft or vessels that have crashed, sunk or been stranded, and any associated human remains'. The Act applies to any

aircraft which has, at any time, crashed while on military service.

29 Winston G. Ramsey (ed.), *The Battle of Britain: Then and Now* (5th ed., London, 1996), pp. 400, 677.

30 See John Hunter and Ian Ralston (ed.), *Archaeological Resource Management in the UK: An Introduction* (Stroud, 1993); English Heritage, *Sustaining the Historic Environment: New Perspectives on the Future* (London, 1997). Protection policy, as outlined by English Heritage, the Countryside Commission and English Nature in *Conservation Issues in Strategic Plans* (1993) and *Conservation Issues in Local Plans* (1996), has placed an increased emphasis on the understanding of the 'total resource' and the importance of distinctiveness. The recent English Heritage discussion document, *Sustaining the Historic Environment*, has emphasised the need for a holistic approach – 'based on a thorough understanding of the historic environment and the options for its management' – as providing the most informed and balanced approach.

31 Planning and Policy Guidance Note (PPG), 15, 3.8.

32 PPG, 16; ibid., 15, 6.40.

33 Winston S. Churchill, *The Second World War*, vol. 2, *Their Finest Hour* (London, 1949), p. 292.

34 Max Hastings, *Bomber Command* (London, 1976), p. 60.

35 Richard Collier, *Eagle Day* (London, 1966), pp. 190–202. For a detailed history of the station, see Graham Wallace, *RAF Biggin Hill* (London, 1957; reprint, 1975).

36 Public Record Office, AIR 28/64, Operations Record Book.

37 Peter Norris, 'Northolt', in Ramsey, *Battle of Britain*, pp. 236–49.

38 Peter Corbell, 'Kenley', in Ramsey, *Battle of Britain*, pp. 46–51; PRO AIR 28/64, Operations Record Book.

39 Wilf Nicoll, 'North Weald', in Ramsey, *Battle of Britain*, pp. 160–75.

40 Jim Beedle, 'Tangmere', in Ramsey, *Battle of Britain*, pp. 30–41.

41 H.T. Sutton, 'Hornchurch', in Ramsey, *Battle of Britain*, pp. 76–87.

42 Alister Raby, 'Duxford Airfield: The Story of a Famous Fighter Station' (unpublished account); Duxford Aviation Society, *Duxford Diary, 1942–5* (Duxford, 1989); Winston G. Ramsey (ed.), *Airfields of the Eighth* (London, 1978), pp. 72–6; Alister Raby, 'Duxford', in Ramsey, *Battle of Britain*, pp. 198–211.

43 Royal Commission on the Historical Monuments of England, 'Historic Building Report on RAF Bawdsey' (unpublished report, 1995).

44 See Derek Wood, *Attack Warning Red: The Royal Observer Corps and the Defence of Britain, 1925–1992* (London, 1996), pp. 82–97.

45 Churchill, *Their Finest Hour*, pp. 293–7.

46 Francis, *British Military*, pp. 46–8.

PAUL ADDISON AND JEREMY A. CRANG

A Battle of Many Nations

In 1940 the British fought on 'alone' after the fall of France. But as the Battle of Britain reminds us, the British were never quite alone. Among those who served with Fighter Command, for example, were scores of airmen from the self-governing Dominions of the Commonwealth and the occupied nations of Europe. Some of the most audacious and prominent combatants in the Battle were from overseas, and the Battle of Britain was, in a sense, a battle of many nations. The argument, however, needs be taken a step further. Britain itself – more correctly the United Kingdom of Great Britain and Northern Ireland – was made up of four nations, and even if England was by far the largest and the most powerful of the four, there were good reasons why the Battle never became known as 'the Battle of England'.

The British Dimension

The United Kingdom was never more united than when it was under threat from Nazi Germany in the summer and autumn of 1940. Within Churchill's 'island fortress' the interests of England, Scotland and Wales were virtually indivisible, though a handful of nationalists continued to think otherwise. The sense of common purpose was intensified by the power of broadcasting. Almost every household had a radio and the BBC's millions of listeners entered into a community of the airwaves of which there had been no equivalent in the First World War. The fortunes of the RAF and the Luftwaffe at the height of the Battle of Britain could be followed every night on the nine o'clock news, with additional bulletins in the Welsh and Gaelic languages.[1] Only Northern Ireland stood, to some extent, outside the national effort. Sectarian divisions remained an obstacle to mobilisation and the absence of air raids during the Battle of Britain tended to lull the province into a sense of false security.

Though the English, the Scots and the Welsh acted as one nation, the impact of war varied greatly between different parts of the country. During the Battle of Britain the main divide was between the south-east of England, where most of the action was concentrated, and the rest of the country, which experienced the ripples and shock-waves of a battle fought elsewhere. At one level, therefore, the Battle of Britain was an authentically British affair; at another a distinctively English drama, played out, in the words of Angus Calder, in a 'Green and Pleasant heartland, "Deep England", which stretched from Hardy's Wessex to Tennyson's Lincolnshire, from Kipling's Sussex to Elgar's Worcestershire'.[2]

In a speech to the House of Commons on 18 June 1940 Churchill declared: 'What General Weygand called the Battle of France is over. I expect that the Battle of Britain is about to begin.'[3] Thus defined, the Battle of Britain was inseparable from the threat of invasion, and it was this above all that created a national sense of emergency. A threat to any part of Britain was a threat to the whole. Nor could anyone be sure where, along the 2,000 miles of British coastline, an invasion or lightning raid would be attempted. Even when the intelligence services detected clear signs of preparation for a cross-Channel invasion, they could not be sure that some deception was not intended. Recent research into the anti-invasion measures of the second half of 1940 has demonstrated how widespread those preparations were. Twenty-seven beaches in Wales and 113 beaches in Scotland were defended with concrete obstacles; inland, the strategically vital heartlands of both countries were protected by a set of interconnected defence lines running for hundreds of miles.[4]

The general public could only speculate or pass on rumours. Many of these rumours were picked up and reported by the Ministry of Information, which had the responsibility of monitoring and sustaining morale. It is interesting to see how sensitive the Ministry was to local factors. Between May and October 1940 its Home Intelligence Division compiled daily reports, based on information gathered from the thirteen regional offices of the Ministry, in which much attention was given to regional aspects.[5] 'There is some nervousness in the Shetlands,' Home Intelligence reported on 26 August, 'due to the fact that these islands are nearer than the rest of Great Britain to Norway, where invasion preparations are said to be in progress.' In a broadcast on 11 September Churchill warned that a full-scale invasion might be launched at any time against England, Scotland, Ireland, or all three. Home Intelligence reported some surprise in Wales because he failed to include Wales in the list.[6]

Once German forces were in occupation of Scandinavia, the Low Countries and the Channel coast, the whole of Britain was within range of the Luftwaffe's bombers. From mid-June onwards, and throughout the Battle of Britain, Scotland, Wales and the north of England were all subject to sporadic air raids. The first raid on Swansea, for example, took place on 27 June, with further raids on 10 July, 24 July, 10–11 August and 1–2 September: in all three raids a total of 58 people were killed.[7] Raids were mounted in and around the Firth of Forth on 25–26 June, 18 July, 22–23 July, 4 August, 27 September, 29 September and 4 October. The bombing of Buckingham Palace in September 1940 is a famous episode; that same month a bomb made a crater in the lawn outside Holyrood Palace in Edinburgh.[8]

Such raids sometimes consisted of no more than a stray bomber dropping a single bomb, and none of them was remotely comparable in duration or destructiveness with the assault on London which began in September. But the effect was to make large areas of Britain air-raid conscious. Sometimes work or sleep would be disrupted when the air-raid sirens were sounded but no raid followed. On other occasions there was indignation when a raid occurred with no warning, or German bombers passed overhead without any challenge from the local AA batteries. The following reports from Home Intelligence's regional offices in Cardiff and Edinburgh give some picture of the situation in Wales and Scotland in July and August 1940:

15 July (Cardiff): The public in the south of the region is acclimatised to warnings and raids, but in the north concern is felt about insufficiency of public refuges and AA defences.

15 July (Edinburgh): Failure to sound siren in Aberdeen during Friday's air raids has aroused intense feeling, and the chief constable who is in charge of civil defence is being booed in the streets . . . There is a strong expectation of intensified air raids in the near future.

16 July (Cardiff): Common belief that fewer air raids during last two days represents lull before the storm. A little trouble has been caused in industry on account of inadequacy of warnings of air raids in which casualties have occurred.

16 July (Edinburgh): Enemy aeroplanes have passed over Clydebank twice in last three weeks, and although held by searchlights met no AA opposition. Communist propaganda, which is effective among the intellectual young artisans, is making full play of this evidence of unpreparedness.

23 July (Cardiff): Lack of shelters in N. Wales causes anxiety. More people staying in bed during raid warnings, which occur almost nightly.

24 July (Edinburgh): Question of chief interest to people on east and west coast is: 'Where are our fighters and AA guns?'; and complaints of absence of opposition have increased from Clydeside. A rumour in Edinburgh last night said that the best guns had been transferred to England, and as a result faith in our defences is becoming undermined.

25 July (Edinburgh): Further complaints from Montrose and Peterhead that enemy bombers are coming over unchallenged by sirens or fighters . . . Complaints of delay in getting shelters from Peterhead and Kincardine.

29 July (Cardiff): In many districts siren policy causes frequent cessation of work and lack of sleep at times when there is no visible or audible enemy action.

3 August (Cardiff): Continuous air raids, although causing lack of sleep, have stimulated morale.

9 August (Edinburgh): In Edinburgh area feeling is growing at absence of our fighters when raiders are over, and an official explanation is requested.

17 August (Cardiff): In some areas crowds which remain to watch and cheer air battles have been the cause of great anxiety to civil defence workers.

20 August (Cardiff): Unlucky salvos of bombs on Cardiff and Swansea when guns were not firing and few searchlights were to be seen has strengthened belief that the aerial defence of the region has been weakened to supplement defence of the south-east coast, and created a sense of grievance.[9]

Both the Welsh and Scottish reports indicate some suspicion of the neglect of local defences by the government in London – a hint that old nationalist grievances could actually be re-awakened by the emergency. As Angus Calder has pointed out, both countries had suffered very severely from the depression of the 1930s, and both contained small pockets of nationalist opposition to the war. In the case of Scotland the Nazis made some efforts to exploit nationalist discontent. The 'black' propaganda department of the German Foreign Office set up 'Radio Caledonia', which claimed to be an independent station broadcasting on behalf of an organisation of Scots working for peace. First monitored on 19 July, Radio Caledonia broadcast every night a ten-minute talk which usually featured anti-capitalist and anti-Semitic themes. Though the station could be heard along the East Coast of Scotland, the early broadcasts revealed little knowledge of the Scottish context.[10]

In the final analysis there was little nationalist dissent from the war on the mainland of Britain. There is no reason to doubt the Home Intelligence Division's claim that the fortunes of the RAF were followed in all parts of Britain with gratitude and admiration. One measure of that admiration was its expression by politicians at opposite ends of the political spectrum.

On 16 August 1940 the fiery Welsh socialist Aneurin Bevan wrote in *Tribune*:

> As wave after wave of Nazi bombers fly to our coast our fighters rise to give them battle. In the hearts of the young men of the RAF there is no qualifying condition, no mean or sordid bargain, no careful weighing of interests, no backward glance, except the last glimpse of the home they have left perhaps for ever, or of the sweetheart with whom they have shared dreams of a future together, maybe not to be fulfilled. In their hearts and minds there is nothing but selfless dedication, a fierce pride in the meteor-like machines they command, and a dauntless determination to protect these shores from the pollution of conquest. Armed with these and with the idealism which is the most precious gift of youth the young fighters of the RAF are performing prodigies of valour infinitely moving to us and an astonishment to the witnessing world.[11]

On 20 August 1940 Churchill paid his own more famous tribute in the House of Commons:

> The gratitude of every home in our Island, in our Empire, and indeed throughout the world, except in the abodes of the guilty, goes out to the British airmen who, undaunted by odds, unwearied in their constant challenge and mortal danger, are turning the tide of the World War by their prowess and by their devotion. Never in the field of human conflict was so much owed by so many to so few.[12]

The 'few' were more numerous than the term suggests. 2,917 Fighter Command aircrew have been recognised as combatants in the Battle and hence able to qualify for the Battle of Britain clasp to the 1939–45 campaign medal.[13] The great majority of them – some 2,334 – were of British birth and came from all parts of the United Kingdom. Since the inhabitants of England outnumbered the total population of the rest of the UK by four to one, aircrew born in Scotland, Wales or Northern Ireland were never likely to constitute more than a comparatively small minority. Of a sample of 1,027 UK members of the 'few' whose precise birthplace has been ascertained, thirteen were born in Northern Ireland, thirty in Wales, and eighty-five in Scotland.[14] Their contribution was, nevertheless, invaluable.

Ulster contributed two Anti-Aircraft regiments to the defence of London and the south coast during the Battle, but Ulster's own 502 Squadron of the RAF was a bomber squadron engaged in anti-submarine warfare.[15] There was no specifically Welsh squadron in Fighter Command, though Pembrey in Camarthenshire was a fighter base during the Battle. In Scotland, however, both 602 (Glasgow) Squadron and 603 (City of Edinburgh) Squadron were long established and both were ordered south to join in the Battle. George Denholm, the commander of 603 Squadron, had been born and brought up in Bo'ness, and educated at Fettes. Although by the summer of 1940 the squadron no longer consisted exclusively of Scots, 'Uncle George' insisted that his pilots drink Drambuie, rather than port, after dinner to remind them of the squadron's identity.[16]

Scots were also prominent at higher levels. Sir Robert Watson-Watt, the pioneer of radar, had grown up in Brechin, and first developed an interest in radio waves at University College, Dundee, at that time a part of the University of St Andrews. Scotland could also lay some claim to the Commander-in-Chief of Fighter Command, Sir Hugh Dowding. A bronze and sandstone memorial in the town of Moffat in Dumfriesshire commemorates his birth there in 1882, the son of a schoolmaster who had set up a boys' prep school in the town in partnership with a Mr Churchill.[17] Sir Archibald Sinclair, the Secretary of State for Air who dismissed Dowding from his post in November 1940, was a Scottish laird with an estate of some 200,000 acres in Caithness and Sutherland. Lord Beaverbrook, who as Minister of Aircraft Production frequently crossed swords with Sinclair during the Battle of Britain, was the son of a minister of the Church of Scotland whose family had lived for generations at Torphichen, near Linlithgow.

One of the publicity campaigns run by Lord Beaverbrook was the Spitfire Fund. The idea was that people both at home and overseas should set up in factories, offices and local communities funds to pay for the production of new Spitfires. The cost per plane, according to Beaverbrook, was £5,000. In August a price list of components was issued: £2,000, for example, bought a wing, 15 shillings the blast tube of a machine-gun, and 6d a rivet.[18] 'Of course,' writes Beaverbrook's biographer, A.J.P. Taylor, 'the fund was an irrelevancy, as the Treasury observed. The shortage was in productive capacity, not in money.'[19]

The Spitfire Fund had little to do with aircraft production but it was remarkable as a demonstration of the desire of civilian spectators to support the RAF and even perhaps to play some vicarious part in the Battle. As one of Beaverbrook's own publicists put it: 'as you put your daily shilling in the collection box, there was the feeling that it connected you – intimately if indirectly – with tremendous and heroic events and in a way that a cheque to the Income Tax collector rather failed to do'.[20]

The Spitfire Fund appears to have exercised a strong appeal across Britain. Virtually every large town set up its own fund. Within a week the 30,000 inhabitants of the islands of Lewis and Harris were reported to have raised £6,400. The Durham Miners sent a cheque for £10,000. From Michaelston-le-Pit, a Glamorganshire village with a population of one hundred, Beaverbrook received a letter from a grieving father whose son had recently been killed while serving with the RAF. 'I cannot provide you with another gallant son,' he wrote. 'The one who has gone was my only son. But I want you to accept from the village of Michaelston-le-Pit the enclosed cheque for £5,000 to purchase a Spitfire.' Every member of the community had subscribed.[21] In August the Lord Mayor of Cardiff opened a Spitfire fund which raised £20,000:

> Collections were made in the clubs, pubs and places of work. A dance, arranged by the Tongwynlais wardens, raised £50 and another substantial sum was raised when villages at Castleton organised a sale of their fruit and vegetables. Two Cardiff lads spent their August holidays collecting golf balls which they sold to raise ten shillings for the fund, while school children sent in their pocket money. Such was the spirit of 1940.[22]

But Cardiff (population 230,000) was outstripped by Belfast (population 440,000), which raised £72,000 by 20 September.[23]

As Home Intelligence reports suggest, the behaviour of Londoners during the Blitz on the capital, which began on 7 September 1940, also aroused sympathy and admiration across Britain:

> 11 September (Edinburgh): People are watching what is happening in London and forgetting their own grievances.

> 24 September (Cardiff): Interest still centres around the bombing of London, and admiration is expressed for the courage of Londoners.

> 25 September (Belfast): The Belfast deputation which has been studying ARP organisation in London has returned full of praise for the fortitude of Londoners in air raids.[24]

The distillation of the Battle of Britain into a distinctively *English* legend has been superbly analysed by Angus Calder in his book *The Myth of the Blitz*. As he explains, the legend grew spontaneously out of the geography of the Battle and the literary culture of the journalists, broadcasters and film-makers whose words and images still have the power to move audiences today.

The south of England lay at the heart of the Battle of Britain. Most of the fighting was concentrated in the area of Fighter Command's 11 Group, and the names of its sector stations were soon to become synonymous with the Battle: Tangmere, Kenley, Biggin Hill, Hornchurch, Northolt, North Weald, Debden. The great majority of the aircrew who fought in the Battle were also, of course, English, including many of the fighter pilots who subsequently achieved fame for their exploits: Douglas Bader, Peter Townshend, 'Ginger' Lacey, Robert Stanford Tuck, 'Johnny' Johnston and others.

The territory over which the great air battles were fought included the landscape, the architecture and the institutions which had come to represent the crown jewels of English national identity. Here were the white cliffs of Dover, the Weald of Kent, Canterbury Cathedral, Lord's Cricket Ground, the Tower of London and the Palace of Westminster. From the grounds of their home at Sissinghurst Castle, a Tudor mansion in Kent, Harold Nicolson and Vita Sackville-West watched the Battle in progress overhead. 'The farm, castle and garden were spattered with the debris of the air battles. Bombs and parachutists fell in the neighbouring fields. On one occasion a German bomber, crashing in flames, missed the Elizabethan tower by only a few yards.'[25] On 12 September an 800-lb bomb landed in front of the steps of St Paul's Cathedral – Wren's masterpiece built after the destruction of Old St Paul's in the Great Fire of London of 1666 – but failed to explode. It was successfully removed by a bomb disposal squad.[26]

In this ancient setting many 'ordinary people' seem to have been conscious of themselves as actors in a great historical drama. 'These were the times', Churchill was later to write, 'when the English, and particularly the Londoners, who had the place of honour, were seen at their best.'[27] The reference to a 'place of honour' sounds highly rhetorical. Who could possibly wish to be in the middle of a Blitz, or imagine that it was a privilege? But a strong thread of evidence does suggest that the fears and suffering of civilians were mixed with a sense of pride and exhilaration at being in the thick of the action.

After the Luftwaffe's attack on Croydon on 15 August 1940, in which eight people were killed or wounded, one of Mass Observation's observers reported the effects on 'Mr M' – a hitherto grumpy and unpopular lodger who had been caught in the raid:

'We were in it! We were in it!' cries Mr M, rushing through the front door at about 10.30 pm. 'We were *in* it!'

His voice rises to a sort of ecstasy, while landlady and fellow-lodgers gather round excitedly. They have been waiting for Mr M's return ever since they heard the 9 o'clock news; for Mr M is an engineer at the Croydon aircraft factory said to have been bombed. Mr and Mrs K, from the top floor, come rushing down the stairs to join the gathering.

Mr K: 'You're back! Here you are! How was it? How did you get on? Did you see it?'

Mr M: '*See* it? We were *in* it! *In* it!'[28]

A few weeks later, during the London Blitz, Mass Observation recorded an elderly Cockney exclaiming: 'We're in the front line! Me own home – it's in the Front Line.'[29]

Anecdotes of the Battle of Britain are no doubt highly selective, omitting the more discreditable aspects of behaviour in a crisis. Even so, the scores of anecdotes which have been handed down cannot all have been fabricated. Many of the participants in the Battle of Britain seem to have known the script before they were called on to perform it: community spirit, social comedy, understatement and the stiff upper lip appear to have been seized on as war weapons.

The poet, John Betjeman, recounted a story told to him during the Battle of Britain of a village in Kent where the local Women's Institute were organising a competition for the best-decorated table centre:

> Bombs and aeroplanes were falling out of the sky, guns thundered and fragments of shell whizzed about. 'I am afraid we have not *everybody* here,' said the head of the Institute. 'You see, several of our members had to be up all night, but we have quite a little show all the same': and there they were, the raffia mats, the bowls of bulbs, the trailing ends of smilax writhing round mustard and pepper pots. God be praised for such dogged calm.[30]

The pastoral setting, the gentleness of English civilisation, the villagers' calm defiance of the terrors overhead, all reflect an era in which, as Jeremy Paxman has written, 'the English had a clear and positive sense of themselves'.[31] A similar point is made by Philip Ziegler in his discussion of the behaviour of Londoners during the Blitz: 'Londoners manufactured their own myth. It is striking how many wrote and spoke in clichés ... They acted out their clichés, too.'[32]

In the spirit of Sir Francis Drake, finishing his game of bowls as the Spanish Armada approached, the English carried on with typical aplomb. At Maidstone Grammar School, the boys regularly had to clear the playing-fields of bomb splinters and cartridge cases before games.[33] When Gordon Farrer, a native of Tunbridge Wells, arrived at a local golf club for a round with his father, a Ju 88 appeared suddenly from the clouds, releasing a stick of bombs which fell on the eighteenth fairway. After clearing the greens of cartridge and cannon shell, father and son enjoyed twelve holes of golf.[34] Whether or not there was a glorious English summer in 1940 is a matter over which opinions differ, but there certainly was according to the legend. Desmond Flower, a young conscript in the Middlesex regiment, describes a typical weekend scene:

> Sunday in Sevenoaks was the same as Sunday throughout Kent, Surrey, Sussex and Essex. The hot summer air throbbed with the steady beat of the engines of bombers which one could not see in the dazzling blue. Then the RAF would arrive; the monotonous drone would be broken by the snarl of a fighter turning at speed, and the vapour trails would start to form in huge circles. I lay on my back in the rose garden and watched the trails forming; as they broadened and dispersed a fresh set would be superimposed upon them. Then, no bigger than a pin's head, a white parachute would open and come down, growing slowly larger; I counted eight in the air at one time.[35]

Out of the Battle there also emerged an image of the Battle of Britain fighter pilot: a dashing English ex-public schoolboy with an upper-crust accent, a silk scarf and a sports car. Courageous to the point of recklessness, he made light of the ordeals through which he had passed by turning them into gripping yarns or funny stories. One of the most celebrated of the aces, Robert Stanford-Tuck, told how, while covered in oil and repeatedly vomiting, he managed to steer his badly damaged Spitfire away from the Channel and over English soil. Forced to bail out when the cockpit erupted in smoke and flame, he came down in a field just outside Plovers, the estate of Lord Cornwallis at Horsmonden. An estate wagon picked him up and took him to the big house, where he was given a bath and a bed and the services of Lord Cornwallis's doctor. After a refreshing sleep and tea with the family he was ready to return to Biggin Hill. As he was about to set off his Lordship uttered a few memorable words of farewell: 'Drop in for a bath any time, m'boy.'[36]

Was the Battle of Britain really like that? Only in part, but the myth proved enduring. 'Deep England' emerged from the Battle of Britain as a model of civic virtue, with its cultural ascendancy over the rest of Britain mightily reinforced.

The Imperial Dimension

In the summer of 1940 the British Empire, with the exception of Eire which remained neutral, was also at war with Germany. Following Britain's declaration of war in September 1939, which committed India and the colonies to the conflict, the Commonwealth countries of Australia, New Zealand, Canada and, after some debate, South Africa quickly followed suit. Robert Menzies, the Australian Prime Minister, proudly announced that the 'British nations' throughout the world were at one: 'One King, one flag, one cause.'[37]

The extent of the support for Britain across the many different parts of the Empire is too complex an issue to explore here. Nevertheless Britain did receive much assistance from imperial sources. During the Battle of Britain the white Empire was, for example, well represented among the 'few': 126 New Zealanders, 98 Canadians – many of whom served in 242 (Canadian) and 1 (Royal Canadian Air Force) Squadrons – 33 Australians, 25 South Africans, 10 Irish, 3 Rhodesians, 1 Jamaican and 1 Newfoundlander fought in the Battle.[38] These included some of the best and bravest pilots. Among the top ten aces of the Battle were two New Zealanders and an Australian. They also suffered some of the heaviest casualty rates. While nearly one in five Fighter Command aircrew who participated in the Battle were killed, over 40 per cent of the Australians and South Africans lost their lives.[39]

Among the best known of the Commonwealth pilots was New Zealander Alan Deere. Born in Auckland, the grandson of emigrants from County

Limerick who had left to escape the troubles in Ireland, he was captivated by the visit to his local town of Sir Charles Kingsford-Smith in his famous tri-plane the *Southern Cross*. In 1937 he applied to join the RAF and was among twelve New Zealanders selected for pilot training. On arrival in Britain Deere and his compatriots were given a frosty reception by their fellow trainees. A game of rugby – 'All Blacks' against the rest – broke the ice. Deare and a number of his team-mates had played first-class rugby in New Zealand and they built up a colossal score: this convinced the British that they weren't such bad chaps after all. During the Battle Deere, who earned a reputation for indestructibility, flew with 54 Squadron and emerged unscathed from countless close shaves. In August 1940 he was shot down by another Spitfire. Swaying in his parachute he landed in a plum tree in Kent and was confronted by an angry farmer brandishing a shotgun. Fearing that his New Zealand accent might be misinterpreted as belonging to a German pretending to be British, Deere pleaded in his most precise English that he was British. The farmer grudgingly conceded, and allowed him to use the telephone, but continued to moan about the damage done to his prize plums.[40]

Johnny Kent was one of the leading Canadians. Born and brought up in Winnipeg, he was thrilled as a boy by the tales of the great fighter aces of the First World War and would bicycle to watch the flying boats operating at the local seaplane base. In 1935 he joined the RAF and became a test pilot. During the Battle he served as a flight commander with 303 (Polish) Squadron and in October 1940 was promoted to command 92 squadron at Biggin Hill.[41] Although this was a high-scoring squadron, it had a reputation for fast living which attracted the attention of an RAF psychologist. Kent had the task of improving discipline. He summoned his officers and gave them a telling off:

> I can't find anything to like about you. You are the most conceited and insubordinate bunch of bastards it's ever been my misfortune to meet in my service career. You dress like bums [their assorted uniforms included check shirts, old school ties, suede shoes and red trousers], you steal air force petrol for your cars, you drink like fishes, you don't sleep and you've made a night club out of your billet, where your girl friends spend the night.[42]

This did not make him popular with the 'playboys' of his squadron, but the tough Canadian persevered and – notwithstanding the occasional night of revelry in the White Hart at Brasted – persuaded the authorities to keep the unit in the fighting line.[43]

The most famous of the South African flyers was Adolph 'Sailor' Malan. Brought up in Wellington, Cape Province, he went to sea as a young man with the Union Castle Steamship Line – so gaining his nickname – before joining the RAF in 1936. Commanding 74 Squadron during the Battle, he was a consummate professional and a most ruthless fighter. On one occasion, when asked how he went about shooting down German bombers, he replied that, if possible, he preferred to let them return home badly damaged: 'With a dead rear gunner, a dead navigator, and the pilot coughing his lungs up as he lands . . . it has a better effect on their morale.'[44] With his fearsome reputation spreading, one of the squadron pilots later wrote to him from a prisoner-of-war camp instructing him to watch his back: 'All Jerries', he warned, 'are after your blood.'[45] After the war he returned to South Africa and, with the same sense of purpose with which he had fought the recent conflict, became a leading member of Torch Commando, an organisation opposed to the disenfranchisement of the coloured voters of the Cape.[46]

Although disowned by neutral Eire, Brendan 'Paddy' Finucane became the most legendary of the Irish pilots. Finucane, whose father fought with De Valera against the British in the Irish uprising in 1916, was a Roman Catholic Dubliner. He developed a love of aeroplanes while on family holidays near the Supermarine factory at Southampton. In 1938 he joined the RAF while working as an assistant book-keeper in London. Although not a born flyer – one of his instructors commenting that 'the ground was never quite sure where Paddy expected it to be' – his determination to succeed carried him through his training. During the Battle he served with 65 Squadron and, flying with a shamrock proudly painted on the side of his aircraft, went on to become one of the most prolific fighter aces of the war. Churchill was so impressed with his exploits that in 1941 he toyed for a while with the idea of creating an Irish wing or squadron in the RAF. In July 1942 Finucane's luck, however, ran out. Leading an attack on a German army base at Etaples, a burst of machine-gun fire struck the radiator of his Spitfire. He turned for home accompanied by his wingman, the Canadian Alan Aikman. About ten miles out to sea Finucane, whose engine was overheating, ditched his plane in the Channel. His last words were 'This is it, Butch' and he was never seen again.[47]

Other key figures associated with the Battle had strong Commonwealth connections. Keith Park, the commander of 11 Group, which bore the brunt of the fighting, was a New Zealander. Born in Thames, a small town south-east of Auckland, his Scots father was director of the Thames School of Mines and later professor of mining at the University of Otago. After a period as a purser with the Union Steamship Company, on the outbreak of the First World War Park volunteered as a gunner and fought with the New Zealand Expeditionary Force at Gallipoli. Later he transferred to the Royal Flying Corps and distinguished himself in the fighting over the Western Front. During the interwar years he occupied a number of RAF posts before taking over 11 Group in the spring of 1940. After his removal from this command at the end of 1940, Park was appointed, in 1942, air officer commanding Malta. There he conducted a successful air battle in defence of the Mediterranean island which bore many similarities to that which he had fought over Britain in 1940. On his retirement at the end of the war he returned to New Zealand and indulged in his favourite recreation: sailing.[48]

Archibald McIndoe, the celebrated plastic surgeon who treated the burned pilots, was another New Zealander. Born in Dunedin, the son of a printer, he was educated at the University of Otago and came to Britain in the early 1930s. On the outbreak of war he was appointed consultant in plastic surgery to the RAF and established a special treatment centre for burned airmen at East Grinstead Hospital in Kent. Among his 'guinea pigs' was Richard Hillary – born in Australia the son of a government official – who was shot down and badly burned during the Battle. On McIndoe's death in 1960 his ashes were laid to rest in the RAF church of St Clement Danes in the Strand: a unique honour for a civilian doctor.[49]

Lord Beaverbrook, the ebullient Minister of Aircraft Production, was a Scots-Canadian who was born in Maple, Ontario, and brought up in Newcastle, New Brunswick. Having worked for a while in his youth as the manager of a bowling alley, he amassed a fortune in the world of finance and came to Britain before the First World War where he built up a newspaper empire centred around the *Daily Express*. In May 1940 Beaverbrook, whose son Max Aitken flew in the Battle with 601 Squadron, was appointed by Churchill to galvanise the aircraft industry. In his later years, he began to regard Canada with increasing notalgia and bestowed generous endowments on his childhood province. He died in 1964 and his ashes were interred in New Brunswick.[50]

The Commonwealth governments also rallied to the 'mother' country during the summer of 1940. Canadian troops, which had begun to arrive in Britain over the previous winter, formed part of GHQ reserve south of the Thames ready to counter a German invasion.[51] A New Zealand force, diverted to Britain on its way to the Middle East, disembarked in June 1940 and was sent to defend the Dover and Folkestone area.[52] Australian troops, sailing in the same convoy, were stationed on Salisbury Plain. On 4 September Churchill paid them a visit: 'It has been very gratifying and refreshing', he was reported to have said to one battalion, 'to have Australians, New Zealanders and Canadians with us in this island during what has been undoubtedly one of the most anxious periods in our long history.'[53]

Another Commonwealth contribution was the relocation of RAF training schools. The extension of active air operations across the country, and the restrictions that had to be placed on flying training, meant that there was an urgent need to transfer a number of schools abroad. Building on the Empire Air Training Scheme which had been established shortly after the outbreak of war, in early August 1940 it was announced that arrangements were being made for the transfer to Canada of the personnel and aircraft of four flying training schools, one air observer navigation school, and one general reconnaissance school. South Africa had agreed to accept two air observer navigation schools, one bombing and gunnery school, and one general reconnaissance school.[54]

The Battle was closely followed in the Empire and many contributed to the Spitfire Fund. The origins of the Fund lay in a letter written by Alec Gordon of St Ann's Bay, Jamaica, to the editor of the local newspaper, *The Gleaner*, in May 1940. Gordon referred to Churchill's appeal for more aircraft to fight the Nazis, and proposed that a 'Jamaica Plane Fund' should be established. The newspaper opened an account at Barclays Bank in Kingston, Jamaica, and money began to flow in.[55] The idea soon caught on and, with the help of Beaverbrook's flair for propaganda, funds were set up across the Empire. At the beginning of August it was reported, for example, that Ceylon had raised £395,000, Natal £201,000, the Falkland Islands £50,000 and Bengal £40,000.[56] In recognition of these fund-raising efforts, a number of squadrons which flew in the Battle were linked to countries or regions which had raised significant sums. Finucane's squadron, for instance, was designated 65 (East India) squadron in tribute to the East India Fund's contribution towards the provision of its Spitfires.[57] A fund was also established in Eire. The Dublin Spitfire Circle, which organised weekly collections from the employees of such firms as Guinness, was singled out for praise by Beaverbrook in the *Daily Express* and the Irish Department of External Affairs sought to put a stop to its activities fearing that it would endanger Irish neutrality.[58] At the end of October 1940 the Home Intelligence reports noted that while there was still a good deal of anti-British feeling in Eire, the bombing of London had produced 'a great if somewhat reluctant surge of admiration for the British people'.[59]

The Anglo-American Dimension

With the fall of France and the withdrawal of British troops from the continent of Europe, the United States became vital to Britain's long-term survival and to any prospect of eventual victory. In his tribute to the 'few' at the height of the Battle of Britain, Churchill – who was himself half-American – recognised that the fate of the British people was closely tied to that of the Americans:

> These two great organisations of the English-speaking democracies, the British Empire and the United States, will have to be somewhat mixed up together in some of their affairs for mutual and general advantage. For my own part, looking out upon the future, I do not view the process with any misgivings. I could not stop it if I wished; no one can stop it. Like the Mississippi, it just keeps rolling along. Let it roll. Let it roll on full flood, inexorable, irresistible, benignant, to broader lands and better days.[60]

The most important contribution of the United States to the outcome of the Battle was the provision of 100 octane fuel, which, as Richard Hallion explains elsewhere in this book, was vital to the operational performance of the Spitfire and Hurricane. Eleven Americans served with the 'few', and in order to facilitate the entry of experienced pilots into the RAF, the British government exempted United States citizens from the requirement of swearing an oath of allegiance to the King.[61]

The best-known American flyer was Billy Fiske. Fiske was the son of a prominent New York banker and studied at Cambridge University in the 1930s. A glamorous figure, he was a champion bobslayer who captained the US Olympic team to the gold medal in 1932, and also broke the Cambridge to London record in his eight-litre Bentley. On the outbreak of war he enlisted in the RAF and served in 601 Squadron during the Battle. This squadron was known as the 'millionaires' squadron' because of the number of well-to-do pilots on its strength. On one occasion, fearing that petrol rationing might interfere with their private motoring, a member of the squadron purchased a local service station, while another, who was a director of Shell, arranged for the pumps to be filled. A brave and skilful fighter pilot, on 16 August 1940 Fiske engaged a pack of Ju 87s and brought his damaged aircraft home, suffering serious burns in the process. Later that day he was sitting up in his hospital bed joking with the squadron adjutant. The next day, however, he died: the result, it was thought, of post-operative shock. On 4 July 1941 a bronze memorial plaque to Fiske was unveiled in St Paul's Cathedral. Inscribed beneath his name were the words: 'An American citizen who died that England might live'.[62]

The Battle also formed part of Britain's effort to bring the neutral United States more directly into the war. At the time of his death the British government had plans to make Fiske into a hero for American school children. Conflict was raging within the United States between isolationists and interventionists over whether the country should remain aloof from events in Europe, and it was believed that the dashing American pilot could be used to promote the British cause in Washington. Although Fiske was destined not to fulfil this role – the focus of attention shifting instead to the RAF's all-American Eagle Squadron, which was in the process of being formed during the summer of 1940 and became operational in January 1941 – the Battle served to emphasise Britain's determination to continue the fight against Nazi Germany, and the RAF's heroism proved a valuable propaganda asset to the British authorities seeking to influence American public opinion. Meanwhile, American correspondents in Britain, most of whom were sympathetic to the British, reported the battles being fought overhead and CBS's Ed Murrow broadcast dramatic eye-witness accounts of air raids over London.[63] While the American public continued to oppose a declaration of war against the Axis powers, it has been argued by Susan Brewer that 'during the Battle of Britain opinion polls registered a shift.

Americans thought that it was more important to ensure Britain's victory than to stay out, and they approved aid to Britain.'[64] Roosevelt, meanwhile, demonstrated greater confidence in Britain. On 3 September 1940, after several months of negotiation, he formally announced the 'destroyers for bases' deal.

The European Dimension

The Battle of Britain inspired bitter feelings towards the leading powers of Europe among the British people. France, it was believed, had let Britain down badly during the summer of 1940. Germany rained down terror from the skies and threatened Britain's very existence as an independent state. Italy entered the war shortly before the capitulation of France and during the last days of October its air force participated in bombing raids over Britain. There was also a fervent belief that Britain was championing the cause of liberty and democracy against the fascist dictatorships of the Continent. This coexisted, uneasily perhaps, with a widespread relief that Britain was now free from European entanglements: 'Never since the days of Nelson', writes P.M.H. Bell, 'had the British been more conscious of living on an island, or happier with that dispensation of Providence.'[65]

And yet the Battle was fought with help *from* Europe. Among the 'few' were 145 Poles and 88 Czechs, many of whom served in 302 (Polish), 303 (Polish), 310 (Czech) and 312 (Czech) Squadrons. 29 Belgians and 13 Frenchmen also served with Fighter Command.[66] Of the top ten aces of the Battle, one was a Pole and one was a Czech. The Czech Joseph Franticek was the highest-scoring ace of the Battle with seventeen confirmed victories. Born in Otaslavice, the son of a carpenter, he served with the Czech air force in the 1930s. When the Germans occupied Prague in the spring of 1939, he fled to Poland and joined the Polish air force. After the German invasion in September 1939, in which he saw combat, he escaped to France via the Balkans and the Middle East. In the spring of 1940 he fought in the Battle of France before departing for Britain. During the Battle of Britain he served with 303 (Polish) Squadron. Although an abundantly gifted fighter pilot, he did, however, lack any sense of air discipline and would often break formation to hunt for the enemy on his own. His exasperated squadron leader eventually declared him a 'guest' of the squadron. As Len Deighton succinctly puts it: 'This gave him the unique privilege of fighting his own war, in his own way, and his own time.' On 8 October his eventful war came to an end. While flying a routine patrol, he was seen approaching an open space near Sutton, apparently trying to make a forced landing, when his aircraft flicked on to its back and dived into the ground. No bullet holes were found in his body or the aircraft. The Czech hero was buried in the Polish air force cemetery in Northwood.[67]

The Battle was, moreover, fought partly *for* Europe. Franticek and his fellow pilots from the occupied countries no doubt believed that the Battle would help to pave the way for the liberation of their homelands. In his eulogy to the 'few', Churchill envisaged that the resistance of Britain would eventually inspire the people of Europe to rise up against their oppressors:

> The fact that the British Empire stands invincible, and that Nazidom is still being resisted, will kindle again the spark of hope in the breasts of hundreds of millions of down-trodden or despairing men and women throughout Europe, and far beyond its bounds, and . . . from these sparks there will presently come cleansing and devouring flame.[68]

The following day Sir Edward Grigg, the Under-Secretary of State for War, introduced the Allied Forces Bill, which gave legal sanction to the establishment of six European armies-in-exile on British soil. He spoke of a partnership with the exiled governments to construct a new Europe:

> We are not fighting for British freedom alone, and therefore we are not fighting for a purely British victory. We do not wish to dominate the Governments that are allied with us, either now or hereafter. We wish them to be our honoured partners in this enterprise, not only in winning the war but in building up a better Europe after the war.[69]

Meanwhile, for the pro-British onlookers in Europe, the dawning realisation that the RAF were gaining the upper hand in the Battle must have provided a psychological boost. As Neville Lytton, a British artist living in a small French town close to the Franco-Swiss border, observed:

> When the Battle of Britain occurred, when astronomical figures of losses incurred by the German air force came over the air, when England lived her finest hour . . . hundreds, thousands, hundreds of thousands, rallied to the belief in victory, and from that moment France recovered her soul. I take this opportunity of saying to my compatriots, those who have stood up to the bombardments in the great cities of England with unflinching courage, that they would feel happy if they knew the effect of their example on the countries of enslaved Europe.[70]

While there were bitter years ahead for those under Nazi occupation, it was Britain's survival in 1940 that provided the strategic base from which the Allies were able to launch the assault which led to the liberation of Western Europe: ironically neither the Poles nor the Czechs were to recover their own independence for decades to come.

On 10 July 1947 King George VI unveiled the Battle of Britain Memorial in Westminster Abbey. The principal feature of the memorial was the stained-glass window extending across the entire east wall of the chapel. At the centre of the window were two panels displaying the flags of all the Commonwealth and Allied nations whose citizens participated in the Battle.[71] As the memorial demonstrated, the Battle belonged to an era in which Britain was both a European power and an imperial power at the centre of the English-speaking world.

Out of the Battle of Britain there arose, in the course of time, a predominantly English legend about the resistance of a liberty-loving people fighting on alone against continental tyranny. The principal effect on post-war British history was to convince many policy-makers that Britain's destiny must always remain separate from that of Europe. In particular, the development of a federal Europe, which appeared to threaten British independence, awoke disturbing memories of 1940.

Of course other interpretations of the Battle of Britain are possible. It could, for example, be argued that the Battle showed that the affairs of Britain were inextricably linked with those of the Continent. It therefore demonstrated the need for Britain to play a permanent and constructive role in Western Europe, and to support a united Europe of which Britain itself must be a part.

Whatever the dilemmas bequeathed to British policy-makers by the experience of 1940, it seems likely that the RAF's victory in that critical year owed much to Britain's diverse international connections and to the multinational solidarity of Britain itself.

Notes and References

We are grateful to Dr Judy Wakeling, Research Fellow at the Centre for Second World War Studies, for her assistance in compiling information for this chapter.

1 Sian Nicholas, *The Echo of War: Home Front Propaganda and the Wartime BBC* (Manchester, 1996), p. 231.
2 Angus Calder, *The Myth of the Blitz* (London, 1991), p. 182.
3 Robert Rhodes James (ed.), *Winston S. Churchill: His Complete Speeches 1897–1963*, vol. 6, *1935–1942* (London, 1974), p. 6238.
4 Neil Redfern, 'Anti-Invasion Defences of Scotland, Wales and Northern Ireland, 1939–1945: Insights and Issues', in *Defence Lines*, no. 12 (July 1999), pp. 6–9.
5 They were superseded from Oct. 1940 by weekly reports. Although Home Intelligence based its findings on a wide range of sources, including the police, the postal censorship, citizens' advice bureaux, and Mass Observation, it is hard to know how much reliance to place on its interpretations of popular opinion. Few attempts were made to survey or quantify opinion, morale remained an elusive concept, and conclusions seem to have been drawn mainly on the basis of

enlightened guesswork. The reports are nevertheless suggestive and also contain much factual information about developments at regional or local level.

6　Public Record Office, Ministry of Information, INF 1/264, Home Intelligence reports, 26 Aug. 1940; 12 Sept. 1940.

7　Nigel Arthur, *Swansea at War* (Manchester, 1988), pp. 21, 27, 34.

8　Andrew Jeffrey, *This Present Emergency: Edinburgh, the River Forth and South-East Scotland and the Second World War* (Edinburgh, 1992), pp. 67–72.

9　PRO INF 1/264, Home Intelligence reports, 15 July to 20 Aug. 1940.

10　Martin Doherty, 'Black Propaganda by Radio: The German Concordia Broadcasts to Britain 1940–1941', in *Historical Journal of Film, Radio and Television*, 14 (1994), pp. 170, 174; Douglas MacLeod, 'Germany calling Scotland', in *Journal for the Study of British Cultures*, 2 (1995), pp. 173–85.

11　Aneurin Bevan, 'Let Us Deserve Our Fighters', *The Tribune* (16 Aug. 1940), p. 12.

12　Rhodes James, *Complete Speeches*, p. 6266.

13　Kenneth G. Wynn, *Men of the Battle of Britain: A Biographical Directory of 'The Few'* (Selsdon, 1999), p. 2. Wynn's book provides biographical details of the 2,917 men awarded the Battle of Britain clasp 'for having flown at least one authorised sortie with an eligible unit of Fighter Command in the period from 10 July to 31 October 1940, both dates inclusive'. We are greatly indebted to Mr Wynn's comprehensive study.

14　We are grateful to Dr Wakeling for calculating these data. On these figures the English were over-represented in relation to population size, and the Welsh and the Northern Irish under-represented, but there could be a range of explanations for this and it would be wrong to draw simple conclusions.

15　John W. Blake, *Northern Ireland in the Second World War* (Belfast, 1956), pp. 80, 163.

16　*The Times* (28 June 1997).

17　'Air Chief Marshall Lord Dowding', Royal Air Forces Association leaflet, n.d.

18　Angus Calder, *The People's War: Britain 1939–45* (London, 1969), p. 150.

19　A.J.P. Taylor, *Beaverbrook* (London, 1972), p. 425.

20　Gordon Beckles, *Birth of a Spitfire* (London, 1941), p. 108.

21　Ibid., p. 98.

22　Dennis Morgan, *Cardiff: A City at War* (Cardiff, 1998), p. 29.

23　PRO INF 1/264, Home Intelligence report, 20 Sept. 1940.

24　Ibid., reports for 11–25 Sept. 1940.

25　Nigel Nicolson (ed.), *Harold Nicolson: Diaries and Letters 1939–1945* (London, 1970), p. 19.

26　Philip Ziegler, *London at War* (London, 1995), p. 122.

27　Winston S. Churchill, *The Second World War*, vol. 2, *Their Finest Hour* (London, 1949), p. 316.

28　Tom Harrisson, *Living Through the Blitz* (Harmondsworth, 1978), p. 56.

29　Ibid., p. 78.

30　John Betjeman, 'Oh to be in England . . .', *The Listener* (11 Mar. 1943), p. 295. We are grateful to Caroline Wellman for this reference.

31　Jeremy Paxman, *The English: A Portrait of a People* (Harmondworth, 1999), p. 2.

32　Ziegler, *London at War*, p. 163.

33　Norman Longmate, *How We Lived Then: A History of Everyday Life During the Second World War* (London, 1973 ed.), p. 115.

34 Oonagh Hyndman, *Wartime Kent* (Rainham, 1990), pp. 152–3.
35 Quoted in John Keegan, *The Second World War* (London, 1989), p. 80.
36 Quoted in Gavin Lyall (ed.), *The War in the Air 1939–45* (London, 1994 ed.), pp. 48–50.
37 Quoted in William Yandell Elliot and H. Duncan Hall, *The British Commonwealth at War* (New York, 1971), p. 11.
38 Wynn, *Men of the Battle of Britain*, p. 2.
39 Len Deighton, *Fighter: The True Story of the Battle of Britain* (London, 1996), p. 234.
40 Group Captain Alan C. Deere, DSO, OBE, DFC, *Nine Lives* (London, 1959), pp. 15–138.
41 Group Captain J.A. Kent, DFC and Bar, AFC, *One of the Few* (London, 1971), pp. 13–127.
42 Tony Bartley, DFC, *Smoke Trails in the Sky: The Journals of a Battle of Britain Fighter Pilot* (Wilmslow, 1997), pp. 56–7.
43 Kent, *One of the Few*, pp. 128–49; also see Kath Preston, *Inn of the Few 1932–1971* (Tunbridge Wells, 1993).
44 Oliver Walker, *Sailor Malan: A Biography* (London, 1953), p. 99.
45 Norman L.R. Franks, *Sky Tiger: The Story of Group Captain Sailor Malan, DSO, DFC* (London, 1994), p. 87.
46 Walker, *Sailor Malan*, pp. 155–82; Franks, *Sky Tiger*, p. 198.
47 Richard Doherty, *Irish Men and Women in the Second World War* (Dublin, 1999), pp. 176–89; A.J. Liebling, 'Paddy of the RAF', in *The New Yorker Book of War Pieces* (New York, 1947), pp. 89–98; Doug Stokes, *Paddy Finucane: Fighter Ace* (Somerton, 1992).
48 D.M. Davin, 'Sir Keith Rodney Park', in *Dictionary of National Biography 1971–1980* (Oxford, 1986), pp. 654–5; also see Vincent Orange, *Sir Keith Park* (London, 1984).
49 Richard Battle, 'Sir Archibald Hector McIndoe', in *Dictionary of National Biography 1951–1960* (Oxford, 1971), pp. 670–1.
50 Katherine Bligh, *Catalogue of the Beaverbrook Papers in the House of Lords*, vol. 1, *Canadian and Business Papers* (London, 1997), pp. ix–xxxix; John Elliot, 'William Maxwell Aitken', in *Dictionary of National Biography 1961–1970* (Oxford, 1981), pp. 8–12.
51 Colonel C.P. Stacey, *Official History of the Canadian Army in the Second World War*, vol. 1, *Six Years of War: The Army in Canada, Britain and the Pacific* (Ottawa, 1955), pp. 288–9.
52 W.G. McClymont, *Official History of New Zealand in the Second World War 1939–45: To Greece* (Wellington, 1959), pp. 23–42.
53 Gavin Long, *Australia in the War of 1939–1945*, series 1, vol. 1, *To Benghazi* (Canberra, 1952), pp. 305–10.
54 Public Record Office, Cabinet Papers, CAB 66/10, Royal Air Force Training, memorandum by the Secretary of State for Air, 7 Aug. 1940.
55 *The Daily Gleaner* (22 May 1940); ibid. (25 May 1940). We are grateful to Linda D. Cameron of the Gleaner Company Ltd for providing us with this information.
56 'The Empire's Part in the Battle', in *The War Illustrated* (2 Aug. 1940), p. 97.
57 The Spitfire and Hurricane Memorial, http://www.spitfire-museum.com/pilot/
58 Robert Fisk, *In Time of War: Ireland, Ulster and the Price of Neutrality 1939–45* (Dublin, 1983), pp. 177–8.

59 PRO INF 1/292, Weekly Report for Home Intelligence, 21–28 Oct. 1940.
60 *The Penguin Hansard*, vol. 3, *Britain Gathers Strength* (Harmondsworth, 1941), p. 190.
61 PRO CAB 66/9, Royal Air Force Training, memorandum by the Secretary of State for Air, 1 July 1940; Wynn, *Men of the Battle of Britain*, p. 2.
62 Nicholas John Cull, *Selling War: The British Propaganda Campaign Against American 'Neutrality' in World War II* (Oxford, 1995), pp. 89–90; Wynn, *Men of the Battle of Britain*, p. 165; Deighton, *Fighter*, p. 44; Norman Franks, *Wings of Freedom: Twelve Battle of Britain Pilots* (London, 1980), p. 169; Norman Gelb, *Scramble: A Narrative History of the Battle of Britain* (London, 1986), p. 143.
63 Cull, *Selling War*, pp. 89–104.
64 Susan A. Brewer, *To Win the Peace: British Propaganda in the United States During World War II* (London, 1997), p. 38.
65 P.M.H. Bell, *Britain and France 1900–1940: Entente and Estrangement* (London, 1996), p. 253.
66 Wynn, *Men of the Battle of Britain*, p. 2.
67 Deighton, *Fighter*, pp. 154–5, 232; Wynn, *Men of the Battle of Britain*, p. 173; Kent, *One of the Few*, p. 126; Josef Frantisek, Hero of the Battle of Britain, by Dariusz Tyminski, http://www.acestory.gdynia.top.pl/frantis/frantis.htm
68 Rhodes James, *Complete Speeches*, pp. 6264–5.
69 *The Penguin Hansard*, p. 160.
70 Neville Lytton, *Life in Unoccupied France* (London, 1942), pp. 24–5.
71 Programme for the unveiling of the Battle of Britain Memorial, Westminster Abbey, 10 July 1947, p. 2. We are grateful to Miss Christine Reynolds of Westminster Abbey for providing us with a copy of this programme.

PART SIX

THE SIGNIFICANCE

RICHARD OVERY

How Significant *Was* the Battle?

In 1980 the historian A.J.P. Taylor defined the Battle of Britain in typically
categorical terms. It was, he wrote, 'a true air war, even if on a small scale,
and had decisive strategic results'.[1] He was speaking for a generation of
Britons for whom the Battle of Britain was unquestionably a turning-point
in the war. Taylor's 'decisive results' were self-evident: Britain had been
saved from conquest and would remain the rallying point for the struggle
against Hitlerism; Hitler turned away from the island he could not defeat
to launch the assault on the Soviet Union which altered the entire nature
of the conflict. Few have doubted, either then or since, that defeat in the
Battle of Britain would have brought about the global New Order to which
the Axis powers pledged themselves in the Tripartite Pact, drawn up and
signed late in September 1940 while the air battle was still being fought.

There is much to recommend Taylor's view. Though recent scholarship
has demonstrated that German victory in the air battle was always unlikely,
it did represent the first major confrontation between air forces fighting
independently. Nor can there be much doubt that British capitulation at
any time between the summer of 1940 and the spring of 1941, when the
bomb attacks finally ended, would have produced an international political
revolution of unpredictable dimensions. It is nevertheless important to
place the Battle of Britain in the wider military and political context in order
to assess just how decisive it was. Many of those 'decisive strategic results'
became clear only with the end of the war and the process of transforming
the Battle into myth. The contemporary evidence suggests that neither side
at the time invested the air conflict with the weight of historical significance
that it has borne in the sixty years since it was fought.

The Military Significance

On 15 June 1940, days before French capitulation, Winston Churchill sent a spirited telegram to the prime ministers of the Dominions: 'I do not regard the situation as having passed beyond our strength . . . Hitler will have to break us in this Island or lose the war'.[2] The German failure to break British resolve during the Battle of Britain and the winter bombing offensive that followed it did not cause Germany to lose the war, even following the most indirect of explanatory routes. But the Battle did have very direct and immediate military consequences, which shaped the strategic choices open to both sides.

In its simplest terms the German failure in the Battle of Britain was the first military reverse suffered by German forces since the onset of German territorial expansion in 1938. (It was, ironically enough, a vindication of Chamberlain's priority for air-defence preparations in the 1930s.) The symbolic significance of this reverse was not lost on those who orchestrated British propaganda, nor perhaps on world opinion, but its military significance should not be exaggerated. The defeat of an enemy air force over its own territory and the establishment, even for a short period, of air supremacy in enemy air space was difficult to achieve against a powerful air force. The asymmetrical conflict in Poland was, in that sense, no preparation for air war in France (where the Luftwaffe suffered heavier losses in the six weeks of fighting than it did in the first six weeks of the Battle of Britain) or over Britain. The balance of recent historical writing on the Battle of Britain suggests that German performance was better than might have been expected given the adverse circumstances under which it operated, but German victory would have been against the odds. By late September the Luftwaffe was temporarily reduced to 276 serviceable single-engined fighters against 665 serviceable single-engined fighters in RAF Fighter Command.[3]

More significant were the military consequences of the German air failure. The Battle of Britain prevented Operation Sealion, the invasion of southern England in 1940, and weakened any prospect that Britain would sue for peace on German terms. That is not to say that other factors were not also important in hindering invasion, but from early on in Hitler's arguments for invading England he had isolated the essential precondition of air supremacy and it was that element of failure that he used to justify postponing invasion. According to the diary of General Halder, German army Chief of Staff, Hitler warned his military leaders on 31 July that an attack on Britain might not succeed: 'If results of air warfare are unsatisfactory, invasion preparations will be stopped.'[4] Although invasion was not formally postponed until 17 September, Hitler had already formed the view by 20 August that 'The collapse of England in the year 1940 is under present circumstances no longer to be reckoned on.'[5]

It is often assumed that the corollary of German failure was Hitler's decision to turn to the east and fight a war with the Soviet Union. The German evidence is nevertheless ambiguous. While it is plausible to argue that the two decisions were sequential – i.e. the failure to force a decision in the west compelled Hitler to turn to the east to eradicate Britain's last hope in Europe – it could also be argued that Hitler never seriously intended to invade Britain and was already planning the next stage of the war for *Lebensraum* in the east at the same time as invasion preparations were used to bring pressure on Britain for a political settlement.[6]

The issue of timing is critical here. For much of June and early July 1940 the German leadership expected Britain to give up a war she had no hope of winning. On 23 June Goebbels announced at a ministerial conference that the Churchill government would soon fall: 'A compromise government will be formed. We are very close to the end of the war.'[7] Hitler was willing to allow Britain to retain her Empire and navy as long as Germany was allowed European hegemony, given back her colonies and the 'wrongs' of Versailles rectified. By the second week of July, in the absence of any indication from Britain of a willingness to reach a political settlement, Hitler began to explore plans for invasion. When the Commander-in-Chief of the German navy, Admiral Raeder, discussed with Hitler on 11 July the prospects for invasion he made it clear that the operation was too risky and recommended instead trade blockade and bomb attacks to bring the war home to the British population.[8] On 16 July Hitler ordered invasion regardless of Raeder's objections. Three days later a final peace offer was made in the Reichstag, which was formally rejected by the British Foreign Secretary, Lord Halifax, three days later. The military solution was approved on 21 July in a mood of growing frustration with British obstinacy. The door was not closed to a political solution, but German leaders now expected this to follow from military pressure. On 22 July Goebbels told his staff: 'With their totally different, un-European mentality the British are unable to believe that the offer made in the Führer's speech was not just bluff but was meant seriously . . . Britain will not see reason until she has suffered the first blows.'[9] On 29 July plans were drawn up to transfer thirteen divisions of 260,000 men across the English Channel at some time between mid-August and mid-September.

There is no reason to assume that Hitler was not serious about the invasion plan. The shift in July reflected real confusion on the German side about how to bring the war in the west to a tidy conclusion. Hitler hoped that Britain would sue for peace, though the terms would be far from favourable, but he also prepared for the military opportunity if, or when, the conditions became particularly advantageous. Yet at exactly the same time a second strategic shift was occurring. During the course of July the German army staff drew up contingency plans for a strike against the USSR, whose forces had used the opportunity of Germany's western campaign to occupy the Baltic states and Bessarabia. On 21 July, when the British operation was approved, Hitler was also presented by the army Commander-in-Chief with a plan of campaign to seize the western provinces of the USSR, a pre-emptive strike to reduce the Soviet threat and secure Germany's eastern empire. Ten days later Hitler called his military leaders together and told them that if pressure on Britain showed that 'the British are crumbling' the attack should be pressed on. Any prospect, however, that Britain might rely on the USSR to help her war effort would be destroyed once and for all by an annihilating attack on the Red Army.[10]

In this sense the two operations were clearly linked. Hitler ordered large-scale army armaments plans for the attack in the east in late July, but he also approved plans to shift to the production of naval and air equipment within six months in order to complete the defeat of Britain and keep the United States at arm's length in 1942.[11] The riskiness involved in a seaborne invasion of Britain in the autumn made the USSR–Britain sequence increasingly likely, but not certain. Hitler made up his mind only as circumstances unfolded. The one thing German leaders could not risk was the messy failure of Operation Sealion, any more than the Allies could run that risk four years later with Overlord. The effect of failure would be to blunt the effort to attack the USSR in the spring of 1941, and to nullify all the diplomatic efforts made in the late summer to isolate Britain internationally. What governed Hitler's attitude to invasion was not his decision to turn to the east, but the operational realities of the plan to eliminate Britain in a brief and decisive campaign.[12]

The failure to force British capitulation had one other significant consequence: it kept a powerful anti-Axis military presence in Europe, which would make possible American entry to the European conflict at some unspecified date in the future. British defeat or surrender in 1940 would have made prospects for American belligerency across 3,000 miles of ocean remote (and would have made continued British Empire belligerency pointless). British survival did not cause America to fight, but it did create circumstances that allowed American statesmen and military leaders to contemplate the prospect seriously. In July 1940 Lord Lothian, the British ambassador in Washington, told an audience: 'Today we are your Maginot Line.'[13] Under the circumstances this was an unfortunate choice of metaphor, but it was consistent with the view expressed by some Washington circles that the American frontier now lay along the English Channel. British efforts, nonetheless, produced little immediate response. It was not until February 1941, almost six months after the Battle of Britain, that Roosevelt sent Averell Harriman to London to 'recommend everything we can do, short of war, to keep the British Isles afloat'.[14]

It is as well to recall at this point some of the things that success in the Battle of Britain did not affect. In the first place it did not end German efforts to pressure Britain into agreement through military means. Following RAF attacks on Berlin in late August, Goering ordered the Luftwaffe on 2 September to switch to the heavy bombing of British industrial cities and administrative centres. At the same time the blockade of Britain from sea and air, which was Raeder's preferred strategy, continued to take a heavy toll of British supplies. The combination of the so-called Blitz and the blockade was an indirect means to secure what could not be achieved by direct invasion. The fear of the 'knock-out blow' from the air did not abate after the Battle of Britain, but on the contrary intensified as German bombing escalated. The Master of Corpus Christi College in Cambridge told a visitor in January 1941 that people still did not realise 'how gigantic the German knock-out blow will be when it comes'.[15]

Even the government was not immune from such fantasies. On the basis of a Swiss Intelligence source which claimed that Germany had kept back a secret force of 10,000 aircraft in order to mount one colossal air attack or 'banquet', Churchill asked the Air Staff to calculate exactly what kind of knock-out blow the Germans could mount. The Air Staff dismissed the idea of 10,000 hidden planes, but told Churchill in February 1941 that if Germany scraped together all her front-line, reserve and trainer aircraft she could dispatch approximately 14,000 aircraft in one attack. When Churchill asked what the RAF could retaliate with, he was told that the maximum was 6,514 aircraft, including 3,000 reserve aircraft and 2,000 trainers.[16] Churchill's concern over German air intentions illustrates the extent to which the Battle of Britain was perceived to be only one part of a longer German assault on Britain, whose dimensions and character remained uncertain across the whole winter of 1940–1.

The air battle also did little for Britain's position in the Mediterranean and Africa, where British Empire forces now faced a belligerent Italy alone, though it did allow a cautious reinforcement of the Middle East. Empire armies found difficulty in containing Germany's weaker ally during the critical months of August 1940, when Italy invaded British Somaliland, and September, when Italian forces crossed into Egypt. It would scarcely be an exaggeration to argue that the British counter-offensive into Libya in December 1940 and the defeat of Italian forces in Ethiopia in April the following year were as important to the survival of the British Empire's global strategic position as the defeat of the Luftwaffe in the autumn of 1940. Indeed the crisis in Africa highlighted just how weak the British population was in the winter of 1940–1, facing the Axis powers in isolation, blockaded by submarine, heavily bombed and stretched taut between Europe, the Mediterranean and the Far East. In late November 1940 Churchill was reported still to be convinced that the Germans 'will strive by every means to smash us before the spring. "We are in for a really terrible ordeal."'[17] In this sense the Battle of Britain ranks with Midway or the German halt at Moscow:

a necessary defensive victory, but a long way from turning the tide of the war.

The Political Consequences

On 29 July 1940 Alexander Kirk, an American long resident in Berlin, wrote to Roosevelt about the rumours flying around the German capital concerning a political settlement with Britain. He expressed his grave concern at the possible political consequences of British agreement: 'any concession on the part of the British Government now would destroy forever the chance of eradicating the forces which are threatening our own civilization . . . with England silenced the force of democracy would be annihilated'.[18] It is tempting to assume that the wider world audience saw the contest in the autumn of 1940 as a decisive political turning point, the forces of democracy triumphant over the dark forces of authoritarianism and militarism. Yet here, too, the impact of the Battle of Britain both on the home population and on international opinion can be exaggerated.

The chief difficulty in assessing the impact of the Battle lies with issues of definition and perception. The 'Battle of Britain' itself is a historical reconstruction, used to describe the air campaign fought from August to October 1940 after the event. When Churchill on 18 June summoned his people to fight the 'battle of Britain' (published later in the year without the capital letter Churchill gave to the 'Battle of France'),[19] he did not have in mind what is now defined as the air battle, but a conflict for the defence of Britain against German attacks of all kinds. The continuous air offensive from July made it difficult to define the precise contours of an air battle. As late as December 1940 General Alexander (Commander-in-Chief of Southern Command) could comment that with the onset of very heavy bombing 'the Battle of England' had begun in earnest.[20] Not until the end of March 1941 did the Ministry of Information publish, on behalf of the Air Ministry, the famous 32-page pamphlet *The Battle of Britain*, which perhaps did more than anything to define the accepted historical image of the battle and to give it a beginning and an end. 'By 31st October the Battle was over,' ran the pamphlet's conclusion. It died away gradually; but the British victory was none the less certain and complete.'[21]

Yet the image of the Battle carried by the British public was not so clear-cut. Fears of invasion persisted, while the onset of heavy night bombing could be construed as the continuation of the Battle by other means. Mingled with the sense of bravado or defiance were very real fears that democracy was still far from safe. On 29 September the MP Harold Nicolson, who worked for the Ministry of Information, complained in his diary: 'Why is it that we are never successful? What we need is a neat little triumph somewhere.' Even in December 1940 he found 'a wave of defeatism' among the public.[22] Popular fears of invasion resurfaced with the coming of spring. Realisation that Britain had won a victory of any lasting significance in the autumn of 1940 perhaps owed as much to the publication of *The Battle of Britain* pamphlet in March as it did to popular perception of the contest, where 'victory' was never so clearly defined. It would be vain to speculate about whether the Battle of Britain kept the British fighting in the autumn of 1940, for the issue of war or peace did not hang on public opinion, any more than it was dependent on the outcome of the air operations that came to be called the 'Battle of Britain'.

The effect of the air battles on foreign opinion was also mixed. British success did not win over potential allies to her cause. The Soviet Union was not beguiled in any sense by the outcome, despite Hitler's fear that she was the last hope for Britain in continental Europe. Soviet leaders continued to distrust Britain more than Germany, since the British Empire represented the epitome of the Leninist imperial antagonist. The formal ideological position was to await the outcome of a war between capitalist states, in the hope that the USSR would profit from the inevitable social upheaval that must follow major war. When the writer Emil Ludwig tried on his own initiative to encourage a Soviet-British-American alliance in August 1940, he was brushed aside by the Soviet ambassador in Washington, Konstantin Oumansky. 'With whom should we ally ourselves, with the British?' Oumansky asked Ludwig. 'Those arrogant milords wash their hands four times after being with us.'[23] The Soviet ambassador to London, Ivan Maisky, made no mention of the air battles in his memoirs, but he did recall telling Halifax in October that the Soviet Union was tired of British 'good intentions' and would only be convinced by good deeds. 'But there were no good deeds,' continued Maisky, 'and as a result Anglo-Soviet relations remained unsatisfactory.'[24] Maisky was among those who feared that Britain lacked the capacity to defeat Germany and would seek a separate agreement with Hitler.[25] Only the onset of the German invasion in June 1941 ended the long period of mutual distrust.

More might have been expected of the reaction in the United States, whose interests were more directly affected by the issue of British survival. It is certainly the case that there existed a much greater fund of good will in the United States over British prospects than was to be found in Moscow, but there was no question of open belligerency on Britain's behalf. The story of the development of closer economic and political ties in the course of 1940 is too well known to bear repeating here. But the extent to which this could be attributed to the Battle of Britain is far less certain. Indeed, during the high point of what came to be regarded as the Battle, the chief issue between the two states was the negotiation over the 'destroyers for bases' deal.

Roosevelt was concerned that the exchange should not take place if there were any chance of British defeat or search for peace. A delegation was sent in the late summer to report back on the state of British morale and the prospects for German invasion. The future US ambassador John Winant reported that the British population could take the air attacks, while his military colleagues, despite the presence of some American observers who believed Britain 'had not got a hope', insisted in their report to Washington that the RAF could not be defeated and recommended that the destroyer exchange should go ahead.[26] The American Secretary of State, Cordell Hull, claimed in his memoirs that the destroyer decision generated the kind of political reaction that has commonly been attributed to the Battle of Britain:

> The transaction enheartened the democracies then under the heel of the Prussian boot ... Hitler could no longer hope that his offer of peace to Britain ... would be accepted. Mussolini realized by now that what he thought an easy chance for booty had turned into a dangerous gamble. Japan, awaiting a British collapse before moving toward the South Sea area, paused and took stock.[27]

Hull almost certainly overstated the case, but it is an interesting reflection of the view of the war from Washington, and it is not inconsistent with the Roosevelt/Churchill correspondence, in which the destroyer deal also featured much more than the air battle in the critical weeks of August.[28]

Hull's assessment of the possible course of the war, which he made before army and navy leaders on 12 October 1940, painted a much bleaker picture of British prospects. Hitler, Hull suggested, held the whip hand: 'He may at any time order a general advance from London to Tokyo, in the air, on the sea, and on the land.' Hull did not rule out the possibility that bombing would continue over the winter, 'until Britain is conquered from across the Channel and through the air'.[29] Hull, of course, hoped to present the worst case as part of the effort to persuade American opinion to follow Roosevelt into a third term of office to safeguard America's safety. Until November Roosevelt himself and the rest of the political elite were absorbed by the presidential contest, whose outcome was thought to affect American foreign and military policy materially.[30] Only with Roosevelt's victory in November could the United States engage seriously again with the European crisis. It was partly for that reason that the Blitz played a much greater part than the Battle of Britain in shaping American opinion on aid for Britain. During the winter of 1940–1 orchestrated propaganda from Britain, particularly film propaganda, jostled with news reports and pictures to present the American public with vivid images of the embattled democracy, images that were mobilised to push through, among other things, the lend-lease legislation.[31]

It is doubtful if American opinion could distinguish the different phases of the air battle until generous quantities of *The Battle of Britain* pamphlet were printed in the United States in April 1941. Bombing touched a chord in popular opinion, as it had done with Spain and China. The propaganda surrounding the Blitz was used instrumentally in Washington to win over doubters on American rearmament or economic assistance for Britain. The new American ambassador, John Winant, was appointed by Roosevelt in February 1941 in part because of his belief in British endurance formed during the air battles in the autumn of 1940, which his predecessor, Joseph Kennedy, had singularly lacked.[32] But even in the spring of 1941 there remained serious reservations about Britain's ability to survive in the face of bombing and submarine warfare. Roosevelt's personal emissary, Averell Harriman, who arrived in London on 15 March 1941, made no attempt to hide from colleagues in Washington the dangers facing Britain if the United States failed to enter the war. On 21 May, when the worst of the bombing was past, Harriman wrote the following to William Bullitt, former ambassador to France:

> Either we have an interest in the outcome of this war or we have not. If not, why are we supplying England with the tools? If we have, why do we not realize that the situation could not be tougher and every day we delay direct participation . . . we are taking an extreme risk that either the war will be lost or the difficulty of winning it multiplied . . .[33]

The Battle of Britain made little difference at the time to American policy towards Britain, any more than it altered Soviet attitudes. The issues surrounding the possibility of American belligerency remained unaltered. The two things that British survival secured, and not until half a year later, were the onset of secret staff talks in March 1941 and expanded economic assistance approved the same month. These additional supplies might otherwise have been reduced for fear that American resources would fall into Axis hands, as they had with French capitulation in 1940.[34]

The effect of the Battle on Britain's enemies is no easier to assess. Despite the failure to defeat the RAF, German leaders remained confident that political initiatives coupled with bombing and blockade would force Britain out of the war with or without an invasion, which the German military had regarded from the start as very risky. On 12 October Hitler issued a directive to that end: 'preparations for "Sea Lion" shall be continued solely for the purpose of maintaining political and military pressure on England'.[35] In conferences later in the year he indicated that an invasion might take place in the summer of 1941, at the same time as the Barbarossa campaign, rather than as an alternative to it.[36] But he envisaged such an invasion, as he had done in the summer of 1940, as something of a mopping-up operation after Britain had been 'crippled to a considerable degree' and Germany had established 'complete air supremacy'. In January 1941 he told the commanders-in-chief that he placed greatest weight on the blockade, which might bring British capitulation in July or August 1941. Above all Hitler still hoped 'to negotiate peace with Britain'.[37]

German strategy towards Britain remained fragmented and uncertain, and consistently over-optimistic, across the autumn and winter of 1940–1. A diplomatic offensive was undertaken to isolate Britain and to threaten her position throughout the Mediterranean and Middle East, with particular emphasis on Spain, whose help was needed to seize Gibraltar. German leaders expected the bombing to complement this political offensive and bring the British to the conference table.[38] On 11 December Hitler reportedly told the assembled Nazi Party gauleiters that 'the war is militarily as good as won'. With Britain 'isolated', 'victory was in the bag'.[39] In the pages of Goebbels's private diary throughout the period there can be traced a persistent confidence that bombing was sufficiently unendurable to bring about British defeat:

> 24 November . . . Grim reports from Coventry and Birmingham. When will Churchill capitulate?
>
> 3 December . . . we have attacked London and Southampton on an extraordinary scale. Pessimistic voices from London and above all from the USA grow stronger . . .
>
> 5 December . . . Frightful reports over the destruction of Southampton. The city is one single ruin as a result, and life there a hell. So it must go on, until England is on her knees, begging for peace.[40]

Alongside the military pressure there remained the hope that the evidence of peace feelers and political dissent in Britain would produce a political revolution and make a negotiated peace a real possibility. Such a view retained sufficient force to persuade Rudolf Hess to fly to Britain on 10 May 1941 to try to detach Britain from the war before the conflict to the east.[41]

A Necessary Battle

The course of German strategy towards Britain from the summer of 1940 suggests that the Battle of Britain was only one strand of German policy, rather than a campaign central to it. Hitler would have preferred a neat end to the war in 1940, but did not think that Britain would survive beyond the defeat of the Soviet Union in 1941. If the Battle of Britain had not been fought at all, German strategy might not have been very different. Blockade, bombing and the political offensive were already in place even before the Battle was waged. It is possible that without the decision to test the prospects for an invasion, Hitler might have been more susceptible to the strong arguments of his operations chief, General Alfred Jodl, and Admiral Raeder that a co-ordinated assault on Britain's

Mediterranean position – Gibraltar, Malta and the Suez Canal – would undermine Britain's strategic position more surely than a campaign against the RAF.[42] On the other hand, the attack on the Soviet Union, with its mixed strategic and ideological imperatives, would have continued whether the air assault had taken place or not. When Hitler one evening in April 1942 lectured his dinner guests on the course of the war, the campaign against Britain was overlooked entirely: 'The two decisive events of the war up to the present have been the Norwegian campaign of 1940 and our defensive struggle in the East during the last winter.'[43]

What if Britain had lost the air battle? This in itself is a problematic idea. The difficulties of achieving air supremacy over the area of southern England destined for invasion were real enough. It could not have been achieved over the rest of the country, and would have been difficult to defend even in the south with shrinking Luftwaffe reserves of men and machines. The real issue is whether the invasion of Britain could have been attempted even beneath an established German air umbrella, given the problems faced by the German navy and the short period of preparation and training. When General Halder heard the navy's operational plans for invasion on 28 July 1940, he commented in his diary: 'If that is true, all previous statements by the navy were so much rubbish and we can throw away the whole plan of an invasion.'[44] On 30 August Raeder insisted that there was still no way the navy could meet the operational requirements of the army. Jodl had already drawn up a memorandum which suggested that unless the navy could meet those requirements 'then a landing in England must be regarded as a sheer act of desperation'.[45] General Blumentritt, who was a staff officer working on Sea Lion, later wrote that the resources assigned to the campaign were quite inadequate for the task:

> Even had we succeeded in landing on the English south coast, the future would still be grim ... It must not be forgotten that we Germans are a continental people. We knew far too little of England. We knew literally nothing of amphibious operations and had no experience. At the time we were preparing the Sealion plans accounts of the campaigns of Caesar, Britannicus and William the Conqueror were being read ...[46]

Even with the RAF defeated, there would have been very real risks, with potentially disastrous consequences. General Jodl prefaced his memorandum on the invasion with the following warning: 'It is imperative that no matter what might happen the operation dare not fail, as failure would have political consequences far exceeding the military consequences.'[47]

Defeat of the RAF did not necessarily mean a successful invasion; nor would it necessarily have forced Churchill's hand in seeking a negotiated peace. Conditions remained perilous enough over the winter months if the British government needed justification for seeking an end to the war. The breathing space secured in September 1940 was confined indeed, for Italian forces and German submarines and bombers kept up relentless pressure on an overstretched British Empire. In November 1940 Harold Nicolson summed up the limited character of Britain's achievement: 'I think we have managed to avoid losing this war, but when I think how on earth we are going to win it, my imagination quails.'[48] The final outcome of the war was only loosely connected to that modest achievement, but to Britain's besieged population the Battle of Britain became and remained the symbol of defiance, a necessary battle for British self-esteem and international credibility. When George Orwell broadcast on the BBC on 19 September 1942 he reminded his listeners that four days before had seen the second anniversary of the Battle of Britain:

> Now that we can look back and see the events in better perspective it is becoming clear that the Battle of Britain ranks in importance with Trafalgar, Salamis, the defeat of the Spanish Armada and other battles of the past in which the invading forces of a seemingly invincible monarch or dictator have been beaten back and which have formed a turning point in history.[49]

For the British people, avoiding defeat and occupation in 1940 seemed nothing less.

Notes and References

1 A.J.P. Taylor, review of *The Air War, 1939–1945*, *Observer* (30 Nov. 1980).

2 D. Dilks (ed.), *The Diaries of Sir Alexander Cadogan, 1938–1945* (London, 1971), p. 303.

3 H. Faber (ed.), *Luftwaffe: An Analysis by Former Luftwaffe Generals* (London, 1979), pp. 191–2. The best account of the battle from the German side can be found in K. Maier et al., *Das Deutsche Reich und der Zweite Weltkrieg*, vol. 2, *Die Errichtung der Hegemonie auf dem europäischen Kontinent* (Stuttgart, 1979), pp. 375–408.

4 C. Burdick and H.-A. Jacobsen (ed.), *The Halder War Diary, 1939–1942* (Novato, Ca, 1988), p. 243, entry for 31 July 1940; see, too, *Führer Conferences on Naval Affairs, 1939–1945* (reprinted London, 1990), p. 115, meeting with Hitler, 11 July 1940 ('considers air superiority a prerequisite'); p. 119, conference with Hitler, 21 July 1940 ('The prerequisites are complete mastery of the air . . .').

5 Imperial War Museum, EDS documents, AL 1492, Aktennotiz, OKW, 20 Aug. 1940. The view was recorded by Georg Thomas, head of the OKW Economics and Armaments Office.

6 See the discussion in J. Förster, 'Hitler Turns East – German War Policy in 1940 and 1941', in B. Wegner (ed.), *From Peace to War: Germany, Soviet Russia and the World, 1939–1941* (Oxford, 1997), pp. 115–33; E.M. Robertson, 'Hitler Turns from the West to Russia, May–December 1940', in R. Boyce (ed.), *Paths to War: New Essays on the Origins of the Second World War* (London, 1989),

pp. 367–82; H. Koch, 'Operation Barbarossa: The Current State of the Debate', *Historical Journal*, 31 (1988), pp. 377–90.

7 W. Boelcke (ed.), *The Secret Conferences of Dr Goebbels, Oct. 1939 to March 1943* (London, 1967), p. 60.

8 *Führer Naval Conferences*, p. 114.

9 *Secret Conferences of Dr Goebbels*, p. 69, conference of 22 July 1940.

10 Förster, 'Hitler Turns East', pp. 120–3; *Führer Naval Conferences*, pp. 122–5, conference with the Führer on 31 July 1940 at the Berghof, C-in-C navy, 1 Aug. 1940.

11 IWM, FD 5447/45, Notiz über die Besprechung bei Chef Heeresrüstungsamt, 19 July 1940; Hitler directive, 'Umsteuerung der Rüstung', in G. Thomas, *Geschichte der deutschen Wehr- und Rüstungswirtschaft*, ed. W. Birkenfeld (Boppard am Rhein, 1966), pp. 413–15, 420.

12 H. Greiner, 'Operation Seelöwe and Intensified Air Warfare Against England up to October 30, 1940', in D. Detweiler (ed.), *World War II German Military Studies*, 24 vols (New York, 1979), vol. 7.

13 *The American Speeches of Lord Lothian* (Oxford, 1941), p. 112, NBC Broadcast, 22 July 1940.

14 W.A. Harriman and E. Abel, *Special Envoy to Churchill and Stalin, 1941–1946* (London, 1976), p. 3.

15 N. Nicolson (ed.), *Harold Nicolson: Diaries and Letters, 1939–1945* (London, 1967), p. 140, entry for 23 Jan. 1941.

16 Public Record Office, AIR 8/463, Portal to Churchill, Feb. 1941; Portal to Churchill, 20 Mar. 1941.

17 Nicolson, *Diaries and Letters*, p. 129, entry for 22 Nov. 1940.

18 W. Kimball (ed.), *Churchill and Roosevelt: The Complete Correspondence* (London, 1984), vol. 1, p. 62, letter from Roosevelt to Churchill, 19 Aug. 1940, enclosing letter from Kirk to Roosevelt, 29 July 1940.

19 R. Churchill (ed.), *Into Battle: Speeches by the Right Hon. Winston S. Churchill* (London, 1941), p. 234, speech broadcast 18 June 1940.

20 Nicolson, *Diaries and Letters*, p. 132, entry for 31 Dec. 1940.

21 Air Ministry, *The Battle of Britain, August–October 1940* (London, 1941), p. 31.

22 Nicolson, *Diaries and Letters*, pp. 119, 130. Interestingly he added in 1947, against the entry for 15 Sept. 1940, 'This was the day we won the Battle of Britain.'

23 F. Somary, *The Raven of Zürich* (London, 1986), pp. 211–12.

24 I. Maisky, *Memoirs of a Soviet Ambassador: The War, 1939–1945* (London, 1967), p. 143.

25 G. Gorodetsky, *Stafford Cripps' Mission to Moscow, 1940–42* (Cambridge, 1984), pp. 71–2.

26 J.G. Winant, *A Letter from Grosvenor Square: An Account of a Stewardship* (London, 1947), pp. 34–6. The key military figure in the delegation was Colonel Carl Spaatz, the future commander of the Eighth Air Force, whose conviction that the RAF could not be beaten in 1940 was expressed with great force to the other members. See R.G. Davis, *Carl A. Spaatz and the Air War in Europe* (Washington, 1992), pp. 48–9.

27 C. Hull, *The Memoirs of Cordell Hull*, 2 vols (New York, 1948), vol. 1, pp. 842–3.

28 Kimball, *Churchill and Roosevelt* vol. 1, pp. 54–68. On 15 Sept. 1940, later designated Battle of Britain Day, Lord Lothian gave a speech at the World Fair in New York which expressed the struggle with Germany as essentially

280 · *The Burning Blue*

a naval contest, and the threat to the United States as an oceanic threat. This was doubtless for American consumption, reflecting the significance attached by American opinion to issues of naval rather than air power.

29 Hull, *Memoirs*, vol. 1, p. 864.
30 Some sense of this is conveyed in R.E. Sherwood, *The White House Papers of Harry L. Hopkins*, 2 vols (London, 1948), vol. 1, pp. 174–201. On the night before the election a Republican radio broadcast included the following: 'When your boy is dying on some battlefield in Europe . . . don't blame Franklin D. Roosevelt because he sent your boy to war – blame *yourself*, because *you* sent Franklin D. Roosevelt back to the White House!', p. 199.
31 See A. Calder, *The Myth of the Blitz* (London, 1991), pp. 209–27, on the selling of the myth in America.
32 W. Kimball, *Forged in War: Churchill, Roosevelt and the Second World War* (London, 1997), pp. 79–80; Harriman, *Special Envoy*, p. 5. Winant himself (*Letter from Grosvenor Square*, pp. 7–8), after briefing Roosevelt on the European situation in a lengthy interview, only learned of his own appointment in the newspapers a few days later.
33 Harriman, *Special Envoy*, pp. 32–3.
34 Kimball, *Forged in War*, p. 77.
35 *Führer Naval Conferences*, pp. 139–40, directive from OKW, 12 Oct. 1940.
36 Ibid., p. 163, report of C-in-C navy to the Führer, 27 Dec. 1940.
37 Ibid., p. 172, report of conferences with the Führer on 8 and 9 Jan. 1941.
38 See, for example, M. Bloch, *Ribbentrop* (London, 1992), pp. 308–12; Maier et al., *Das Deutsche Reich und der Zweite Weltkrieg*, vol. 2, pp. 409–16.
39 E. Fröhlich (ed.), *Die Tagebücher von Joseph Goebbels: Sämtliche Fragmente*, 4 vols (Munich, 1987), vol. 4, p. 429.
40 Ibid., pp. 410, 415, 420.
41 See, for example, P. Padfield, *Hess: Flight for the Führer* (London, 1991).
42 See Greiner, 'Operation Seelöwe', p. 11, for Jodl's view of indirect war against Britain; *Führer Naval Conferences*, pp. 132–5, report of the C-in-C navy to the Führer, 6 Sept. 1940; pp. 141–2, report of the C-in-C navy to the Führer, 26 Sept. 1940 ('Gibraltar must be taken. The Canary Islands must be secured beforehand . . . The Suez Canal must be taken . . . an operation against India can be feigned . . . action must be taken against Dakar.' Raeder recorded that 'The Führer agrees with the general trend of thought').
43 H. Trevor-Roper (ed.), *Hitler's Table Talk, 1941–1944* (London, 1973), p. 418, entry for 24 Apr. 1942.
44 *Halder War Diary*, p. 255.
45 Greiner, 'Operation Seelöwe', pp. 10–12.
46 G. Blumentritt, 'Operation "Sealion"', in Detweiler (ed.), *German Military Studies*, vol. 7, pp. 10–11.
47 Greiner, 'Operation Seelöwe', p. 10.
48 Nicolson, *Diaries and Letters*, p. 126.
49 W.J. West (ed.), *Orwell: The War Commentaries* (London, 1985), p. 153, broadcast of 19 Sept. 1942.

Notes on Contributors

Paul Addison is Director of the Centre for Second World War Studies at the University of Edinburgh. He is the author of *The Road to 1945: British Politics and the Second World War* (1975), *Churchill on the Home Front, 1900–1955* (1992) and editor (with Angus Calder) of *Time to Kill: The Soldier's Experience of War in the West 1939–1945* (1997).

Tony Aldgate is Reader in Film and History at the Open University. He has published extensively on British cinema history and is the author of *Cinema and History* (1979) and *Censorship and the Permissive Society* (1995). He is the co-author of *Best of British: Cinema and Society from 1930 to the Present* (2nd edition, 1999) and *Britain Can Take It: The British Cinema in the Second World War* (2nd edition, 1994).

Hans-Ekkehard Bob was born in 1917 and joined the Luftwaffe in 1936. Having trained as a fighter pilot, his first combat took place over Poland in 1939. He then flew in the war against France in the spring of 1940. Serving with 9/JG 54 during the Battle of Britain, he displayed great skill as a squadron leader. By 11 November 1940 he had scored nineteen of his sixty confirmed aerial victories during the war. In March 1941 he was awarded the Knight's Cross of the Iron Cross. He participated in operations on the Eastern Front from mid-1941 to early 1943 and, after duty in France, returned to Russia as commander of IV/JG 51 from June 1943 to May 1944. He then commanded II/JG 3 until August 1944. He ended the war as a member of JV 44, flying the Me 262 jet fighter in Adolf Galland's 'squadron of experts'.

Brian Bond is Professor of Military History at King's College, London, and President of the British Commission for Military History. He is currently a Visiting Fellow of All Souls College, Oxford. His books include *British Military Policy Between the Two World Wars* (1980) and *Britain, France and Belgium 1939–1940* (2nd edition, 1990).

Horst Boog is a former Senior Director of Research and Head of Research Department II (Second World War), Militärgeschichtliches Forschungsamt. He is the author of *Die deutsche Luftwaffenführung 1935–1945* (1982) and editor of *The Conduct of the Air War in the Second World War: An International Comparison* (1992). He has also made extensive contributions on operational air war, strategic bombing and German home air defence to the multi-volume *Germany and the Second World War*.

Angus Calder is a former Reader in Cultural Studies with the Open University in Scotland. His books include *The People's War: Britain 1939–1945* (1969), *The Myth of the Blitz* (1991) and *Wars* (1999), an anthology of writing about warfare in Europe in the twentieth century.

Theodore F. Cook is Professor of History at the William Paterson University of New Jersey and a Visiting Scholar at the Edwin O. Reischauer Institute of Japanese Studies at Harvard University. Among his publications on the military and social history of Japan's wars is *Japan at War: An Oral History* (1992).

Sebastian Cox is Head of the Air Historical Branch (RAF) at the Ministry of Defence. He has recently edited and published Sir Arthur Harris's official *Despatch on War Operations* (1995) and the report of the British Bombing Survey Unit, *The Strategic Air War Against Germany* (1998).

Jeremy A. Crang is Lecturer in History and Assistant Director of the Centre for Second World War Studies at the University of Edinburgh. He is the author of a forthcoming book on *The British Army and the People's War 1939–1945* (2000).

Wallace Cunningham was born in Glasgow in 1916. He volunteered for the Royal Air Force Volunteer Reserve in September 1938. Called up a year later, he joined 19 Squadron in June 1940. On 16 August he claimed a Me 110 destroyed, on 7 September a Heinkel 111 destroyed and another damaged, on 9 September a Me 109 destroyed, on 15 September a Me 109 destroyed and a Me 110 shared, on 18 September a Ju 88 shared, and on 15 November a Me 110 shared. On 23 September he was awarded the DFC – the first Glasgow airman to be awarded this decoration during the war. In August 1941, while escorting Blenheims on a low-level attack on shipping in Rotterdam harbour, Cunningham was shot down by ground fire and taken prisoner. He spent the rest of the war in prisoner-of-war camps.

Owen Dudley Edwards is Reader in History at the University of Edinburgh. Born in Dublin in 1938, his first visit to the United Kingdom was in 1955. He co-directed with Paul Addison and Tony Aldgate the

Inter-University Historical Film Consortium's *The Spanish Civil War*. His most recent book is the Penguin Classics edition of Oscar Wilde's *De Profundis* and related writings (2000).

Adrian Gregory is Tutor and Lecturer in History at Pembroke College, Oxford. He is the author of *The Silence of Memory: Armistice Day 1919–1946* (1994) and of several articles about the First World War.

Richard P. Hallion is The Air Force Historian at Headquarters, United States Air Force, Bolling AFB, Washington, DC. He has published widely on the aerospace revolution and air power history, and his most recent work is *Air Power Confronts an Unstable World* (1997).

Sergei Kudryashov is Editor-in-Chief of the Russian archival journal *Istochnik*, Moscow. He is the author of a number of articles on the history of the Second World War, and his forthcoming book, *Nazi Occupation of the Soviet Union and Collaboration*, is due for publication in 2000.

Jeremy Lake is an Inspector of Historic Buildings at English Heritage. He is responsible for the assessment of a wide variety of building types, including in recent years those of the military estate.

Klaus A. Maier is a former Director of Research Department III (History of the Bundeswehr), Militärgeschichtliches Forschungsamt. He has published on the Spanish Civil War, the European Defence Community and the control of nuclear weapons in NATO. He is the co-author of *Germany and the Second World War*, vol 2, *Germany's Initial Conquests in Europe* (1991).

Richard Overy is Professor of Modern History at King's College, London, where he has taught since 1980. He is the author of numerous books on the Second World War and the Third Reich including *The Air War 1939–1945* (1980), *Why the Allies Won* (1995), *Bomber Command 1939–1945* (1997) and *Russia's War* (1998). He is currently writing a book on the Nazi economy and is preparing the Oxford History of the Second World War.

Nigel Rose was born in Newcastle-upon-Tyne in 1918. He volunteered for the Royal Air Force Volunteer Reserve in December 1938 and was called up on the outbreak of war. He joined 602 Squadron in June 1940. On 25 August he claimed a Me 110 destroyed and on 7 September he shared a Me 110. He was wounded on 11 September and began flying again on 9 October. He claimed a Me 109 destroyed on 29 October. In September 1941 he joined 54 Squadron and, having completed his tour of flying duties, was transferred to 57 Operational Training Unit in November. In January 1944 he took command of 14 Air Practice Camp and in June was posted to the Middle East. There he was in charge of the single-engine component of the Advanced Bombing and Gunnery School at El Ballah. He remained in this post until the end of the war.

John Schofield has been an Inspector with English Heritage's Monuments Programme since 1990, working on the protection and appreciation of England's historic environment. Since 1995 this has involved recent remains and specifically twentieth-century military sites.

Malcolm Smith is Senior Lecturer in History at the University of Wales, Lampeter. His publications include *British Air Strategy Between the Wars* (1984), *British Politics, Society and the State* (1990), and *Democracy in a Depression* (1998).

Index